Three Years in America
I

הנוסע העברי ישראל בן יוסף בנימין השני

I. J. BENJAMIN II.

THREE YEARS
IN AMERICA

1859-1862   *Volume I*

by

[I. J.] BENJAMIN

translated from the German by
CHARLES REZNIKOFF

with an introduction by
OSCAR HANDLIN

Philadelphia
THE JEWISH PUBLICATION SOCIETY OF AMERICA
5716 - 1956

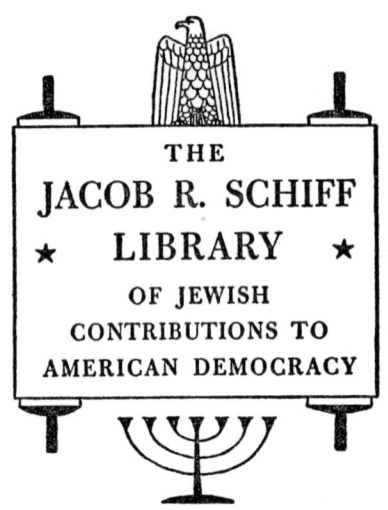

THE
JACOB R. SCHIFF
★ LIBRARY ★
OF JEWISH
CONTRIBUTIONS TO
AMERICAN DEMOCRACY

Library of Congress Catalogue Card Number: 56-7957

MANUFACTURED IN THE UNITED STATES OF AMERICA BY

BOOK CRAFTSMEN ASSOCIATES, INC., NEW YORK

Foreword

This record of an extensive journey through the United States a hundred years ago has long been out of print in its original German and never existed in English translation. Yet it is full of interesting facts and observations which the average reader of American history, not to speak of the scholar, is certain to find both entertaining and informative. The Jewish Publication Society of America believes that it is performing a service by making Benjamin's, or Israel ben Joseph's, report of his American visit available to the general public.

The translation is faithful to the original. No attempt was made to correct the author's statements or to improve upon his observations. Corrections were made, wherever possible, in the spelling of names and occasionally where the mistake was clearly due to the German printer's misreading of the author's writing. The reader must realize that the author's understanding of English was not perfect; that he jotted down his observations in German, or possibly even in Yiddish; that he transcribed his notes more than a year after he had made them and, finally, that the printer was unaccustomed to English words and names. Under the circumstances mistakes are to be expected. Without attempting to produce a scholarly edition of this work, the translator and the editor made only the most obvious corrections.

Thanks are due to Professor Oscar Handlin for providing an interesting description of the historical background of the period in which Benjamin made his way through the United States, and to Charles Reznikoff for his lively and thoroughly readable translation.

Contents

Introduction

by Oscar Handlin

———

THE ACCOUNT OF THE TRAVELER IN A STRANGE LAND PRESENTS US WITH a reflected image. We see the shape of the objects at which he looked, but only from the perspective of his own point of observation. To understand that image fully we must come to know both the traveler and the place through which he passed. Knowledge of the man whose eyes we use will make clear the biases and distortions that originate in his peculiar background and antecedents. Knowledge of the place, drawn from other sources, will reveal what matters caught his attention most prominently, what matters he slighted through ignorance or inattention.

In the case of the book which follows, such clarification is particularly necessary. For the wanderer who composed it described a society altogether different from that in which he himself was reared. The contrast often lent depth to his observations; but it also calls for caution and understanding in using them.

Of the early life of this traveler practically nothing is known. His own late recollections are the only sources of information, and the accuracy of these cannot be accepted with unqualified certainty.

Israel Joseph Benjamin was born in 1818, in the town of Falticeni, part of the Turkish Province of Moldavia. A few Jews had lived in this section of what was later to be known as Rumania for centuries. But Israel Joseph's parents appear to have been relatively recent arrivals; most likely they were among the numerous Jews who fled southward, early in the nineteenth century, away from Poland and Russia toward the relative tolerance of the distant Ottomans and the easy-going local nobility. Falticeni itself had been established in 1780, by Prince Morouzi, to attract Jews and to stimulate the commerce of the region. That favorable attitude persisted through Benjamin's early life.[1]

The Jewish newcomers found a tolerable place in the commercial life of the small towns and cities of that region. In the midst of a pre-

———

[1]   Bernard Stambler, *L'Histoire des Israélites roumains* (Paris, 1913), p. 54; Joseph Berkowitz, *La Question des Israélites en Roumanie* (Paris, 1923), p. 73.

I

dominantly peasant society they found themselves one of the accepted groups, along with Germans, Magyars, Greeks, Armenians and gypsies, who performed special artisan and trading functions for the husbandmen and landlords. In this ordered society, where there was a fixed place for many different kinds of people, it was not surprising that the Jews should retain the manners and attitudes, as well as the language of their Polish background. Within the context of that traditional background Benjamin grew to maturity.[2]

The essence of that background was a distinctive and consistent way of life that extended to every aspect of the Jews' existence. From their religious orthodoxy, derived from Torah and Talmud and embodied in the *Shulhan Arukh,* came an elaborate code of practices and attitudes. From the peasant society within which they had lived for five centuries were drawn a variety of beliefs and forms of behavior that were by now thoroughly identified as Jewish. In the days of Benjamin's youth, it was all of a piece that man should live by study, prayer and trade; that ritual should permeate every act of the day; that the sharpest reasoning powers should be joined to credulous superstitions; and that the proper modes of acting and thinking should be rigidly unchangeable. Traces of these attitudes were to emerge later in the writings of the grown man.

No doubt, the future traveler had the customary education of boys of his time and place. How long he remained at his books or how deeply he was carried into them, it is difficult to tell now. But his later writings are replete with references and allusions to the well-known texts; he had certainly acquired some familiarity with them in his youth.

As a matter of course, also, he entered upon the career of the trader relatively early. By his own account, he appears to have had some initial success. When he was little more than twenty he found himself a prosperous dealer in lumber. Unfortunately, as he would often reflect later, the pursuit of wealth was seldom rewarding; his own prosperity did not last long. At the age of twenty-five or so he lost what fortune he had accumulated and discovered he was well-nigh penniless, without any dependable means of support.

The failure shocked the young man. Whatever its immediate cause, it came in relatively prosperous times while others among his contemporaries continued to thrive. Why should other, less worthy, men have been more successful? That question long echoed in his mind, as he continued to brood over the cause of his failure. His later writings find frequent occasion to reflect upon the vanity of the worship of Mam-

[2]   S. F. Bloom, "The Peoples of My Home Town," *Commentary* III, (1947), 329.

mon; his bitterest comments are reserved for those who heap up fortunes without proper talents either to have deserved or to enjoy them. On the other hand, his own failure may have seemed providential; perhaps he had not succeeded in business precisely because he had another mission in life.

Casting about for something to do, the young man seized upon the romantic thought that he was the second Benjamin. His task was to emulate the great medieval traveler, Benjamin of Tudela, who had made a circuit of the known world (about 1170) to seek out and to describe the scattered remnants of the tribes of Israel. The motivations of Israel Joseph's decision to become a wanderer are clouded in obscurity. He was no doubt influenced both by his failure in trade and by the romantic-heroic notions of the period. But the determination to take to the road was also influenced by Benjamin's lack of place and status in an environment in which both were of crucial importance. The man was temperamentally unable to remain where he was as an inferior in his community, at the rank his business failure compelled him to take. He was no doubt also moved by influences diffused by the *Haskalah;* for the Enlightenment was then opening before the Jews of Southeastern Europe the vision of the wide, secular world outside the gates of their towns. At any rate, he now styled himself Benjamin II and made ready for his journeyings.

The decision to become a wanderer was not altogether novel. Throughout the countryside of eastern Europe there drifted a host of such familiar peripatetic figures. The bulk of the population in the Rumanian villages and towns was sedentary; but through it there moved a variety of itinerants, well-known and accepted, though peripheral to both Jewish and peasant society. There were traders by the scores whom Benjamin must have encountered in his earlier career — venders of horses and livestock, of timber and tinware and of every other kind of goods. Along the dusty roads there wandered also every manner of masons and smiths and bakers and cobblers. And all these found the company, now and then, of artisans, beggars and pilgrims of every species. With these ill-assorted characters, Benjamin resolved to throw in his lot.

Benjamin had too much self-esteem to think of himself as one of the company of beggars and tinkers. But among the denizens of the road there was a model he undoubtedly counted worthy of emulation. For it was the pattern of the *maggid,* or itinerant preacher that Benjamin took up, in order to realize his high-flown ambitions.

In the crowded synagogues of Rumania, the exhortations of an eloquent preacher were always among the more attractive portions of the

3

Sabbath afternoon. Through most of the acts of worship, the Jew addressed himself directly to God; in the sermon he found the relevance of religion to his own condition. Twice, or occasionally more often, in the year, the rabbi spoke to the congregation. But the rabbi was essentially preoccupied with another task, that of studying and understanding the sacred books and of acting as judge in the affairs of the community. It was only on the most important days that he undertook to preach himself.

Therefore the Jews were eager, from time to time, to welcome the *maggid*, an itinerant preacher who moved from townlet to townlet (studying a little where he went) and speaking on the Sabbath in the Synagogue. He lived by the hospitality of the well-to-do in the community; and might even, if his eloquence sufficed, carry off a small contribution to help him on to the next congregation. Among these wanderers Benjamin probably hoped to take his place.[3] He differed from the usual *maggid* in that he had a goal other than merely earning a livelihood; he saw himself as a living link, joining the Jews of distant lands to those of Europe. When addressing Jews in Europe, he spoke of the Jews in Asia and Africa; and, when among the Jews of the non-European continents, he spoke of those in Europe. He became a *maggid* on a world wide circuit.

By the early nineteenth century, the *maggid's* style of preaching was fairly well fixed; Benjamin adopted it as a matter of course. That style became so much a part of his way of thinking that it persisted to give form to much of his writing. The *maggidim* were not men particularly known for their learning in the scholarly sense. They were acquainted, as most Jews were, with the texts of Torah, Talmud and Midrash; and they possessed in addition an endless stock of oft-repeated stories, legends and traditional folk tales. Finally, they brought also to the congregation, circumscribed in the orbit of its own limited neighborhood, a touch of familiarity with distant lands and strange peoples. As they spoke they conjured up wondrous visions, mingling myth and reality, past and present.

The sermons had, however, a religious end appropriate to the Synagogue. Their form was hortatory and moralistic. The *maggid* was not telling idle stories. He was teaching a lesson; and the sermon, in style, was directed at that objective. Generally that involved a series of stinging rebukes for the transgressions of the community which explained the difficulties in which it was eternally involved. The stiff-necked folk were called to account for their selfish absorption in worldly goals,

---

[3]   Salo W. Baron, *The Jewish Community* (Philadelphia, 1948), II, 97.

for their neglect of piety and learning; and the all too abundant disasters were recalled as warnings were they slow to mend their ways. Yet the harshness of the *maggid's* judgments was tempered by the tales of the fresh outside world that he brought to the closed circle of the little towns.

In what light Benjamin saw his ultimate future is difficult to say. But his immediate role was one in which he would move from community to community of Jews supporting himself by his preaching and by the generosity of his co-religionists, wherever he met them.

In 1844, therefore, he set off on his journey, first westward to the Hapsburg capital at Vienna. There he remained for several months soliciting the funds necessary to take him further. In 1845 he had accumulated enough; he then embarked upon the more serious part of his travels. Proceeding to Constantinople, Benjamin made a long, slow tour of the Near East, moving successively through Egypt, Palestine, Syria, Babylonia and Persia and finally reaching as far as India, Kabul and Afghanistan. After all these years of wandering, at last in 1851, at the age of 33, he made his way back to continental Europe. He returned at that time to Vienna. In that community he lingered a while. But his travels had not prepared him any better for a sedentary career than when he started. Before long he had taken to the road again. This time his path was southward to Italy, Algeria, Morocco and then back to France.

In the course of these last travels, the idea occurred to him that he might make a book of his observations in all the distant ends of the earth through which he had passed. Traveling through Algeria, he struck up an acquaintanceship with Daniel Lévy, the director of the Jewish school at Algiers, a restless character whom Benjamin would later see once more on the other side of the globe. Together these two had conceived the project of publishing an account of the persecution of the Jews in the seventeenth century revolt of the Cossacks under Bogdan Chmielnicki. This venture took the form of a translation of Nathan Hannover's Hebrew chronicle, *Yeven Metzula* ("Mire of the Deep," 1653), an account that dealt with the events of the years, 1648-1652. In the collaboration Benjamin supplied the knowledge of Hebrew, and Lévy of French. The work was published in Tlemcen in 1855.[4] To it, Benjamin attached an account of a sect of Russian Sabbath observers who were suspected of "confessing the law of

---

[4]   *Quatre années de guerre des Polonais contre les Russes et les Tartares (1648-1652). Persécutions des Israélites de la Pologne.* Traduit de l'hebreu *Javan Messoula* par Daniel Lévy. Israel-Joseph-Benjamin éditeur. Suivi de; *Les Schobatniks en Russie (1800-1814)* par Israel-Joseph-Benjamin. Tlemcen, 1855.

Moses" and persecuted on that account.[5] These rather gory narratives followed an introduction, also from Benjamin's pen, which called upon Poles of his age to forget the divisions that separated them from the Jews and to unite against the common oppressor of all, the Tsar of Russia.

The first venture into print was most encouraging. It led Benjamin to try his hand at a more extended effort. Already while still in Algeria he had composed the first draft of the story of his travels to the East. There was, however, no suitable publisher on that side of the Mediterranean; and in any case the task was hastily done, and incomplete. Furthermore, in 1854, Benjamin lacked the resources to see it into print.

The next two years saw all these defects rectified. By the time Benjamin reached Paris he had supplied himself with the means of publishing the work. As he traveled through the towns and villages of Algeria, Southern France, Alsace, Lorraine and the Rhineland, he accumulated not only the usual donations but a string of subscribers to the forthcoming book. Wherever he saw a Jew, there he found a customer. Indeed the list of subscribers printed in the opening pages of the book as it finally appeared supplies an itinerary of Benjamin's travels through the French and North African countrysides. In Paris, also, he secured the advice of more competent critics in the process of revising his manuscript. There, too, Daniel Lévy appeared to translate it into French. In 1856, at last, the book came forth from the presses of Michel Lévy Frères, *Five Years of Travel in the Orient, 1846-1851*, by Benjamin II, traveler and author.[6]

In the volume, Benjamin described his travels from his departure from Rumania to his return to Europe. There were long accounts of Jerusalem, of the rest of Palestine, of Damascus, of Kurdistan and of the more exotic lands of the East. In each case Benjamin took particular pains to present an account of the situation of the Jews. The author, however, also felt free to include occasional digressions on the condition of the Jews in countries such as Abyssinia, which he had not visited, drawing his material from a variety of sources, reliable or not.

The book was no model either of succinctness or of literary grace. But it achieved a moderate currency and gave Benjamin the basis of a reputation of sorts in France and later in Germany. For, the traveler showed no disposition to settle down. Instead he continued his peregri-

---

[5]   S. M. Dubnow, *History of the Jews in Russia and Poland*, Philadelphia, 1916, I, 401.

[6]   Israel-Joseph Benjamin II, *Cinq années de voyage en orient 1846-1851*. Paris, 1856; German version, 1858; English version, 1859.

nations, venturing now into the heart of Germany in the quest for fresh audiences.

Benjamin had by now resolved to make a tour of the entire known world with the same objective as his medieval forerunner, that of seeking out the scattered remnants of Israel. The idea was by no means an impossible one. Benjamin was still only about forty years old. He was vigorous, brash and aggressive, and needed only the financial resources to take him on his way. The years between 1856 and 1858 he seems to have spent raising funds throughout Germany. In that period he acquired some acquaintanceship with the German language, although his familiarity with it was always limited; his writing showed strong traces of his Yiddish background and was replete with errors of grammar and spelling.

In his travels through Germany, he also acquired a valuable portfolio of letters of recommendation, many of which are reprinted in the author's introduction to this volume. The letters themselves express no great enthusiasm for Benjamin or for his project, but the distinguished names with which they were signed were nonetheless useful. One can well imagine Benjamin bustling into the study of some learned professor in one university town after another, introducing himself with his volume already published, and extorting a note from the acquiescent savant as the price of being rid of a garrulous guest. Benjamin's great coup was the letter from Alexander von Humboldt, which served as the opening wedge in securing all the others.[7]

One way or another, by 1859 Benjamin had acquired the means to take him to the New World. In July 1859, Benjamin left Hanover, sailing to New York by way of Bremen. An uneventful crossing brought him to the American metropolis where he remained fully a year. His own account is not altogether clear as to why he lingered so long, or as to what he did. But in the summer of 1860 the desire to see the West set him to traveling again. He then started out for the Pacific coast, proceeding by the usual route, by ship to Panama, then across the Isthmus by rail, and on to California by sea.

His stay in the West afforded him the opportunity to travel along the coast and some way into the interior. Finally, in 1861, he resolved to return to Europe. On this occasion he went overland, coming eastward through the Northern states to New York where he embarked for the voyage back to Hanover.

Now an experienced author, he forthwith set himself to writing an

---

[7]   Friedrich Heinrich Alexander von Humboldt, naturalist and traveler (1769-1859), author of *Cosmos* and of numerous works on geology, botany and zoology.

7

account of his travels through the United States. He published the volumes here translated, in German, in Hanover in 1862. With the appearance of this work he was on the verge of enjoying the reward for all his efforts. He acquired a substantial reputation and also decorations from the kings of Sweden and Hanover. In 1864 he resumed his travels, but got no farther than London, where he died in May of that year. His journeyings and his labors thus came to an end.

Benjamin's description of America mingled somewhat incongruously all the qualities of his earlier works, all the characteristics of his background. At the core of the book are his actual observations. He was an acute and perceptive spectator of men and events that interested him. He had a sharp eye for local traits and these he wrote about with verve. But he was not content to limit himself to what he actually saw. He had a ready imagination and a strong sense of self-confidence that blinded him to the extent of his actual ignorance. Along with the accurate observations, therefore, there come distressing examples of lack of understanding of the conditions with which he dealt.

Furthermore, Benjamin was not one to let false pride stand in the way of filling out his account by helping himself liberally from the writings of others. Copious extracts from contemporary almanacs, directories and local histories were translated and incorporated into the body of his text. This was one of the usual practices of the travelers of his day; and often the information was enlightening and useful, although there must remain some question as to the utility of long lists of names and of statistical tables. Generally the copying was accurate, although marred, now and then, by mistranslation and by the errors generated by over-confidence.

Above all, the qualities of the *maggid* characterized Benjamin's writing. Accuracy was less important than the good story. And both weighed less in the balance than the opportunity for moralizing and for delivering sententious ethical judgments. The volume is full of generalizations about American life and about Jewish life in the United States. These must be taken with considerable caution; as was often the case, they reflected less what the traveler saw than the prejudices he brought with him. All this apart from the fact, as the pages that follow will illustrate, that Benjamin was not above settling scores with personal enemies and antagonists in his acrid comments on men and events.

Nevertheless, taken as a whole, his book is useful. It is the only coherent account by a Jewish traveler of American life in the period before 1870. Furthermore, Benjamin penetrated areas of the country not commonly visited by travelers before 1865. His observations, at their best, have a pungency and point that is not usual. And, handled with the caution which all travelers' accounts demand, his observations provide us with a lively commentary upon society in America in the middle of the nineteenth century.

The America to which Benjamin came was a land on the verge of a great conflict that would try its institutions and test the innermost beliefs as well as the character of its men. In the years before 1861 all the great hopes that had surrounded the Republic since its formation seemed about to come to naught. The crisis, long in preparation, was troubling not simply because it threatened to disrupt the nation; but more, because it brought into question the very ideals for which the country stood.

It was not, therefore, simply a sectional war that was about to burst upon the land; this was also the decisive trial of American democracy and of the way of life it embodied. Long since, American statesmen and writers had conceived of their country as the model the rest of the world would ultimately follow. The seventeenth century Puritan had regarded his primitive cluster of rude huts as a city upon a hill upon which the eyes of all men would ultimately fasten; the generation of Jefferson had thought the cause of America the cause of all mankind; and the boisterous exponents of Manifest Destiny in the 1840's had been confident that the superiority of their institutions would quickly win recognition everywhere. For it had been assumed that the special merit of the New World was the opportunity it afforded, in its openness and freedom, to develop the institutions of the future without the trammeling restraints of medieval, anachronistic superstitions and despotism.

Until this fateful decade of the 1850's every fact of American history had seemed to confirm these assumptions. Unexampled material prosperity and general tranquility of government had justified the fondest hopes of the founding fathers. There seemed every reason to believe the people of the rest of the world would adopt the pattern set in the mother of republics.

The crisis that led to secession planted the seeds of doubt in the minds of many because it appeared to be not susceptible to democratic solution. All the years of debate and compromise had at last produced only an impasse. Was that not a reflection upon the validity of democratic ideals as well as upon the forms of American government?

Therefore the outcome of the war would affect, not simply the future of the United States, but also that of democracy throughout the world. So the issue was viewed in America; so it was viewed by the more perceptive observers in England and on the continent of Europe. That explains the sense of impending momentous events with which the country passed through the election of 1860 and entered, the following year, upon the Civil War.

These circumstances Benjamin dimly understood as they broke out into the open during his visit. But he did not altogether comprehend the long chain of events that drew the nation over the brink of the crisis in 1861.

These events were more than a decade in the making. In a narrow sense, they originated in the war against Mexico and in the results of that war. But in a more meaningful sense, they had roots in the very nature of American society, fertile in expansive elements. By 1840 the republic had extended itself deep into the continent away from the shores of the Atlantic; the old West was rapidly filling with settlers, and even the imperial Louisiana purchase, less than a half-century in American possession, had already received its first wave of pioneers.

In Jefferson's day it had been possible to imagine that this great domain would remain available for settlement for generations to come. By 1840 a vast westward movement that had rapidly filled in great tracts of this open land had drawn the line of settlement to the edge of the Mississippi, and in some places well beyond it. No one, in view of the rapidity of this growth, could be certain how long there would yet be room for the ever-advancing line. While there was still empty land in American possessions across the Mississippi, there was little inclination to think that future expansion would be limited to those areas alone. Americans were not disposed to believe that existing political borders would long restrict the ultimate spread of the population. On the contrary, there was a widespread assumption that it was the manifest destiny of the United States eventually to reach from one ocean to the other, and before long to encompass the whole continent of North America.

These were not simply imperialist dreams. They were expressions of confidence in the superiority of American life and institutions which were inherently so attractive that all neighboring peoples would instinctively welcome their extension. If "corrupt" governments stood in the way, as in Mexico or Canada, then it was the duty of the United States to liberate those territories and to offer them the advantages of freedom as parts of the union.

The results of this expansive sentiment were already visible in Texas in 1840. A handful of Americans had moved into that Mexican province early in the century. By 1830 these newcomers exerted decisive

10

power in the area. Too late the Mexicans recognized the danger. The attempt by law to prevent further colonization touched off a revolution that earned the Lone Star Republic its independence. Although it was clear from the start that the fortunes of the new country would be closely linked to those of the United States, it was almost a decade before annexation was consummated. Meanwhile the process of negotiation provoked a long series of acrimonious controversies with Mexico. A disputed boundary supplied the incident that touched off the clash.

The war against Mexico was conducted without military difficulty; the decisive defeat compelled the Mexicans to recognize the annexation of Texas and, in addition, to hand over to the United States the vast territory that included New Mexico, Arizona and California, in which gold had already been discovered.

Victory had been easy; but disposition of the fruits of victory was to involve a painful reckoning. For these territories, already growing in population, threatened to upset the long-standing political balance that had maintained an uneasy peace within the country. Until 1848, the southern states, united by the institution of slavery, had a voice as strong in the Senate as did the northern states, in which free labor was characteristic. The new territories would ultimately become states; and whether they became free or slave states might decisively affect the whole structure of political control.

Slavery was a troubling element. Manifestly the institution ran counter to the spirit of a democratic republic which had, from its establishment, insisted that all men were created equal. In the early days of the republic, there had not been any disposition to defend slavery. Even in the slaveholding states, this was rather regarded as a necessary, temporary evil, doomed to disappearance, although the means of its eradication were not yet clear.

The compromises embodied in the Constitution had rested on the assumption that slavery might, for the time being, continue where it was. But the founding fathers had accepted those compromises because they looked forward to a future when the whole problem would vanish along with the institution of slavery itself. The pattern of compromise had been extended temporarily in 1820 in the case of Missouri. But the issues presented by the new territories conquered from Mexico in 1848 were not so readily adjusted, for men's conceptions of slavery had, by then, been radically altered. Many southerners in 1848, were not content to request the tolerance of slavery where it was, but rather demanded its extension into new territory as an institution that was positively good and worthy of support.

11

From the beginning of the war, therefore, a substantial body of opinion in the free states had adopted the objective of excluding slavery from the new territories. The places in which bondage was recognized, they argued, would attract slaveholders, repel free farmers. The states that would ultimately rise there would thus be lost to slavery. The free-soil efforts provoked a bitter political controversy that brought the country close to disunion and which was not allayed until 1850, when a series of compromises temporarily closed the issue.

But only temporarily, for deep resentments continued to boil beneath the surface. Some northerners bitterly objected to the provisions for return of fugitive slaves, while some southerners were unwilling to accept the principle that there were any territories to which slaves could not be taken. In 1854 these resentments broke into the open when the Kansas-Nebraska Act raised anew the whole question of the place of slavery in the territories. This measure reversed the whole line of earlier legislation, by removing the decision as to whether a territory should be slave or free from the hands of Congress and placing it in those of the future settlers.

The appearance of logic in this scheme for "squatters' sovereignty" was quickly dissipated in the attempt to put it into practice. It was all very well to affirm that the people of a territory were to decide its future for themselves. But what if the territory were as yet uninhabited? At what stage was the decision to be made?

The stakes in Kansas were large. As far as the free states were concerned this was the critical point at which to halt the advance of slavery; as far as the South was concerned this was the line at which to hold the advancing power of the North. There followed five turbulent years of battle, with each section striving to encourage settlement in the disputed area. Contested elections, rival constitutions and rival local governments, even bloodshed, marked every stage of the struggle. Ultimately the weight of numbers was on the side of the free settlers; but the outcome was less important than the fact that in all those years Kansas remained an irritating reminder of the nation's disunity.

Furthermore, the price of the compromise of 1850 had been a revised fugitive slave law to assist southerners to recapture slaves who fled to freedom along the underground railroad. Through the next decade, therefore, men in Boston and New York were compelled to see the manacled victims of the slavecatchers dragged through their streets back to bondage — a further indication that the effects of slavery could not readily be confined to one section of the country. If some hotheaded southerners also began to speak only of slavery as a natural good and to advocate its extension through the conquest of Cuba, that only increased the apprehensions of moderate northerners and lent point to the old abolitionist warnings of a slaveholders' conspiracy.

By the same token, the long bitter quarrels stimulated fears in the South, not merely that the spread of slavery would be halted, but, even more, that the institution would be attacked in its stronghold at home. Uneasy at the necessity of justifying slavery, the dominant whites came increasingly to fear a future in which they would be ever on the defensive. When John Brown carried his guerrilla warfare from Kansas to outright rebellion in the very heart of Virginia, in 1859, that was a further sign that the era of compromises was running out.

Everywhere, the forces of stability and adjustment were in retreat. The old Whig Party, which had furthered some degree of cooperation across the Mason-Dixon Line, declined as it lost its national support. On the one hand, southern plantation owners moved increasingly into the Democratic Party, convinced this was the best means of protecting slavery. On the other hand, the conscience Whigs, no longer able to compromise, moved out, first into the Free Soil Party, later into the Republican Party.

The last-named organization had made its mark in the election of 1856 when its candidate had been the western hero, General John C. Frémont. It had shown then the evidence of potential power at least in the North. By 1860 it had added substantial bodies of strength, in the industrial states by supporting a protective tariff, in the West by favoring a homestead law to give free land to settlers, and among some Germans by repudiating the nativism displayed earlier by the Know-Nothing Party. It was in a position that year to assert its fullest force in the presidential election.

Its task was made easier by divisions among the nation's Democrats. Jackson's party had split on the slavery question; and all efforts to heal the breach proved vain. Two candidates approached the polls that autumn under the Democratic designation — Stephen A. Douglas, on behalf of the conciliatory northerners, and John C. Breckenridge for the extreme southerners. In addition the votes cast were shared by John Bell of the Constitutional Union Party, a group that stood for compromise above existing political lines.

Against these divided opponents, the Republican Party under Lincoln won readily, although its votes came entirely from above the Mason-Dixon Line. For the first time a party in which the South had no effective voice carried off the presidency.

Almost at once the Dixie radicals demanded that the slave states

13

withdraw from the union. This step, long in contemplation, they justified by the theory that the United States was a federation of sovereign states each of which had voluntarily joined and each of which retained the power to secede. In the early winter, the states of the deep South, led by South Carolina, through conventions, severed their ties with the national republic, and readied themselves to form a new confederacy. The border states, Virginia, Kentucky, Tennessee and Missouri were, however, hesitant. Important interests drew them to the union, yet the desire to preserve slavery made them fearful lest secession of the other southern states leave them isolated in a rump republic over-whelmingly anti-slavery in sentiment.

The crisis continued through the winter and early spring. The lame-duck Democratic administration under Buchanan was ineffectual. It had no plan for dealing with the situation and it was riddled with treachery. The Republican administration, not due to take office until March, was neither able nor willing to take the responsibility for decisive action. Meanwhile individuals and groups unofficially explored the possibilities of compromise, but without success.

The gravity of the situation oppressed Lincoln as he took office at last in March. His sole concern was to preserve the integrity of the union. But he could see no clear means of drawing the disaffected states back into the union, for he was incapable of agreeing to the only terms that might have satisfied the southerners — the opening of the territories to slavery and a constitutional guarantee of the inviolability of the peculiar institution. Lincoln was no abolitionist; but neither could he bring himself to recognize slavery as a permanent, ineradicable feature of American life.

His policy was therefore to wait, to recognize in no way the legitimacy of secession, but also to provoke no aggressive action. Perhaps he cherished the hope that he could thus hold the border states and in time proceed somehow to the restoration of the union.

The impasse did not continue, however. The period of restless inactivity after the election came to an end over the question of the federal forts in the seceded states. Lincoln could not hand these over as the southerners wished, without recognizing the validity of secession; he felt obliged to retain and defend them. Yet to the southerners, in the full flush of their nascent nationalism, the continued hold on their territory by what they regarded as a foreign government was offensive; the very sight of the stars and stripes over Fort Sumter in Charleston Harbor was an insult to those who had come to regard it as the banner of a foreign power.

So it was on that April day in 1861 that General Beauregard, at the head of the South Carolina forces, ordered the firing across the harbor. Few in the holiday atmosphere of that Spring day in Charleston envisaged the disastrous train of consequences that followed upon that order lightheartedly given. At this point, the long-delayed decisions would have to be made; and men and states were drawn into the opposing ranks that faced each other in bitter battle for four bloody years.

Of these events Benjamin had a general knowledge. As he landed in New York, the drama was in the last stages of preparation; and as he traveled through the country its first act unfolded. Here and there in his wanderings he would see the signs of it, become acquainted with its leading protagonists and acquire an understanding of at least the surface issues.

What he never learned was the extent to which this conflict extended deep beneath the surface political issues to the fundamental social and economic forces that made the two sections of the country what they were. There was a relationship he did not altogether grasp between the character of the people and the institutions of the various regions of the United States, and the position taken on the political questions that led to the Great War.

From time to time Benjamin saw, partially understood and commented upon cultural traits, upon social and intellectual habits, which were intimately wrapped up in the crisis. In effect there had developed within the nation two disparate societies which viewed the most important issues of the day from altogether different perspectives. That the two societies would clash was well-nigh unavoidable; that insight had been in Lincoln's mind when he warned that a house divided against itself could not stand. That the clash should ultimately take the form of war was certainly not inevitable. But the conflict was nonetheless bound to come to a head; to that extent it was irrepressible.

One of these societies Benjamin did not get to see at all. By the time he reached the United States the South was already on the verge of war and travelers could not readily move across the Mason-Dixon line. Benjamin had visited several Southern cities, but did not have the opportunity to examine at first hand the plantation society that had come to revolve entirely about the institution of slavery.

Economically, it was true, the slaveholders in the South were a minority; and the number of large slaveholders worthy of being designated masters of plantations was smaller still. Certainly they were far outnumbered by the yeoman farmers, by the poor whites, by the mountain folk in the back country who struggled for a livelihood in the isolation of the hilly little patches.

15

Yet, in a meaningful sense it was the slaveholders who set the dominant tone of southern life. It was they who were responsible for the concentration of southern capital in agriculture, and particularly in the production of the great staples — cotton, tobacco, rice and sugar. In the plantation they worked out a rationalized form of organization for slave labor that enabled them to control large numbers of hands to raise crops in ever expanding abundance and to maintain for themselves a life of increasing dignity, leisure and elegance.

The hidden costs of that way of life were paid by the whole section. Earlier in the century, the South had buzzed with projects for industrialization and internal improvements. But the planter ideal did not encourage these schemes. Whatever capital was accumulated went into land and slaves; and foreign investors were not disposed to send their funds here, particularly after a number of southern states repudiated their debts. Manufacturing therefore took no root in the region; and the system of railroads and canals developed but slowly. Generally, men of ability shunned business; as would-be aristocrats, they looked down upon the tradesmen's ways. What few entrepreneurs and managers there were, were recruited from among outsiders — transplanted northerners, or the foreign-born.

The mass of southerners were not, of course, plantation owners. The yeomen operated family-sized farms, sometimes with a few slaves, sometimes alone. There were substantial numbers of poor whites in the hills and back of the most fertile lands. And in such thriving cities as Baltimore, Louisville and New Orleans were a variety of urban folk. But all these people found the dominant patterns of their economic life shaped by the plantation.

The slaveholders in addition were dominant politically. In some states there were long intervals in which other social groups contested their control. But the agitation of the slave question, particularly after 1850, tended to subordinate all other issues in public interest. The questions that provoked the internal divisions within the South yielded to the necessity of closing ranks against the threat of the abolitionists.

In Georgia, in North Carolina, and in the western states there remained, even in 1860, sensitive spots of opposition. But in the crisis a preponderant sentiment identified the political interests of the section with those of the planters.

That decision was the easier to reach because it had already been made more subtly in many other aspects of southern cultural life. The spectre of abolitionist ideas had convinced many earnest men of the necessity for fighting dangerous doctrines. With the exclusion of northern books and loss of contact with northern educational institutions, southern thinking became narrow and ingrown; only thus could it escape unpleasant criticism of slavery. In religion, the problem of whether slavery was sinful or not split almost all the great national denominations on sectional lines; and that left the southern churches exposed as defenders of the institution of slavery and of the way of life that depended on it.

The tragic impact of slavery and of the necessity of defending it against attack had molded every feature of southern life to conform to it. Consequently, the southerners faced across the Mason-Dixon line an altogether different society in the North.

Not that uniformity or homogeneity in any sense characterized the North of the decade before the Civil War. Indeed, it is more appropriate to use that term to describe a combination of sections held together by their common opposition to the South — by the common support of the system of free, as distinguished from slave, labor.

The patterns of northern economic life involved three distinctive features, each strikingly in contrast to the productive system of the South. Northern economy was shaped by its system of free farming, by the rapid development of industry and by the growth of great commercial cities.

Northern agriculture was free. Here were no large plantations, no slave laborers, very few tenant farmers or even hired hands. The last remnants of servile institutions had disappeared in the 1830's during the "anti-rent War" in the Hudson valley of New York State. Predominantly all the northern regions were areas in which freeholders owned a family-sized farm that they operated through their own efforts.

There was considerable diversity of condition, of course. New England farming had been on the decline since the end of the eighteenth century. The rocky soil was not propitious and the attraction of fresher western land perpetually drew away the best energies of the region. With the development of communications — first by turnpikes and canals, then by railroads — the New England farmer faced, in addition, the necessity of competing with the cheaper, more abundant products of the West. Yankee agriculture had therefore declined steadily except where the most enterprising and industrious could piece out a livelihood by fishing or by toiling at some household trade for extra income.

In all too many places, however, no such expedients were available. The sons of the farmers could escape the grim prospects of steady economic degradation only by emigration. First from the hill country of northern New England, then from Massachusetts, Connecticut and

Rhode Island, they drifted away, as individuals and in groups, to the superior lands of western New York State, Ohio, Indiana and Illinois.

In the middle states, New York, Pennsylvania and New Jersey, the situation was far more encouraging. Here were frequent tracts of fertile soil, where thrifty agriculturists managed to resist the competition of the West, and to build a competence for themselves. Particularly in the great valleys of the Hudson, Delaware, Susquehanna and the Mohawk rivers, thriving farms yielded gratifying crops of grain and animal products. The descendants of the oldest English settlers there mingled harmoniously with the offspring of Germans, Scots-Irish and Yankees attracted by the richness of the land.

But the region of great agricultural growth lay to the west. The rolling plains between the Allegheny Mountains and the Mississippi River came under cultivation between 1820 and 1860. Fertile and attractive, abundant with wood and water and close to markets, the area drew to it an unabating stream of settlers both from the East and from south of the Ohio River. Here empty plains and virgin forest in a handful of years became prosperous farm sites.

Throughout its course this westward thrust was assisted by an impressive development of means of communications. A variety of new forms of transportation helped the settlers on their way in and brought their products readily and cheaply to the cities of the eastern seaboard. Already in the 1820's canals were supplementing the river waterways; and soon the steamboat had become familiar in places where not long before only the Indian's canoe had made its appearance. The development of the railroad after 1830 wrought a transformation that was more remarkable still. By 1860 a number of parallel lines tied the Northwest directly to the cities of Boston, Albany, New York, Philadelphia and Baltimore. These were the channels by which the unceasing outpouring of agricultural products that originated in the Northwest flowed to eastern and transatlantic markets.

This westward movement had by no means slackened in the decade before 1860. Indeed, it crossed the Mississippi to Iowa, Wisconsin and Minnesota and was aggressively seeking further outlets. Here was the true explanation of the gravity of the question of slavery in the territories. At this point the aggressive westward thrust of free labor encountered and came into irrepressible conflict with the equally aggressive westward thrust of slavery.

Industry had, from the start, been related to free agriculture. In the very earliest days many farmers had also been handicraftsmen and artisans. In eighteenth-century New England it was usual for the assiduous tiller of the soil to use the intervals of leisure away from the labor of the fields, manufacturing, with the aid of their families and in their own homes, shoes, shingles, nails or other goods. Later some of the husbandmen participated in the development of mill sites; now and then, they invested in grist, saw, fulling and slitting mills, and thus became involved in the first factories.

But in the four decades before 1860, the development of manufacturing in the United States took on a radically new aspect. Industrial production was still rural; but it was carried on in integrated factories rather than in the household, it used unskilled rather than skilled labor, and it depended upon the power-driven machinery even then being invented in England and in America.

The new manufacturing appeared first in the textiles, then spread to the fabrication of a wide variety of other goods, and ultimately created a new type of industrial wealth in the United States. In the interior back country of New England and the middle states, in small towns at Lowell and Fall River, Massachusetts, at Utica, New York, and Patterson, New Jersey where the falls of the rivers made power available, and where the labor of the farmers and of their children could be harnessed at low cost, there arose the gaunt shapes of long factory buildings and around them the clustering shacks and boarding houses of the mill town. Meanwhile in Boston and New York and Philadelphia, the stockholders who had supplied the capital and the merchants who acted as selling agents for the new enterprises discovered they had hit upon a remarkably profitable form of production. By 1840 this was a substantial interest — and one that continued to grow.

American manufacturers competed in a financial and commercial situation that, they thought, left them at a disadvantage when compared to the more developed industries of Europe. The mill-owner's readiest temptation was to seek the protection of a tariff for his home market; and the demand for such an impost was a persistent source of conflict between the North and the South. For the tariff was an abomination to planters whose cotton went to world-wide markets, who needed no protection at home, and who were convinced that the sums they paid out in taxes on manufactured goods went largely into the pockets of avaricious Yankees. In 1832 the issue had driven South Carolina into the desperate, though futile, nullification controversy. On the other hand, the tariff tended to draw together the eastern and western sectors of the North. Henry Clay's American System had convinced a good part of the agrarian West that protection could be to their advantage too. The tariff, Clay had urged, was a means of creating a great home market that would unify East and West. The proceeds of the tariff could build valuable internal improvements, at no cost to the taxpayer, that would bring the western farmer into close and profitable relationship with his eastern market. Throughout the period a substantial body of westerners continued to support protection. Although the influence of the southerners kept the tariff relatively low, the issue was still alive in 1860. The high tariff was one of the important planks of the Republican platform, and would be translated into a new national law shortly after Lincoln took office.

In the interim American industry had also developed in quite another direction. After 1840, it found its way into a number of cities which had theretofore been mainly commercial centers. Until then places like Boston, New York, Baltimore or Pittsburgh had been primarily markets. The earliest cities had risen on the harbors along the seacoast; economically their function was to supply facilities for the ever-growing trade with Europe. By the end of the eighteenth century these were substantial towns, wealthy and bustling with business. Other cities had arisen at the internal points of exchange — at the falls of the great rivers, as at Albany or Pittsburgh, or at the crossings of important transportation routes as at Cincinnati, Chicago, St. Louis and Milwaukee.

All these places had been commercial in character. There goods were bought and sold, processed or repacked, and transferred from ship to train, from river to road. The residents were mainly such folk as were occupied in trading pursuits, merchants, clerks, seamen, shipbuilders and ropemakers. Whatever industry existed was that of tailors, shoemakers, bakers, cabinet makers and carpenters who served the needs of the inhabitants of the town. These were the pursuits of artisans, skilled craftsmen who worked in their own shops and with their own tools, generally as individuals or with a journeyman or two to assist them. In addition there were also a sprinkling of professional men who helped to make urban life commodious. But manufacturing in any larger sense had as yet no place in the cities.

After 1840, however, the nature of the American city began to change. In New York, Philadelphia. Boston and elsewhere, the ready-made clothing, furniture, meat-packing and machine industries developed rapidly. These branches of manufacturing displayed traits very similar to those that had already emerged in the textile mills of Lowell or Patterson. The new industries were also organized in factories; they used large sums of capital and machinery operated by power; and they were operated by an unskilled labor force rather than by the skilled artisans. These industries expanded rapidly in western as well as in eastern cities. The value of their products and the number of hands engaged in them rose rapidly. By 1860, they had transformed the pace of urban America. Where the trader's counting-house once stood was now the cavernous factory; where the clerk's cottage has been was now the darkly-looming mill; and everywhere the smoke of steam power cast a pall over the old lanes and little squares of green. This was the cost of industrial growth.

Not all the consequences were yet clear. The demand for power would stimulate coal mining, the call for rails and machinery would make room for the products of the new iron and steel plants. Here were the sources of the great industrial potential that would, after the war, further alter the nation. Already, in the 1860's it had decisively set the northern apart from the southern sections of the country.

The rapid expansion of American agriculture, industry and urbanism, dramatic and sudden as it was, was yet not extraneous to American life as a whole. Indeed, this growth drew its energy from qualities long characteristic of the United States. They operated more freely in the North than in the South, but that was also an aspect of a more fundamental divergence in social experience.

The sources of expansion were multiple. In part rapid economic growth derived its force from the natural resources of the country, from its abundance of water power and of fuel concealed in the earth, from the fertility of its soil and from the excellent disposition of its rivers and harbors. In part it derived its force from factors general to all western society, forces also operating in Europe; many of the inventions and new processes that proved so stimulating on this side of the Atlantic had indeed originated in the Old World. In part, however, expansion proceeded from the impact of forces peculiar to the characteristics of the American people and of the society in which they lived.

The restraints upon innovation and expansion which hampered some of the European economies certainly did not exist on this side of the ocean; there were no restrictive relics of feudal or mercantilist practice here. On the contrary, the spirit of the country encouraged newness. The government imposed few restraints upon industry; indeed, the state often regarded as its function the stimulus and encouragement of enterprise. No rigid social lines attached any sort of stigma to the tradesman's career; nor did any arbitrary barriers prevent the entrance of talented individuals into any desirable pursuit; for freedom of opportunity distinguished every operation of the productive order. Most important of all, Americans had accepted as a mission the task of transforming themselves; and that task they interpreted in economic as well as in social and political terms. Since they were, by virtue of their superior institutions, to be a model for the rest of the world, that superiority must display itself in the factories and fields as well as in the legislatures and courts. The rising volume of wheat and shoes would be as much evidence of the advantage of Americanism as orderly elections or a free press.

That accounts for the high regard with which these people viewed the life of trade, and the premium they placed on the search for wealth. To Europeans, like Benjamin, this concern with success often had the appearance of crass materialism. In actuality it represented a realistic estimation of the value of economic achievement in an environment in which there was almost no premium on social or hereditary distinctions.

Finally, since the Americans considered their society capable of continuous and indefinite progress, they could not conceive that expansion might have set upon it any previous limits, derived from history or from ancient institutions. All things existed so that they might be improved upon — the means of production, as well as all else.

These attitudes help to explain America's economic growth; they help also to explain why that growth was northern rather than southern. Below the Mason-Dixon line, the defense of slavery had cast doubt upon the idea of progress and upon the utility of expansion, had nurtured aristocratic ideals and had encouraged the ideals of stability and conservatism.

Among the most prominent features of the changing North, and to a lesser degree of the South, was the noticeable increase in the number of the foreign-born, both in the industrial cities and the rural countryside. Americans had always been ready to welcome as future citizens any newcomers who came to the United States. This policy had been set long before the opening of the 19th century. Even in the Colonial era the American colonies, as subject territories of Great Britain, had permitted every type of future settler to make a home in the New World; by the time of the Revolution it had been altogether appropriate for the "American Farmer" (Crèvecoeur) to assert, "We know properly speaking no strangers; this is every man's country."

The new republic consistently adhered to the same policy. Men had been free to come to the United States without any distinction as to place of origin or national characteristics. As Franklin had pointed out, Americans held out no inducements to newcomers, but were willing to welcome industrious individuals without prejudice.

This open attitude was rooted in part in an assumption as to the nature of American nationality, in part in the concrete benefits that the immigrants brought to the United States. The assumption as to nationality followed logically from American history. The Americans were a people not because of common heredity or ancestry. They were a people because, whatever their origins, they had lived under the common free institutions that made them one. It followed from that premise that any persons of whatever origin, who came to live under the influence of these institutions, would in the same way be Americanized. The desirable qualities of immigrants then were not those of heredity or origin, but those related to their willingness and capacity to live as free citizens of the republic.

The material benefits of immigration were readily understood. Repeatedly, in the years after 1815, Americans had their attention drawn to the advantages that accrued to both agriculture and industry from the addition of the newcomers to the population. In the whole period, no one seriously proposed the least curtailment of the existing policy. Nor was there any effort to reduce the total volume.

When the quarter-century of European wars ended in 1815 after Waterloo, the tide of immigration already in preparation began to flow. The volume of entering newcomers mounted steadily after 1820 as shipping became increasingly available. Down to 1840 the migrants were drawn mostly from two sources. Some of them were artisans displaced by industrialization in their homelands, most frequently English, but also some Irish and German. Another component of the flow consisted of peasants who had lost their place on the land in the course of the changes in the agricultural organization of England, Ireland, Scotland, Western Germany and Scandinavia. By 1840, more than a half-million immigrants had entered the United States.

After 1840 still another stream was added to the current that moved across the Atlantic. Everywhere in Europe, a large group of landless peasants lived on the periphery of the economic system. Poor and without the means of improving their condition, they were only slowly set in motion; often it took great disasters, such as the potato rot of 1846-47, to dislodge them. But in this decade there were disasters enough; and those, combined with the cheapening rate of transportation, brought the peasants in hundreds of thousands to the United States. Together with the artisans and the more fortunate peasants who still continued to come after 1840, these newcomers rapidly accelerated the rate of migration; in the next two decades, fully four million were admitted.

Among the immigrants were some Jews who left England, Holland and Germany to find homes in the New World. Generally they were swayed by the same considerations that moved the other migrants; but some felt, in addition, religious restrictions that heightened the attractiveness of American freedom. The numbers are difficult to estimate since no statistics were kept on a religious basis and since the Jews moved largely in the company of their compatriots. However, it seems likely that by 1860 there were in the vicinity of one quarter of a million Jews in the United States.

Whether native or foreign-born, these Jews were widely scattered throughout the country. There were, as always, substantial clusters in the large commercial cities. But it was more characteristic of these years to find Benjamin's co-religionists dotted in isolated families and little groups throughout the length and breadth of the land.

The nature of American opportunities encouraged that diffusion. The hasty spread of settlement in the decades between 1820 and 1860 left many agricultural communities without adequate facilities for trade. The farmers of the West and the planters of the South welcomed both the goods the pedler brought by their door and the stocks displayed on the counters of the village store. Settling down, the Jews became a part of these communities and absorbed many of their attitudes; some became rabid abolitionists in the North, others fire-eating champions of slavery in the South, in a pattern common to most immigrants of the time.

Immigration had a pronounced effect on the whole American economy, stimulating both farming and manufacturing. The newly-arrived immigrants did not proceed directly to the frontier; few among them had the funds to set up a going farm, and even fewer were capable of maintaining themselves in the wilderness. But to find a place on the land was the ultimate goal of almost all the newcomers, even though to succeed might require an initial period of residence in some city, while working to accumulate the necessary capital. Not all of them — probably not most of them — did at last become the proud owners of their own acres. But enough did attain that status to influence the course of American settlement.

The immigrant farmers stood in a complementary relationship to the natives, who were often disposed to press onward to a newer frontier. The American settler was likely to be impatient with the ways of settled agriculture. He planted hurriedly and mined the soil for what he could get from it with as little labor as possible; often he drew a large part of his subsistence from the fish of the streams and the game of the forests. Improvident, he frequently found himself in debt. His salvation then came from the immigrants who were not capable of moving directly to the frontier, but who were eager to purchase the cleared or partially cleared land of the pioneer at a good price. The American farmer was thus able to move onward to newer lands, while the European took up the task of establishing a more permanent settlement and more stable ways of agriculture.

The industrial effects of immigration were more complex. There were some skilled artisans like the English iron workers, or the German brewers and bakers, who brought their crafts with them to the United States and introduced here new branches of manufacturing, or helped expand old ones. These men, valuable as were their contributions, were, of course, exceptional. The great mass of newcomers brought with them no usable industrial skills. These were peasants, incapable of getting at once to the land and compelled therefore to spend a greater or lesser period of residence in the cities where they could find no other place in the labor force than as unskilled laborers ready and willing to sell their toil at any price. Such immigrants accumulated in a great pool of surplus hands, depressed by frequent unemployment and by a pitifully low level of wages.

Whatever problems of social adjustment this fund of available labor created, it proved remarkably stimulating to American industry. This was the manpower that staffed the new factories. The pool of immigrant labor combined with the capital seeking new channels of investment and the burst of mechanical invention to create the conditions that brought the industrial revolution into the American cities. Immigration was thus intimately involved in every phase of expansion.

As if these expansive influences were not enough, the fortunes of discovery added fresh resources to the American economy. California had fallen into the hands of the United States as a result of the Mexican War. Shortly thereafter, the exciting news came out of the hills, of the discovery of gold at Fort Sutter, near Sacramento. The discovery touched off the great Gold Rush that persisted through the next few years. By steamship and rail across the Isthmus of Panama, or by clipper ship around Cape Horn, or overland across the plains and mountains, hundreds of eager prospectors hurried to the Pacific Coast to seek fortune in the goldfields. A few succeeded, and the vast mineral resources they uncovered added substantially to the wealth of the nation.

But perhaps more important was the sudden emergence of a fully developed civilization along the shores of the Pacific. The Gold Rush significantly hastened the westward movement. The edge of the frontier had theretofore extended gradually across the continent, with each stage of settlement contiguous to its predecessor. Now as it were, the frontier was lifted across the mountains and the desert and planted almost full-blown in California. The state grew by migration from abroad and from the eastern part of the United States. By the side of the Yankee and the Southerner, could be found Frenchmen and Germans, Englishmen, Irishmen and the Chinese, all attracted by the same hope.

In San Francisco, a thriving metropolis quickly took form around the old Spanish town. This had been a place of call for whalers and China-bound ships, and in the 1840's had boasted a modest population engaged in a modest trade. Now enriched by the gold seekers, the city swelled suddenly, and its trade, as Benjamin pointed out, expanded phenomenally. The gold seekers needed supplies and were willing to pay for them at any rate. The rapid growth in number of residents created a demand for housing and for a variety of services and put a premium on labor. For the time being, almost every form of enterprise enjoyed prosperity.

Sudden growth also created a multitude of problems. The territorial government inherited, in part, from the earlier Mexican régime was incapable of enforcing the law upon such a diverse multitude of people. The compromise of 1850 made possible the admission of California as a state, but did not at once lend effectiveness to local government. Hence there developed a system of direct vigilante action that Benjamin described graphically. In the rough, unsettled conditions of the period, formal courts of justice were sometimes inadequate and the people were often tempted to take the law into their own hands. Down almost to the end of the decade this trace of violence persisted, one of the unexpected results of rapid American growth.

What happened in California was only the extreme of a tendency apparent elsewhere in many other phases of life in the United States. Given the mobility and expansiveness of their society, Americans were by no means disposed to rely only on the efforts of government to achieve communal ends. There were too many places where settlement outran government and where rapid change made established forms anachronistic. Riots and the spontaneous recourse to violence were frequent in every part of the country.

By the same token, Americans saw no reason to limit more peaceful types of joint action to those patterns embodied in the polity. They were instead often accustomed to achieve common purposes through spontaneous voluntary societies. "Americans associate as freely as they breathe," wrote Frederika Bremer, an unusually perceptive observer of the period.

These associations were as variegated as the functions and the people who brought them into being. Many had a religious focus to their activity, for this was an area in which the state took no part at all and

26

which was therefore entirely reserved to voluntary societies. There was no established church in the United States and by 1840 there was no part of the country in which any special denomination held any special relationship to the government.

To such Europeans as Benjamin, then, American religion presented a curious and anomalous picture. Since no church was established, men were entirely free to belong to whatever denomination they chose, or to none at all. They could maintain membership in old churches or create new ones; and any man who wished was capable of taking unto himself the dignity and style of a minister. To Benjamin all this smacked of sectarianism and charlatanism, if not of worse.

What Benjamin could not understand was the nature of the adjustment Americans had made to religion. That adjustment included at least three critical elements. In the first place, membership was voluntary, unlimited by any legal restrictions. Americans were free to join or to withdraw from religious bodies to their heart's content. To some observers it seemed these people changed their affiliations as easily as they changed their hats. In the second place, there was no limit to the capacity of any group to constitute themselves a religious denomination; a new sect could be invented as readily as a new machine. In the years before the Civil War there was indeed a remarkable increase in the number of such bodies, each apparently serving a peculiar need in the lives of its members. Finally, American thinking about religion was characterized by a widespread latitudinarianism, by the belief that salvation could be attained by a variety of roads. It followed from that assumption that creedal doctrines and articles of faith were less important than ethical practice, that the good man would be saved whatever were his beliefs. To the stranger, these qualities seemed evidence of widespread apathy; but to Americans these were the elements of a formula that permitted great numbers of people of diverse origins to live harmoniously in the same society.

No religious denomination held a majority of Americans, or close to it. But the various sects did fall into a number of clear categories. The congregational churches were made up largely of New Englanders by birth or antecedents. The rigorous Calvinism of the original Puritans had been substantially modified by now. The orthodox trinitarians throughout the country were probably still in a majority; but they no longer held to the doctrines of predestination, human depravity and the clear demarcation of the saints from the sinners. Furthermore, orthodoxy had been dealt a staggering blow by the development of Unitarianism and Universalism, which accepted the congregational form of church organization and worship, but which rejected the idea of the Trinity and adopted a rationalistic and optimistic view of the place of man in the universe. Given the spirit of the age, even the orthodox were compelled to make significant concessions to the demands for the affirmation of human goodness.

The same necessity for compromise affected also the Presbyterian sects, which had spread mostly from out of the middle states and among whom were some Scottish and Scotch-Irish immigrants. In some places, the Presbyterians tended to merge with the Congregationalists, although the former held more tenaciously to orthodox Calvinist notions.

In rather sharp contrast to these groups were the Baptists and Methodists. These denominations were evangelical in emphasis; they minimized the importance of creedal niceties and stressed the necessity of some act of conversion that came as an act of will through appeal to the emotions. They resorted often to revivals and camp meetings and were less likely than the Congregationalists or Presbyterians to insist upon an educated ministry. Therefore the Baptists and Methodists were particularly effective in the frontier regions and the rural South; and these sects were likely to absorb the great mass of unchurched individuals who drifted through American society in these years.

The Episcopal Church was weaker. It suffered still from the odium of its connection with the Church of England and from a general American prejudice against bishops and hierarchical ecclesiastical organizations. This denomination was therefore confined mostly to the South and to a few centers in northern cities where it drew much of its support from English immigrants. It was, however, in a few places beginning to attract the interest of the wealthy, to whom its orderliness, discipline and conservatism appealed.

The influence of religious bodies was not altogether measurable by their numbers. The Society of Friends, for instance, had an influence upon American culture quite disproportionate to the size of its membership. Its conceptions meaningfully entered the thinking of such writers as Whittier and Whitman and supplied also significant impetus to the developing reform movements.

As striking to the outsider as the variety of existing churches was the ability of men to develop entirely new religious systems. The most dramatic, in Benjamin's eyes, was the Mormon Church of the Latter Day Saints.

The sect originated in the "burned-over district" of western New York, a region settled by restless Yankee immigrants from northern New England and much given to the enthusiasms of religious revivals. There, Joseph Smith, a young farmer, claimed to have discovered a set of gold plates which he deciphered with the aid of special divine revelation. The translation constituted a new book of the scriptures. The doctrines therein proclaimed attracted a substantial following which Smith organized in the new Church, promising a solution to economic and social, as well as religious problems.

Smith promised the converts the opportunity to create a new society in which the Kingdom of Heaven could be realized on earth. Fulfillment of that promise called for a move to the open spaces where the new order could freely be established. The Mormons pitched on several sites in the Middle West and finally, in 1839, came to rest at Nauvoo, Illinois. In the next few years they prospered. Governing themselves with rigid discipline, and recruiting immigrants from the East and from England, they grew to a community of 15,000 by 1844.

That success roused the jealousy of their "gentile" neighbors who feared that the sect would become a political power, dominating the government by its wealth and organization. Constant friction and bitter feelings ultimately led to an outbreak of violence against the Mormons. Smith himself was killed, his followers driven out of their city, and Nauvoo subjected to the torch.

In the crisis, leadership fell into the hands of Brigham Young, a native of Vermont. Young understood that only removal to a region remote from hostile outsiders would give the sect the opportunity to create a society in accord with its distinctive ideas. After sending ahead a scouting party, he led the remnants of the Mormon community in a great overland trek across the plains to Utah where they proceeded, in 1846, to build a new settlement in Salt Lake City.

Again fortune favored the group. By industry and ingenuity they made a success of agriculture; innovations in irrigation and dry farming enabled their farms to flourish in what had once been a desert. Furthermore, the Mormons thrived from the transcontinental trade that the Gold Rush set off. Salt Lake City was the one civilized place between California and the edge of settlement in the east, and the city took a toll, as it were, of all the traffic through the region. Tight control by the Church, under Brigham Young, permitted the Mormons to make the most profitable economic use of their situation.

Utah had become a part of the United States as a result of the Mexican War. The Mormons therefore faced the necessity for finding a constitutional place for their own imperium. There was a period of tense relationships between them and the American government that came to a head in the brief Mormon War. But ultimately Brigham Young accepted territorial status for Utah, with the actual machinery of control in his own hands. The compromise which lasted until after the Civil War illustrated the capacity of American life to adjust to the development of new religious bodies, even to one like the Mormon Church, which ran counter to many fundamental assumptions as to the nature of society and the family.

Immigration added still other religious groups to the American scene. Lutheranism had been established in New York and Pennsylvania in the 18th century. But the newcomers from Germany after 1820 were not satisfied with the form that Church had acquired in the United States. They therefore established a synod of their own, closer in spirit to the practices of the homeland. That did not, however, satisfy the Norwegian or Swedish Lutherans, who followed and who insisted upon building on this side of the Atlantic churches on the precise model of those they had left in their native villages.

In the same way, Irish and German Catholics strengthened the Church of Rome in the New World; yet within the communion each group made the effort to reconstruct the patterns of worship familiar to it. Within this context it was not surprising that Benjamin should observe that the Jews, too, would follow the identical development; once those from England, Germany, Holland and Poland, reached America, they created congregations reminiscent of their familiar synagogues of Europe.

The seeming anarchy of this Babel of worshippers never failed to astonish outsiders like Benjamin. Accustomed to the ordered society of the Old World, where the place of religion was clearly established by law and where each individual was identified with a church by birth rather than as a choice of free will, Europeans were prone to disregard the solid strength diversity and multiplicity gave religious life in the United States.

Those were characteristics general to the structure of American society. In every sphere of action variety was the rule rather than the exception; and that reflected the freedom of men voluntarily to form whatever organizations they deemed most appropriate. Every significant difference in origin, in cultural heritage and in social and economic condition could therefore receive legitimate expression. The vast array of philanthropic, fraternal, benevolent, literary and political societies that enlivened the American scene was the end result. And the appearance of social disorder and social disunity upon which Europeans commented was due less to the failings of the system they observed than to their own faulty perceptions. For, only thus could Americans preserve the mobility and freedom of their society.

Mobility and freedom and the patterns of voluntary action they

30

produced kept alive important differences within the American population. Since uniformity was neither an ideal nor a reality, the people of the United States regarded themselves as organized in meaningful groups that expressed those differences.

The foreign-born were the most recognizable, since they were set off by manners, language, dress, as well as by their distinctive associations. So it seemed not unexpected that the Irish, the Germans and the English should stand apart from one another and from the rest of the population. Benjamin encountered and described some of these folk, but overlooked others such as the Scandinavians who settled in parts of the country he did not visit.

Curiously, Benjamin was more sensitive to the question of color than many Americans of his day. His references to the Negro are hardly flattering or fair. In the South, of course, the Negro was degraded; and some whites were attempting to justify his degradation on the grounds of his innate racial inferiority. Yet Benjamin must have met Northerners who expected that the black men, once freed, would become respected citizens with all the rights of other Americans. His comments nevertheless are superficial and hostile.

Nor is he more tolerant of the Chinese. Some Californians had already given way to expressions of bitter prejudice. But the more usual assumption at the time was that the Orientals served a useful purpose in the United States and could be expected ultimately to adjust peacefully to the society about them. The great wave of anti-Chinese feeling, even along the Pacific Coast, would not come for fifteen years after Benjamin left the United States.

Indeed, hostility toward foreigners emerged in this period only on a few sporadic occasions and then mostly as a result of peculiar local conditions. Brief flurries of anti-Catholic sentiment in the 1830's and 1840's, in New York, Philadelphia, and Boston, had almost no effect.

Nativism in the 1850's was somewhat more consequential, but still did not permanently disrupt the harmony of group life. Between 1850 and 1853, a number of secret lodges were formed to combat Catholic influences in the United States. Since immigration strengthened Catholicism, these societies tended to view foreigners as their enemies, and as threats to American institutions.

The disorderly political situation of 1854 gave these lodges unexpected importance. With the existing parties disrupted by the confusing issues of slavery, many men found it tempting to seek the true source of the nation's difficulties in the foreigners. In the face of the shocking divisions that endangered the union, there was a vague hope that perhaps the only real peril was from the outsiders, a desire to believe that if only Americans could unite against those outsiders, all the troubling problems of the times would somehow resolve themselves.

In the elections of 1854, the American or Know-Nothing Party, without any public campaign, swept into office in many states and acquired enough seats in the House of Representatives to hold the balance of power there. Although the Know-Nothings professed no hostility to immigration as such and claimed they wished only to limit the political influence of the foreign-born, their success was an indication of widespread nativism in American society.

Their success was limited, however. Within two years their influence evaporated and the Party fell to pieces. It disintegrated because it had been held together by an accumulation of contradictory fears rather than by any positive unifying attitudes. Thus, at the first national convention of the party in 1856, when members from various parts of the country had the opportunity to meet one another, it became apparent that the Massachusetts men were Know-Nothings because they were abolitionists and thought the Irish supported slavery, while the Texans were Know-Nothings because they approved of slavery and thought the Germans opposed it, and the New Yorkers were Know-Nothings because they did not wish to take a stand on slavery and considered the foreign question a useful diversionary issue. Under these circumstances, the convention produced only dislike at first sight; and the Party collapsed shortly thereafter. No organization that belied the fundamental diversity of the nation could then long survive.

The characteristics that shaped the forms of religious and social organization also influenced the country's culture. This was probably Benjamin's blindest spot. Accustomed to thinking in terms of European achievements and imbued with particular respect for German scholarship, he approached American culture expecting the worst and found little to contradict his expectations. Philosophy, education, journalism, literature and the theater in the United States alike earned his contempt.

Yet American culture was not to be understood through comparisons — invidious or favorable — with that of Europeans, but through the functions it served in the lives of the people. Newspapers, for instance, were not distinguished for literacy and were not free of mercenary motives. But neither were they restricted in circulation and interest to a tiny segment of the whole society, as were the great exemplars of the European press. The American journals already aimed at a mass public and attempted to supply every element of society with a medium of expression. Some, like the New York *Post* appealed to the literate and leisurely merchants. Others like the *Sun* and the *Herald* strove to bring the news and issues of the day down to the comprehension of the common man, to reach as wide an audience as possible. In addition the newspaper, cheap and readily published, supplied every cause with a convenient organ of expression. They supplied political, religious, social and ethnic groups with an invaluable instrument of communication, to be read in the slums of the great cities, in the hovels on the edge of the frontier, as well as in the neat parlors of the well-to-do.

A similar mass basis distinguished every feature of American culture. American writers and thinkers were not to be measured by the degree to which their achievements were comparable to those of their European contemporaries, but rather by the degree to which they succeeded in understanding, and being understood by, their own society. Against the giants of German philosophy, for instance, Emerson would cut a poor figure indeed. But he assumes his true stature as a man who appeared on the lecture platform of town after town, and explained to thousands of simple folk the nature of their own aspirations. The great landmarks of this culture, therefore, were not the monumental treatise or the classic work of literature, but the lyceum and the public school.

Benjamin was rather harsh in his comments on American oratory and education. Within his own terms, those criticisms were probably justified. But his terms were not appropriate. Whatever the estimation of its oratory by classic standards, the lyceum was an effective instrument of popular instruction. Into hundreds of American towns it brought discussion of serious issues in a manner that was not only informative, but that also habituated its audience to the practice of thinking seriously about a wide range of problems outside its immediate concern.

It was the same with education in the more formal sense. American schools suffered from many inadequacies when it came to training the exceptional few for the life of scholarship or the professions. But their dominant preoccupation was with another task — training everyone for the life of citizenship in the republic. To that end a succession of great reforms, after 1830, had transformed education in the United States. Horace Mann and his colleagues had labored to put the support of the state governments behind the public schools, to establish adequate standards and to train competent teachers, all with a view to the critical role of education in a democracy. The state universities that emerged in these decades accepted the burden of the same responsibility. These were not merely imitations of European institutions, or even of the older eastern colleges; and they did not take as their goal pursuit of knowledge in any abstract sense. Rather they were dedicated to public service, and that objective would lead them into areas of teaching utterly unlike any with which Benjamin was familiar.

Behind the multiplicity of these strivings was a single social aim, often unexpressed but nonetheless consciously adhered to, to assist every individual to improve himself. The same spirit animated the excited reform movements of the period. Benjamin, like many European immigrants and travelers, failed fully to comprehend American reform, because he was struck mostly by such exotic manifestations as the women's rights movement which offended his conservative sensibilities. Yet reform was a product of impulses whose sources were deep in the fundamental ideas of the era.

Essentially reform rested upon a pervasive sense of optimism and a certainty of the inevitability of progress. Americans could not question the assumption that man was innately good and that he was capable of indefinite improvement. If there were, at the moment, evils upon the earth, these did not originate in any fault inherent in man's nature; they were rather the products of bad institutions, which were themselves the heritage of earlier, unenlightened ages. The task of man in society, therefore, was to reform those institutions so that they would no longer restrain the individual and hold him back from the improvements of which he was innately capable.

Reform took a variety of shapes. Some men insisted upon a total alteration of their society. At Brook Farm in Massachusetts, a group of intellectuals withdrew entirely from the world to create for themselves a community that would be a model of correct economic and moral principles. Similar communitarian experiments attempted to realize in practice the utopian dreams of Fourier, Owen and other social theorists.

More characteristic and more influential were the efforts to eradicate specific evils through reform action. So, the immoderate use of spirituous liquors seemed to limit the ability of many men to advance themselves; earnest advocates of temperance set about to rectify the situation. The movement gained adherents rapidly, directing its energies first at moral exhortation, but later calling upon the support of prohibitory and regulatory laws to compel the people to be good — in their own interest.

A host of other zealots each found his own cause. Some fought to secure for women equality before the law with men; others wished to teach the criminal to walk in the ways of righteousness, to provide

34

proper facilities for the care of the insane, to abolish imprisonment for debt, to educate the blind and the dumb, or to lay down new principles of diet or medicine. "What a fertility of projects for the salvation of the world!" exclaimed Emerson.

The brightest star in the constellation of reforms was the abolition movement. Slavery was the greatest of all evils, for it most completely denied the dignity of man. To wipe out human bondage was the most crucial task on the way to progress and perfectibility. Efforts to liberate the Negroes had begun early in the century, but had then been limited largely to Quakers. For a long time, too, those who disapproved of slavery had consoled themselves with the hope that the institution would disappear by itself and the black men migrate to Liberia or elsewhere.

After 1820 that consolation was less and less adequate. Cotton culture, the plantation and slavery were fixed in southern life. The realization dawned that this form of servitude would not vanish of its own accord, might even spread, unless it were abolished. At the same time, its sinfulness became more apparent. The wave of revivals set off by the preaching of Charles G. Finney and his followers supplied a religious impulse; slavery was a sin that had to be rooted out both for the sake of the slave and the slaveholder. Societies devoted to that end grew in number and influence in the succeeding decades.

Abolition gained strength also from the general diffusion of humanitarian reform sentiments. It was as a spokesman for those sentiments that William Lloyd Garrison was significant. Many moderate people were often shocked by Garrison's radicalism, and he himself had little direct influence upon the active political organizations. But he did give direction to the movement as a whole. Abjuring every compromise and consistently maintaining the extreme position, he restated over and over again the ideal to which no American could be insensitive. His harsh words kept clear and unambiguous the implications of democracy, for the solution of this, as for the other problems of American life.

There was the source of the tragic events that were in process as Benjamin came to the United States. From its establishment, America had been a democracy in the sense that it was dedicated, as a government of the people, to the advancement of its citizens. From the start, slavery had been a contradiction in a free society. As the years went by and the hope disappeared that the contradiction might vanish of itself, as the South, in defense of slavery, found itself alienated from the spirit dominant in the Republic, it became clear that slavery and the Union could not both survive.

Yet all but the most radical abolitionists were also limited by the democratic and constitutional means to which they were devoted. Benjamin saw and understood some of those limitations. The American government found it difficult to make incisive decisions and was perennially plagued by corruption and inefficiency. It teetered along, responsive to the winds of popular opinion and to the pressure of a multitude of interests, attempting to move in the direction the majority desired without overstepping the bounds of minority rights. These were the price of the democratic ends which the government served.

Hence the crisis and the disaster of war. The nation devoted to the attainment of dignity for all men had reached the point at which compromise was no longer feasible. The two sections then plunged into the long war that would significantly alter the society Benjamin witnessed.

Hence too, however, the inner health of the nation. Despite the immense exertions of the war, the nation still had the energy to go forward with its productive pursuits. Long after the peace, the gaping wounds caused by the conflict would show through American society. But by then, the means of healing those wounds would also have been created.

Three Years in America

Recommendations

The author had the pleasure of receiving from several of the most important contemporary scholars flattering letters that might be in place here.

* * *

In an introduction to the excellent and important work which the bearer of these lines, the traveler, Mr. I. J. Benjamin (from Falticeni, in Moldavia), published in 1858 under the title *Acht Jahre in Asien und Afrika*, I (together with our great geographer, Professor Karl Ritter, and the distinguished botanist, Berthold Seemann) pointed out in London, the noble and lofty purpose which Mr. Benjamin pursued in his travels: finding and investigating the settlements and communities of Hebrews who, in those distant lands, drag out an unhappy existence, the victims of political intolerance. Following in the footsteps of Benjamin of Tudela, the worthy Mr. Benjamin is now about to undertake a similar journey, and I therefore take the liberty of asking officials, consuls, and all those who honor me and my work with their sympathetic interest, to take an active interest also in his new undertaking and to contribute to whatever will make possible and further a journey completely unselfish and undertaken solely for a philanthropic purpose.*

Berlin, October, 1858.

Baron Alexander von Humboldt.

* * *

Through my work in the geography of the East and particularly in the countries of the Arabs, Malays, and Chinese, one can readily see the interest I take in renewed exploration among the inhabitants of those lands, for which the experienced and learned Mr. Benjamin has prepared himself with such persistent zeal and striving for knowledge. Although my opinion has neither the weight of the foregoing nor is it as far-reaching, still I take the liberty, at the request of Mr. Benjamin, of joining in the testimonial of Alexander von Humboldt and of recommending most heartily the purely patriotic and scientific efforts of this traveler to the assistance of all men of education and culture.

Berlin, November 26, 1858.

Professor Carl Ritter.

* * *

Although my recommendation after such names as those of the two coryphaei just before me can carry no weight, still I feel that I have to, in view of the request of Mr. Benjamin, recommend most warmly, as they do, his noble purpose and express the hope that his tireless striving to achieve it will be crowned with the utmost success.

Berlin, November 26, 1858.

Professor H. Petermann.

* * *

Often it is not the great and expensive expeditions that achieve the greatest results but the journeys of zealous and self-sacrificing individuals. Inasmuch as I greet the new journey of the enterprising and tireless Mr. Benjamin with interest and sympathy, I wish him from the bottom of my heart the success and the happy return of a Barth and a Livingston.

Gotha, May 2, 1859.

A. Petermann.

---

*   The original is in French. Tr.

The investigation of the conditions of the Jewish Diaspora in those distant regions where, under the oppression of Mohammedans and heathen, they remain Jews even though they have assimilated so many varied shades of speech and custom, and the discovery of Jewish writings of which the most worth-while are important documents for the history of the text of the Old Testament, particularly its punctuation and Masora — as the recent elucidations based upon Karaite manuscripts from the Orient show — that must still be brought out of distant corners: both these ends of exploration that Mr. Benjamin has set for himself and for which he has in many ways already shown himself most gifted, strongly bespeak the sympathetic interest of Christian scholars, so that he can be most heartily recommended to such for aid towards a second journey of exploration, particularly in the interior of Arabia and Ethiopia.

Erlangen, February 26, 1859.

Professor Dr. Delitzsch.

* * *

I join in the above recommendation with pleasure.

Erlangen, February 26, 1859.

Professor Dr. von Hoffmann.

* * *

After the precedent set by such competent judges of the endeavors and efforts of Mr. Benjamin as A. von Humboldt, Petermann, and Ritter, I have no hesitancy in recommending him likewise.

Munich, March 6, 1859.

Dr. Justus Liebig.

* * *

The undersigned wishes the journey undertaken by Mr. Benjamin all the more success as it is devoted to the study of ethnographical questions that are not only of limited Israelite interest, but of general interest. It may be expected, from what Mr. Benjamin has previously accomplished, that he will continue to accomplish excellently in the future.

Munich, March 7, 1859.

Dr. B. Haneberg, O.S.B. abbot.

* * *

The commendatory opinion of his friends, Drs. Delitzsch and Hoffmann, of Erlangen, and Dr. Haneberg, of Munich, experts of the first rank, is concurred in with pleasure and of his own conviction by

Dr. A. H. von Schubert.

Munich, March 7, 1859.

* * *

Should these lines be read by one of my friends anywhere and thereby help provide Mr. Benjamin — I do not have to call attention to his merits after the above testimonials more important than any I could give — with a hospitable reception, thus in some way promoting his noble undertaking, I should be greatly pleased.

Munich, March 11, 1859.

Frederick Bodenstedt.

* * *

I gladly concur in the above.

Munich, March 12, 1859.

Professor Dr. von Lasaux.

* * *

At the request of Mr. Benjamin, I, likewise, beg leave to recommend to friends, in the interest of humanity as well as research in geography and ethnography, the furthering of his laborious and dangerous undertaking (of which interesting results

are already to be seen in his writings).
Munich, March 12, 1859.

Franz Loeher.

* * *

Mr. Benjamin is undertaking a new journey to the Orient. Should he show these lines to one of my friends and patrons in the East, namely, in Armenia, India, and China, and should they wish to be helpful to him in his research, the undersigned would be very much obliged to them.

Munich, March 12, 1859.

Professor Dr. Neumann.

* * *

In the above desire joins

M. Joseph Mueller, professor-in-ordinary.

* * *

The noble striving of the tireless searcher, Israel Joseph Benjamin, is recommended to all friends of learning for all possible aid by

Michael von Deinsein, archbishop.

Bamberg, on the 11th of April, 1859.

* * *

In the above concurs

Dr. A. Anton von Stahl, bishop of Wuerzburg.

Wuerzburg, April 22, 1859.

* * *

Likewise the undersigned.

Wuerzburg, April 22, 1859.

Dr. Urlichs.

* * *

I have seen several extracts from the writings of Mr. Benjamin that contain some very interesting details of various peoples of Israelite origin scattered through India and other countries of Asia. This information has unquestionable authority, and the devotion of the tireless traveler deserves the greatest encouragement.*

Paris, July 29, 1855.

S. Munk.

* * *

Flevimus, cum recordaremur tui Sion.
We wept when we remembered you, O Zion.

John N. Neumann, bishop of Philadelphia.

* * *

It gave me pleasure to welcome Mr. Benjamin in Cambridge on his journey through the United States. I hope he will be able to carry to the Old World a good impression of the progress of knowledge in the New.

Cambridge (suburb of Boston), February 11, 1862.

Louis Agassiz.

---

* The original is in French. Tr.

Preface

by Dr. H. Guthe

IT IS WITH PLEASURE THAT I COMPLY WITH THE DESIRE OF MR. BENJAMIN that I introduce the present work to the public just as I recommended his earlier work dealing with his experiences as a traveler in the Orient. The author, bent on traveling, the equal of the well-known Ida Pfeiffer in endurance and courage but much her superior in knowledge of languages and in the power of observation, has journeyed in the years just past in every direction throughout the United States; he presents his experiences ond observations in this work. Not only those of his faith will find in it reliable information on the situation of the Israelites in that land; it will be quite as interesting for every one who is interested in a new development — particularly that of California.

Quite apart from this, I hope the author of this work will see it sell in large quantities because the profit will put him in a position to undertake a second journey to the Orient, during which he intends to wander through the interior of Arabia as a "geographical pathfinder." Knowledge of the speech and customs of the Orient, a physique accustomed to hardship, an energetic though easily satisfied spirit, plus the fact that as an Israelite he finds help for his plans everywhere among the widely scattered members of his faith, all lead to the expectation that his journey will have the happiest results for science.
Hanover, July 1, 1862.

Dr. H. Guthe.

The Author's Preface

THE PRESENT WORK IS THE RESULT OF MY TRAVELS IN THE UNITED States of North America. I know full well that many excellent reports of travel in that part of the world have been published recently and I do not fail to appreciate that I did not have at my command the help of scientific knowledge of such breadth as to enable me to claim for my book such merits as many of those writings have acquired in so rich a measure, especially in the furtherance of the science of natural history. In spite of this, if I venture to make public my experiences in and across America and to indulge in the hope that this report will be favorably received, I do so on the assumption that my book, because of the special nature of its contents, has something new to offer the world of learning and culture.

There are many factors, of course, which have gone into the wonderful and unique development of the United States of North America and which have shared in the merit of having created and supported this mighty realm with its great and learned institutions. Among these factors the settlement of the Jews certainly need not be considered the least.

The historical significance of the Jewish people did not end with the downfall of their state but rather became all the more important for the spiritual and material interests of the world with the unprecedented growth of its dispersal. Certainly the extensive settlement of Jews in the young country beyond the ocean was of no little influence upon it. Where everything was just beginning and in the process of becoming — and, to a certain extent, still is in that condition; where it is still possible to plant the seed of civilization in virgin soil; where the foundation of the structure of the new state of necessity implied the acknowledgment of the common origin of all men and their common right to equality, there the example and activity of that race which knew how to use the delicate ties of family and the firm bonds of the religious community in order to unite into a single whole the cultures of the earth's varied areas would be of great and telling significance.

In our day the development of California bears witness to this very situation.

This element, however, is either completely missing in existing publications or is touched upon only superficially. I have paid special attention to it and presented in my book a comprehensive picture of the condition of the Jews, beginning with their immigration. The fact that I am a Jew myself qualified me all the more to do so.

For fifteen years I have not put the wanderer's staff from my hand, and my constant intercourse with various peoples of the earth has made my eye the keener, perhaps, to recognize strange situations and national characteristics. Therefore, my observations and experiences, even if they are unable to offer any direct service to any special branch of science, are not wholly without value and contribute in general to the clarification and the extension of one's acquaintance with strange, little-known lands and nations.

The friendly and favorable reception of my earlier work concerning the Orient by men such as Humboldt, already among the immortals, and Ritter, who has likewise gone to his rest, the great geographers, H. and A. Petermann, and others, permits me to hope that, in similar fashion, much that is worthy of notice will be found in the present book as well.

The following is treated in the first part here published: the history of the Jews of North America; the development of their religious and communal conditions; their charitable institutions; general conditions in America; the settlement of San Francisco and geographical observations as well as observations of natural history; in the second part: my travels in California and a detailed description of conditions there; my journey to the northwest coast of the Pacific Ocean; my visit to about thirty-five Indian tribes; in the third part: my wandering through the plains and prairies of the North American wilderness and along the Great Salt Lake; a history of the Mormons and their condition. May this have a friendly reception!

As soon as I have completed the publication of this work, I shall, with God's gracious help, enter upon my second pilgrimage to the Orient, namely to Arabia, Malabar, Afghanistan, and China.*

Hanover, July 4, 1862.

Israel Joseph Benjamin II.

---

* My best thanks to Dr. S. Kayserling for his ready undertaking to correct the proofs of most of my book.

Volume I

*The Eastern States of the Union
and San Francisco*

Chapter I

Departure from Europe to America

ENCOURAGED BY THE FLATTERING JUDGMENT OF SUCH MEN AS Alexander von Humboldt, Carl Ritter, Professor Petermann and others, who expressed the highest praise for my work, *Eight Years in Asia and Africa,* and fired by the requests of other European scholars to undertake new journeys, I decided this time to turn my attention to the West. My journey was directed towards the continent of America; I wanted to become acquainted with the customs, habits and the degree of culture of its inhabitants.

Inasmuch as the best and most profound writers of our time have already published so much valuable material on the land of Columbus so that almost every European schoolboy is quite familiar with its history and geography, little, indeed, is left for me or any other traveler to say. My attention, however, was called to an aspect which, at least to my knowledge, no traveler had as yet taken into account: namely, the history of the Jews in that land of political and religious freedom.

Besides, since the exploration of the interior of China and Arabia is part of the further undertakings I have in mind, it seemed to me most important to visit, in addition, various sections of the western part of the United States and the coasts of the Pacific. Accordingly, I turned to California, stayed there for some time and had sufficient leisure to become acquainted with the characteristics of that land and its inhabitants. Inasmuch as little that is worthwhile has appeared as yet about this part of the American continent, I hope to offer the educated public no unsubstantial service and to furnish a pleasant as well as an instructive discourse if I set down here, in a fairly large work, the sum of my own experiences as well as what I was told and the information that I gathered.*

---

* Before I left Europe, I had still an important duty to perform. I could not leave for so long a time without, as a father, providing faithfully for my son. As Jacob said to Laban: "If not now, when will I provide for my own house?" So I had to consider first of all how to provide for my only son, Meyer Haym (who was still

45

On the fifth of July, 1859, I left Hanover and my many friends and patrons, who had stood beside me so helpfully with rede and deed and through whose contributions I was in a position to undertake a new journey. I had to wait in Bremen until the ninth, on which day the ship sailed. Early in the morning, I boarded the steamship *Roland* that was to carry us toward the open sea where the ocean steamer *New York*, that was to bring us to North America, received us. About three in the afternoon, the steamer *New York* began to move and towards the evening we were in the North Sea and crossed it in twenty-four hours. We passed through the English Channel and went past the Isle of Wight where the famous astronomer Tycho Brahe had lived in the fourteenth century. On the twelfth of July we reached the Bay of Southampton, and here the sad news of the disaster to the steamers *Arago* and *Canada*, because of floating icebergs, darkened our gay traveler's mood. Towards eleven in the morning we sailed on until we stopped opposite an old church in order to take on board more freight. The cannons were fired; it was time to say farewell to the continent; this was really the departure.

There were about five hundred passengers on board the ship *New York*. That very night we suffered a most unpleasant accident: a stoker, employed on the steamer, met a horrible death by the fall of a heap of coal that buried him. The weather until then was favorable, but on July 13 the fog became so thick that our ship had to make signals to warn others of our approach. In the afternoon, the fog cleared up to our delight, and we were crossing the great Atlantic Ocean.

The air became piercingly cold, and the inseparable companion of sea travelers, namely seasickness, made its appearance: many of the passengers were sick below. I and a fellow traveler* remained on our feet and did not let this enemy near us. In spite of the raw air, we marched up and down the deck, protected by our winter cloaks, and

---

at that time in Moldavia, in a land where the beneficent reviving rays of knowledge had not yet penetrated), that which neither time nor place could disturb: a spiritual education. Therefore, I brought him to Hanover on April 4 to leave him under the supervision of the official rabbi, Dr. S. G. Meyer, and the head-teacher, Dr. S. Frensdorff, that he might share in the higher education of the seminary for Jewish teachers in that place. After spending two months in Hanover with my dear son whom I had not seen for a long time in order to provide him with an introduction to educated families, I left him in the hope that through tireless industry he might reach that degree of spiritual education that would satisfy all my wishes.

* Abraham Kaufmann, born August 1820 at Urdenbach near Duesseldorf, came to America in 1849, returned to Europe in 1851 and married the daughter of Solomon Kaufmann of Cologne and again went to America. On his return journey he was shipwrecked without suffering any injury; later, he brought all his family over to join him. After the death of his first wife, he married her sister, Emma. It was my pleasure and happiness to become acquainted with this family, to whom I owe much.

46

our thoughts and glances wandered far and wide. The captain of the ship provided me daily, at my request, with a geographical reckoning of our journey as well as with an exact account of the miles we left behind us. On that day we found ourselves at 49 degrees, 51 minutes latitude, 5 degrees, 35 minutes longitude, and covered 165 miles. About noon on July 14, the strong northwest wind fell and mild weather began. On July 15 we were at 50 degrees, 12 minutes latitude, 18 degrees, 47 minutes longitude, and covered 254 miles. The following night we were troubled by storm and foul weather; towering waves, roaring frightfully, arose and then I understood very clearly the words of Psalm 107: "Those who travel at sea become aware of the wonders of the Almighty."

The next days passed quietly. On the sixteenth we were at 49 degrees, 52 minutes latitude and 25 degrees, 26 minutes longitude, and had covered 255 miles; on the seventeenth, at 49 degrees, 16 minutes latitude, 31 degrees, 30 minutes longitude, equal to 250 miles; on the eighteenth, 47 degrees, 52 minutes latitude, 37 degrees, 33 minutes longitude, equal to 254 miles; on the nineteenth, 46 degrees, 30 minutes latitude, 43 degrees, 30 minutes longitude, equal to 255 miles; on the twentieth, 45 degrees latitude, 49 degrees, 17 minutes longitude, equal to 252 miles.

We passed Newfoundland, where we were made uncomfortable by the story of one of our passengers, the captain of a ship. He told us that he had passed forty-three icebergs in that area and that his ship was damaged there on one of his last voyages. Such information was not calculated to arouse a cheerful mood, since we were so near the scene of danger and going towards it. However, we passed it, with God's help, without the least accident. On the twenty-first we were at 44 degrees latitude, 53 degrees, 50 minutes longitude, equal to 210 miles. On the twenty-second of July we found ourselves at 43 degrees, 1 minute latitude, 57 degrees, 38 minutes longitude, and had only gone 180 miles farther. At noon a complete calm descended.

On the twenty-third of July, at half-past twelve European time or six o'clock New York time, a pilot-boat came into sight. The happiness of the passengers was very great. All gathered on the deck to greet the pilot who soon stepped upon our ship. On the twenty-fourth of July we could make out Long Island through a telescope. Brooklyn, a great city on that island, is too well known to need a closer description. On the morning of the twenty-fifth we passed Sandy Hook, a fortress of considerable importance, and towards evening sailed at last into New York harbor. The joy and jubilation at entering a harbor has been so often described that I may well omit saying anything at all about it here.

As a second-cabin passenger* I was compelled to spend the night on board the ship. Upon the order of the commissioners of New York, all of whom are German, the deck and second-cabin passengers of a ship that arrives after five o'clock spend the first night on board. These commissioners made it their duty to care for the arriving deck and second-cabin passengers and to escort them to all parts of the city or wherever they wished to go. This is an arrangement to be highly grateful for, a precaution to protect poor aliens from many deceptions and swindles to which they were formerly exposed. Hundreds of people, formerly, waited at the wharfs for the arrival of an immigrant ship to lure the inexperienced into their dens where not only was everything that was sold them reckoned at doubled prices, but where one finally robbed the poor people of all their possessions that had any value.

I myself witnessed a scene of this kind which I would not have thought possible if I had not seen it with my own eyes. A Frenchman arrived in New York and refused to be warned but, in his excessive curiosity, insisted on visiting the city at once. He soon fell into the hands of a hotel-runner and before another day dawned was already robbed. Whatever little money he had, his little bundle of clothing, all his little mementos from home, fatherland and friends were all gone. When he complained, he was beaten up in addition and thrown out into the street. I must add, however, that here, too, justice was done and at his complaint in court everything had to be returned to him and those who had cheated him were severely punished. Thousands of similar occurrences had happened previously and women particularly were placed in the greatest danger. Fortunately, such and other shocking scenes have now, for the most part, been done away with, ever since the great number of Germans in New York caused measures against the prevailing evil to be taken and organized the "German Society."

On the morning of the twenty-sixth of July, I left the ship together with my dear friend and companion, Kaufmann, and his wife. To my great regret, however, we had to part almost at once. To be rid of the crowd of riff-raff that surrounded and hounded me with their solicitations, I hired a carriage and drove to a convenient hotel in one of the quiet neighborhoods of the great city.

It is no part of my plan to treat in this work of New York, of its eight hundred thousand inhabitants, its public buildings, the commercial advantages which it enjoys over all other cities of the American continent, and to show its bright and dark sides. This theme has been dealt

---

*   Through the good offices of Mr. Cohn of Bremen, the banker, to whom I was recommended by his uncle, Mr. Alexander Cohen of Hanover, I had the privilege of traveling in the second-cabin.

with often enough and is quite exhausted. I limit myself only to a picture of New York as it was sixty-six years ago, and take this from the description of Mr. Grant Thornburn, now eighty-six years old, a resident of the city. He says:

"I landed in New York on the sixteenth of June, 1794, after, as it was called in Lana's *New York Gazette*, an unusually short voyage of nine weeks. We disembarked at the corner of Front Street and Governor Lane. South Street at that time was under water. At the foot of Broadway was the Exchange, built before the Revolution, and in an upper story was Jobenn Baker's museum. That was before a Barnum was ever thought of. What was then the Exchange is now a fishmarket. At the eastern corner of Exchange and Broad Streets was the only station-house in the city. The city hall was where the custom-house is. There were only two banks in the city, the Bank of New York at the corner of William and Wall Streets and, right near it, a branch of the old Bank of the United States. The first city hotel was still being built: it extended from Cedar to Thomas Streets and faced Broadway. That house was the first building in America to have a slate roof; now it is a warehouse. In this hotel entertainments consisting of music and dancing were held in the winter, and there the Governeurs and Kimballs, the Franklins and Robinsons, the Leroys, Bayards, McEyers, Livingstons, Schermerhorns, Leonores, Beekmans and Hamiltons, Tays, Depeyrs, Clintons, Yaricks, Anzwerps, Kips, Dickers, and so on, assembled and met one another.

"At that time the 'upper tens' lived for the most part in what is now farthest downtown, many of them in Wall Street. At the corner of Pine and Nassau Streets stood an old Dutch farmhouse in which lived a man ninety-eight years old with his daughter. It was his father's house and his father had been born there, too. The farm ran from Nassau Street along Pine Street down to the East River and extended in width to Maiden Lane. The old farmer still had a vivid recollection of the Negro plot, the execution of twelve pirates, and the 'Doctor mob' of 1794. The Osnego market was in Maiden Lane. The poorhouse and the penitentiary were where the city hall is now, and the prison and gallows were where the surrogate's office is at present. We had only four little fire-engines, and wooden pumps, set up at the street-corners, furnished the water. The engines were supplied with water in a cumbersome way: the citizens formed two rows through which buckets were sent forward and back; these buckets held about three gallons each. Every householder was obliged by law to have as many buckets in his house as there were fireplaces; the buckets had to be hung up in the entrance as near as possible to the door."

Out of such small beginnings, with such small-town regulations, New York has built itself and in the space of half a century worked its way up to become one of the great cities of the world, exciting the wonder and astonishment of all travelers.

Chapter II

The First Immigration of Israelites into North America

On all my travels i have, naturally enough for a jew, paid particular attention to my Jewish coreligionists, in order to follow, wherever possible, the path of their wandering through all lands and to trace their relationships and their origins in the far-flung regions of their habitation. In New York, likewise, I made it a matter of great importance for myself to provide myself with as detailed a history as possible of the Jews of that city, as well as of the entire continent, and I believe I have found worthwhile material.

The first Jews who migrated to America went from Portugal to Brazil. I take this from the geography of South and North America by William Rapz (Philadelphia, 1857, 2nd edition). Page 358 reads as follows:

> "Brazil was discovered in 1500 by the Portuguese Pedro Cabal. In the beginning, only the Jews who had been driven out of Portugal settled there, until the Portuguese government sent over Thomas de Souza as governor. He improved the welfare of the colony by his excellent measures and founded Bahia. During the time that Portugal was a Spanish province, the Dutch took possession of the seven northern provinces of Brazil (1630). However, in return for an indemnity, they were relinquished in 1689 to Portugal which, in the meantime, had regained its independence."

In the same work on page 124, we find, that in 1614 New Amsterdam, now New York, was founded by the Dutch. It seems that by the capture of the Brazilian provinces by the Dutch the port of New Amsterdam became known in the South and very likely, as a result, several Jewish families emigrated from Brazil to New Amsterdam. Here the Jews, as everywhere, directed their chief attention to the improvement of commerce. Later, when Brazil fell into the hands of the Portuguese again and new persecutions were to be feared, almost all the Portuguese Jews emigrated to North America to the more liberal Hollanders. The Jews might have been especially attracted there by the government because it wished to build up the new port.

The settlement of the Portuguese Jews might well have taken place directly from Holland. Although weak as proof, I must not fail to file here what was told me of one of the oldest families by a member of it. In my journey through Cleveland, Ohio (North America), I made the acquaintance of a merchant, Benjamin Franklin Peixotto. The name caught my attention because I had met with it in Aleppo on my journey in the East (EIGHT YEARS IN ASIA AND AFRICA, 3rd edition, page 44), and I asked for detailed information on his family, a request which he most readily granted in the following sketch:

"The forefathers of Moses Levy Maduro Peixotto emigrated probably from Spain in the beginning of the seventeenth century. Unfortunately, the writer of this sketch has no definite dates and cannot state exactly when the family of M. L. M. Peixotto migrated to Curaçao, an island of the Dutch West Indies. Because of the fact that this island was occupied by the Spaniards in the sixteenth century and captured by the Dutch in the seventeenth century, one may draw the conclusion that the Peixottos either went directly from Spain to Curaçao, or from Spain to Holland and from there came to the island. This would be ascertained if members of the family who have continued to live until now on the island and in Amsterdam could be consulted. Moses Levy Maduro Peixotto, the first of the family with whose life the writer of this sketch is fully acquainted, was born on Curaçao. Here he received a liberal education and was brought up an active, well-educated man. He visited Europe towards the end of the last century and during his stay in Amsterdam became friendly with Jewish families. He married the daughter of an old Portuguese family, Lopez Salzedo, and from this marriage was born Daniel Levy Maduro Peixotto on July 18, 1800. I have more to say about him below.

"Moses Peixotto returned to Curaçao in 1805. Here he conducted an extensive business. In the year 1807 he visited the United States and came to New York on one of his own ships that, heavily laden, he planned to bring back with American products as its freight. It was at the time when that well-known law of Congress was passed at the suggestion of President Jefferson placing an embargo on all foreign freighters. Moses Peixotto had several ships in the port of New York and in other ports and was accordingly prevented from returning at once. So he remained in the country and, although he undertook still other journeys, became a citizen of the American republic. The fame of his hospitality and philanthropy soon spread among all foreigners. When the Portuguese congregation lost its minister, Moses Peixotto generously assumed the duties of this office for a number of years for the benefit of the widow of the dead *hazzan*. When his own means, later, were destroyed by evil fortune, he was elected *hazzan* and held this office until his death. He died at the age of sixty-two. A number of his sermons in manuscript are still in existence and show him to have been well-grounded in Jewish learning and of Orthodox inclination.

"Daniel Levy Maduro Peixotto, his oldest son, who later became famous as a physician and writer, was, as mentioned above, born in Amsterdam in 1800. He received the beginnings of his education from his mother, Judith Salzedo, a highly gifted woman. She taught him Latin and French and in these branches of knowledge he reached, even as a boy, great proficiency. He continued his studies in America under his father's supervision and was later placed under Professor Strebeck to continue his education. In the year 1815 he entered Columbia College and was graduated four years later, when he was nineteen. Since he was to be a physician, he betook himself to the famous Dr. Hosack of Washington and remained with him until he received the degree of doctor of medicine. His health, however, had suffered because of his tireless and zealous industry. He, therefore, went on a trip to the West Indies where he visited his relatives and was received in the highest circles of Curaçao and Caracas. Upon his return to New York, he began to practice and, after only a few years, enjoyed a wide reputation.

"In the meantime, he became a member of several societies and published a number of contributions to science and medicine. Together with Drs. B. Beck and John Bell, he published in the years 1823-25 the *New York Medical and Physical Journal*. He was also an industrious co-worker for literary publications. In 1825, there was founded in New York an academy of medicine, a society for fostering the science of medicine and its related branches, and Dr. Peixotto was elected the first secretary. Dr. Felix Pascalis was the president, Drs. Watts, Steam, and Joseph M. Smith, vice-presidents, and Dr. Samuel W. Moore, treasurer. In 1831, Dr. Peixotto was named president of the New York Medical Society that numbered among its members the distinguished physicians David Hosack, John R. B. Rodgers, John Redendonk, William Hammersby, Felix Pascalis, and others. At this time, I believe, he edited Gregory's *Practice* and other works. He spoke and wrote many languages with great facility: Hebrew, Greek, Latin, French, Dutch, Italian, English, and several oriental languages; his works include a large number of volumes and will soon appear in a collected edition. He was also brilliant as a speaker. A journal of 1831 said in judging one of his speeches: 'Yesterday evening we had the pleasure of hearing a most excellent and persuasive address by Dr. D. L. M. Peixotto. We regret only that we cannot provide our readers with this beautiful and learned address. Profound in its comprehension, beautiful and glowing in its presentation, Dr. Peixotto's lecture on "The Universal Influence and Usefulness of Literature" belongs to the best given in this city this winter.'

"A few years later, in 1836 I believe, Dr. Peixotto was appointed to the presidency of Willoughby Medical College and after that lived in

Willoughby. He died of consumption in 1843, after his return to New York, and left behind him a widow, the daughter of a rich New York merchant, Benjamin Seixas, and seven children."

One of his sons is Benjamin Franklin Peixotto, with whom I had the pleasure of becoming acquainted and to whom, as remarked above, I am thankful for this sketch. Although a merchant of importance, he cherishes learning with great affection and has devoted himself to the care of communal institutions: he is at present president of the Hebrew Literary Society of Cleveland. I hope that the information he has given us will be welcome to one or another among my readers.

We document our view, expressed above, with still other evidence leading to the same conclusion. On the eleventh of July, 1859, the Portuguese congregation of New York, Shearith Israel, laid the cornerstone of a new synagogue. On this festive occasion the rabbi of the congregation, Dr. A. Fischell, a native of Holland belonging to the Leeren family, delivered the following address which I furnish here because it has some bearing on the history of the immigration of Portuguese Jews:

"More than two hundred years have gone by since our ancestors, the founders of our congregation, set foot for the first time on this island. They came from Brazil, where they were part of a flourishing Jewish colony. The colonists had sought on this continent refuge from the religious persecutions of their native country, but were driven away also from this new settlement by the victorious Portuguese. As a result, a few emigrated to the West Indies, while others came to this place which the Dutch had purchased shortly before.

"After several energetic attempts to secure civic rights here, these were granted on two conditions. The first was that they were to provide for their own poor. Our forefathers assumed this obligation gladly. They were themselves too well accustomed to suffering not to have learnt to be sympathetic to the poor, the miserable, and the victims of calamity. Those who had been driven from one continent to another, and from one island to another, could not find the undertaking of this duty in any way burdensome, so that they would have gladly assumed it even if it were not an obligation required of them. The second condition was that they were to build no synagogue, but were to practice their devotions in their own homes and for this purpose build them close to each other. This condition, which had rather too much of the odor of the age's bigotry, would have involved our forefathers in insurmountable difficulties if the object of their worship had consisted of idols of stone or cement. However, since their worship was directed towards the Being whose all-pervading presence is as approachable in the humblest huts as it is in buildings resplendent with gold, they could find it as surely in the privacy of their homes as in the open, in that most splendid of all temples that has the heavens for its roof and God Himself for its architect.

"Although this requirement also seemed in no way a heavy burden to our forefathers, it shows, nevertheless, quite clearly how blinded the view of our brothers that was held at that time. The government officials of those days had been made to believe that the teaching of our religion of a universal salvation kept us back from the systematic participation in the creed of others. According to our religious view, the just Judge of the world will reward or punish mankind according to their deeds which He can easily perceive, but not according to their views or opinions of religion which He cannot control. Out of fear that synagogues would endanger the most widespread religion of the state, they tried to prevent the building of them; but that was simply to ascribe to these innocent walls of wood and stone powers of conversion that even the most superstitious of our brothers never believed. It is a comforting feeling to turn from the antiquated follies of old to the more enlightened views of modern times in which man has learned to perceive that religious belief cannot be gained by legal regulations or sectarian persecutions and that the survival of a creed depends upon the conscientious conviction of its followers and not upon the violent oppression exercised against the members of other religions.

"The first synagogue in this city was built one hundred and thirty years ago, and since then Congregation Shearith Israel has met for religious services. An interruption occurred only when the English captured this island. At that time our forefathers, enthusiastic supporters of the national cause, left the city and went to Philadelphia. Their minister dedicated the first synagogue there. I have all the more pleasure in citing this fact inasmuch as the congregation then organized is still in existence and has just built for itself a new and more spacious house of worship. Now for us, too, the time has come when removal from our synagogue has not only become desirable but an unavoidable necessity.

"Only the unusually deeply-rooted reluctance to leave the old, dear, and accustomed place could have postponed this undertaking so long. I mention this not to find fault, for I confess and readily admit that the same feeling also dominated me: I surrendered to it not out of superstition but rather for religious reasons. The place to which we come in joy or sorrow to seek our Creator becomes for us a memorandum-book in which the memory of past occurrences and the life we have passed through is recorded. It has seen the enthusiasm and the ecstatic hopes of youth as well as the earnest meditations of old age. Bride and bridegroom have brought to it their offering of thanks and there those who mourn have poured out their grief in words. There the orphaned could see the place where parents, gone to their sleep, paid their devotions and, as they themselves bowed in awe to take their seats, the old, revered face appeared again before them and awakened love, esteem, and a sense of duty. The venerable old building reminded others of the beloved figure of a friend or relative whose voice, once heard among the multitude praising the Lord, is now forever at discord with the earth in order to sing more harmonious hymns in the kingdoms of eternity.

"All these memories are to be extinguished! Only a few months more, and the center of our religious gatherings will become a heap of ruins. It will be replaced by a building that will proudly show itself more artistic in its structure and more fully decorated, but to which our memory will not be chained by the magic of grateful and sublime memories. From this point of view, the disappearance of our synagogue must appear as an irreparable injury, even if we have other motives that outweigh this. For it happens, not seldom, that ties that draw us closer to a place of divine worship claim so much of our attention and sympathy that we forget the principal object for which the place was consecrated. The disappearance of our personal recollections compels us to return again to fundamentals and to think of the much wider spheres in which our religious activity should function. We must think of ourselves not only as men but as members of the Jewish people, as witnesses of the Divine revelation.

"To one point I wish to direct your attention particularly: the time is already here when the Jews who live in this country must show more earnestness and activity and should not permit differences in nationality to disturb their unity and joint co-operation. What does Portugal or Poland, Spain or Germany really matter?* Have we not suffered persecutions enough in all those countries? Must we, because of this, divide into so many divisions and allow these names still to persecute us in so free a land? No! Let us gather together under the single name "American Israelites' and let this motto become the cornerstone on which we shall be able to build, and will build, successfully the splendid structure of Israelite unity, Israelite strength, Israelite civilization, and, above all, Israelite religious activity."

Frank Leslie's *Illustrated Newspaper* for September 29, 1860, has the following report:

"On September 12th, 1860, the 26oth anniversary of the landing of the first Jewish settlers in New York, the dedication of the new synagogue on West 19th Street was celebrated. This house of God was built by Congregation Shearith Israel ('Remnant of Israel') that follows the so-called Portuguese ritual. The congregation of Shearith Israel is the oldest and richest in New York; its members are chiefly American and English who are joined, however, by many Spanish, Portuguese, Germans, and West Indians. In 1729, this congregation held its first religious service in Mill Street. In 1833 the synagogue was removed to Crosby Street. Since the building on that street no longer

---

* Names for the various rituals.

answered the requirements of the congregation and was also rather badly in need of repairs, it was decided to sell it and to build a new temple. The sale of the property on Crosby Street brought the congregation $58,000. The new building on 19th Street cost more than $100,000."

The writer of the foregoing speaks of the 260th anniversary but does not tell us of the source of his information.

Of this congregation we find further mention in the *Jewish Calendar*, published by Jacques J. Lyons and Abraham de Sola (Montreal, 1854):

"The first settlement of Jews in the city of New York is supposed to have been about the year 5410-1650. The earliest known official records are copies of a petition of Salvador d'Andrada, dated December 17, 1655, to the Directors-General and Council of the Netherlands and of a remonstrance signed by Abraham de Lucena and others, dated March 10, 1656. In the Documentary *History of the State of New York*, Volume I, Governor Andros, in his answer to certain inquiries about New York in 1678, included Jews amongst the inhabitants, and in Volume III mention is made of the Reverend Abraham de Lucena applying as a Jewish minister to his excellency Governor Hunter, in 1710, to be exempted from militia and civil duties, stating that these privileges had been allowed to his predecessors. The first minutes of congregational affairs at present in possession of the Congregation Shearith Israel, written in Spanish and English, are dated Tishre 20, 5489-1728 and have reference to certain wholesome rules and regulations adopted 5466-1706, twenty-three years previous. Before the erection of a regular synagogue, prayers were read in a frame building in Mill Street in the first Ward, about one hundred feet east of the lot on which the first synagogue was built in 5489-1729 and consecrated on the eve of the seventh day of Pesach, 5490-1730. This place of worship was taken down, rebuilt on the same site in 5577-1817 and consecrated on the eve of the *Shabbath Hagadole*, 5578-1818, the congregation in the interim worshipping in a large room in an engine house in Beaver Street, a few doors west of Broad Street. During the prevalence of the yellow fever in 1822, service was performed in a schoolhouse, corner of Henry and Oliver Streets. In the spring of 5593-1833, the property in Mill and Beaver Streets was sold, but the materials of the old synagogue, having been reserved by the trustees as far as possible, were used in the erection of the present place of worship in Crosby Street, which was consecrated on the eve of the first day of Shabuot 5594-1834. The congregation worshipped in the meanwhile in a large room fitted up for that purpose over the New York Dispensary, corner of White and Centre Streets, which without interruption has ever since been used by various congregations as a temporary synagogue. The first *Beth Haim*, so far as is known, was on the corner of Madison and Oliver Streets, purchased in 5441-1681, and stood on a high hill adjoining the ground purchased in 5489-1729, extending to Chatham Street, then called the King's Highway. Interrment having been prohibited by the Common Council, a portion of this ground that had not been used was sold and the entrance made in Oliver Street, facing Henry Street. The second *Beth Haim* in Eleventh Street, near Sixth Avenue. The third *Beth Haim* in Twenty-first Street, near Sixth Avenue, was dedicated November 5589-1820. Interrment was discontinued in accordance with an ordinance of the Common Council prohibiting burial in the City 5611-1851. The fourth *Beth Haim, now in use,* is situated on Long Island, in Kings and Queens Counties, opposite Cypress Hills Cemetery, five miles from Williamsburg ferry, consisting of nearly seven acres, dedicated August 3rd, 5611-1851. It was chartered by the legislature 5613-1853."

From all that has been presented above it follows sufficiently that the immigration of Jews to America took place in the seventeenth century.

During my stay in New York, I tried to search (at the Portuguese congregation, since I had learnt that this was the oldest) for various documents that dealt with Jewish history. I became acquainted with the former *hazzan* of the Greene Street synagogue, Mr. Leo, the son-in-law of the late president of that congregation. Mr. Leo's wife has some old documents as part of her inheritance. Among them was a letter that the Jews of Malabar sent the Portuguese Jews of New York, written in Hebrew and in the square Hebrew alphabet. Here it is, word for word:

אלו המעשה של היהודים שבאו לארץ מלב"ר:

מגלות בית שני תו"בב שהיה בשנת ג' אלף תתכ"ח ליצירה יצאו הרבה יהודים
איש ואשה ובאו לארץ מלב"ר ונתיישבו בד' מקומות ואלה שמותם. כנ"גנור
.. פא"קלור .. מדי .. פולוטה .. ורובם היה בכנגנור הנקרא שינ"גילי והיה תחת ממשלת
שיר"ה פרימ"אל. ובשנת ד' אלפים קל"ט ליצירה שהם שע"ט לנוצרים. ניתן להם
מן מלך שיר"ה פרימ"אל ושמו איר"וי ברמ"ין חוקים ופרטגמאות בטס של נחושת
הנקרא שיפ"רו למנהגם ולגדולתם. ובאותו הזמן היה להם ע"ב בתים בכנגנור והנשיא
שלהם שמו יוסף רבן. וזה המלך שיר"ה פרימ"אל שחילק כל ארצו ונתן לשמונה
מלכים שהם מלך טירב"גנור .. כריכנגור .. כליכ"וט .. אר"גוט .. פלכט"שירי ..
כולאס"טירי .. כורבינט .. ומלך קוגין ..

וזה העתקה של טס הנחושת שנעתק מלשון
מלב"ר ללשון הקודש.

בשלום האלוה הוא מלך שעשה הארץ כרצונו. ולזה אלוה אלו נשאתי ידי איר"וי
ברמ"ין שגזר בפריטגא זה שהרבה מאות אלף שנים נהג הממשלה שנה ושני שנים
בזה היום יושב בכנגנור וגזור שהם ל"ו שנים למלכותו. בגבורה אמיץ גזר. בגבורה אמיץ
הרשה ליוסף רבן ה' מיני צבע. תותא. רכיבת פיל וסוס. וקריאה לפנות הדרך.

57

ולגייר מן ה' אומות. גר היום. מצעות בארץ. מצעות הקשוטים לנוי. ומגדל הפורח. צל. דמאן. חצוצרות. תוף שמכה בשני עצים. ואת הכל נתתי לו ולע"ב בתים ושכירות ארץ והמאזנים עזב. ושאר המדינות שיש בהם תושבים ובתי כנסיות יהיה הוא ראש ומושל. ובלי שום שינוי וערעור עשה טס הנחושת ונתן לאדרון של ה' מיני צבעים הוא יוסף רבן לו ולזרעו בנים ובנות חתן וכלה. כל זמן שזרעו קיים בעולם. וכל זמן שהירח קיים. וזרעם יקיים קיים ויברך האלוה. ולזה העדים ח' מלכים הנז' והסופר שכתב כילא"פיז וזהו חתימתו ‏‏⁂

ונתיישבו היהודים בכנ"גנור עד בא פורטוגיז וכיון שבא פורטוגיז היה להם לפוקה ולמכשול ויצאו משם ובאו בקוגין בשנת ה' אלפים שכ"ו ליצירה ומלך קוגין נתן להם מקום לבתים ולבית הכנסת סמוך לפאלאטין שלו כדי להיות להם לעזרה. ונבנה פה בית הכנסת בשנת ה' אלפים שכ"ח ליצירה ע"י ד' אנשים גדולים שמואל קשטיאל. דוד בלילא. אפרים סלח. יוסף לוי. ועדיין היו בגלות מפני פורטוגיז שלא יוכל לילך בחוקינו ולא יוכל לילך למחייתם במקומות שלהם והיה להם הרבה צער עד שבאו אולנדיז בקוגין בשנת אלף תרס"ג לנוצרים ח' ינוארו ונתקררו דעתם והיו שקטים ונחים עם אנשי מלב"ר

בעזר בקוגין יע"א

ובשנת אלף תרפ"ו לנוצרים בא פה קוגין ד' אנשים מן [א]משטרדם משה פיריאירה. יצחק אורנש. אברהם בורטה. יצחק מוכַט. והם יהודים ספרדים סוחרים וראו כל המקומות שיושבים יהודים ושמחו וכתבו ל[א]משטרדם כל העינינים וגם חסרון הספרים וכיון ששמעו שלחו מן ק"ק אמשטרדם מתנה לק"ק קוגין חומשים מחזורים ושולחן ערוך ואיזה ספרים אחרות [אחרים] ושמחו כל הקהל.

ומאותו הזמן היו לנו אוהבים באמשטרדם ואנו כותבים להם ומביאים ספרים שאנו צריכים עד היום ויש פה ספרים הרבה גמרות מדרשות וספרי קבלות ואין אנו בקיאין כל כך באלו הספרים. אבל אנו הולכים כפי השולחן ערוך שחיבר יוסף קארו ומנהגינו מנהג ספרדים.

בקוגין אנו הנקראים יהודים לבנים שהם אנשים שבאו מגלות ארץ הקדושה תו"בב כמו מ' בתים וא' בית הכנסת ולא יש עוד בכל ארץ מלבר . . אבל יהודים הנקראים יהודים שחורים הם אנשים שנעשו במ"לבר מן גרות ושחרור ובלי שחרור בערבובייא. וע"ז אין אנו נותנים נשותינו [בנותינו] להם ואין אנו לוקחים נשותיהם [בנותיהם]. אבל מנהגיהם ומשפטידם הכל כמותינו ויושבים בשבעה מקומות.

בקוגין יש כמו ק"נ בתים וג' בית הכנסת. באנגי כאימל יש כמו ק' בתים וב' בית הכנסת פרעור יש כמו ק' בתים. א' בית הכנסת. שינוט יש כמו נ' בתים א' בית הכנסת. מאלה יש כמו נ' בתים א' בית הכנסת. טירטור יש כמו י' בתים א' בית הכנסת. מוטס יש כמו י' בתים א' בית הכנסת

יציע ליד השם הטוב הנבון אל מול פני האדון רבי שלמה ששמשן שמו לעד אכי"ר סעיר קונין לעיר נייוארק יע"א [מישאן] סוחר
ולור קרוב"ץ

History of the Jews in the Land of Malabar

"In the course of their wanderings in exile after the destruction of the Second Temple, which took place in the year 3828, many Jews, both men and women, came to the land of Malabar and settled in four places, namely, Kangnur, Paklur, Modi, and Pä-luta. Most of them settled in Kangnur, which was called Senegal, and were under the rule of Sira Primal.

"In the year 4139 after the creation of the world (that is, 379, according to the common chronology), King Sira Primal, who was also known as Iru Brahman, gave them laws and privileges, and these were engraved on a tablet of brass which, according to their customs and appearance, were called *Seferu*. At this time they had in Kangnur seventy-two houses and their prince (*nasi*) was Joseph Rabban. The king, Sira Primal, divided his kingdom and gave it to eight kings whose names were Tirbengur, Krikengur, Klikut, Argut, Plaktsiri, Kolastiri, Kurbiut, and to the king of Kugin (Cochin?).

"This is a transcript of the brass tablet, translated from the language of the land of Malabar into Hebrew: In the peace of God, the King, Who has created the world according to His Will! To this God Who has ruled and reigned many hundreds of thousands of years and years and years,* I , Iru Brahman, lift my hands in an oath. I reign at Kangnur now and have ruled thirty-six years since I ascended the throne. With mighty power I order and with a mighty power I allow Joseph Rabban to wear five kinds of colors and to ride elephant and horse and to have cried out before him that men make way before him,** to make converts among the five peoples who live here, to spread carpets*** and have couches for ornament, a flying tower (?),† flutes,**** trumpets, and kettledrums that are struck with two sticks: all this I have permitted him and the seventy-two families, as well as to rent land and weights.***** He shall be prince and lord over all the provinces in

---

*   From this it is to be concluded that they believe in a creation of the world to which they ascribe a great age.

** To this day, it is forbidden the Jews of Persia to ride freely in the city streets. Since a similar prohibition probably existed here, special permission had to be granted.

*** In many places in Africa, Jews are not permitted to ornament their houses (see *Eight Years in Asia and Africa*, p. 263).

†   Benjamin did not know the meaning. It was perhaps a standard borne by the princely retinue. [ed.]

**** The text reads צל דמאן which I do not understand. Perhaps it stands for צלצל .

*****A custom exists in Asia to this day that larger quantities must be weighed by one who is vouched for by the government and has rented the right.

which the tolerated people dwell and synagogues are found. Without change, without condition attached, he has prepared this tablet of brass and given it to the lord of the five colors, Joseph Rabban to him and his descendants, his sons and daughters, sons-in-law and daughters-in-law, as long as his descendants exist in the world, as long as the moon exists.* May his race last long and God bless it. To this the eight kings are witnesses and the scribe who has written it — Kilafis. This is his seal: ⅃ ⅃

"The Jews remained in Kangnur until the Portuguese came. These were for the Jews a snare and a stumbling-block. Therefore, the Jews left and came to Cochin in the year 5326 after the creation of the world. The king of Cochin assigned them a place for their houses and their synagogue near his palace so as to be able to come to their help. A synagogue was built then, in the year 5328 after the creation of the world, by the aid of four distinguished men: Samuel Kastial, David Blilia, Ephraim Zelach, and Joseph Levi. They were still oppressed because of the Portuguese so that they could not live according to the commands of the Torah and could not go about their business as in their former dwelling-places: because of this they suffered greatly. In the year 1663 (common era), the Dutch arrived at last and the hearts of the Jews were lightened. And so, by the help of God, they lived in peace and in quiet among the inhabitants of Malabar in Cochin.

"In the year 1686 (common era), four men came to Cochin from Amsterdam: Moses Ferrara, Isaac Irgas, Abraham Burata, and Isaac Muchata. They were Portuguese Jews, merchants, who visited all the places where Jews lived. They rejoiced and reported everything to Amsterdam, above all, that there was a great lack of books. When that was learned in Amsterdam, that community sent, as a gift to the community of Cochin, *Humashim* (copies of the Pentateuch), *mahzorim* (holiday prayer-books), copies of the *Shulhan Arukh*, and other books, to the joy of the whole community.

"Since then we have friends in Amsterdam. We write to them and to this day they send us the books we need. Accordingly, many volumes of the *Gemara* (the Talmud) may be found here, *midrashim*, and also Cabalistic works. We are not well versed in these, but we do regulate ourselves according to the *Shulhan Arukh* which Joseph Caro prepared; our ritual is that of the Portuguese.

"In Cochin we are called the "white Jews." We are those, namely, who came as exiles from the Holy Land; we are about forty families strong, with a synagogue. There are no more in all the land of Malabar. But there are also the so-called "black Jews." They are descended from

---

* Evidence that they measure time by moons.

those who became Jews in Malabar — as freemen and as slaves. We do not give them our daughters in marriage nor do we take our wives from among them; but their way of living and their pursuits are quite like ours. They live in seven places: in Cochin are about one hundred and fifty families and three synagogues, in Bangi Kaimel one hundred families and two synagogues, in Ferur one hundred families and one synagogue, in Shinut fifty families and one synagogue, in Malah fifty families and one synagogue, in Tirtur about ten families and one synagogue, and in Muts ten families and one synagogue.*"

In a business letter which I found, the foregoing writing is mentioned. Since the letter itself is of no great importance, I present it here only as an exact copy, in English, without translation:

Cochin, 13. January 1790.

Mr. Solomon Simson, Newyork.
    Dear Sir.
    Embrace the oppty of acknowledging the favor reception of Your favor of Decbr. 88. And duplicate of Yours of Juny 87 the original not having come to hand.
    Juny 87. Am obliged for Your generous offer of service and am sorry that had not the pleasure of seeing Mr. Haley to whom and Capt. Moore think myself much indebted for their recommending me to Your acquaintance as Mr. Haley is not here to refer to for the particulars concerning the trade of Your place. I shall say little on that subject except acquainting that trade here is declining so fast as puts it beyond any hopes of its answering to our mutual or even to one of our advantages.
    Dec. 88. Am happy to learn that Mr. Haley being recovered. My respects to him also to Capt. Helme, am obliged for all the information You gave and agreeable to request enclose here in the particular of our persuasion. Should Capn. Sarly touch at this post he shall meet every attention from   Dear Sir
Your Most Devoted H. Servant
**שמואל בן מהורר אברהם זצ"ל*

P.S. Saleth the sort You required is not procurable here. Best compliments from my ten Abraham Samuels and his spouse and Mr. Solomon Norden from London to You and all Your friends.

The letter is without a date and was sent from Malabar, via a sailing-ship, to London. From there it was mailed on January 13, 1787, to New

---

*   This document contradicts the account in the *Mikveh Yisrael* of Manasseh ben Israel, folio 24, page 1, Lemberg 1847, and the information of the Meassefim (for the year 5550, 1790 C.E., Sivan and Shebat). The former has the immigration as from Mongolia; the latter as having taken place from Yemen to Malabar.
**   It seems to be either a Polish or a German name.

York, as the seal of the post-office shows.* It contained the history of the immigration of the Jews of Malabar and the account of the privileges granted them by the kings. From this it is clear that the Jews of Malabar, after the destruction of the Second Temple in the year 3828 (in the year 67 according to Christian chronology), consequently in the first century of the Christian era, emigrated directly from Palestine to Malabar.

I found another letter, dated seven years afterwards (1794), which the Portuguese Jews of New York sent to the Jews of China. I made copies of both letters which I quote here.*

ב'ה נייא יארק ר"ח שבט תקנ"ה באלף הששי
ליצירה
אליכם בני ישראל אקרא לשלום: אך טוב
וחסד ורב שלום

ראו ראינו וקרינו מספרי מסעות אשר נדפסו מחדש מן גלח אחד ערל שמו
אלכסנדר גרוסטיאן: שהיה במדינתכם נקרא טשעני [חינא]: ומצא שם יהודים:
והוא היה בבה"כ שלהם וראה שם י"ג' פתחים לארון הקודש אשר בתוכו תורת משה:
לכן בקשנו מאתכם לכתוב לנו אם אמת אתו: ולהודיע לנו מספר בני ישראל
שיש שם ומאיזה שבט את [אתם]: ומאיזה עת אחר חורבן אתם גולים לשם: ומה
מנהגכם: ואם יש אתכם ספרי תורות ושאר ספרים: ואם יש לכם שלוה או גלות:
ומה מעשיכם: כמו שאנו קבלנו כתב מן ארץ מלבר מן אחינו ב"י: אשר המה יושבים
שם בשלוה גדול: ויש להם נשיא אחד בשמו יוסף רבן: והרשה המלך מלבר לו
ה' מיני צבע: ולגייר מן ה' אומות: והוא יהיה ראש ומושל על כל בני ישראל
הדרים שם: כל זמן שזרעו קיים וירח קיים: ואגב הננו מודיע לכם שאנו יושבים בכאן
מדינת אמעריקא בנייא יארק ובשאר מקומות בשלוה גדול: וישראלים יושבים עם
ערלים על הדין דיני ממנות הן דיני נפשות: בכאן יש כמו ע"ב בעלי בתים ויש
לנו בה"כ הנקרא שארית ישראל: ושאר מקומות עם בתי כנסיות וכולם יושבים
בשלוה גדול: לכן אם יש אפשר לכם לכתוב תשובה עם מהות וניקום של מדינתכם
והיה לנו לנחת גדול ולמשיבת נפש: ועלינו לשרתכם ככל אשר תצונו עלינו כה
דברי הכותב הדורש שלומכם
הקטן אלכסנדר בר צבי ז"ל
הקטן שלמה בר יוסף שמשון ז"ל

ע"ש אם יש את נפשכם לכתוב לנו תשובה: אזי שימו כתבכם בנייר חלק המונח
בתוך אגרת זו אשר כתוב מבחוץ בלשון אנגלטירה לשמי ובודאי יגיע לידנו ממש

לעיר קעפאנג במדינת הַאנאן
ליד פרנסים וקנים בעיר הנל בטשעני

---

* A third letter is dated January 13, 1790, and deals with business matters.

62

The letter to China read:

New York, New Moon of Shebat 5555
(after the creation of the world)

Children of Israel, I greet you for peace: may only happiness and favor and the fullness of peace be your lot.

We have seen and read in descriptions of travels published not long ago by a Christian clergyman, Alexander Christian by name, who was in your land of China, that he found Jews there. He was in their synagogue and saw thirteen openings in the holy tabernacle in each of which was a Torah of Moses. We request you, therefore, to inform us if he reports the truth and at the same time to tell us the number of the children of Israel who are to be found there; from what tribe you are; when, after the Destruction, you migrated there; what your ritual is; if you have books of the Torah and other books; if you live in peace or are oppressed; and what you do for a living. In like manner, we have received a writing from the land of Malabar, from our brother-Jews there. They live in fortunate circumstances. They have a prince whose name is Joseph Rabben; the king of Malabar has permitted him five colors and allowed him to make converts among the five peoples; he is to be the chief and lord of all the Jews who dwell there as long as his family lasts, as long as the moon lasts.

At the same time, I inform you that we, in America, live much at peace in New York and in other places, that Jews act as judges beside Christians in suits involving money as well as at the trial of capital crimes. Here there are about seventy-two families.* We have a synagogue which is called Shearith Israel. In other places are other synagogues, and we all live in great peace. If it is possible for you to inform us about the usage and ways of your province it would please us greatly. We are always at your service.

These are the words of the writer who wishes you well.

Alexander Hirsch
Solomon Joseph Simson**

If you wish to send us an answer, place your letter in the enclosed envelope, on which is an address in English. It will then reach us without fail.

To the city of Kaifang, in the province of Honan, for the heads and elders of this city in China.

They gave this letter to Captain Howell, to whom they wrote the letter that follows. Upon his return, later, he noted down that he could not find those to whom the letter was addressed and sent it back.

---

*   What a huge growth! Now there are almost 40,000 Jews there!
** These names seem to have belonged to Polish or German Jews.

New York, Juny 22, 1795.

Sir.

You have herewith a letter in Hebrew directed to the Elders of the Jewish Congregation at Cac fong or Cac fong ford, in the Province of Honan; these people are not called Jews by the Chinese but are called Tiaokin kiao by which name You will please to inquire for them. If You should not meet with any of them, then please to get some person to direct it to them in Chinese agreeable to the above. Your complyance may bring some accounts from this people that may serve to amuse the literati and will in a particular manner oblige me. Sincerely wishing You a prosperous voyage and safe return, I am,   Sir,

Your H. & H. Servant

Solomon Simson.*

This letter was directed to

"Capn. Howell

Bound for China."

On the cover the following words are written: "Captain Howell could not discover them."

Before we tell about the second Jewish immigration, we shall first have another glance at the congregations and charitable institutions of New York.

This city has twenty-three Jewish congregations with as many synagogues. *The first is Shearith Israel*, mentioned above. This is the richest congregation, following the Portuguese ritual. At present it has sixty members, but of these only about twelve or fifteen families are of Portuguese descent; the others are English and Spanish who, because there was no other synagogue at that time, joined this Portuguese congregation and therefore are likewise called Portuguese Jews, although they are not really such. The congregation's income amounted to $91,136.30 from July 1, 1858 until July 1, 1859; its expenses, $62,442.42; so that there was a surplus of $28,693.88. The capital of the synagogue fund amounts to $18,500. The real property of this congregation consists of thirty-four lots on Seventy-first and Seventy-second Streets; as well as a lot on Nineteenth Street, six lots on Sixth Avenue between Twentieth and Twenty-first Streets, four lots on Twentieth Street between Sixth and Seventh Avenues; besides the cemetery on Twenty-first Street, the cemetery on Eleventh Street, the cemetery on the New Bowery (formerly on Oliver Street), and the cemetery on Long Island.

I hear from various sources that the capital of the congregation was derived from the legacies of rich Jews who intended them for char-

---

*   This is the way the letter is to be found in Benjamin II's book. [Tr.]

64

itable purposes among all the brothers of their faith, but that this congregation, because it had the upper hand from the beginning, appropriated the money so that other, later congregations would very likely have an action at law against it if they had possession of trustworthy documents to be able to prove how the money had come to Shearith Israel. It would be a difficult matter to obtain these documents from the hands of the Portuguese Jews, because they permit no one into their archives.

The Second Congregation: Bnai Jeshurun

Polish ritual. Organized in the year 5586 (1825). The synagogue is on Greene Street, between Houston and Bleecker Streets, and was consecrated in September 5612. Cemeteries: the first, on Thirty-second Street near Sixth Avenue, no longer in use; the second, on Long Island, adjoins that of Congregation Shearith Israel. The ministers are: Dr. M. J. Raphall, rabbi, and Amsel Leo, cantor, whom we mentioned above. President: Mr. David Sampson. The aforesaid Dr. Raphall is the only rabbi that the Orthodox have to show. Because of his scholarly attainments and his beneficent character he is highly respected by Jews and Christians. In the past year he was called to Washington, as the representative of his religion, to deliver the prayer at the opening of Congress on February 1st. The prayer was printed in a number of newspapers and runs as follows:

"Almighty and most merciful God, we approach Thy presence this day to thank Thee for Thy past mercies, and humbly to beseech Thee to continue and extend the same to Thy servants, the Representatives of these United States in Congress assembled.

"Lord, great and manifold have been Thy bounties to this highly-favored land. Heartfelt and sincere are our thanks. While the vast despotisms of Asia are crumbling into dust, and the effete monarchies of the Old World can only sustain themselves by yielding to the pressure of the spirit of the age, it has been Thy gracious will that in this Western hemisphere there should be established a Commonwealth after the model of that which Thou, Thyself, didst bestow on the tribes of Israel, in their best and purest days. The constitution and the institutions of this Republic prove to the world that men, created in Thy image and obedient to Thy behests, are not only capable, fully capable, of self-government, but that they know best how to combine civil liberty with ready obedience to the laws, religious liberty with warm zeal for religion, absolute general equality with sincere respect for individual rights. In acquiring and carrying out these most wise institutions, Thy protection, Lord, has been signally manifest. It was Thy right hand that defended the founders of this Commonwealth, during the long and perilous struggle of right against might. It was Thy wisdom that inspired them, when they established this Congress, to be what Thy tabernacle, with the urim and thummin — right and equity — were intended to have been for the tribes of Israel — the heart of the entire nation, where the wants, the feelings, and wishes of all might become known, to be respected by all, so that union might create strength, and concord keep pace with prosperity.

"Lord, the ordinary life-time of a man has barely elapsed since this Constitution came into force, and under its auspices our country, from being feeble and poor has become wealthy and powerful, ready to take rank with the mightiest, and Thou, O Lord, wilt realize unto it Thy gracious promise unto Thy chosen people: *Wehosircha Adonai letobah* — the Lord will distinguish thee for that which is good.

"Supreme Ruler of the universe, many days and many weeks have gone by since thy servants, our Representatives, first met in this Congress, but not yet have they been able to organize their House. Thou who makest peace in Thy high Heavens, direct their minds this day that with one consent they may agree to choose the man who, without fear and without favor, is to preside over this assembly. To this intent, Father most gracious, do Thou endow them with Thy spirit; the spirit of wisdom and of understanding; the spirit of counsel and of amity; the spirit of knowledge and of fear of the Lord. Grant, Father, that amidst the din of conflicting interests and opinions, Thy grace may direct them so that each one of them and all of them may hold the even tenor of their way — the way of moderation and of equity; that they may speak and act and legislate for Thy glory and the happiness of our country; so that, from the North and from the South, from the East and from the West, one feeling of satisfaction may attend their labors; while the whole people of the land joyfully repeat the words of Thy Psalmist: "How good and how pleasant it is when brethren dwell together in unity."

"Lord God of Abraham, of Isaac, and of Jacob, I, Thy servant, beseech Thee, bless these Representatives, even as Thou has directed Thy priests to bless Thy people:

Yevarekhekha Adonai ve-yishmerekah
Yaer Adonai panav elekha Vi-yehuneka
Yissa Adonai panav elekha v'yassem lekha Shalom
May the Lord bless ye and preserve ye.
May the Lord cause his countenance to shine upon ye and be gracious unto ye.
May the Lord raise his countenance unto ye and grant ye peace.

"May this blessing of the One who liveth and who reigneth forever rest upon your counsels and yourselves this day, and evermore. — Amen."

66

The Third Congregation: Anshe Chesed

German ritual. Organized in the year 5590 (1830). This is the largest German congregation, not only in the United States, but on the whole American continent. The synagogue is on Norfolk Street, between Stanton and Houston Streets, and was consecrated in May 1850. The cemetery is on Long Island, near Cypress Hills Cemetery. Ministers: the post of rabbi is at present vacant; earlier, Dr. Lilienthal was the first rabbi. He is now the rabbi of Congregation Bene Israel in Cincinnati. The second rabbi was Dr. Bondy; the cantor, L. Sternberger; the second, J. Hecht. The president is Mr. E. A. Stern.

Fourth Congregation: Shaarey Zedek

Polish ritual. Organized in the year 5600 (1840). The synagogue is at No. 38 Henry Street. The cemetery is in Yorkville, at Eighty-sixth Street. Minister: H. A. Henry. President: Mr. Joseph Levy.

Fifth Congregation: Shaarey Hashamayim

German ritual. Organized in the year 5601 (1841). The synagogue is at No. 122 Attorney Street, between Rivington and Stanton Streets. The burial-ground is in Salem Fields Cemetery, near Cypress Hills Cemetery, and adjoins the cemetery of Congregation Bnai Jeshurun. Ministers: Dr. M. Lilienthal, rabbi emeritus; I. Falkenstein, *hazzan* (cantor). President: Mr. Moses Wallach.

Sixth Congregation: Rodeph Shalom

German religious service. Organized in 5603 (1843). The synagogue is on Clinton Street, between Houston and Stanton Streets. The cemetery adjoins that of Congregation Anshe Chesed. Minister: Rev. N. Davidson. President: Mr. H. T. Weinschenk.

Seventh Congregation: Emanu-El

Organized in 5605 (1845). For some time the synagogue was at No. 56 Chrystie Street, between Walker and Hester Streets. It was later removed to Twelfth Street, between Third and Fourth Avenues. Cemetery: Salem Fields Cemetery in the northerly part of Brooklyn and Jamaica Street; it adjoins that of Congregation Bnai Jeshurun. Ministers: Rev. S.* Merzbacher, preacher; Rev. A. Rubin, cantor. President:

---

*   Should be *L*. [Tr.]

Mr. A. Michelbacher.

This congregation is the first Reform congregation in America. The above-mentioned rabbi has also written a new prayer-book, *Seder Tefillah*. It was revised by Dr. Adler in 1850. The principal prayers are in Hebrew; the others in German. The synagogue has a choir and an organ. It is very crowded on the Sabbath and holidays. This congregation is the most charitable in all America and many of its members are much interested in noble and superior matters. It is, as I have convinced myself, the only congregation in all America that is distinguished by both of these characteristics.

At present the well-known, learned and profound Dr. Adler occupies the post of rabbi of this congregation. His merits are too well-known among the learned rabbis of Germany to require any further elaboration here.

Eighth Congregation: Shaarey Tefilah

Polish ritual. Organized in 5606 (1846). The synagogue is at No. 112 Wooster Street, between Spring and Prince Streets. The cemetery is at 105th Street. Minister: Rev. Samuel M. Isaacs. President: Mr. John I. Hart.

Ninth Congregation: Beth Israel

Polish ritual. Organized in 5606 (1846). At present the synagogue is above the New York Dispensary, but it will soon be removed to No. 56 Chrystie Street, between Walker and Hester Streets. The cemetery is in Yorkville. The post of preacher is at present unoccupied. President: Mr. S. Pinner.

Tenth Congregation: Bnai Israel

This is a Dutch congregation, organized in 5607 (1847). The synagogue is at No. 63 Chrystie Street, between Walker and Hester Streets. The cemetery is in Yorkville, at Ninety-fifth Street. Minister: Rev. M. S. Cohen. President: Philip Levi.

Eleventh Congregation: Ahabat Chesed

Bohemian ritual. Organized in 5608 (1848). The synagogue is at No. 33 Ridge Street. The burial-place is in Cypress Hills Cemetery. Minister: Rev. Falkman Teberich. President: Mr. Ignatz Stein.

Twelfth Congregation: Shaarey Rachamim

German ritual. Organized in 5609 (1849). The synagogue is at 156 Attorney Street, between Stanton and Houston Streets. The burial-place is in Cypress Hills Cemetery. Minister: Rev. L. Heilner. President: Mr. L. Federlein.

Thirteenth Congregation: Bikur Cholim

German ritual. Organized in 5610 (1849). The synagogue is at 514 Pearl Street, in Monroe Hall, at the corner of Center Street. The cemetery is at Ninety-third Street in Yorkville. Minister: Rev. Wolf Stamper. President: Mr. Isaac Levy.

Fourteenth Congregation: Beth Abraham

Polish ritual. Organized in 5611 (1850). The synagogue is at No. 9 Henry Street. The burial-ground is in Cypress Hills Cemetery. Minister: Rev. L. Kantrowitz. President: Mr. Isaac Peiser.

Fifteenth Congregation: Beth El

German ritual. Organized in 5613 (1852). The synagogue is at No. 1104 Broadway, near Thirty-third Street. The cemetery adjoins that of Congregation Emanu-El. Minister: Rev. I. Schiekler. President: Mr. Edward Nathan.

Sixteenth Congregation: Beth Elohim

Polish ritual. Organized in 5614 (1853). The synagogue is at 51 Division Street. As yet the congregation has no cemetery of its own. Minister: Rev. Jerachmiel Chuck. President: Mr. M. Greenthal.

Seventeenth Congregation: Neve Zedek

This is really a charitable and aid society. It has a place at No. 9 Henry Street that is arranged as a synagogue. The cemetery adjoins that of Congregation Beth Abraham. The president of the society is Mr. Schillink of Mulberry Street. The presiding official of the synagogue is Mr. Jaffe.

Eighteenth Congregation: Bnai Zion

German ritual. Organized in 5614 (1853). The synagogue is at 202 Houston Street. Minister: Rev. J. Leon. President: Dr. Weiler.

Nineteenth Congregation: Beth Hamidrash

Polish ritual. Organized in the month of Sivan 5612 (1852). Religious services are held in Monroe Hall, 514 Pearl Street at the corner of Center Street. President: Mr. Isidor Raphael, 405 Pearl Street. Minister: Rabbi Abraham Myers. The burial-ground is near Cypress Hills Cemetery and adjoins the cemeteries of Congregation Anshe Chesed and Rodeph Shalom.

Twentieth Congregation: Beth Hamidrash Livne Yisrael Yelide Polin

Organized in 5613, in the month of Heshvan. Religious services are held at 132 Walker Street. President: Mr. J. Middleman. The burial-ground is in Cypress Hills Cemetery.

Twenty-first Congregation: Beth Hamidrash
Twenty-second Congregation: Beth El
Twenty-third Congregation: Shaarey Beracha

Organized in 1859 by French Jews.

There are two synagogues in Brooklyn. Likewise, two in Williamsburg. There is one synagogue in Hoboken.

The Jewish Charitable and Educational Societies of New York City

1. *Hebra Hased Vaamet.* Its purpose is to visit the sick and to be helpful at funerals and in the house of mourning. It associated itself with Congregation Shearith Israel and was organized in the year 5562 (1802). President: Mr. Isaac Phillips.

2. *Polonies Talmud Torah** of Congregation Shearith Israel, under the supervision of its trustees. Organized in the year 5568 (1808). The school is in the basement of the Crosby Street synagogue.

3. *Female Hebrew Benevolent Society of Congregation Shearith Israel.* Organized 5580 (1820). First "directress": Mrs. J. J. Lyons.

4. *Meshibat Nefesh,* charitable society, organized in 5582 (1822). President: Mr. H. Aronson.

5. *Hebrah Gemilut Hesed,* society for mutual aid, organized in 5586 (1826). President: Mr. A. S. Van Praag.

---

* Benjamin II has "Polnische Talmud Torah" (Polish Talmud Torah). [Tr.]

6. *Society for the Education of Poor Children and the Relief of Indigent Persons*, organized in 5588 (1828). It was allied to Congregation Shearith Israel. President: Mr. L. J. Cohen.

7. *Hebrah Terumat Hakodesh*, a society for the purpose of collecting and transmitting funds for the poor in the Holy Land, organized in 5592 (1832). President: Mr. Solomon I. Isaacs.

8. *Hebrah Ahavat Achim* is allied to Congregation Anshe Chesed. Organized in 5592 (1832). President: Mr. L. Rotacher.

9. *Hebrah Gemilut Hesed shel Emet*, a society for mutual aid, allied to Congregation Shaarey Zedek. Organized in 5601 (1851). President: Mr. Isaac Levy.

10. *Mendelssohn Society* for mutual aid and assistance at burial, organized in 1842. The burial-ground is in Salem Fields Cemetery. President: Mr. Jonas Heller.

11. *Montefiore*, a charitable society for the benefit of widows, orphans and the sick, organized in 5601 (1841). President: I. D. Walter.

12. *Hebrah Neshe Hesed Veemet*, charitable society of the women of Congregation Shaarey Tefilah, organized in 5603 (1843). President: Mrs. J. M. Davies.

13. *Hebrah of the Ladies of Congregation Shearith Israel* for the care of the sick and dead, organized in 5601 (1841). President: Miss Zipporah Hart.

14. *German Hebrew Benevolent Society*, organized 5604 (1844). President: Mr. Joseph Seligman.

15. *Ladies Sewing Society*, organized in 1847. President: Miss J. Palache.

16. *Hebrah Ahavat Achim*, the society of brotherly love, allied with Congregation Bnai Israel. Organized in 5677 (1847). President: Mr. H. B. Hertz.

17. *Bachelors' Hebrew Benevolent Loan Association*, organized in 5608 (1847). President: Mr. B. Benrimo.

18. *Hebrah Terumat Hakodesh of Congregation Bnai Israel*, to collect and transmit funds for the poor in the Holy Land, organized in 5608 (1848). President: Mr. J. A. Leon.

19. *Young Men's Hebrew Benevolent and Fuel Association*, to provide the needy with wood in winter, organized in 5609 (1849). President: Mr. H. B. Hertz.

20. *Bnot Jeshurun*, a charitable society of Jewish women for the benefit of the female poor, organized in 5609 (1848). President: Mrs. David Sampson.

21. *Hebrah Bikur Cholim ve-Kadisha*, a society for mutual aid, af-

filiated with Congregation Bikur Cholim. Organized in 5610 (1849). President: Mr. Joseph Levy.

22. *Mutual Benefit and Burial Society of Congregation Shaarey Tefilah*, organized in 5610 (1850). President: Mr. John I. Hart.

23. *Hebrah Re'im Ahuvim*, a society of brotherly love, organized in 5610 (1850). President: Mr. S. Hyams.

24. *Hebrah Gomle Hesed*, affiliated with Congregation Emanu-El, for the care of the sick and dead. Organized in 5611 (1851). President: Rev. Dr. Merzbacher.

25. *Hebrah Neshe Gomle Hesed*, a women's society, affiliated with Congregation Emanu-El, for the care of the sick and dead. Organized in 5611 (1851). President: Rev. Dr. Merzbacher.

26. *Bnai Jeshurun Institute*, organized in 5612 (1852). The school-house is next to the Greene Street synagogue. President: Mr. Joseph Falman. Superintendent: Rev. Dr. M. J. Raphall.

27. *Hebrah Ezrat Yetomim ve-Almanot*, a society for the assistance of widows and orphans, affiliated with Congregation Anshe Chesed. President: Mr. Marx Wash.

28. *Hebrah Sheerit Bnai Israel*, for the care of the sick, affiliated with Congregation Shaarey Hashamayim. President: Mr. S. Oppenheimer.

29. *Hebrah Bikur Cholim*, affiliated with Congregation Rodeph Shalom. President: Mr. Marx Wash.

30. *Hebrah Ahavat Nashim*, affiliated with Congregation Rodeph Shalom. President: Mr. A. Semel.

31. *Hebrah Ahavat Ahayot*, affiliated with Congregation Shaarey Hashamayim. President: Mr. S. Rosenfeld.

32. *Hebrah Shaarey Tikvah*, affiliated with Congregation Anshe Chesed. President: Mr. N. Rossman.

33. *Hebrew Young Men's Literary Society*, organized in 1851. President: Mr. Isaac Seligman.

34. *Hebrew and English School of Congregation Rodeph Shalom.* Mr. H. American, superintendent.

35. *Hebrah Anshe Emunah*, a mutual aid society of Congregation Shaarey Rachamim. President: Mr. Isaac Jeitels.

36. *Constitutional Grand Lodge of the Order of Bnai Brith* ("Sons of the Covenant"). The subordinate lodges in the Union are under its control. The former "grand *sar*" (grand master) was H. Jones of New York. The present "grand *sar*" is Mr. Bien, lithographer.

37. *District Grand Lodge of the Order of Bnai Brith.* Grand *Nasi Ab* ("elder"): Dr. S. Waterman. This is a secret society, like the Freemasons, with password, signs, and the like, and was quite a new phe-

nomenon for me. All its officials and lodges have Jewish names. Although the essential character of this society is a beneficence — whoever becomes sick receives four dollars a week, medicine, a nurse, and so on, and this the rich who belong to the society must also receive in case of sickness so as not to put the poor to shame — still, I think the existence of such a society not at all necessary, because it is an established principle of the Jewish religion that a poor man receives help and this, indeed, without shaming him, even as King Solomon has said: *Matan besether yichpeh-af* ("a gift to the poor in secret is a shield against the anger of the Court," *Proverbs* 21. 14).

38. *Jewish Dispensary*, a private philanthropic undertaking of several doctors who profess the Jewish faith. It was founded in 5612 (1852). President: S. Abrahams, Doctor of Medicine.

39. *Hebrah Etz Haim*, a mutual aid society belonging to Congregation Bnai Israel. Organized in 5612 (1852). President: Mr. Joel Isaacs.

40. *Jews' Hospital of New York*, organized in 5612 (1852). Its building is on Twenty-eighth Street, between Seventh and Eighth Avenues. President: Mr. Sampson Simson.

41. *Jewish Theological Seminary*, organized in 5612 (1852). President: Mr. Sampson Simson.

42. *Jewish Asylum for Orphans and Needy,** New York. Organized in 5613 (1852). President: Mr. Sampson Simson.

43. *The Jewish National School*, belonging to Congregation Shaarey Zedek. Organized in 5613 (1853). The school building is in back of the synagogue on Henry Street. Superintendent: Rev. H. A. Henry.

44. *North American Relief Society for Poor Jews in Palestine.* Organized in 5613 (1853). President: Mr. Sampson Simson.

In addition, there is in New York an organization of women whose purposes, however, are kept secret so that I can give no information about it. In this city there are also several other small societies for the purpose of aiding the poor and in the suburbs there are, likewise, similar societies.

With so many organizations of this nature, it is not difficult to form a conclusion about the generous spirit that moves the Jews of this city, so that it is not necessary to furnish more details.

---

* Grinstein's *Rise of the Jewish Community of New York* has no record of such a society. The Hebrew Orphan Asylum was not organized until later. [Tr.]

Chapter III

I left New York on the third of October 1859, to visit Philadelphia, Baltimore, Washington, Richmond (Virginia), Cincinnati, Louisville, New Orleans and several other places. In this I had a double purpose in mind: I wished to become acquainted with the development of various Jewish communities and, at the same time, to obtain impressions of the spirit of America. On July 24th, 1860, a day before the first anniversary of my landing, I returned to New York from my trip.

If anyone has any doubts about the ever fresh and youthful strength of our religion that flourishes in all zones and regions of the earth rich both in blossoms and in fruit, let him go to the United States and see what it has effected and produced there also. The rapid expansion which Judaism itself has undergone, the magnificent institutions that it has called into life, the great increase of congregations, which their members joined out of personal inspiration, the variety of religious viewpoints that are expressed with neighborly patience and without animosity and with the greatest freedom — all these manifestations prove that Judaism there is full of hope and is advancing towards an exalted and prosperous future.

The second Jewish emigration from Europe began in the year 1836 and increased from year to year. The oppression that then still burdened the Jews of various lands, the education that they had gained but which made them feel all the more the injustice of the political and civil disparagement of them, the religious distaste for the proselytizing measures of the Jesuitical hierarchy and of the reactionary states, an awakening and ever greater sense of human rights and human dignity — these were reasons enough to spur the Jews on to search for a new home where they might live freely as men and as Jews: their gaze was bound to fall first of all on the modern Promised Land.

Bavaria with its Pharaoh-like registration laws — the first to be revived in recent times — and its restriction of trade stood first in the

74

row of intolerant states and made marriage and the right of residence almost impossible for Jews; naturally it furnished the first emigrants, just as it has since supplied the largest number. The statistics of these states in 1860 show clearly that Bavaria is the only land in which the number of Israelites has decreased by several thousands.

The first Jewish immigrants were workers, poor men looking to earn their bread by the sweat of their brow, without any more knowledge of the world than what they had managed to acquire in their schoolyears and as journeymen, without any more education than that offered them in the German elementary schools, and without other means than the scanty possessions locked in their knapsacks or traveling-bags. But as stay and staff to help them at the beginning of their bitter journey, they had a cheerful spirit together with sound commonsense, trust in God and their own arm, as well as tireless industry, inexhaustible patience, and the thrift and sobriety characteristic of Jews. These attributes had weight in America, where credit is easily had and capital is quickly increased.

A few fellow-countrymen, who had arrived earlier and were working as clerks in places of business, helped the aliens with rede and deed, provided them with goods and credit, and advised them to peddle out in the country. This business is not at all in disrepute in America: the Yankee was always engaged in it and the farmer, who then had no opportunity to find goods at his door, received the peddler with hospitality and gladly paid him good prices. The Jewish immigrant, with his inherited knack for business, threw himself into this calling with zest and was happy that at every crossroad a German policeman did not make life miserable for him. His earnings increased his zeal; within a few weeks he had saved his first hundred dollars, paid off what he owed the merchants, and increased his credit through his honesty. He made rapid progress and soon provided himself with a horse and wagon to do business on a larger scale. Profits accumulated daily; and from his profits he sent, as a token of love and a sign of a fortunate beginning, sums to help his old impoverished parents; other sums went along with these to pay for the passage of dear friends. The letters and money so received were the missionary tracts of freedom, and immigration grew at an incredible rate.

This rich aftergrowth enabled those who had arrived earlier to go into business for themselves and with their own credit to help those who came later. The name, "German Jew," soon fell pleasantly upon the ears of American importers, manufacturers and wholesalers; credit and profit increased rapidly, and in a few years the poor immigrant workingman was a respected and well-to-do merchant in his new fatherland. North and east, south and west, there arose countless Jewish firms, many importers in New York, wholesalers in Philadelphia, Baltimore, Cincinnati, St. Louis, Chicago, New Orleans, San Francisco and so forth; while thousands of flourishing firms in other cities, towns and villages gave evidence of the prosperity that the Jews had gained in twenty-five years.

The political position of the Jews kept pace with this rapid commercial development. Every office was open to all without distinction of religion or birth. As a result, the Israelites were represented, not only in all the states in the municipal and state offices, but they were also members of Congress, in the Senate as well as the House of Representatives.

The southern states, however, for natural reasons, outdid, in many respects, the northern states in hospitality. The white inhabitants felt themselves united with, and closer to, other whites — as opposed to the Negroes. Since the Israelite there did not do the humbler kinds of work which the Negro did, he was quickly received among the upper classes and easily rose to high political rank. For this reason, until now, it was only the South which sent Jews to the Senate. Benjamin came from Louisiana; Yulee from Florida; Louisiana has elected Hyams lieutenant-governor; and in Charleston Israelites occupy the most distinguished places. On the other hand, we must also admit that the Israelites in the North seek political office less because there official position is neither so highly respected nor so profitable as that of merchant, manufacturer or craftsman.

To proceed to the founding of individual congregations: New York with its many synagogues will serve as an illustration of the larger cities. There were several reasons for the withdrawal by the non-Portuguese from the original, Portuguese synagogue. To begin with, there was the different *minhag* (traditional usage) as well as the aristocratic character of the Portuguese. The prayerbook and the manner of praying were strange to the immigrants. Furthermore, the Portuguese claimed a sort of patronage over the immigrants; they had helped the latter generously and now wished to maintain their supremacy — at least in the administration of the congregation.

Accordingly, the immigrants founded a new synagogue on Elm Street. Here those of English origin among the founders introduced the London *minhag* with a sermon and discussion of congregational matters in English. The Germans and the German character, however, could not endure the English; the Pole could not endure the Germans; and so there was soon division and separation in all directions.

The beginning of the third congregation, Congregation Anshe

Chesed of New York, was the next result. It was organized for the most part by immigrant Bavarians. Nevertheless, the separation aroused no jealousy on the part of the older congregations but was encouraged and aided by them in the friendliest manner. The founders of this congregation, which now numbers more than three hundred families and is rated the largest, numerically, in the Union, still like to tell how it was founded and how weak was its beginning. The first fifteen or twenty members had turned a miserable "hall" into a synagogue and when, on a Friday evening in winter, they went to "Schul," each brought along under his cloak some wood to lessen the burdensome expense to the congregation by this contribution to its heating.

New York, however, spread ever more rapidly; distances became too great, the synagogues too small. An exceedingly large number of Jewish and Christian Germans had made their homes on Houston and the neighboring streets so that in a short time it was possible to open a second German synagogue on Attorney Street.

However, the bad aspect of the "growing-pains" of freedom had a shattering effect on the young congregations. The unlimited freedom which religious congregations enjoy in America led to abuse in the beginning: the slightest insult suffered, or an unsuccessful bid for a congregational office, would mislead disappointed men into founding a new congregation to satisfy their ambition. So, instead of blessed religious freedom, there was at times unbridled license. This evil and the national divisions brought from the other side resulted in the growth of many congregations. In the large cities, particularly in New York, the evil results of this were, it is true, obviated by the rapid and numerous immigration. The congregations and synagogues of New York, which has about 40,000 inhabitants, are fairly strong and well-established. It was only among the younger congregations in the smaller cities and in the country that this imported nationalism and divisive quarrelsomeness were disturbing and harmful.

In addition, there was a factor, specifically German, which exercised a new influence upon the congregations of the United States: this was the spirit of "Reform." The Portuguese, with their aristocratic prejudice, clung to their *minhag* and the old ways which they had brought with them; the English, who also cling with tenacity to everything that is traditional until a revolution forces them forward, wished to hear nothing of any "reform" and insisted on maintaining their orthodoxy. They knew nothing of the writings of the German-Jewish theologians that had so strong an influence upon Judaism; for this reason, every utterance of the late chief rabbi of London, Herschell, has an authority for the present generation of English Jews which they would not disobey at any cost. This reverence for the traditional shows itself also in their family life, animated by the warm Jewish feeling for the Sabbath and holidays; and the cheerful satisfaction which such a life affords them, combined with their ignorance of German cultural progress, keeps them far from every innovation. The same is true of the Polish Jews. The latter, moreover, consider themselves superior in learning and, proud of their origin in this or that place, where this or that *gaon* or rabbi flourished, they hold fast to their *minhag*.

The cornerstone of the Reform movement was laid in New York in the congregation of Temple Emanu-El, and the example there furnished was followed in Albany and Baltimore. The influence of the Emanu-El congregation made itself felt more and more, and all the congregations of the metropolis were forced by its example to improve their form of worship. The religious service of congregation Emanu-El forced its sister congregations to appoint preachers and introduce choirs; its magnificent cemetery, laid out in family plots, compelled the more important of the other congregations to take similar steps; the order which distinguished their conduct of congregational business, the peaceful spirit which dominated every member, taught the others to desist, more and more, from party quarrels and dissension. The Reform movement is powerfully felt in Philadelphia, Baltimore, Albany, Cincinnati, Chicago and San Francisco, and there is no doubt that in the next generation Reform will gain the upper hand and that Judaism will be transformed much faster than people in Europe imagine.

The old conservative congregations have sought to avert the threatening danger by erecting splendid synagogues and thus trying to hold on to their vacillating members. However, a second reason for building new houses of worship has been the increasing immigration and the growing prosperity of the Israelites. Many American synagogues excel those of Europe in magnificence and splendor. New York has among its synagogues five truly splendid buildings: those on Greene Street, Wooster Street, Norfolk Street, Twelfth Street, and the Portuguese synagogue on Nineteenth Street. Philadelphia, New Orleans, Baltimore, Charleston, St. Louis, Cleveland, Cincinnati and so on, also have large and richly-furnished synagogues.

Religious instruction in Jewish schools does not yet flourish as desired. In New York, the temple congregation is the only one that has an organized religious school. Cincinnati has the so-called Talmud Yelodim Institute, the best organized school in the United States; Philadelphia has a school that is supported by the Hebrew Education Society and another that belongs to the congregations of German origin; Baltimore, Chicago, Cleveland, Hartford, Louisville and other congregations have only congregational schools.

The charitable institutions, in spite of their youthfulness, are splendid. In addition to the countless *hevrot* that every congregation has for the mutual assistance of the members, societies and institutions have been founded for the aid of the poor and sick that have no equal in Europe. New York has two benevolent societies which annually divide more than $20,000, a splendid hospital, just built, and an orphan-home; Philadelphia has its Foster Home; Cincinnati a hospital; New Orleans a home for widows and orphans; and every important city has its charitable society that divides thousands of dollars annually and dispenses help and blessing.

In the smaller cities and in the countryside, the rise of congregations proceeds slowly, for here only a few have settled and at that singly. It was, therefore, impossible for them to follow the Jewish precepts and only one or two, here and there, have joined a congregation in a city. On the Passover, if possible, they provided themselves with *mat-zoth* from the cities at great expense, but along with it ate the usual food. If a boy was born, a *mohel* was sent for by letter at great cost or the child was brought into the city after several months. This kind of life exercised and still exercises a harmful influence, but the love for Judaism was too deeply rooted, was too thoroughly entwined with their whole way of thinking for them to turn their backs lightly upon their inherited faith. Here it was impossible for them to follow all the Jewish precepts and regulations, and so they silenced the warning of their conscience with only the weak hope that one could live as a Jew without fulfilling the traditional precepts. This way of acting and thinking was a most effective preparation for the Reform movement.

In a short time, the number of such settlers increased everywhere and the impulse not to be estranged from a Jewish life — for the sake of their children — spoke with an ever stronger voice. The settlers themselves had brought along from their native environment the holy jewel of religion, often the only jewel they had carried away, and it had manifested its wonderful power many times; now it had to be handed on to their children also. The immediate economic needs having been provided for, one did not wish to be, and could not be, ungrateful to the faithful Guardian of Israel, Who had shown Himself so gracious here as well. The changing conditions of life forced them to a decision and institutions for the general welfare began to be a necessity.

If a Jew died somewhere, the shipment of his body was a great expense and very troublesome. Besides, one did not wish to see a friend, who had become dear, buried in a distant place; one wished to know that the grave that held one's dear father, one's beloved mother, was close at hand. Since land was very cheap, it was decided to buy some land as a burial-ground: what had happened to one today might very well happen to another tomorrow — no one escapes death. One had also to acknowledge oneself as a Jew; the old love awoke new and strong; one began to discuss Jewish conditions and the first steps toward improvement were taken. All the dear, slumbering memories of the past awoke and wished to live again; one thought about the celebration of the very moving Day of Atonement, and deliberated how one might, on strange soil, celebrate again in the old way the ritual of that Fast and of the New Year. A room was prepared, a *hazzan* (cantor) was found, familiar with the old, well-known melodies; he was elected, and the first religious service, exalting and exhilarating, was held, accompanied by tears of pain and joy.

In many places they did not get beyond this beginning; in other places, however, they went farther, driven along by circumstances. The Jewish heart with its most beautiful blossom, parental love, thought in its happiness of parents living in need in the old country and would bring them over from Germany. But the old father and the pious little mother would not, in the late evening of their lives, have any part in eating forbidden food. The sons had no choice, then, but devoutly to accommodate themselves to true Jewish piety, according to the wishes of their parents, and also to appoint a *shohet* (slaughterer of animals according to Jewish ritual). The institutions that a Jewish community usually organizes were, accordingly, soon in existence. So arose one Jewish institution after another; and now the northern states, especially, are full of young, flourishing and ever stronger communities. The Union has today at least 200,000 Jews, who are scattered over all the states, and who have brought their religious institutions to life everywhere.

The organization and development of the Jewish communities all over America, as pointed out above, everywhere followed the same pattern.

The Portuguese communities are distributed among the following cities: New York one; Philadelphia two; Charleston two (one of these Reform — so far as I know the only one in the world); Savannah one; Richmond (Virginia) one; New Orleans one. Reform congregations are to be found in: New York one; Philadelphia one; Baltimore one; Charleston, as mentioned above; Cincinnati one; Chicago one; St. Louis one; San Francisco one. Among these, the New York temple congregation of Reform Jews is especially noteworthy because of its charities.

A month after my arrival in New York I heard that many Jewish orphans, because there was no Jewish orphan asylum in the city and no Jew interested in them, turned to the missionaries and were sheltered by them. This grieved Dr. Adler, the rabbi of the Reform congregation, as it would any man of feeling; and, at the following festival of Tabernacles, on *Shemini Atzereth* (5620), the anniversary of the death of the first rabbi of the congregation, Dr. Merzbacher, Dr. Adler delivered an address in honor of the festival, in which he brought home to his congregation that, if they wished to set up a permanent memorial to the beloved man, they should found a home for orphans, in which helpless orphans who ran the danger of becoming estranged from Judaism might find shelter. This suggestion, happily phrased, was made in so suitable a manner that it found general approval and within half an hour $8,000 was subscribed. The Orthodox congregations also could not refuse their mite for so generally useful an institution, and they also contributed, although, on the whole, they gave very little. Thus did the orphan asylum come quickly into existence.

The following circumstances also contributed. There were two charitable organizations in New York: the Hebrew Benevolent Society, founded by Polish and English Jews, and the German Hebrew Benevolent Society which, as the name indicates, consisted only of Germans. The former had accumulated the sum of $12,000, but the latter had only $4,000 because it had made greater disbursements. It was clear on a number of occasions, that it was unsatisfactory to have two such organizations in the same field, and the Rev. Dr. S. Adler had tried to effect a union. The difficulty lay in the greater means of the Hebrew Benevolent Society, since because of that the society was unwilling to enter the union. The Rev. Dr. S. Adler tried to use his personal influence with the presidents of the various congregations and stirred up individual preachers to support his proposal from the pulpit. In this he was completely successful — if we except two important congregations, who refused to go along for reasons unknown to us.

The Hebrew Benevolent Society made it a condition of the union that the name of the united institution should be The Orphan Asylum and that $20,000 should be on deposit as a reserve fund. With the rest, they bought a house in which for the time being thirty-four orphans found a refuge and where they had bodily and spiritual care. A charitable man, Mr. Joseph Seligmann, a distinguished merchant of New York, was named president. Upon his suggestion to the management,

$30,000 was guaranteed and seven acres of land allotted to erect a large building for the institution. May the Father of Orphans reward the charitable and defend and protect the institution!

No one could take exception to these good works of Reform Judaism, and it would be best for Judaism if Jews did not direct their attention to the abrogation of traditional customs and only tried to ennoble the spirit and improve the heart. Since the author himself, by conviction and in his way of life, is no believer in Reform, he wishes passionately that all the congregations of America would at long last try to attain a firm foundation again. At present, they sway this way and that, without cause and without stop.

The Reform rabbis do insist, however, upon the strict observance of the Sabbath and festivals. For example, a few years ago (5620), Dr. David Einhorn, at present in Philadelphia but then rabbi of a temple in Baltimore, showed, in a sermon on the Day of Atonement, the importance of keeping the Sabbath holy as a principal point and pillar of the Jewish religion. He brought home to his congregation the folly of throwing away lightly the treasure of the Sabbath. The result was that since then, as I myself witnessed, more than half of his congregation have observed his wishes strictly and do no more business on the Sabbath. So Reform, perhaps, after many a deviation, steers a proper course.

The learned Orthodox rabbis are very poorly represented in all of America. I have already mentioned Dr. Raphall in New York and, if he stands in the first rank, next to him we find Dr. Hayyim Hochheimer of Baltimore, a native of Ichenhausen in Bavaria, and Dr. Illoway, formerly of Baltimore, at present in New Orleans, a good Hebraist and Talmudist. With this ends the list of learned rabbis in a land that numbers more than two hundred Orthodox congregations.

The Reform congregations number eight, as indicated above. At their head are the following very well educated men as rabbis: Dr. Adler, who has been mentioned several times, leader of the temple congregation of New York; Dr. Deutsch of Philadelphia; Dr. Einhorn of Baltimore;* in Cincinnati, Dr. Isaac M. Wise and Dr. M. Lilienthal (although appointed by an Orthodox congregation, he belongs, nevertheless, to the Reform movement — I had plenty of opportunity to learn his views);** in Chicago, the teacher Baruch Felsenthal; in St. Louis, Mr. Kuttner Baruch, a man who performs the

---

* Dr. Einhorn is at present in Philadelphia. Dr. Deutsch lives as a private person in Syracuse.
** I have to thank Dr. Lilienthal and Dr. Wise for observations about the Jews of America which they made for my benefit and of which I have made use.

various duties of his post very well; in Charleston (previously), Dr. Meyer; in San Francisco, Dr. Elkan Cohen.

The principal objectives of all Reform rabbis are to re-establish the observance of the Sabbath and festivals and to spread the spirit of charity. The Reform synagogues are, therefore, crowded on the Sabbaths and holidays: this is not at all the case with respect to the Orthodox synagogues. These tower up like Solomon's temple, but it is painful to see how throughout the whole year, except for the Day of Atonement and New Year's, they are half empty. And on these days also, few as they are, they would not be so assiduously visited if one were not afraid of the Incorruptible Judge, Who judges without regard to person. They make the unimportant their chief concern and of the most important a secondary matter. If a bit of *piyyut* (religious poetry) is omitted, there is a great outcry in the congregation that reaches to high heaven, and it has happened that such excitement has often divided a congregation into two parties; but the essentials of the religion — observing the Sabbath and the festivals — are pushed into the background. To such a state of affairs the words of the prophet might well be applied (Isaiah 5. 20): You change darkness into light and light into darkness!

How often my heart has bled when I visited these synagogues on holidays and found them empty; here, in a land where Israelites do not encounter the least obstacle to the full practice of their religion and where the best opportunity in the whole world offers itself to bring Judaism to its finest blossoming — so that the words of the prophet could be most beautifully fulfilled: Israel, you are my pride and my boast! — unfortunately, all is here in vain! The sun of religion is in darkness and the heavens covered with clouds. Under such conditions, what is to be expected of the future? "How long will you still waver between two opinions?" (I Kings 18. 21). If Orthodoxy, the path which your fathers have beaten out, is dear to you and precious, then do not leave it; but, if this way is no longer pleasing, declare yourselves for another and seek a prop for your Judaism that it does not vanish out of your hands! Do not think, my brothers, that I will show the world only your shortcomings; I solemnly declare in the name of the All-Knowing, Almighty, and All-Merciful God, Who has given us life and has saved us from all difficulties, that what I say is uttered by me only out of love for my brothers and that I write these words deeply moved and almost in tears!

The Torah has imposed upon me the duty of declaring the truth (Lev. 5. 1). "If one has fallen into sin and another hears or sees it and does not correct him, the sin is his who fails to do so." All hope is not lost yet that, perhaps, in a short time, Judaism in America will recover; for the many charitable institutions there, without equal in any other land, show that the Jewish spirit still lives; and we may hope that the other two pillars of Judaism, *Torah* and *Abodah*, religious study and religious service, which along with charity, *Gemiluth Hesed*, have been declared by our sages to be the foundation of our religion, will soon rise up again, in their full splendor.

With respect to religious service it is to be noted that there are six kinds of prayer-books in use: the Portuguese ritual; the Polish ritual; the Ashkenazic (German) ritual; another prayer-book arranged later in New York by Dr. Merzbacher in German and Hebrew, in which the use of the former language is proposed; still another, *Olath Tamid* (1857), by Dr. Einhorn, mostly in German with only little Hebrew; *Minhag America* (1857), the prayer-book of Dr. Wise, in Hebrew and merely a shortening of the old service.

The Jewish periodical literature consists of: *Jewish Messenger*, in English, edited by the Rev. S. M. Isaacs in New York, a weekly; *The Occident*, in English, edited by Isaac Leeser, and *Sinai*, in German, edited by Dr. D. Einhorn, both monthlies and published at present in Philadelphia (the former used to be a weekly); in Cincinnati two periodicals, *The Israelite*, in English, and *Deborah*, in German, both edited by Dr. Wise; in San Francisco two weeklies, *The Gleaner*, edited by Dr. Julius Eckmann, and *Pacific Messenger*, edited by Dr. Bien and Henri. The latter is no longer published. In New Orleans there appeared until lately the *Cornerstone*, in English, edited by the Rev. Jacob Salomon: he died a year ago, and with his death the publication came to an end.

The principal congregations are to be found in New York, Philadelphia in Pennsylvania, Baltimore in Maryland, Charleston in South Carolina, Savannah [in Georgia], Richmond in Virginia, Cincinnati in Ohio, Louisville in Kentucky, New Orleans in Louisiana, San Francisco in California, and in other cities as I will detail below.

The principal cause for the decline of Judaism, about which we lamented so bitterly above and which will always embitter our lives as long as we draw breath in this world, is due, as was already pointed out, to two sources. One is materialism. The grubbing for, running after and hunting for money and gold, which is hardly interrupted by night, and allows the soul neither rest nor peace, almost buries it and chokes it to death in the slime of the earth; it permits no higher thoughts to spring up and kills with the bitter frost of winter all nobler and sacred feelings which stem out of eternity and lead back to it again. The second source, out of which likewise no water of life streams, is the unscientific mentality of many rabbis and teachers, who have knowledge neither of the Talmud nor of the literature of Judaism. It happens, not infrequently, that he, who at home enjoyed not even the benefits of a superficial education, in this country holds his head high and proud and makes a lot of noise, like an empty ear of grain. The passage of the Talmud might apply here: *Kat ragiz ra'ayah 'al ana abid linegida sumaita* (if the shepherd is enraged with his flock, he pierces the eyes of the bell-wether, so that the flock plunges into the pit).

It is to be hoped that the words of the Prophet Ezekiel (36. 25-28) will also soon apply to this country: And I will sprinkle clean water upon you, and you shall be clean from all your filthiness; I will also give you a new heart, and a new spirit will I put into you; and I will take away your stony heart, and I will give you a heart of flesh. And I will put My Spirit within you, and you shall keep My ordinances and obey My laws.

Chapter IV

About the Upbringing of Jewish Women in America

Of all the inflexible demands which his religion and his duty make on each Israelite, the first and foremost is to give his child a good education; to equip it for the journey through life and give it the means to find its way. The American schools, of which we are about to speak, certainly guarantee this in part; but it is much to be regretted that, because they exclude all religion and confessions of faith — not with an unwise purpose — I must say with the deepest regret that the study of the Holy Scriptures, particularly, is much neglected among the daughters of Israel.

Jewish boys after a fashion — for that is the established way — are instructed in their religion, as is also the case with the sons and daughters of Christians. The Jewish boys attend some Hebrew school or other, or are instructed privately; but in this respect, what does the situation look like for the daughters of Israel? What a great difference! How sad is the provision for the religious instruction of these Jewish housewives and mothers of the future! How little do they learn of their duties towards God and man! What do they know of what our faith requires and of the commandments that they must obey as daughters of Israel? Should not those who are to perform the holiest religious duties be thoroughly prepared for such performance? These duties are indeed many and noble and it is with regret and astonishment that one learns that half of the American Jewesses are at present unable to undertake and fulfil worthily the place in life for which they are intended; nevertheless, it is unfortunately all too true. And why? The reason for this lies in their neglected education.

To throw more light on this statement and confirm the truth of it, let us describe the upbringing that the American Jewish women of today receive, and then let us proceed to show how the evil may, and should be remedied.

The mother of a little girl, a good-hearted, rather well-to-do woman, let us say, will try to impress on the young spirit of her child as much good instruction as ever she can. This private care lasts until the child is five. Then the child, it is obvious, must be sent to a public school or, what is more respectable, to a so-called "institute." Accepted by the "institute," the child begins the usual course of studies, makes the acquaintance of girls of other religions and has friends among them, and may well, without any objection or even realization of its significance, kneel during morning prayers which are arranged for those of other faiths, before classes begin. After school, she studies her lessons for the next day or, like all children, plays. Upon going to bed or arising in the morning, she may very likely recite for her mother some Hebrew or English prayers; but as for Judaism, the child experiences nothing and knows nothing.

In this manner the girl continues to be brought up until she is fifteen, except for the unimportant difference that in time she leaves the institute to attend a high-school or college. On her fifteenth birthday a new life begins; the longed-for day arrives at last; Papa and Mamma have promised her that on this day she shall be free and shall leave school, and she "graduates," to her great joy. What useful knowledge has she gained during this time? Extremely little in fact. She has spent ten years of her precious life among all kinds of books, and, with all that, she has not advanced in the least; the time is lost, indeed, forever. What she has learned is of no use to her and of no profit. She does not know how to sew, has no knowledge of household affairs, and still less of higher things. Ask her who has created her, who clothes her, who gives her her daily bread; and she may have the correct answer — perhaps, but it is more likely that she will say: "That was not in my book."

Her good parents have increased their wealth during these ten years and have taken the commendable resolution that their daughter should not forget all that she has learnt. Accordingly, they provide her — to complete her education — with a music-teacher, a singing-teacher, a drawing-teacher, and a governess to continue the practice of French; the latter also teaches her how to sew, knit and the like; and, to give it all a final touch, they assign a teacher to give her Hebrew lessons. He must make her acquainted with the alphabet of a language in which, as a child, she should have lisped the name of God. She will find this last teacher, as is only to be expected, a bore. She will find Hebrew too dull and also too difficult; she will weep over her lessons so that her yielding parents, who will be touched by her tears and moved to pity, will give the teacher notice — he whom they should have engaged first and dismissed last. But they took the opposite course, out of their own lack of true religious feeling, and so they engaged him last and, again, dismissed him first.

Since, in this manner, the girl has come to the end of her religious upbringing, she continues to recite in English the few prayers which she has learnt from her mother. Should she, quite by accident, attend synagogue, she takes a book in the same language. Her other teachers soon share the same fate as her former Hebrew teacher. Because of the parties, balls, soirées, and so on, which have now become the important questions of the day for her, and at which she remains until the last, the girl becomes full of whims, her mind is distracted. She listens to the chatter of young men and all thought of study and the desire for it is gone. The young lady — she will no longer permit herself to be called a girl — believes that her upbringing is now completed in every respect, considers herself qualified to take her place in the world, able to make a man happy and to become a Jewish mother. I must remark that, unfortunately, this can serve as an example for a thousand cases that occur in this land with only slight variations.

Who is to blame for this completely inadequate upbringing? The girl with her whims or her over-indulgent parents? I answer: neither. The girl is like all other children; the parents are doing all in their power to give their child the best upbringing: they would give their wealth, their energies, their time, yes, even their lives, to provide her with the highest possible education; and they imagine, without doubt, that they have done so. But, alas! To their horror, they will soon discover their mistake — and it will be too late.

I blame neither the young woman nor her parents; rather are all those who are members of the Jewish religious community to blame: as a body, as is the case in England, France and Germany, they should have supplied the general need and have founded a "Jewish school" for girls as well as for boys. There girls would be provided, from their early years, with a thoroughly good upbrihging that would make them familiar with their duties towards their Creator. This is the most urgent need; for I am quite convinced that such an arrangement would have as beneficial an effect on the generations to come as any other that might be hit upon.

Napoleon the First, the greatest benefactor that France ever had, understood very well the value of schools for the daughters of the land and of the influence of mothers, well brought up, upon future generations. When he came to power, one of the first acts which he pursued, energetically, was to establish institutions for the education of women. He himself visited them often and distributed very valuable prizes among the outstanding students in the various institutions. To this I most certainly ascribe the wonderful ability and the cleverness of the present generation of French women in the sphere of their activities. It would be well to consider the example of Napoleon the Great and to establish a "Jewish school" in America: the blessings of such an institution would be innumerable.

Having spoken, as above, of the upbringing of Jewish women, we should like to follow this with a few remarks about the upbringing of Jewish young men. This, unfortunately, is not much better. A Jewish boy is sent to school from the age of six until he is sixteen to learn reading, writing and arithmetic. But no father is culturally alert enough to have his son provided with some degree of general knowledge, or have him acquire a higher education. As soon as he has acquired the above-mentioned rudiments, he is sent to business, naturally without having gone to a commercial school — for that is not necessary: commerce consists simply in the practical and mechanical knack of making money; if he is sufficiently clever at this, he soon earns the reputation of being an educated man.

It is only in the larger cities, as already indicated, that provision has recently been made for religious instruction and for teaching Hebrew. But it is clear enough that men of great learning will never arise among the Jews of America. It is especially remarkable how quickly Jewish children find themselves at home in American ways. Among other things, this can also be seen in the fact that they speak only English to their parents, neither German nor Hebrew, and will only answer in English, even if spoken to in another language. So they become part and parcel of the American way of life — and this we will describe in the next chapter.

Chapter V

The Women of America in General: A Further Cause of Deterioration

America worships two idols: one is Mammon — who is deaf, dumb and blind; before whom the multitude of that land bow humbly and kneel down, forgetting all honor, thinking only, day and night, how to heap up riches and to build themselves palaces. The second idol that is prayed to sees, hears, walks, speaks, and — above all — is full of life: this is the female sex. Both idols are in a constant feud with each other. What one builds the other tears down; what one heaps up the other scatters again; what one improves the other spoils, as the reader will discover in the chapter on luxury.

Let me draw a parallel here. Alexander the Great went out with his host to conquer various lands and is said at last to have reached a land where women ruled; they summoned the men or dismissed them, as they pleased, and generally regarded them as slaves. I journeyed through several parts of the Old World through which Alexander's army went and nowhere did I find a land to which this tale might apply. Accordingly, I thought of the whole story as fiction, until I found it verified in America.

Here, indeed, government by women has been established and it is only in Jewish circles that the old ways, except for the rivalry in luxury, are kept up: in these circles, the privileges of women in America and the power they exercise have limits. Improbable as it sounds, it is nevertheless true that even in a court of justice the word of a woman of the lowest class is more readily believed than that of the most respectable man. I was told in New York that a few years ago these feminine rights were carried to such an extreme, or rather abused to such an extent, that if girls met men in the street who pleased them, they would find out their name, residence and station in life, go to court and accuse the men of having promised to marry them and then failing to do so. The men would then be forced into a marriage against their wish, without any consideration paid to the consequences of such a "shotgun" marriage. If married women cannot satisfy their passions, their love of dress, indulge their idleness or whatever else they have in mind, they leave their husbands and pay no attention even to their children. Such cases are of daily occurrence and they provide constant headlines in American newspapers.

Let us examine more closely the women who are capable of causing such evil. American women have dignity and refined features, are very delicate in physique and, above all, are those who of all women in the world know best how to dress. Their conversation is very cheerful; they are always lively and are passionately fond of music, singing and dancing. We have already informed the reader what little benefit they had from instruction at school and how little they know about bringing up their children. Many do not even wish to have children because they are afraid of losing their beauty, and ways of preventing this are often resorted to. A physician in New York asked me if the evil custom of the Orient, that women use a drug to prevent having children, is still in existence. There is also a passage in the Midrash (*Bereshith*, chapter 23) which says that women took a drug, called *kos shel akarin*, to remain childless. A physician in America, he said, would surely make a million dollars in one year with this substance. I told him that I had given this subject no attention, but I would not fail to look into the matter on my next visit.

The women have a characteristic, inherited and ineradicable aversion to any work or household management and delight in sweets and tit-bits. As a result, nowhere in the world are there so many dentists as in America, and yet they are all doing well. They are indispensable because the excessive use of sweets is harmful to the teeth and artificial ones must take the place of natural teeth. Many women, therefore, often have rows of their teeth pulled, as I myself witnessed, to obtain more beautiful ones; and well-known as this is, and as much at it should frighten away men, their beauty and charm are alluring with an irresistible power. The women know nothing of love — that salt of marriage — for if a man has only money enough to serve their love of luxury, he is good enough for a husband, whether he is young or old, handsome or ugly, religious or atheist. If his money vanishes, naturally so does her loyalty and love. In this connection, I will cite a passage from the Talmud (*Sanhedrin*, 38a): "When God wished to create man, he took earth from all parts of the world and out of this created Adam." Then He let him fall asleep and out of one of his ribs created Eve. She ate of the apple and gave some of it to her husband, so that like her, he became mortal. It seems that this rib, out of which Adam's wife was created, consisted of American earth, and therefore carried in it the lust for pleasure. Since Adam was poor and could not satisfy Eve's love of luxury, life was a burden to her and she tried to do away with him and herself. Perhaps she gave him the apple out of jealousy that he might not marry another woman. In America, at least, such cases are not rare.

I tried to find a cause for all this and believe that the reason for this situation lies in the fact that, when America was first settled, there were so few women that a man thought it a stroke of luck to find a wife. He had no choice and had to ignore her weaknesses and deficiencies; on the contrary, he idolized her. Although now there is no longer any lack of women, this attitude has continued from generation to generation. At the same time, I must remark that in some places this evil is not so great and that there the relation between man and wife is normal. In California, however, these customs may be observed in all their crudeness.

For the sake of truth, I must also set the bright side beside the dark and confess that unmarried girls live very properly before marriage. They are charitable, give thought to the higher pleasures of life, and take delight in hearing good lectures and sermons. Time passes very quickly for them: at fourteen they are marriageable, and at sixteen, seventeen, or eighteen they marry.

It is interesting to compare the women of various lands and to note the differences among them. The American women seem to be born only for fine clothes and luxury, as has already been said several times. The women of Asia and Africa find their purpose in life in bearing children and consider many children, especially boys, a great good fortune. The greater the number of children the more they are elevated in the eyes of their husbands and the worthier of their love. This spirit seems to have prevailed in the Orient from the most ancient times. Thus we find it mentioned by Leah in the Bible (*Genesis* 30. 20; 32. 34), for after she had given birth to her sixth son, she cried out in joy: "Now will my husband love me!" It is a pity that they cannot give their children a good upbringing; they understand their household duties, to be sure, very well; but they trouble themselves about nothing else so that a husband is king in his house. At the same time, the family life is very affectionate and cheerful.

The women of Europe may be divided into several classes. In France, for example, the women are good housewives and bring up their children well. Many women are also very industrious and help their husbands even in business. But the pleasure of family life is broken up for them, for the husband goes out much and too often runs away from his hearth. The Polish women are like the French; like them, they are good housewives and also bring up their children well; likewise, they help their husbands in business. But their status is a lower one; the husband does what he likes and very seldom asks his wife for advice; he is the lord and master. In fact, there is a proverb in their language: *Gdzie Zona rzazi, tam Diablo blazi* (where the women rule, the devil is at large). The fear of a petticoat tyranny has here produced the opposite. The Bible seems to be directly opposed to this notion of what is proper, for we find, for example, that Jacob took counsel with his wives (*Genesis* 31. 4-16).

German women are endowed with a combination of most of the virtues: they are very good housewives; they bring up their children well; and they are true to their husbands, in misfortune as in good fortune, in sorrow as in joy.

As for beauty, the prize must be awarded to the women of Bagdad in Asia, Tunis in Africa, and those of America. The women of the first two places are beautiful by nature and excel all others; the American women are beautiful by art rather than nature. But good, genuine women are to be found only in Germany, and if God had only used German earth when He created woman, there is no doubt that only the apple of life would have been offered to Adam. They are very much like the women of the Jews of whom Solomon said (*Proverbs* 31. 30): "Grace is deceitful and beauty is vain, but a woman who fears God shall be praised."

A land which suffers from so great an evil, where every noble impulse is nipped in the bud, must become incapable of all that is lofty, elevated and noble, and, if no remedy is provided, great harm must come of it.

Chapter VI

THE SPIRIT OF AMERICA AT PRESENT

WE HAVE, BEFORE US, A LITTLE BROCHURE, A LECTURE ON "AMERICA and its Destiny," delivered by a lady in New York, because — so she says — "the spirits" determined that she deliver the lecture there. The statement was believed, and people came streaming from all sides to listen to the revelations of the spirit that ruled the lady. That single fact characterizes the spirit of America. It is to be regretted that such a crude delusion could find admirers and partisans among a people whom Morse and Mitchell in their geography call "the most enlightened." How can one still be angry at magic, witchcraft, or the other superstitious notions which mankind has cherished all along, if "the most enlightened people" find pleasure in such frauds, and have Mormons, Millerites and similar strange sects among them! Why still speak of the delusions of the Middle Ages, if with our own eyes we see that "the most enlightened" people run to the representative of such superstition and if one can be sure that the more absurd and sillier a thing is, the more numerous its admirers, helpers and defenders! The peaceful and serene spectator at such exhibitions might almost completely doubt the existence of sound common-sense and is almost ready to believe that the world is most easily ruled by the swindlers and the sly. It is harsh to say this, but it must be said: he is no true friend who only flatters his neighbor and gilds the spots in his character or excuses them. He is also no friend of the American people who increases and supports the self-delusion and self-complacency from which the Americans suffer. A true friend says a truthful word at the right time even if it has a bitter sound (Proverbs 12. 17).

The writer of these lines loves this land and this people as his own and has chosen both out of a free choice without compulsion. He should consequently be permitted to speak freely, provided he does not speak out of a mania for blaming and fault-finding.

Above all we must — as a naturalized American permit me to say "we" — make mention of the fact that it is a great self-delusion to maintain that we are "the most enlightened people." In our fatherland we have not a single seat of learning that can be compared to the little universities of Padua, Jena, Goettingen or Halle, to say nothing of the famous universities of England or France, those in Berlin, St. Petersburg and Vienna. This is one of the surest measures of culture. Enlightenment is not a plant that grows wild, that springs out of the ground without any trouble and labor; it is rather a blossom that will never flower without the helping hand of man. From what sources, then, have we drawn the unusually illuminating principles, opinions, or doctrines? Enlightenment must have its conductor as well as electricity if it is to become part of a vast community; and the best conductor is the schools and the press.

Our public schools are no more than twenty years old and are still handicapped by the lack of that which new institutions lack generally. The superficiality of our colleges, academies and seminaries has become proverbial. Young ladies study astronomy before they can spell properly; young men receive their doctorate after they have gone through a thoroughly confused mass of Greek, Latin, Mathematics, French, German, physics, chemistry, history, geography, logic, metaphysics, ethics, and still other studies, in two or three years, and that without a firm grasp of any one of them. Tailors, cobblers, farmers, or clerks in stores are turned into physicians in thirty-two weeks; policemen, watchmen and constables suddenly become lawyers; every man feels that he has the ability to be a preacher, teacher, politician, statesman and diplomat and soon finds his public and his sphere of influence. This utterly ridiculous superficiality is nevertheless by far not so stupid and disgusting as the pedantry of our self-educated schoolmasters and pedagogues who kill the spirit with words and formulas. Can we regard this as a fountain of enlightenment which has educated us to be "the most enlightened people?" What then are the merits of the model schools, gymnasia and universities? One must not deceive oneself: the schools are still too young and the colleges too superficial to make an enlightened people of us.

The press likewise is not strong enough to make up for what the schools lack. Only too often it is governed by inadequate principles so that it only aims at making money; or by superficiality, so that by means of pictures and other ways it tries to supply what it otherwise lacks. In this, too, other nations are far ahead and there is still no paper that can be considered the equal of the press of London, or the French and German periodicals. We are also far behind in this respect: every kind of depravity finds its defenders and patrons in the press if they only pay well enough. Thus it is that our press is not always a lighthouse for the community, not always the great lever for noble and illustrious purposes, not the honest and faithful expounder of the events of the day, not the torch that carries progress and knowledge; but rather at times merely a commercial enterprise in the hands of a group which publicizes only such things which, according to all expectation, will yield the most profit. One often looks in vain for the serious or the love of truth; so much the oftener one runs into articles that are merely sensational, into bombastic words and immoral announcements. The press here is not the mistress but too often only the wretched handmaiden of the people, picking up the crumbs of news that fall from the richly laden table of mankind. Such a press could never, and can never, lift a people to the highest degree of enlightenment.

A glance at the current literature likewise does not make us happy. If we except a few names with a good old reputation, we have no better authors, no scholars more brilliant, no men of talent in the arts more illustrious, to point to. We shall be answered by those who point to the greatest, loftiest blessing of our land, saying: "It is the freedom for which our fathers bled and died, it is the Constitution and the laws which the wise men, our ancestors, have left us, that have made us the most enlightened of people." It would be more correct to say: "That should have made us such." In such a school quite another kind of student should be found; with such examples to shine before us, quite another spirit should animate us. Our Constitution and institutions merely show that the Fathers of the Republic were very enlightened. What is the condition now of that Constitution, in theory and in practice? We must be silent. Where is the Constitution? Where is our freedom? We ask this often and receive no answer.

Future generations, will be astounded to learn from history that from 400,000 to 500,000 volunteers took up arms to defend the Constitution of their land and that nowhere could this most enlightened people find a man to lead these mighty columns, this mountain rolling onward to victory, so that it might in a short time shatter its weaker opponent, and that immigrant Germans and Irish had to be summoned to act as spearhead. The generations to come will read to their amazement how twenty-two million free men, who arose in the majestic strength of a lion and were aided by the wealth of a Croesus, who stood up with the firm conviction that they were defending only their sacred possessions and that the iron dice of death were rolling only for the sake of right, could suddenly remain motionless, utterly inactive, that the lion would no longer shake his mane in anger and terrify the foe by the paralyzing thunder of his voice.

Is there, in the history of the world, another page on which the like is to be read? The great army of the Persians which invaded Greece was not inactive; the great army of Napoleon, which poured over Russia, fought; the Austrians in Italy defended themselves. Where in history did a nation ever rise to such great fame and mighty strength without begetting great and mighty spirits who took over the leadership? One has only to think of the generals of the French Revolution. We stand with all our might, with our love for the Constitution, with our longing for peace and unity and with our myriads of soldiers, our mighty arms — have we no one who can lead us, guide us happily to victory, and must we now live to see defeats like that of Manassas? Who knows how much time must still pass before the old spirit re-awakens, when more illustrious deeds will cause the first defeats of this struggle to be forgotten.*

Our present distress arose out of no organic defects of the government, but has its origin in a kind of demagogism to be found in many lands . . . The present situation in the northern states — the misfortunes that they have suffered, blow upon blow, at the beginning of the war just broken out — has encouraged the enemies of the American Constitution to condemn it utterly and to represent it as a vain effort. Without wishing to appear as its defender, I cannot refrain from mentioning the present state of affairs and to shed some light on its various aspects. The current state of mind, brought about and continued by the war, emphatically calls for such an explanation.

From the outset the baser passions of the volatile multitude were aroused and bloody feuds were the natural and necessary result. Our struggle then began because of the abuse of freedom and of wealth, just as a man, through excessive pleasure and immoderation, can kill himself.

This abuse of the boundless wealth of our land and of freedom occurred in two ways: first, through materialism and then through the neglect of learning. Fast as our steamers speed at sea and our locomotives fly over the western plains, faster still we raced into materialism and corruption. To make money! This has, at present, a magnetic charm and enchantment! Public officials accept positions and others long for them simply to enrich themselves. They care nothing about working for the common good, and have set no noble goal for themselves; no pure motive animates them. True enough, there are exceptions. For a few, honor and the public good are the stars that guide them; but, for the great majority, the important thing is the money that this service provides. Did anyone ever hear of so many officials turned traitor as we have had in the few months of our political dis-

---

* To our joy the fortunes of war have turned for the better (beginning of 1862).

96 /

turbances? The reason is elementary: treason is more profitable than loyalty, and he who is only loyal for money quickly turns traitor if the seducer pays more. Money makes a man respected here, honored and prized; people ask: what is he worth? And, according to the amount of his possessions, he is a statesman, a scholar. An honorable man without money is not respected at all; he is considered a nobody; he is treated as though superfluous. On the other hand, we heap all honors on a rich scoundrel, on a well-to-do blockhead, on a wealthy ignoramus, and almost crawl before him. Only at election-time, when every one has his right to vote, does respect for the poorest comes into its own.

Almost every man is therefore driven to try to become a merchant, a banker, a speculator, a manufacturer, or tries to capture a position that will yield money. The child hears from its father, the pupil from his teacher, the student from his professor, that gold creates an all-mighty power in every circle of society. The greed for it is thus nourished with our life's blood at the expense of all nobler, better and higher feelings, and at the sacrifice of our spiritual capacities and our happiness. Thousands sacrifice their health and their lives to the service of Mammon and as a result of this general and prevailing passion the human spirit is completely neglected. Tied to the making of money ever since childhood, the beauty of nature is stunted and so is the charm of education in the humanities, the truth of science, the sublimity of art, the holiness of religion, morality, truth, honor and virtue. Everything is pushed into the background and takes a subordinate place. This is the focal point of our corruption, around which it revolves. How can one still wonder at the multitude of dishonest officials and traitors? They walk along the same path as the others; they, too, are making money like the rest; and in no way are they different from the multitude. How can one still be surprised that the most impudent demagogues try to stir up the basest passions so that, once the election is over, they might find compensation in a well-paid post. When these things happen, why should one complain that neither talent nor true greatness exist? Everyone only wishes to make money and that as fast and as safely as they can.

Herein, as I said, lies the root of the sickness and this is the dangerous cancer. The spirit of the American people is sick in a fashion that must arouse the greatest anxiety and that should never have occurred in a constitutional state. Thus it has happened that now, after we have done business for fifty years, and, to be sure, most successfully, we stand on the brink of an abyss and run the danger of plunging down if someone or other does not soon appear to help us with rede and deed.

We come now to the second point mentioned above — knowledge. This, too, like everything else, is only the slave and the handmaiden of the passions that can only be goaded on by the pursuit of money. We have no love for knowledge for its own sake; we do not turn to it as to the sun that illuminates our path, but look on it as merchandise. We find shops for politics, working-places of professional politicians who manufacture politics, and working-rooms of priests in which religion is dispensed. The occupation of a professor, a scholar, a clergyman, a rabbi and preacher, is regarded as his business. "That is his business." We have no time to do anything for ourselves and want our fellow-creatures to earn money like ourselves. We are pleased to find ready, for our comfort, the shoes, boots, clothes, caps, even medicines, magnetic pills, galvanized chains, health, morals, religion, truth, or any other article which they have manufactured. Therefore any absurdity or madness, if only mad enough, creates a stir in this country and men have faith in it. Deception, quackery, misrepresentation, ridiculous or childish superstition — they all pay and whatever its name it is profitable for a while until it must give way before something newer, from Barnum down to a fortune-teller, from Dr. Townsend's sarsaparilla down to the different bitter cordials made by Jon Smith and Mueller, to Mr. Lederer of New York. We are so often deceived because we want to be deceived.

Knowledge cannot flourish under such conditions and since this is the situation that prevails generally we came to the conclusion that is reached everywhere: everyone knows everything and can do anything. The facts here teach that we know everything and understand how to set to work at anything without having studied it or engaged in it before. We met a professor in this country who stepped down to become a bookbinder and bookseller, that is to say, to become a good man. Having failed in the mission of his life, instead of devoting himself to knowledge, to perfecting himself and developing his knowledge further, he had to drive himself, like the rest about him, to make the most money in his own fashion. We met an astronomer, who was excellent in his field but who, in addition, engaged in the ordinary work of an engineer. Many doctors who never studied a thing do best of all; they rely on boasting and bragging and in this they do not miscalculate. Quacks, swindlers and the great native intellects brag and are, in almost all places, the representatives of the intelligentsia. Everyone must admit that our learning is still on a very low level. To be sure, we are still too young a nation to enter the ranks of other nations and to be able to match their men of distinction with names of equal importance, but if we continue on the same way that we have gone, if our young people continue their studies as until now, knowledge will never blossom here.

The students have no time to busy themselves for long with earnest studies, but must hurry on. And yet, nothing can be studied thoroughly in a hurry.

It is no trick to be a captain when the sea is quiet. But, when the storm rages, the experienced seaman proves himself. As long as peace and unity reigned upon our ship of state, every man was good enough and capable for a public office. But now, at the first storm, the result of our foolish system can be seen: everyone understands and can do everything. Nevertheless, the judgment of God, through which we now must pass, will show us how small we are in our inflated pride; it will teach us that there are loftier and more important interests than gold and luxury. For as little as it is the highest calling of an individual to amass goods and chattels, no more can it be the highest calling of an entire nation which, after all, consists only of individuals. It will teach us that man has been chosen by Providence to progress in the good, the true and the beautiful and also that upon this blood-soaked place of God's election welfare and blessing will blossom forth for America and all mankind.

Chapter VII

School, Church and State

THE PROUDEST AND MOST SPLENDID POLITICAL STRUCTURE EVER ERECTED by the hand of man on the solid foundation of religious and political freedom, of personal and municipal liberty, is threatened with collapse — caused by its own sons.

We tried above to give general causes for this danger and now we ask the reader to follow us in a brief examination of particular institutions. Three of these exercise the greatest influence on the public generally and on individuals: school, church and state. I must blame them too, in part, for the faults pointed out above. Let us examine them more closely.

1. The School

More than once the press has called the attention of the public to the fact that the public schools and academies are merely hot-houses for memory, calculating craftiness and cold reason and leave all the higher capacities of youth, the noble impulses and the lofty feelings of the young, wholly untouched and undeveloped.

A child's love of learning, his tendency to reflect and think for himself having been stifled by the eternal "spelling" lessons, his mind is stuffed with a mass of names — geographical, historical and grammatical. These remain only words without being understood, without becoming flesh and blood. The child retains nothing but words. In this he has the help of his textbook which the unfortunate pupil must study without understanding it. In this manner his memory is exercised and overloaded for six or eight years at the expense of his higher faculties for thought, and nine times out of ten the pupil forgets in one year what he has learnt in six because he has gone ahead without any brainwork.

The study of arithmetic also belongs to this type of study of dead words. In most cases it, too, is nothing but drill in testing the memory. Granted that it is properly taught with the objective and goal of developing the mind, it develops at best only the ability to calculate coldly, earnestly and cunningly, and is in no way natural or elevating for the youthful spirit.

What then of the moral tendencies of youth that should also be cherished and protected? What is done for them? What attention do they get? What nourishment? Nothing! They are considered not worth a glance in this kind of education. Here, too, we may judge the inside by the outside, for the place and construction of the school-house characterizes the spirit of the school. We saw school-houses in the country that had no tree or blade of grass growing near them. In Europe, on the other hand, a wealth of flowers and plants grow, for the most part, next to a school in the country, and in the larger cities unusually large sums are spent on gardens to teach botany and particularly the care of fruit-trees and gardening and to awaken the love of nature. In the schools of America there is also no instruction in natural history — not the slightest hint of it. Everything that surrounds the pupil is dead and deadening. He is offered only words and more words and gloomy calculation that is alien to his spirit, that promise nothing for his feelings of morality, that take no notice of the many thousand beauties of God's creation nor of the noble virtues that slumber in the breast of man or live in the figures of history. In this condition, the pupil leaves the public school and joins the common herd.

We will now glance at the chosen few — very few in fact in comparison to those who attend the elementary schools — who go to the academies, seminaries, high-schools, colleges, or whatever a place of higher education is called.

We begin with the young ladies who are kept at the study of Latin, Greek and mathematics and who were not included in our earlier discussion.

Can one think of a greater perversion of nature? A young woman, whose every nerve is sensitive, whose heart is full of noble impulses, who has an innate admiration for the good and beautiful, must stamp upon her memory the formulae of mathematics and the paradigms of Latin and Greek so that, after she has been graduated with all honor, she might forget them in a year! The same is true of history. The teacher of it does not call attention to the connection between cause and effect to point out the wisdom of foresight or to use history cautiously as a guide for life: there is nothing of that. The teacher says only: "For your next lesson study ten pages." And so the poor being burdens her memory without having the slightest use in return for all her torment.

A few study music (piano), drawing and painting, mechanically. But the true appreciation of the beautiful, so close to the feminine soul, is a circumstance completely neglected in such institutions. Others lose themselves in the study of physics and chemistry, though, to be sure, without instruments and laboratories; they exercise themselves in the study of astronomy without observatories; in winter they study botany in their rooms and in summer the formation of the crystals of snow and ice; the thought of favoring the students with nature herself and her charms through the study of the Book of Nature occurs to no one.

Is not such an education to be rejected?

If we turn to the institutions for young men, we find again all the above-mentioned deficiencies in a like degree. Along with this there is also a superficiality which results from the neglect of the old and later classics. Of all the branches of learning, only mathematics is really studied.

Nobody studies in school for the sake of study. The great problem that has to be solved is how to pass one's examinations. One becomes alienated from art as well as nature: everything is done only for the sake of its usefulness.

As a result, we encounter among men who have enjoyed an education so much egotism, so little interest in the public good, and all the more interest, therefore, in what is of benefit to oneself. A gentleman, to whom I expressed one day my astonishment at so much perjury and public fraud, remarked: "Not all are tainted, not all are spoiled: only those, incredible as it may sound, who have enjoyed an education. We get sound men from among the uneducated people." Here, then, stalks an evil that must be cured at the root if this republic is not to come ever closer to ruin.

2. The Church

Religion has proved itself to be that element which was usually attended by civilization and humanity. Neither the sciences nor the arts brought the savages out of the woods into a society of law and order: only religion accomplished this. The blessings of religion, which gives contentment to the individual and stability to society, are so numerous that the worst religion is better than none. France, during the Revolution, was the most striking proof of this assertion. It is undeniable that religion, falsely used, breeds fanaticism; and that religion, misunderstood, leads to absurdities; that both, absurdities and fanaticism, have caused much evil in the world; but yet not as much as the lack of all religion would have caused.

The practical result of religion must be morality — the elevation of mankind. The object of divine Revelation is to teach mankind the good, the right and the just, and their opposites; and so the chief object of a synagogue, church, or mosque is contained in this revelation: to awaken the germ of goodness in the soul, to suppress the baser passions, and to turn a man into a useful member of human society — this is their goal.

Is it attained?

If a man goes into this or that church, when and as often as he will, he will find too much of sectarianism and too little religion, too much dogma and too little faith. Seldom does the preacher make it his task to talk on, or spread fundamental principles of justice and goodness; instead, every one is occupied in finding as many dogmas as possible. Seldom does the preacher take as his text for a sermon honesty, uprightness, integrity, faithfulness, the sacredness of a promise and an oath, modesty, respect for parents and teacher, gratitude and the like. Nowhere is this heard. But the preacher preaches what he wishes: that one should believe in this, or not believe in that, in order to become immortal after his own particular pattern. The child receives from its mother, from the minister and in Sunday-school, religious instruction that cannot stir it or inspire it. "Pray and read the Bible" or "memorize a catechism"; religious instruction consists chiefly of such sentences. The child goes to church and hears singing that he does not understand; then he hears from the pulpit how evil and corrupt man is. Instead of a man receiving strength and encouragement and gaining faith in himself and his Creator, he is depressed and loses what little faith in himself he has left.

Religion is pictured as a prescribed way of conducting oneself towards God, for which every one gets his particular reward. Looked at closely, it must be confessed that such a religion nourishes only egotism and actually works against all morality. Accordingly, one hears of many church members that they are immoral, greedy, egoistic and faithless in the highest degree, yes, that even priests become guilty of all sorts of crimes. One must tread another path: our preachers should teach morality and our children should be made aware early of the holiness of an oath, the inviolability of honor and chastity, the sanctity of human life and of a good name, respect for parents and teacher, and so on; prayers should be offered up out of complete conviction and loving hearts. Religion would then be implanted in truth, and fanaticism as well as egotism stamped out.

3. The State

The progress and the fortunate condition of a people that was governed for the seventy years just past by the Constitution of the United States, as well as the express wish of the majority to continue to be governed by it in the future, proves that it is the best means ever devised by man to govern a nation. The best example of this is in the way the seceding states framed their own constitution. Their representatives found no reason whatever for changing any of the principal features of the Constitution itself, but had only the *improvement* of it in mind, so that it would correspond to the needs and conditions of the time — at least according to their ideas. This Constitution of the United States was evolved out of vigorous conflict of views and, like pure gold fresh from the furnace, satisfied all parties. The basis of our public life is, accordingly, sound, and there can be no ground for blaming the governmental system for any social evils which may exist. One should not compare this social unit, which has hardly an independent history of its own but is to a great extent a pell-mell gathering from various nations in various stages of development, with European society. The unqualified condition of freedom in which the people here find themselves has no place for the wishes which move us constructively to a life of idealism, and in the meantime the selfish drive for self-preservation and material gain remains the impulse for every action and explains its one-sidedness. Only the slow building up of a class, sure of its possessions, will in time provide an aristocracy above the common people, an élite which will devote itself exclusively to higher aims and be able to lead the masses.

We have run into the following who, among others, have an influence on the actual working of the government: the officials of the various branches of the government; the office-seekers; the politicians by profession; *the gentlemen with influence*, who buy votes; the demagogues with, and without, principles; the press; the public speakers; and so on.

Until now, the most deplorable corruption was to be found among the officials of the government. Why? Before a man receives an office in the government, he must pass through every degree of corruption. He must make himself popular by any means, even the most ignoble — by intrigues and tricks, by entering into bets with politicians of single municipal districts (ward politicians), and by currying the favor of *influential men* — and so try to show that he is suitable for the office. At election time, he must under all circumstances know how to distort the truth into lies and, on the other hand, give every lie as much plausibility as possible. These are facts, and it is only surprising that the officials of the government are not really worse than they are.

Furthermore, a poor man cannot be elected to any office, for a rich man must squander everything, often until he has spent his last cent, before he can hope for a nomination or election. As a result, it follows naturally enough that when he is finally in office, he tries to reimburse himself. The people cannot complain about it after they have stripped the candidates almost to their shirts; this teaches the official, indeed compels him, to exploit his authority and power for profit.

In addition to this evil, there is still another: no official of the government is responsible to the people, but most of them are under the control of an executive department which, for its part, is in turn responsible to the party that put it in power and not to the people who must maintain it. "What will the Party say? What impression will this make on the Party?" These are the urgent questions everywhere. Since the officials are not responsible to the people, they pay no attention whatever to the opinion of people who do not belong to their political party. If they are accused of some injustice or other, the members of their party defend them, and the Press serves those who pay it.

It is not a question of ability. Second-rate and third-rate lawyers, and merchants who have lost their standing, are good enough and able enough to govern a country although they could not manage their own affairs.

A fundamental defect of America is that there is no prevalent general public opinion. There is nothing but party spirit. Almost every man is hitched to the cart of some political party and, without really being aware of it, he must keep hauling the office-seekers who sit in the cart. The moral sense of the community is not strong enough to despise and condemn men who are guilty of crimes against the republic. As long as a man becomes rich, even if he steals thousands or millions, and robs widows and orphans of their property, he passes everywhere as a respected man. These are the faults and crimes of the country! The corruption of those on top having in this manner for so many years seeped into the people below, there is no morality whatever in politics, and this is the cause of the sickness and decadence from which we suffer. When the moral strength of the nation is strengthened again and Mammon has put down his sceptre, everything will return to its proper and orderly condition again.

Let the philanthropists, first of all, work for the reform of school and church. Let the candid man speak out unafraid — he who uncovers the mistakes and degeneration into which men have fallen and exhibits them in the proper light — and all may yet turn out for the best.

Chapter VIII

The Situation in America Illuminated in Another Way

THE NEGLECT OF LEARNING IS THE PRINCIPLE CAUSE OF ALL THE MIS-
fortunes in which the United States has suddenly and unhappily found
itself. No sensible and intelligent man has ever doubted that the progress and prosperity of society keeps step with the degree of education
and knowledge that has been spread among all the people. Society in
the Middle Ages had all the material wealth that it could wish for;
nevertheless it was pitiful, crippled and unhappy, and that merely because learning and knowledge were principally limited to a very small
section of the people. If such is the case, then backwardness in knowledge and useful learning must hasten, above all, the misery of the people
generally.

We often hear complaints that among the officers of the United
States army and navy so few are from the northern states. The reason for this is obvious. In our northern and commercialized states
Mammon has reached such a degree of sovereignty that every other
interest has vanished before this all-powerful idol. The schools and
academies there are only institutions which prepare students for the
great and practical art of making money, yes, for making as much
money as possible. Every higher interest of mankind is subordinated
to this great problem of gathering wealth. The lad of fourteen or fifteen must clean a store, hop around a bar, watch an office, be the humblest underling in a bank, or do something or other like that, to earn
money. He is sent to a commercial school to learn bookkeeping, arithmetic and writing, for no other purpose than that he might become
more adept and quicker at making money. Thus thousands, and more
than thousands, of young spirits are lost and the nation robbed of its
strength.

Many young men attend a military or naval academy and complete
their studies with distinction, but then the question immediately arises
as to how much money will the position of a lieutenant in the army
or of a naval cadet yield annually, and how much that of a lawyer,
merchant, or banker. Since the last-named occupations offer better

prospects than that of serving the state, Mammon makes prisoners of the young men, drives them into his own service, and seduces them from the service of the army or navy of their fatherland — the United States.

Furthermore, there is much complaint about political wire-pulling, the demagogues, and the speakers who arouse political passions, and of other similar cancerous sores of society. It is said that they mislead the people, that they have, first of all, only their own interests at heart, and never that of the general good. How does that happen? One never takes the time to pay any attention to public affairs; day and night there is only one subject, one object to devotion: how to make money. And all other interests are surrendered to the hands of those who use them for their own profit. There is not sufficient will-power to give children a good education at a college, early to implant in their hearts the lofty principles of humanity, and, above all, to teach them that there are things far more desirable and precious than all the gold of Ophir.

Will America be able to become a nation of princes without the education of a prince, without the exalted principles of patriotism and unselfishness without which no republic can endure? Never. Its young people are brought up to be merchants, bankers, farmers and mechanics, but not independent men. The exceptions are too few to change the general color of the whole. We therefore reiterate what we stated at first: the neglect of teaching and of knowledge is the principal cause of the present calamities.

We also wish to add that all the standing armies, fleets, divisions of the national guard, arsenals, fortresses and fortifications of this republic will be utterly unable to save it from certain ruin if the nation itself does not become convinced that there are more precious and desirable ends, more sacred and durable interests to which man must direct himself than the disgusting and, in the final analysis, widely injurious object of making money. As long as money remains the principal object of the efforts of private citizen and public official, the republic will always be in danger no matter how many armed defenders it may number. This greed for money will only yield before the might of knowledge, the might that lifts mankind above the low horizon where egotism has placed him and which teaches him that he is only a part of the whole upon the soundness of which his own well-being depends.

We turn, once more, from the prevailing Church to our own Jewish congregation. It has a new foundation under the sunshine of freedom and has utilized this freedom in many ways. We Jews are scattered and divided into many congregations, as if the fate of our people must also be re-enacted here, on a lesser scale. Each community is concerned only with itself and has nothing to do with any other. The religious feelings of our brothers are strong enough to spur them on to the organization of congregations, to the building of synagogues, to the establishment of philanthropic and educational societies in order to satisfy their religious and philanthropic needs; but they have separated themselves from each other, and each congregation stands alone and without help; each congregation is sovereign. Every one can see, easily enough, the evils that arise out of such separation, but no one has suggested a practical plan to heal it.

Quite contrary to the spirit of Judaism and the experience of the times, American congregations adopted the system used by the Methodists who, in very little time, turn into a preacher the first, best tradesman who comes along. A shoemaker, tailor, furrier, harness-maker, village schoolmaster, butcher, or anybody of almost any occupation or handicraft has on occasions been transformed into a shepherd of souls. The task of such men has been to conduct the services and to supervise the observance of the laws concerning food; some of them also preach, write and become men of importance without the least knowledge of Judaism and its sacred writings. These pseudo-preachers were greatly pained when by chance a few ordained rabbis set foot upon this shore of the Atlantic — men who had a different conception of the essence of Judaism and did not reject the demands of the times. All too soon, the pseudo-preachers were at odds with those who insisted on their own views, and were only too quick to attack them, confusing persons and issues. A struggle broke out and was carried on by both sides with bitterness. Two parties came into existence; one called itself Reform and the other Orthodox, and Israel was divided into two camps. Every attempt to heal the breach has been avoided or openly attacked.

Such a condition of affairs cannot last long and it is to be hoped that, in the not too distant future, difficulties will be cleared up as men turn to the study of theology more than they do now and ignorance is no longer able to have its say. Teach the Jew fully about the essence and history of Judaism and he will at once distinguish what to accept as part of Judaism and what to reject, so that Judaism will show men the way to proper conduct before God and the world. He will soon perceive that all observances and ceremonies lead us into the Holy of Holies of truth, light, morality and humanity. Once again I insist, therefore, that the neglect of instruction is the principal cause of the present difficulty and that here, as everywhere at every time and at every place, only our ignorance has defeated us.

Permit me to tell you, Israelites, that neither your synagogues nor your temples, neither your *hazzanim* (cantors) nor your *shohetim* (slaughterers of cattle and poultry according to religious laws), are able to make Judaism continue to grow in this land if you yourselves do not set to work with all your energy and labor for the spread of knowledge through schools. Not such knowledge as learning Hebrew or quoting a few sentences from some catechism is useful and helpful, but a thorough acquaintance with the sources of Judaism, the chief of which is the Bible, indeed the whole Bible, in its original language. Furthermore, let me say that until then there will be no unity of opinion and no harmony in the management of the community. Experience has taught that the union of more than twenty communities, organized in 1860 under the name of "Board of Delegates," has remained ineffectual and has not brought to maturity the fruits that were expected, because Reform was against it and undermined its effectiveness. As long as the cultivation of knowledge is not more general, no one can tell how this breach in America will be healed.

We could add another list of facts to support our contention, but these hints may be enough and give the reader food for thought.

Chapter IX

Journey from New York to California

THE JOURNEY THROUGH THE UNITED STATES TOOK ME A WHOLE YEAR. The East with its industrious and intelligent inhabitants, the West with its unpretentious prairies and woods, the sunny South and the stern North arrest in equal degree the attention of the traveler.

On August 1, 1860, I said farewell to the noise and bustle of the city of New York and set out on my journey to California on board the steamer *Ariel*. The Pacific Company let me have the very best accommodations free to San Francisco, thanks to Mr. William Seligman and the references for which I am indebted to the most illustrious scholars of Germany. At the stroke of twelve noon, the thunder of cannon announced our departure, and after the lapse of an hour we were in the bay. Towards evening we lost sight of the continent. As if in compensation for this loss, we saw, through a spy-glass, a ship from California with which we exchanged signals.

On the second of August, a mild southerly wind favored our journey, so that we could hoist all sails and steam ahead briskly. In the twilight of evening we passed Cape Hatteras. On the third, we approached the Bahamas. San Salvador, discovered by Christopher Columbus on October 12, 1492, is one of the islands. Here the captain is required to exercise great caution, for many rocks, hidden under the surface of the water, are to be found in the neighborhood of these islands and can prove very dangerous to seafarers and have often caused great loss. Many of my fellow-travelers became seasick and had to leave the deck. But I, who had made a number of journeys by sea and, it seems, am not easily inclined to this sickness, was not troubled by the least feeling of sickness and, in addition, was able to assist my suffering fellow-passengers when they were sick and to care for them.

On the fourth of August a remarkable phenomenon in the sky attracted our notice. A fiery object, like a planet afire, with a long tail of blazing light, rose from the distant horizon and came nearer and nearer to us until at last it stood directly over the steamer; and then, with a deafening noise, it fell into the ocean a short distance away.

On the sixth and seventh unusually large birds flew about our ship. Towards seven o'clock of the second day we had to struggle against high waves caused by the many little islands here. On the seventh, we passed the island of Cuba, discovered on October 28, 1492, by Columbus: this and the little island of Puerto Rico are all that are left in this hemisphere of the once mighty Spanish dominions. Even these narrow strips of land will not escape their fate and will soon be annexed to the free states of North America in order to round off the territory of these states and ensure the safety of their southern ports.

In the afternoon we passed the island of San Domingo that was discovered by Columbus in 1492. It is the only island that has not, as yet, become the booty of the European powers. Lately, however, Spain has made her influence felt.

We found ourselves among a group of islands! What a splendid spectacle! One could still sense the joy of the discoverers at the sight of them! How many thousands had their ships shattered and sunk along these islands in those days when new dangers awaited them at every knot they made! Those who with sacrifice and devotion ex-plored and discovered are no more; they do not enjoy the fruits of their undertakings and their industry. The islands and continents, dis-covered for the good of man, are thickly populated and flourishing, but the memory of their discoverers quickly falls into oblivion.

The general atmosphere of today is one of teeming activity — boats constantly coming and going, provide a most worthwhile spectacle. To go from one island to another is almost like a pleasure trip.

At two o'clock in the afternoon we noticed — not exactly to our joy — a school of porpoises tumbling about in the ocean: the sign of a violent storm close at hand. In the morning of the ninth of August, a violent and heavy rain poured down on us. In many places the sea was covered with floating grass.

On the tenth we reached Aspinwall — two thousand miles from New York. On our arrival I had a special surprise: a Negro greeted me as a fellow Jew, and for a moment I believed that I had reached the coast of Malabar. In reply to my question where he was from, I learnt that he came from Jamaica, an English possession in the West Indies, where there was an entire community like him, and that they had their own synagogue. It is very likely that they are the descendants of slaves that were converted to Judaism.

Chapter X

Aspinwall

ASPINWALL WAS FORMERLY KNOWN AS NEHA BAI. ITS PRESENT NAME is that of the founder of the city and the president of the railway that crosses the isthmus from Darien to Panama. The city belongs to the republic of New Granada, and its harbor is very well protected against the attack of enemies. It has from three to four thousand inhabitants, of various nationalities and among them also a few Jews. The natives are a lazy pack of thieves who live chiefly on native fruit which grows wild, such as bananas, pineapples, oranges and the like, of which there is more than enough. Although the natives are in one sense better off because of the construction of the railway and the discovery of gold in California, their condition has become much worse because of the wickedness of their wives and the avarice and greed of the men themselves. No one can be sure that what he has is safe, for the native slyly lies in wait to take possession quickly of the traveler's property, no matter whether this is permissible or not. The city is built on a swamp, and the only street that is paved is that where the principal business is transacted.

After I had stopped two hours in Aspinwall, I took the railway to Panama. We reached it in two and three-quarter hours.

A stranger is charged $25 for the trip to Panama, although a resident pays only $5. The banks of the Chagres river are now joined by an iron bridge over which the cars of the railway can pass in all conceivable safety and many accidents are thus avoided. Many an emigrant with a heart full of brave hopes in the years '49 and '50 lost his life in this stream on the way across the isthmus; on the back of a stubborn mule the journey was not as easy as one might think. For us, in cars of a train, the trip was nothing less than comfortable. For the first fifteen miles the air was heavy and the sky cloudy and both sides of the railway were surrounded by thick vegetation. We could not discover even a bird — that might have brought some life into the landscape. But the picture changed when we left this dismal neighborhood behind and we were on a beautiful even plain; the sky above was mild and transparent; and the air was balmy and fragrant. Fruit, such as only the tropics can show, gladdened the eye; gaily-feathered birds flitted about; alligators and lively monkeys particularly delighted those passengers who had never seen them before. All along the way we saw log huts in which graceful Creoles or naked Indians lived.

We were offered sugar-cane, boiled eggs, sweet cakes, and many other things to refresh and sustain us. The natives hurried up to the train whenever we stopped to take on water. As we approached Panama the weather became still pleasanter and more refreshing although hot, and the heat itself was no longer as oppressive as in Aspinwall. The view expanded into a marvelously beautiful landscape: now mountains and now gardens, now pretty dwellings and now little huts. I was completely enchanted by the paradise we saw and it increased in abundance and splendor the closer we came to the city.

Panama

This city was built several centuries ago and, because of its location, its chief inhabitants have been pirates and Jesuits. The former had to go out of business because of the many ships which now run in and out of the Bay of Panama, but the latter still live upon the credulity of the churchgoers whom they lead by the nose. The city was built by Catholics and churches are its most striking characteristic. Gold, diamonds, men and women — all these are to be found in church, even if nowhere else. The natives have learnt from their European and American neighbors the habit of dressing handsomely and, in order to pay for the expense of it, are forced to work. But the lowest class has no expenses; they need no clothes, since they sun themselves under the open sky, and the finest fruit that the world has ever seen nourishes them and they need only stretch out their hands for it.

Steamers bound for San Francisco lie about three miles out to sea, for the harbor of Panama is not deep enough to receive large ships. Accordingly, we were taken in a little steam-tug to the splendid "Golden Age."

Panama has about ten thousand inhabitants. Among them there are also a number of Jews who in 1852 organized a charitable society. They carry on important business with the towns in the interior of New Granada as well as with passengers who cross the isthmus.

Chapter XI

CONTINUATION OF THE JOURNEY TO CALIFORNIA

ON THE ELEVENTH OF AUGUST WE LEFT PANAMA AND PASSED SEVeral islands. The following evening we saw the farthest headland of South America. From there a lighthouse sends its beam over the quiet waters of the Pacific Ocean. This day was marked by wind, rain and seasickness.

August 13. At daybreak the rain stopped and it looked as if the weather would become calm and pleasant. However, the rain began again at noon.

August 14. We entered the Bay of Fehantupan. All day the wind came from the southwest, accompanied by rain.

August 15. A stormy day: the waves were high and our ship was tossed about like a ball.

August 16. The rain poured down in a flood; but, towards noon, the clouds parted and the passengers dared to walk the deck again. At the first glance about us we saw great tortoises. A streak of water, of a different color than the rest, caught my eye. Closer examination showed that this slimy substance, mixed with an oily stuff, came up from the ocean bed. Apparently it consisted of infusoria and served to feed the whales. We saw several in the afternoon. At seven in the evening we entered the harbor of Acapulco to take coal and water on board. The natives brought fruit and shells to sell on the ship. Towards midnight we left Acapulco. The night was close and dark.

August 17. The rain continued to pour down. We saw the mountains of the coast. Sea-monsters and sea-gulls surrounded us in great number.

August 18. The sun rose in all its splendor and under these good auspices we entered the Gulf of California. The evening was spent on deck and young and old enjoyed themselves in dancing to the music of a good band.

August 19. Accompanied by flying fish we reached Cape St. Lucas in Lower California. The climate changed and the air was of that heavenly purity and clarity of which we often read but seldom have the opportunity to breathe.

For the twentieth of August I had saved for myself an added pleasure: I wished to see the sun rise. This spectacle of nature upon the Pacific is too splendid to be adequately described. Carried away by admiration, absorbed in that majestic sight, blinded by its splendor and glory, one can only exclaim: "For you and your Creator silence is praise!" I was humbled before such grandeur and felt my spirit elevated again only at the thought that as man I was favored above all His creatures and was able to gaze at all this and admire it.

Towards seven o'clock in the evening, a monstrously great cloud, like a mountain in the distance, stood over the sea in bold relief. We approached it partly in fear, partly in pleasure at the thought of being able to contemplate a phenomenon of nature which is not to be seen ordinarily. The ship sailed on and suddenly we were enveloped in clouds: all about us was dim and dark, just as the Bible describes the Egyptian darkness (*Exodus* 10. 22, 23); even the lanterns on the steamer were no longer visible and the fog was so thick it could almost be grasped. For two hours we kept sailing through this cloud, until at

114

last the soft light of the moon and the stars was again visible and the blue sky of a beautiful summer evening spread out above us in all its splendor.

On August twenty-first there was no land in sight. The sea was like a clear, unclouded looking-glass. Towards sunset a wind from the west drove foaming waves with white caps past us.

On the twenty-second the waves were still high. It was very cold and we had to take refuge in the cabins.

It was still colder on the twenty-third. Heavy waves flooded the deck and the morning was not at all pleasant. About ten o'clock we approached Point Conception. A fairly large number of small whales, as well as rocks and little islands, gradually became visible, and at noon we had the entire mountain range along the coast of California before us with its many lighthouses and other tokens of civilization and progress. We found ourselves near the "Golden Gate" and opposite the entrance to the Bay of San Francisco. Here we saw a single sea-lion of considerable size, its eyes shining, stretching its head boldly out of the water in its curiosity while the rest of its great bulk remained under water.

On the twenty-fourth, at about eight o'clock in the morning, we sailed through the Golden Gate and an hour later landed at the great capital of the West — San Francisco.

After I had worked my way successfully through a mob of drivers of carriages for hire, agents for hotels, and others who crowded about us, I made my way to the New York Hotel on Battery Street. That very morning I visited Dr. Julius Eckmann, publisher of the *Gleaner*, as well as Mr. Daniel Levy, a native Frenchman, who, in Algiers in 1854, translated my first travel-book into French. The joy of Mr. Levy and myself was great as we met again after our long separation, twelve thousand miles from the place where the brief time we spent together had securely tied the bonds of our friendship. There is really something wonderful in a friendship formed in a foreign land, then broken off for a time through circumstances, and renewed again in another foreign land; it becomes warmer than ever. We sat and gossiped; we had so much to tell each other we did not notice how soon the day passed; but we did not stop talking, as though we feared to be parted for ever and that if every minute were not utilized it would be lost eternally. My stay in California, however, was fortunately prolonged beyond my expectations so that not a few evenings were devoted by Mr. Levy and myself to the memories of the past.

Before we proceed to the description of particulars, we should like to describe San Francisco briefly as it appeared until 1849. The harbor of San Francisco was discovered as early as 1769, it is generally thought, and probably named after Francis Drake, the seafarer, who discovered the coasts of Upper California (1578). On June 17, 1776, the Jesuits founded a mission on the site of the city of San Francisco; but, for a long time, it had little or no political or commercial importance. Most of the trade was in tallow and skins. The first warehouse was not built until 1836. It is estimated that as late as 1844 there were not more than about fifty inhabitants in the place, living in about a dozen houses. So it went on until California was yielded to the United States by Mexico. With that the city began to grow quickly, so that at the end of 1847 it numbered seventy-nine houses and in the spring of 1848 had grown to two hundred. At this time the gold-fever made itself felt and immigration increased phenomenally.

About seven houses were of unburnt brick* dried in the sun, with tile roofs, each house surrounded by an arcade; these buildings dated from Spanish or Mexican days. The rest were of wood, with roofs of boards, shingles, or sail-cloth. The other dwellings were merely tents, except that here and there one saw on the streets huts from the decks of ships and cabins that the owners had turned into dwellings, saloons and shops. Wood was extraordinarily dear: boards, an inch thick, cost $200 to $300 a thousand square feet, and the demand was so great that all that arrived was instantly bought up. Goods lay heaped high in the streets, so great was the need for dwellings and space. Many hundreds of the new arrivals, constantly pouring into the city, had no shelter at all. Necessity made them inventive and taught them to set up tents and find places where they might stay without having to pay rent or being driven away. Accordingly, places suitable for building that were not as yet used, and were even beyond the city limits in those days, were occupied by a multitude of squatters.

Here and there they organized orderly colonies: New Boston, for example, founded in a steep ravine of Telegraph Hill by a group of Americans, newly arrived on a small ship called "Boston"; New Mexico, on the heights of Pacific Street, where most of the Sonorans lived;

---

* Dr. Berthold Seemann (*Journey Around the World*, vol. I, p. 53) has the following comment about these air-dried bricks: "These bricks are undoubtedly of the same sort and shape as those that the children of Israel had to make for the Egyptians (*Exodus* ch. 5). In fact, there is a group of Hawaians (Sandwich Islanders) who make these bricks, and the implements they use for it are an exact replica of what we see illustrated by the four-thousand-year-old hieroglyphics. "Adaub," the Egyptian word for these bricks, is still used by the Copts. The Saracens undoubtedly brought the manner of making them from Egypt to Spain; from there it came to America and farther still to the Sandwich Islands. Should it continue its journey westward, it might well reach the land of its birth."

New Sidney, in a valley between Bush and Market Streets, a settlement of Irish families, most of them immigrants from Australia; New Canton or Little China, high up beyond Clay Street, where the sons of the Celestial Kingdom camped for the time being; and so on. Some of these colonies still remain, if no longer in the original tents, yet with the old residents. Where the building lots were fenced in but not yet built upon, the tents and huts of the squatters stood in the streets outside the fences, but, yielding to the owners of the land, they had to move on time and again.

Place and space were extraordinarily dear: a building lot, fifty feet in length and sixty-five to one hundred and thirty feet in depth, rented for $100 to $500 a month, according to location; to store a trunk or chest somewhere under a roof cost one dollar for each a month; and whoever was lucky enough to get a room, ten foot square, on a court — a room that was not unlike a pig-sty, in which to leave his baggage and to sleep — had to pay at least $25 a month for it.

This lack of space caused the residents and owners of houses to use the available space in such a way as to make the most of it, and events that then occurred over and over again would seem incredible to one who arrived only three years later; after three years San Francisco was quite another city. These quick changes brought many surprises now and then, and many a queer story is told. For example, the captain of a ship who was engaged in trading with the Indians and Mexicans in skins, agricultural products and other objects, returned to San Francisco after an absence of about four years. It happened that he reached the Bay of San Francisco at night. He saw a multitude of lights and could not decide whether or not he had made a mistake. He was puzzled; according to his chart and compass, he had held a true course and this was where San Francisco should be — a San Francisco, he thought, as small as it had been four years previously. He was no little astonished, however, by the many lights and almost believed in magic or witchcraft. What was he to do? He spent the night on board his ship where it anchored and at dawn, to his astonishment, he saw a city spread out before his eyes. The magic was gone and the riddle solved.

On Dupont Street (between Pacific Street and Broadway) there stood originally a great round tent which was a saloon during the week but served as a Presbyterian church on Sunday. The cabin of a ship, eight foot square and seven high, set up on Pacific Street, was a saloon during the day and at night the sleeping-quarters of four or six people; in addition, a dealer in hardware lived there who displayed his goods before it during the day. I was shown a very fine house on Montgomery Street in the cellar of which is a ship. At one time ships could go as far as this and one was left behind as a memorial. At the upper end of Jackson Street stood a very small tent that seemed hardly large enough for two persons. Nevertheless, a physician and a druggist lived there and in it salted bacon in barrels, brandy in bottles, and hot coffee could be had at any time. In several of the wooden houses the lower rooms were fixed up as offices; and in such a house six, and as many as ten, desks stood close to one another. They were used by persons in various kinds of business — merchants, money-changers, lawyers, doctors, land commissioners, brokers, notaries, and the like — and each paid from $25 to $50 a month for the privilege. Places to sleep, narrower than bunks in the holds of ships, were in tiers of three or four. On the floor of a house, that might be as much as twenty by thirty feet, more than sixty persons were often seen trying to sleep. The owner of the place made a clear profit of thirty dollars every night, for each guest had to furnish his own bed and quilts.

Because of the high prices of building materials and the unusually high wages of carpenters, who made from $16 to $20 a day, speculation in wood and buildings naturally resulted, and it was not long before a good deal of wood was imported from the Atlantic states, from Germany, Sweden, and Oregon on the Pacific. In a few days, apparently, complete streets were built; tents and sheds were replaced by decent-looking houses. By 1850 one saw such an assortment of different houses, inhabited by people of all nationalities, as was never before seen anywhere in any one land. The rapidity with which the buildings were erected bordered on the miraculous. With astonishment one often saw houses standing on an evenly-leveled part of the city where only a week before, it seemed, were only hill and dale and bushes. The Eldorado, three stories high, built, to be sure, of a light wood, was completely ready in sixteen days and already on the tenth day there were gamblers on the ground floor who spent their dollars and gold-dust freely to the sound of drums and trumpets, while above them the carpenters with ax and saw finished the building. California was certainly the land of wonders!

Such a sudden growth in the space of not more than ten years borders on the miraculous and bears witness to the enterprise of the Anglo-Saxon race. Not only has something been produced from nothing, but San Francisco, particularly at present, is striding forward with giant steps; houses and streets come into existence, industry is growing, and it is to the latter that the flourishing state of the city is chiefly to be ascribed. Building is going on everywhere; hills vanish and valleys are filled up and along the principal streets one wooden house after another is moved to the suburbs to make room for palaces of stone.

118

Not long ago, California was of little or no importance in the field of industry; everything was imported and there was no talk of local manufacture. This has changed, and the activity of its great factories, foundries, machine-shops, sugar refineries, and so forth, should not be valued lightly; they employ a multitude of workers and day by day efforts in this direction assume greater proportions. Thus California is making use of its own resources and it is no longer only its wealth in precious metals, which gives the young state prominence, but rather its industries; and it is the progress in these that makes the great future of San Francisco a certainty.

Chapter XII

SAN FRANCISCO, THE CAPITAL OF CALIFORNIA, AND ITS EARLIEST HISTORY

The etymology of the name, "California," is uncertain. Some writers have stated that it is derived from the two Latin words *calida fornax* or the Spanish *caliente fornalla*, that is, "a hot oven." However, this derivation was doubted by Michael Venegas, a Mexican Jesuit, in his *Natural and Civil History of California* (2 vols., Madrid, 1758), a work of great learning and much respected. According to his view, the Spanish discoverers did not name lands found by them in this pedantic fashion. "I am therefore inclined to the view," he remarks, "that this name is due to some event; perhaps to some Indian words which the Spaniards did not understand." This has, at times, been the case. Dr. Berthold Seemann, in addition, calls attention to the fact that our "califonium," resin derived from the fir-trees of that country, might have given the land its name. Captain Beechey also advances this view.

The name "California" was first used by Bernal Diaz del Castillo, who served as an officer under Hernando Cortez during the conquest of Mexico and published a history of this extraordinary expedition.

In his view California consisted only of a single bay on the coast. But Jean Bleau, in another interpretation (Amsterdam, 1662), understood this term to refer to all the immense stretches of land that lay west of New Spain and New Galicia and the entire coast from the northern parts of South America to the Strait of Anian (Bering Strait). In this broader meaning of the term, several writers of geography agreed with Jean Bleau. Whatever the actual boundaries of the land might have been, its name was changed at various times. On some English maps, it is called New Albion, because the famous English admiral, Sir Francis Drake, a German by birth, who is supposed to have introduced the potato to Europe and who touched the Californian coasts in 1578, called it that. About a century later it was called "Carolina Islands" (Islas Carolinas) in honor of Charles II of Spain, since the peninsula of California was mistakenly considered an island — a name adopted by several famous writers and geographers. Later, the original name of California was revived and soon generally accepted.[*]

No period of life is more interesting to the scientist than that of childhood. Even the loftiest heights of success, the highest distinctions of a career, the highest grade of culture which a man often reaches as he grows older, does not please the philosopher who observes life in the same degree as the first development of childhood. A wreath of honor about the frosty brow of age as the proper reward of a life use-fully spent has a pleasing aspect — but it is no more than a memorial. In such a wreath is woven little of earthly hope; one sees forebodings come true or hopes disappointed; memories alone have reality, and these memories are generally grave if not sad. On the other hand, the cradle and a child's play are under the protection of the smiling god-dess, Hope, and nothing of a withered past throws its shadow on the buds and blossoms of youth. Life is a joyful future, and we look for-ward to all its developments even as the nursery-gardener cares for the sprouting plants, or he who tends an orchard watches the twigs he has grafted when they are bearing buds.

Cities are like human beings; they have their period as suckling babes; their childhood; their gray old age. Yes, many even die and, after the silence of many ages of mankind, they find their "friends" who clear away the rubbish on their graves, brush the dust from their gravestones, in order to decipher their epitaphs and to tell their story to a later world. Nineveh, Pompeii, Palenque had their beginnings, matured, flourished, aged, fell, and were forgotten in their graves until Lanard,

---

[*]   Fr. Soulé, J. Gihon, and James Nisbet, *Annals of San Francisco*, N. Y., 1855, pp. 23, 24.

Stephens, and others gathered their dust and preserved it in their classical urns.

All the stages of development in their history would certainly be of great interest, if they could have been preserved in the language of a Gibbon, Hume, or Prescott; for nothing is so delightful as to follow the first indications of future greatness. Dark woods are cleared away, barbarous customs and usages vanish before the rays of civilization; the clipper makes the slow-sailing ship unnecessary; the sail of the white merchant vessel takes the place of the Indian's paddle. The rattling wheels of the steam-engine press forward farther and farther where, only a short while before, the slinking step of the savage broke the silence of the night. Eagerly we behold the bold landing of new, daring, thinking and civilized men upon shores which, until then, were trodden only by the uncivilized natives, the scurrying buccaneer, or the sailor making a single visit to fetch wood and water; and soon the sound of the battle-horn gives way to that of the saw, the hammer and the shaving plane. The firmly-fastened tent follows the original hut, a friendly dwelling takes the place of the smoking fire-place of the native, row after row of buildings group themselves on the sides of the hill until they reach down to the seashore. Timber, brick and sandstone are used instead of cane, bark and brushwood; for roofs of smoked hides and sooty willows, walls with frescoes and paintings; for Indian huts, buildings with marble façades. The busy hands of man and his intelligence have changed the threatening face of nature itself into a picture which the visitor greets with a smile and which leaves a pleasant memory in the minds of those who go their way.

The triumphant signs of trade and traffic take the place of the trophies of barbaric war; rustling silk that of a bloody scalp. To follow all this to its sequel and to watch it was the fortunate lot of those who lived in San Francisco over a number of years. They were witnesses of scenes which no other place, perhaps, and no other period had to show; for never before were the springs of human action set into motion at such a rate; never before did such a prospect for gold offer itself to the adventurous of all nations, and yet never as here were the obstacles to obtaining it so slight. Old myths became real, the vaults of the romanticists were opened, El Dorado was found.

The cry of treasure, gold discovered — and that in immeasurable quantity — rang in the ears of the weary workingman like a message from Heaven itself, compassionate and full of blessing. The great, deep, common passion was stirred: the longing for wealth had some prospect of satisfaction. Gold had a tongue and spoke to the world and entered upon its mission; well-chosen words of fervent monks left their listeners cold in comparison with the soul-shaking speech that was read into in the delightful promises of gold. Its call found ready and attentive listeners; a general migration began, as if a new Jerusalem was to be besieged, its golden temple robbed, its golden sepulchre captured, and its rich inhabitants driven away. With a wild adoration for that which lay buried in the mines of California, an adoration in its strength nothing less than that of a religious enthusiasm, they streamed to the promised land of California.

They came from all the four corners of the world and the dangers of the sea did not deter them. All the races of mankind, the five great races, were represented. The Caucasian traveling on the railway of one empire; the Mongolian turning his back on another; the Malay leaving behind his piratical freedom; the Negro running away from his bonds; all met on the shore of the American Indian, and all, except the Indian, became worshippers of the same holy thing — all on fire to bow humbly before the same god, all crusaders in the service of Mammon, all for the time being surrendering the disagreeable differences of blood, caste, and color in the common passion that here sought its satisfaction. From the "northern beehive" itself, which had sent out its swarms of conquering Goths and Huns over the fruitful plains and proud cities of classical Italy fourteen hundred years ago, came the planning, industrious, well-brought-up emigrant from northern Europe. The descendants of Brennus' countrymen forgot Napoleon and the barricades for a while in their fervor to storm the ramparts of rock that nature had hidden in the strongholds of the Sierras. The Scotsman turned his back on classical Edinburgh and his native heath; the followers of St. Patrick forgot the hills of Howth, and John Bull banished himself from Bow Bells, that they might gather gold under the Manhanita bushes and on the banks of Californian streams. They came from the zones of Kamchatka, from the land of the Cid, from the gold-ridged kingdom of Montezuma and from the silver-veined hills of the Incas; the Tahitian wearing his *tuppa* and the Russian wrapped in fur; the French Canadian who lived on the St. Lawrence and the Hindu who prayed to the Ganges; the disappointed followers of Kossuth and Mazzini, battalions of the Mobile Guard, and soldiers from the troops of General Flores; the imported coolie and the transported "Sidney duck": all turned their faces to the rays of hope that vanished as quickly as they appeared — namely, gold.

In this manner, San Francisco had become a mosaic of races, the like of which had never been seen before. All religions were represented. The Jew and the follower of the Prophet of Mecca lived side by side with the follower of the Cross, the enthusiastic disciples of

Buddha, Brahma and Vishnu, and those of absolute faith in the apostolic succession to St. Peter. Gold is the great equalizer, fusing into unity the melting-pot of mankind, bringing all castes, religions, and sects into one congregation of its worshippers. This was the case in California. Here appeared all kinds of legislation, moral and unmoral. The homicide and the Turner; the unarmed Shaker and the Mormon with many wives; the man unable to resist temptation and the stickler for his honor and righteousness; the honest borrower and the sponger; the spendthrift and the miser; the generous and the stony-hearted. From all points of the compass, all parts of the earth, all nations and tribes — they felt themselves drawn to this great magnet. No thinker should be surprised that such a confused combination of human beings of widely-varied character resulted for a time in disorder: of morality, government and, indeed, of the whole scale of human values. Only a reliable element could instil order into so remarkable a confusion of individuals: it was the Anglo-Saxon race that formed the kernel about which the elements of religion, morality and enlightened progress gathered and crystallized.

We omit the earliest history of San Francisco and its original condition, of which nothing is known and nothing remains except some of its ruins and the remnants of its Indian villages, and turn to its recent discovery — probably in the year 1769 — its settlement at the missionary-station, "Dolores," in 1776, by the missionary Franciscans and the dreamlike Christian life of the laity and the new converts. With this period the history of San Francisco really begins.

The preponderant principle of an orderly society is to be found, from earliest times, among the races that populated the eastern side of North America. To be able to evaluate properly the state of the city in all its aspects and in all stages of its development during its brief but brilliant existence, it is absolutely necessary to understand the character of a settlement that gathered together as this did and to see clearly the ingredients that went to make up the community; this is why we have had to spend so much time on this subject. No chemical laboratory ever received a greater variety of material for analysis, mixing, or separating, and perhaps none has contained elements so mutually repellant. If their contact resulted in the flaring up of violent passions, boiling in the melting-pot is as common; and it is a pleasant surprise to follow the progress that has been made in so few years.

Through untold centuries the site of San Francisco had remained bare and barren, except that it was overgrown with stunted bushes and twisted oaks which, struggling against strong winds and dry soil, battled for life and became extinct. Here wild tribes led their dreamlike existence and left no trace behind except the fragments of pottery and other articles that indicate the antiquity of those who made and used them. The barren sand-hills, the rippling waters of the bay, the thick underwood, the flowers that quickly followed the winter rains — these made the history of this place until men, strangers to the soil but filled with a strong faith, left home and the society of civilized men and plunged into this solitude to bring civilization to barbarians and to enlighten the heathen.

This was followed by mission life in all its various aspects — self-denial, diligence, toil, the cunning of the statesman and the courage of the soldier. Little by little the confidence of the savages was won, their natural indifference partly shaken, and their life of laziness and hunger changed by stimulating their appetites to one that was, to some extent, industrious and comfortable. The savage was taught to provide himself with food by plowing the soil, and his feeble notions of God were used to awaken in his soul ideas of moral and religious responsibility. All these poor heathen and their teachers have vanished and have left hardly a trace of their history. But no one can deny that the account of what the Franciscan missionaries and their savage Indian pupils did and tried to do might well put to shame, in the large history that follows, the greater results of our more modern missionary and political activity.

Seventy years — the span of life allowed to man — glided away, and only a few acres of land were cultivated, only a few Indians had the desire, and gave their promise, to permit themselves to be joined to the mission's flock, more out of the hope for food than out of religious impulse, or an understanding of the Gospel they heard. A few soldiers were stationed at the fort; a few vessels visited, from time to time, the harbor to fetch water, skins and tallow; and there was little other progress in civilizing the region than that mentioned above. Although the methods of the Catholic mission are excellently devised — namely, to bring the Indians into the fold in order to teach them the skills of mankind and to surround the heathen traditions of the Great Spirit with religious forms of Catholicism — it has seldom, or perhaps never, made any progress beyond this and has been only partially successful. The faults of the system itself may be to blame or, as seems more likely, the dull, incapable — in spite of every inducement — stagnant nature of the Indian which is intractable.

Not much more fit for the demands of progress than the nature of the Indian, was a great part of the Mexican population who first took possession of California and who, at the time when the Americans took it over, formed its ruling class. As a rule, their character was as far removed from that of their ancestors, whether Moorish or Castilian, as they were in time, or as the adobe *haciendas* and missions were when compared to the palaces of Granada or Madrid. Their capacity for civilization, progress and industry seemed to be incapable of developing beyond a certain point, a point that was soon reached after the erection of the missions when sufficient Indians were lassoed to provide, by their hard labor, for the priests and their hangers-on. A few of another kind are to be recognized as exceptions to the general rule; but whatever nobler perceptions they had died under the prevailing craftiness of bigots.

So the process of civilizing the Indians went little higher than that which teaches the wild ass to lower his head to the bread-basket; his conversion to nothing higher than the grafting of religious forms upon the existing mold of heathen superstitions. The Spanish priests and overseers were well content with such results of their attempts at progress.

Chapter XIII

CONTINUATION OF THE HISTORY OF SAN FRANCISCO

THIS SITUATION COULD NOT LAST FOREVER. SO SPLENDID A BAY COULD not remain merely the stopping-place of a rarely-appearing whaler or a clumsy drogher; rather were its waters destined to be dotted with the sails of merchantships, to carry on its way the long, graceful form of the clipper, and to let its shores echo the cannon of the warship. The splendid site of the present city could not be surrendered forever to the dull savage or Spanish-American civilization. Destined by nature for a great future because of its bay — one of the most splendid on earth, at the healthiest of latitudes, nine days journey from the Sandwich Islands, one month from China, adjacent to Japan and the archipelagos of the southern as well as the northern Pacific — this locality was bound to attract the attention of the Anglo-Saxon race and to fall into their hands, as ready to possess as they were mighty to win.

The time drew near. The traffic of the merchants hastened it; the whaler on his occasional visits came away with a high regard for the locality; even the beaver and the otter helped, for they attracted the hardened fur-trader. Several of these adventurers, after they had crossed the Sierras, tasted the feel of silver coins and of the dreamlike life on the western side; they set up their residence in that land or returned home with favorable reports. Gradually the next generation began to dot the land with scattered settlements, and a few settled in San Francisco.

Among the first settlement in the presidio and the mission of Dolores — now within the boundaries of the city and the county of San Francisco — few events of historical importance occurred in a period of almost seventy years; life revolved around the missions and the occasional war-like skirmishes of the Mexicans. The present-day San Francisco had few residents during all that time that it was known as Yerba Buena. It had received this name because of a fragrant plant that grew in abundance between and all over the sand-hills. The reason for the present name, in place of the one used for so long, is very much in dispute; the choice of a better and more agreeable sound probably had little to do with it.

In 1816 the British war-sloop, *Racoon*, sailed into the bay and the harbor. From 1822 on, whaling ships began to visit the place to take fresh supplies of food on board; and even before this, there was traffic in merchandise between this land, Mexico and the Sandwich Islands. Warships of various nations arrived, but only at intervals. It is safe to say that twenty years or so passed before regular traffic in merchandise was established. But by 1835 the harbor and its traffic was considered important enough to merit the honor and attention of a harbormaster, and Capt. W. A. Richardson was appointed to the post. He was engaged at the time in the business of handling the freight between various points on the bay and the ships that visited the harbor of Yerba Buena to take on board food, or shipments of hides, tallow, soap, or grain. At this time, he erected the first dwelling — or rather tent: it consisted simply of a few posts covered with the sails of a ship. This was the beginning of a village that, within fifteen years, was destined to astonish the world with its fabulous wealth, its abundance of gold, its adventurous commerce, business and speculation; with its harbor of a thousand ships and its forest of vessels; with its wonderful growth, its unexpected strokes of luck, its remarkable flow of events, and its active life.

Chapter XIV

WE HAVE NOT TOUCHED UPON SOME OF THE INSIGNIFICANT EVENTS: for example, the earthquake of 1812 and, at a later date, the cloudbursts that flooded the land in 1824 and 1825; the quarrels among the inhabitants, and the mild excitements that hardly disturbed the monotony of the district. Our treatment is not supposed to be a history, but only a sketch, and because it is the growth of the American city which most appeals to the public, it is that to which we have devoted our attention.

In May 1836, Mr. Jacob P. Leese arrived at Yerba Buena to set himself up as a merchant; his partners were said to have their residence in Monterey. This separation prevented him from taking legal possession, according to Governor Figueroa's order of two hundred *raras* of land along the coast of the harbor. He returned to Monterey and knew how to obtain from Governor Chico the title to such land as he might select as suitable for the conduct of his business. On the following July first, he went again to Yerba Buena, unloaded his timber, and selected a hundred *raras* for a building site. Later, the St. Francis Hotel was built on it. The building of a house was commenced and it was completed on July fourth. This was the first building of the city that was to arise later, and the first that could really be called a house.

That day was celebrated with a banquet and ball by as many gentlemen, American and Mexican, as could be gathered together. It was the first such event to be publicly celebrated here. Those who take pleasure in omens will find in this event, as well as in the festivities, a sign of the future. Captain Hinkley of the American long-boat *Don Quixote*, together with the captains of other vessels, American and Mexican, that happened to be in the harbor just then, supplied the decorations by means of the flags of both countries, and the band of the *Don Quixote* played gaily among them. More than fifty of the most respectable residents and strangers were present; a great dinner was served, toasts were drunk, and a ball followed. Everyone rejoiced: American civilization, commerce and pleasure were inaugurated.

In the course of the year 1838, Mr. Leese erected a large building on the spot where at present Commerce and Montgomery Streets meet. Captain Richardson, likewise, built in the course of the year the adobe house earlier known as the "Casa Grande," somewhat west of the line along which Daport Street runs. After it had been there for seventeen years it was broken up to make room for more modern buildings and so vanished the most famous of the old Mexican landmarks. Although no Mexican had built it, it was nevertheless built in the true Mexican style which the Mexican upper class used. On the fifteenth of April of that year (1838), Mr. Leese rejoiced in the birth of a daughter. She was named Rosalie. I mention her because she was the first child of civilized parents to be born in Yerba Buena. Her mother, a sister of General M. G. Vallejo, had been married to Mr. Leese on April seventeenth of the previous year.

In the year 1839, the first survey of Yerba Buena was undertaken by Capt. Juan Vioget upon the order of Governor Alvarado: the survey included the area which was not included in the original limits of Pacific, Montgomery, Sacramento and Dupont Streets. Mr. Leese sold a large part of his land to the Hudson Bay Company in 1841 and moved to Sonoma. Three years later, the place had only ten or twelve houses and about fifty inhabitants. In another two years, the Hudson Bay Company gave up its trading-post and moved away. These changes had not the least harmful effect upon the place, for its buildings and inhabitants had increased fourfold within the space of four years by annual additions; and from that time on the increase continued at a much greater pace, for on July eighth the American flag was run up over the plaza by Captain Montgomery from the American war-sloop *Portsmouth*. This was upon the order of Commodore Sloat who, a few days before, had hoisted the same symbol at Monterey.

The population made giant strides forward under this flag. Its shadow meant protection; and the people sensed in its waving and fluttering the murmur of a great stream of people that would soon appear, to found a realm great because of its wealth, freedom and well-being. On the last day of the same month the ship *Brooklyn* arrived at San Francisco with a rich replacement in number for those who had departed, consisting of Mormons and other travelers. One can see in this the vanguard of a fleet laden with immigrants which was now to enter the harbor annually. The multitude that began to enter this newly discovered wonderland, and whose appearance resulted in a great variety of events, seemed inexhaustible.

The rest of the year 1846 passed quietly indeed, without any event that deserves mention. The population was in the first stage of its development, grew only gradually, and assumed the form of a social group. Balls were held. Commodore Stockton had a public welcome; foreigners and natives united gladly in this show of respect, and a peaceful atmosphere prevailed.

When Americans emigrate, the printing-press goes along in the vanguard and a newspaper appears as soon as the press is set up and able to furnish a report of the first sermon delivered. Yerba Buena, inhabited mostly by Americans and Europeans, had for some time felt the need of a newspaper and in 1847 saw itself in a position to establish one. On the seventh of January of that year, Mr. Samuel Brannan published the first numbers of the *Star of California* under the editorship of Dr. E. P. Jones. It appeared weekly; not a large but a most suitable newspaper for a new land "so far from home." It was the second newspaper to be published in the state. On August 15, 1846, the *Californian* had been launched by Messrs. Colton and Semple. On May twenty-second, Mr. Semple moved his publication office to Yerba Buena which, even at that time, overshadowed Monterey.

On January 30, 1847, the settlement of Yerba Buena was christened San Francisco; the old name was given up as the result of a government order from Washington. A. Bartlett became the chief magistrate or the alcalde — he was the first to occupy this post under American rule. When he was ordered to return to his ship, Mr. George Hyde officiated temporarily as alcalde. On February 22, 1847, Edwin Bryant, who was later to write *What I Saw in California*, was installed as the successor of Mr. Bartlett.

During the year 1846, a regiment of volunteers for service in California was raised in New York City. Col. J. D. Stevenson was placed at its head. The first detachment and its leader arrived in San Francisco on the sixth of March on board the *H. Perkins*. Many of the officers of this regiment, as well as many of the privates, still live in the state and not a few of them occupy very influential positions. With their arrival, not only were Americans predominant in the city, but a thoroughly American sentiment prevailed. This harmony found expression on the twenty-eighth of May when the place was illuminated for the first time in honor of General Taylor's victory at Buena Vista. Light and joy flooded the place; all forces were put to work; houses, hillsides, vessels, air and sea were brilliant and warm with light, comparable only to the patriotism that found expression in this manner.

General Kearny, governor of California, according to an order dated March tenth, released the district between Clark and Rincon Point for sale, and on March sixteenth Alcalde Bryant set the date of sale for June tenth. The sale was postponed until July twentieth. On that day almost half of the 450 building lots were sold at a price that ranged from $50 to as high as $100. In the course of five or six years several of these lots attained a value of more than $50,000. The building lots on the higher land, fifty *raras* square, were disposed of that summer for $12 each, so that including the charge for legal registration each cost $16. This was only a short time before many lots sold for $16,000 apiece and when prices, too fabulous to mention here, were being asked. The precautionary rule, according to which no person was to own a lot measuring more than fifty or one hundred *raras*, was disregarded by the speculators. Alcaldes and council, seized by the fever of speculation and at the same time throwing aside scruples of conscience which seemed an intolerable burden, declared this ordinance enacted against "landgrabbing" null and void and plunged head over heels into land brokerage and speculation.

This way, a few managed to get hold of almost the entire region; became immeasurably rich in a short time; formed a landed aristocracy; and forced all others either to pay enormous prices for land to build on, or to surrender almost larger sums in the form of rent. The most sensible system was the Mexican, and if a similar ordinance had been passed, namely, that each resident was permitted to have only a single building-lot, the city of San Francisco would be worth millions more than it is today. No monopoly hinders the prosperity of a community more than that of land, and in San Francisco it has been most harmful. If the injury was not so obvious at first, it certainly assumed greater proportions as time went on.

The population in June of that year amounted to 460 persons, among them 140 women. The majority of the inhabitants consisted of those who were still in the early stages of active life, or were minors: a fiery, bold and courageous people, half of them American by birth, the rest having drifted together from almost all the nations of the world. Thus, at the very beginning, this place set the pattern, with respect to its population, for what it remained later — with perhaps the single exception that, in proportion to its numbers, the American element obtained ascendancy over the rest. It is well known that certain kinds of crossbreeding, in the case of horses and other animals, improves the breed; in this respect, man is like the animals. Whether or not such improvement will prove to be the case in the population of this city only the years to come will show. But, just as the interbreeding of the crusaders with people other than their own was for Europe the means of advancing civilization and its Dark Ages were changed, as a result, into the fairer age of modern culture with its art, science, literature and freedom, so we may anticipate that this interbreeding of the population of San Francisco will also prove to be a blessing for all. Without probing too deeply, here favorable opportunities exist for acquiring knowledge and for studying the characteristics of other peoples without having to travel in foreign lands; opportunities to adapt one's own ways to whatever intellectual and mechanical superiorities they disclose; and this will certainly contribute much to the enrichment of our knowledge and increase the resources of city, state and people.

The use of the steam-engine, as of the printing-press, is part and parcel of American civilization. The first steamship that adorned the bay made a trial run in November. During the last three months of this year, exports amounted to $50,000 and imports to somewhat more. In the beginning of the year 1848, the *ayuntamiento* attempted to put an end to gambling through ordinances which called for fines and confiscations; but at the very next meeting of the council these resolutions were made ineffective. It is not known what influences induced the council to do what it did. The city assumed, more and more, a commercial aspect. On the fifteenth of March, a list of wholesale prices was made known. Now the population grew rapidly and amounted to more than 800 persons — among them sixty children of school age. A school was opened on the third of April under the direction of Mr. Thomas Douglas. On the same day, Dr. J. Townsend was installed as alcalde, since Mr. Hyde had resigned. The little town slowly rose to the rank of "a place." It had firms of merchants, places of amusement, public buildings, and to all appearances promised to become a city of 10,000 inhabitants in the course of a decade or two.

Suddenly there entered into this quietly growing society the Seducer — gold. Gold was discovered in January at Coloma on the American River. Rumors of the discovery and particles of the gold dust came, from time to time, to San Francisco. Presently miners arrived with "piles" that they had quickly made, and the race to riches was on. All other occupations suddenly lost their attraction. The prize of the golden apple was in this modern contest, however, not awarded to "the most beautiful" but to the strong of heart and the willing of hand. Diligence, endurance, energy, hope and, as some believe, luck decided who should win.

Chapter XV

THE DISCOVERY OF GOLD MINES AND THE FURTHER HISTORY
OF SAN FRANCISCO

IN THIS MANNER BEGAN AN EXCITEMENT THAT OTHERWISE ONLY PHE-
nomena such as, perhaps, an avalanche, earthquake, a victorious army,
or a flood could produce. Who had any more desire to toil and drudge
for some trifling reward at dry-goods or the printing-press, on ship
or shore, when fabulous wealth lay waiting in the beds and banks of
streams ready to surprise those who approached with its golden smile?
The craftsman and the mechanic left; the merchant's clerk and the
merchant himself set out; business in the city was at a standstill. The
tents were empty; the houses were locked. The Brazilian vulture
squatted in the streets; grass grew where the foot of man had formerly
trampled it; ships lay at anchor without an owner; newspapers were
no longer published, for printer and compositor had fled, and the
publisher had exchanged his pen for a crowbar, his scissors for a pick,
and instead of writing leaders for gold he now hurried to the pits
and washed it out of his pan. With the residents gone, the government
ceased. The city was almost like a deserted wilderness.

On July fifteenth the *Californian* was published again. A month
later, on the eleventh of August, a great illumination was arranged in
honor of the conclusion of peace with Mexico. On the ninth of September, a public meeting fixed the value of an ounce of gold dust for
business purposes at $16, and it was further resolved to urge Congress
to build a mint in the city, so certain was the confidence of the people
— a large number had returned from the miners' pits — that the supply
of gold would become enormous.

The price of food was high and the wages of the workingman rose
constantly. The value of land did not rise accordingly; it may be said
to have leaped from negligible amounts to princely sums, inasmuch
as it might be doubled within twenty-four hours and in many cases
increased at a much greater rate. Entire shiploads of goods were
unloaded and customs duties reached the sum of $200,000 in one year.
The value of imports was almost a million dollars. Cash value attained

that sum. The export of gold during the last half of the year reached almost the sum of two million dollars. From then on it increased three-fold every month. As one can easily imagine, the world was astounded at such a result so soon after the discovery of gold, and thousands of adventurers throughout the civilized world had already begun to prepare themselves to emigrate.

Many who had tried their luck in the mines returned to San Francisco. Their gold had not been won without the expense of many privations; without the ever-present danger of falling sick; without heavy work and a rugged diet. And the shrewd merchant discovered that, although gold-diggers became rich, the city offered him a more lucrative field for heaping up treasure. The high prices and the great increase of various goods and foods and other indispensable things, opened up for those who preferred to be merchants rather than hunters for gold the most glorious of prospects. It was seen, moreover, that those who came from the nearest surrounding territories were only like a small point in comparison with those who would stream there from beyond once the enthusiastic reports of rich gains of gold penetrated the eastern states, Europe and the tribes of Asia, and there found believers. So, many prudently selected the gold mines in the city to coin wealth for themselves there, in preference to the mountain gorges and the beds of streams where they would have to dig for the raw material. They continued to enjoy this state of affairs after experience proved the wisdom of their choice. For the gains of these merchants were enormous and in the course of a year their trade yielded great wealth.

The influx of strangers was extraordinary. The news of the discovery of gold had spread abroad and the echoes came back in the hum of hundreds of thousands of gold-seekers and in the stir which their trade and their business activity caused. Cadmus had sown the dragon's teeth and now on all sides sprang up men armed for the battle for gold against all obstacles — ready for the dangers at sea; for the longer and dangerous journeys on land and water; through wildernesses; among Indians; in sickness, hunger, thirst, famine, heat, cold, hard labor, absence from those near and dear; carrying with them solitude and death. The peoples were aroused, the sea swarmed with ships, the ships with multitudes of men; the wilderness heard the voice of mankind; the mountains felt the hurrying steps of myriads journeying west; and this host was soon in a position to reach the shore, walk the wastes of sand, and fill the streets, tents and shops of San Francisco with the stir of business.

The year 1848 inaugurated a series of changes in the Press as follows: the *Star and Californian,* under which name the *California Star* and the *Californian* appeared jointly during the last part of the year 1848, took the name of *Alta California* on January 4, 1849, and this newspaper at present has the largest circulation in the State. In the second half of that month, the civic aspect of the city assumed a more confused and uncertain color; the election of a new city council was held. The members of the existing two councils resigned and fourteen new members were elected, as well as three judges. This took place on February twenty-first. At the end of February the steamer *California* arrived, forerunner of the mail-packets of the Pacific Mail Steamship Company, and was heartily welcomed. On March thirty-first, the steamship *Oregon* arrived and brought the first regular mail as well as the first postmaster of California — Col. John W. Geary.

During the first half of that year the municipal affairs of the city were in great confusion. In fact, there was no orderly government, for the people opposed the claims of Mr. Leavenworth, whereas the alcalde, as well as Governor Riley, supported him. The governor finally issued a proclamation for an election of municipal and other officers and for delegates to frame a constitution for the State. On August first, the people assembled and denied Governor Riley's right to name the time and place for the election of such delegates but, out of political expediency, accepted his proposal and order. The law-making assembly finally dissolved and left the alcalde together with his council in undisputed control.

The population kept growing rapidly. New arrivals made their purchases and left the place to go to the mines; gold-diggers, who could rejoice in a lucky strike, came back with their quickly gained wealth and squandered their money, partly at the gaming-table, partly at other amusements, or used it to set themselves up in business as merchants. The people seemed to resemble one of the tribes of Israel when they lived in tents, or the Arabs who sleep upon the sand under the open sky. It was a time of violent progress. There was no orderly society but "every man did what seemed good in his eyes."

In midsummer there was great disorder: depraved persons terrified the well-meaning, formed a sort of organization known as the "Dogs," and spread fear and terror throughout a city that then numbered at least 5,000 persons. They committed all sorts of violence, seized tents and shops, robbed them and supplied themselves, without money or payment, with all they desired. Their violent acts finally enraged the inhabitants. They formed a sort of police and military organization. It arrested many of the "Dogs," or "Regulators," as they called themselves, and brought them before the court it had set up. Nine were convicted of robbery and other crimes, and imprisoned or fined by way of punishment. This organization of the people may be considered the first vigilance committee of San Francisco. It not only broke up the gang of "Dogs" but put an end to that evil.

At the election of August first, in accordance with the proclamation of Governor Riley, Horace Howes was elected prefect and John W. Geary first alcalde. The council met, the alcalde and prefect made their requests, and the city was organized with a properly constituted and duly elected government. The Baptists consecrated their first church on August fifth of that year (1849). Other religious denominations were already organized and about to erect buildings for religious services.

Trade made new progress at this time that was to prove most beneficial. During October, forwarding purchases by steamer became a customary provision in business arrangements, inasmuch as the iron-built steamers — Pioneer, the Mint and the old propeller *MacKinn* — had begun their trips between San Francisco and the cities inland. The *Senator* was put into service to care for the traffic between Sacramento and San Francisco and ran for several years with a reliability and at a profit that it probably never surpassed again. On the twenty-fifth of the same month, a democratic assembly on the Plaza instituted a definite method of procedure for political matters. Row opened his Olympic Circus on the twenty-ninth of the same month, and this was the beginning of theatrical entertainments. One month later, in accordance with a proclamation by the governor, a day of thanksgiving and of prayer for the existence of the new State of California was set, and in this way the stability of the Pacific coast was brought to the attention and approbation of the Eastern States.

On November 13, 1849, an election was held to designate the first officials under the new constitution of the State, and a register of the votes for the acceptance or rejection of this instrument was set up. In San Francisco only two votes were surrendered out of 2066. Gabriel B. Post and Nathaniel Bennett were elected State senators and William van Vorhies, Edmund Randolph, Levi Stowell, J. H. Watson, and J. A. Patterson members of the State assembly. This was the first election for State offices.

A court of first instance was organized at the order of the governor on December twelfth, under Judge William B. Almond. His jurisdiction was limited to civil suits and claims that exceeded $100. The purpose of the order was to lessen the burden upon the regular court, which had become very heavy. Lively scenes took place before Judge Almond. His decisions were marked by an acumen and the achievement of satisfactory results that often astonished lawyers, witnesses and litigants.

The twenty-fourth of December is memorable as the day on which the first of those great conflagrations broke out that, from time to time, turned to ashes the buildings and hopes of many citizens of San Francisco. At six o'clock in the morning Dennison's Exchange was found to be on fire, and almost all the blocks bounded by Kearny, Washington, Montgomery and Clay Streets were burned down. The damage amounted to a million dollars. If one considers that no fire department had been organized and that the nature of the buildings exposed them readily to destruction by fire, one is surprised that it did not spread much farther than it did. The Parker House was also destroyed by this fire; at that time it probably brought in more rent than any other building in the United States.

The condition of the streets at that time left much to be desired. The first heavy downpours of rain began on October eighth and continued the next day. Although this made them impenetrable during those days, the condition of the streets was back to normal within a short while. About the fourth of November, the rains began again, and from then on until April the mud was really dreadful. The streets, almost without exception, were as nature made them, without pavement or planks, and the constant traffic of wagons made them look like bogs in which man and beast were in danger of sinking and suffocating. Those who had recently arrived from the well-paved avenues of the eastern cities were most aware of the condition of the streets.

By this time, this great inconvenience is remedied by the fact that many streets are laid out with boards. But, since this is not very skilfully done, the ladies have to suffer because of the iron nails, silk trains being treated so badly that new ones have to be made every two or three months. The owners of the silk stores have not as yet, to the best of my knowledge, complained about the condition of the pavements; some of the inhabitants, however, have succeeded in obtaining stone pavements in certain parts of the city, as well as properly-dug ditches for drainage. In Market Street and the adjoining streets in the southern part of the city, the conditions described above continue as bad as ever: sand still lies there, inches deep, over long stretches of road and, in a strong wind, threatens to blind the passer-by. In this way the shoe dealers lose on the one hand what the silk merchants gain on the other, as long as the former are not able to do better by themselves.

136

Chapter XVI

THE YEAR 1849 BROUGHT A FAIRLY LARGE INCREASE IN THE POPULATION of the city. More than 30,000 persons had come to San Francisco by water — of these more than two-thirds in the last half of the year — for the Atlantic States and Europe now poured their adventurers over California. There were now at least 20,000 residents in the city and without doubt more than 10,000 transients who were there on the way to the mines, or returning from a business trip, or a trip for pleasure or health. The city seemed to have a population only of men, for there were few women and still fewer children.

At that time, the men lived in the restaurants or in their lonely cloth tents, and the only comfortable places were furnished by the gambling-houses which were warm and dry, even if they were also full of the vile smell of clouds of tobacco smoke, of Holland gin and other spirits. The music of bands added to the excitement and banished any searching of one's soul or reflection on the part of anyone who found himself within these enticing gulfs of hell. Few could see the heaps of gold lying on the gambling-tables and breathe easily at the sight, or resist the influences at work about them and before them. A man might step in just to get out of the rain and to warm himself, or because he was moved by sheer curiosity; he watched, bet and was soon a lost man. Most of the inhabitants at that time were gamblers. At present it is fashionable and considered right to condemn this passion. The temptations to gamble are also far less seductive than they were then; moreover, the urge to gamble is strongly curbed by the severity of the law. In spite of this, there are secret gambling-houses in several cities in the country: I have convinced myself of that.

The last months of the year 1849 were the golden age of the city. Almost everybody had money, and there were still more than one who were dazzled by the hopes of mountains of gold that they would some day have. There was plenty of work and the payment for it was very good, for there was plenty of gold — more than enough. Everything was expensive: rent, interest, goods and pleasures. This picture of plenty had its dark sides, too; for among so much abundance there were also the forsaken and the sick, and the situation of a sick man was pitiful — without a wife, sister, doctor, without a nurse. No one was there to ease his pain, to help him and to bring him food. Many a poor fellow whose life had been spent in comfort, among the pleasures and the luxuries of civilized society, became sick and died in want — a stranger in a foreign land. Thus, as everywhere in life, we meet the contrasts here, too: the miserable hut beside the palace; the barracks leaning against the splendid cathedral; the groans of the sick and the dying penetrating the walls and windows of the dance-hall; the beggar jostling the millionaire; rags and splendid ribbons; poverty and wealth; rich comfort and squalid want; wailing and laughter; lamentations and shouts of joy; the bridal gown and the widow's weeds; health and sickness; life and death. This is the varied substance of the world.

In spite of the prevailing lack of consideration for others, many of the inhabitants were not unmindful of the obligations that a common humanity demands and gladly gave their mite to aid those in distress as often as they were asked. But this only made an evil situation worse: for almost all those who were well off were so engrossed in their business that they could hardly find a thought for the destitute.

On January 3, 1850, the sale of 430 building-lots "on the water," as the result of an order of the *ayuntamiento,* brought the sum of almost $650,000, so that on the average the price of each came to almost $1500: a sign of prosperity that is truly astonishing if these prices are compared to those which similar property brought hardly two and a half years before and when one realizes that it represents an increase from fifteen to twentyfold. These so-called "water lots" were made possible by a machine imported from England, that scooped the ground from the sand-hills, so that it could be used for filling. In this way, many lots were made as stable as any on firm ground; but others really remained lots under water. Piles were driven into these and wooden structures built on them which were used for business. On the eastern side of the city there are still rows of such lots.

On January eighth, an election was held for a state senator, members of the state assembly, the first alcalde and other officers. The result was the election of D. C. Broderick as senator, Samuel J. Clarke as member of the assembly, and John W. Geary as alcalde. At this time, at the end of January, the appearance of *Alta California* as a daily was a further indication of the progress of the place. Shortly afterwards the *Journal of Commerce* was published daily, according to a prospectus issued by Mr. W. Bartlett. The appearance of news-papers, whose columns were usually for sale, was so common at this time and afterwards that they were considered unimportant and no particular attention was paid to them.

The first conflict with respect to the settlement of unoccupied land by squatters occurred at Rincon Point on February twenty-eighth. The United States reserves at the above place were leased to Mr. Alexander Shillaber. When he went to take possession, he was pre-vented by those who had settled on the land. Accompanied by a small detachment of troops, Captain Keyes was able to regain possession of the property. The courts sustained him.

During March, the proceedings between the *ayuntamiento* and the prefect, Horace Hawes, with respect to the Colton grants, also came up for further consideration. In this action, the former brought charges against the latter. As a result, the governor suspended him from the further performance of his duties as prefect. Shortly before, he had given Mr. G. Q. Colton, justice of the peace, the right to sell the flat lands belonging to the city upon his responsibility as prefect. Under such circumstances, the lots were ridiculously cheap; as it was said in a joke: they went for a song. The authorities of the city found this "music" to be profitable on more than one occasion.

Colonel Jack Hays, the "Texas Ranger," was elected sheriff on April first in the first county election held. On this occasion there was great enthusiasm for "Jack" and no one had anything to say against the popularity with which he was generally regarded. On the fifteenth of the same month, the legislature gave San Francisco its first charter. The charter fixed the boundaries of the city; according to this, they included a district extending about three miles north and south and about two miles east and west. The city was divided into eight wards. The charter was accepted by the city on May first and J. W. Geary elected mayor together with seven heads of departments, eight alder-men, eight assistant aldermen and eight assessors.

We now come to the unfortunate day of the second great conflagra-tion of San Francisco — May 4, 1850. On that day property worth about four million dollars was destroyed. The fire broke out at four in the morning and within five hours turned three blocks into ashes, each covering 56 raras — more than seven acres. It was probably a case of arson. Great though the loss was, the young and hopeful energy of the citizens — who knew neither despair nor despondency — stimu-lated them to begin the courageous work of rebuilding before the last smoldering embers had been extinguished. This courage was always a characteristic of the people and the place, and showed itself on the occasion of all similar calamities. Indeed, there have been cases where agreements for new buildings to be erected were concluded before the fire had consumed the old, and where timber for a new house was delivered to the site before the smoke of the burning building had disappeared. Leave the spirit and the energy of man unfettered, inspire his soul with the fire of hope — and his enterprise will be subject to no barriers!

On the ninth of May the city government was regulated by providing for the joint meeting of the two boards of the city council, the election of officials, the naming of committees and the reading of the report of the mayor. According to a public report, financial conditions were very favorable. Another conflagration on the fourteenth of May caused greater damage than both of the former: the damage was estimated at more than five million dollars. The fire destroyed almost all the buildings and the goods within the district bounded by Clay, Kearny and California Streets, and the harbor. It was a hard blow, but the spirit of the inhabitants had such resiliency that persons who had left the city shortly before the fire found no traces of the destruction on their return in July. They missed only certain buildings which had been there when they left and were now replaced by completely new ones. The burnt-out district was completely built up again.

The members of the city council now began to discuss the question of receiving fixed salaries; this caused much discussion among the people and in the Press. The council paid no attention to this and set high salaries for the heads of the departments, fixed at $4,000 for each of them. Mass meetings were held at which dissatisfaction at this was voiced and it was demanded that the council reduce the salaries or resign. The meetings had their effect and salaries for municipal officials were finally refused: the regulation by which each member of the common council was to receive $4,000 was vetoed by the mayor.

An approximate idea of the business and trade of the place at this time may be had from the fact that in July more than five hundred vessels, for the most part fairly large ships, were in the harbor. It was very difficult, however, to get the crew of a ship to return, for the gold-mines and the high wages for labor were enough to induce a sailor to abandon his ship and to keep him from hurrying back to it. The result was that when a vessel reached the harbor it remained at anchor for a long time, more for lack of a crew than because of its ground-tackle. Temptation led Jack from the forecastle and changed him into a land-crab.

At this time, many of those who had been among the first to land in California began to see the usefulness of establishing an organization for social pleasures and the like, and as a result the Society of California Pioneers was organized in August. Wm. D. M. Howard was elected president.

A piece of bad news troubled the city. It was said that uprisings of settlers were taking place in Sacramento and Brighton, resulting in the death of several persons. The California Guard and Firemen's Company No. 2 went to Sacramento on August fifteenth, in accordance with a proclamation of the mayor. Before they arrived, however, the disturbances had been put down.

The twenty-ninth of the same month was set as a day of mourning for these riots and as a memorial-day for President Taylor. A very long funeral procession, in which the military and fire companies took part, made its way through the streets to the plaza where the Hon. Elcan Heydenfeldt delivered an address which was an inspired eulogy of the departed hero. The Chinese, who the previous day had received as gifts, Chinese tracts, books and newspapers from the mayor and other persons in the plaza, made a striking group in this procession. They were dressed in their gaily-colored and brilliant national costume and aroused great interest. Progress and flourishing growth were visible on all sides and continued to advance swiftly and surely.

The first directory of the city, published by Charles P. Kimball, appeared in September.* It contains about 2500 names and 136 pages in duodecimo. It may be of interest to compare this first edition with the present state of the city and its 28,000 dwellings, a long list of schools, colleges, churches, mercantile firms, iron-foundries, miles of streets, wharves, cemeteries, hospitals, charitable societies, halls, fire-departments and railways: all signs of a progressive state of development which, it is hardly believable, was reached in the short space of ten years.

The results of the speculations of the previous and the current years were now seen. A reaction set in: possessing land and merchandise was

---

* This account is set down according to the information I was given, but it is not quite accurate with respect to the date and the number of pages. I have before me a copy of the first edition of the book referred to — I could only get a copy after a great deal of trouble, for most of the edition was lost in repeated fires — and I see that the year of publication was 1852, that there were 125 pages, and that the name of the publisher was A. W. Morgan and Company. This was expressly stated in the foreword of the book, as follows: "We here present to the Public the first San Francisco Directory yet published. etc. San Francisco, Sept. 8. 1852. A.W.Morgan & Comp." The reader will observe, from this little incident, that I do not have absolute faith in whatever information I am given, but that, so far as I am able to, I investigate everything most carefully without sparing trouble or expense.

like being burdened with damaged goods; prices fell; credit sank; there were runs on banks; merchants and bankers, contractors and entrepreneurs failed, and many on the heights of apparent prosperity and wealth were plunged in a day into want and poverty. These occurrences were closely followed, on the seventeenth of September, by the horror of the fourth great conflagration. It destroyed almost the entire four districts that lay between Montgomery, Washington, Dupont and Pacific Streets. Most of the buildings consisted of wooden shanties so that the damage was probably not more than half a million dollars; but it completely ruined many an industrious, but unlucky, man.

But hope revived quickly and the smoking ruins were replaced by new improvements. In this period, the city extended rapidly along the shore of the bay on the eastern side; not only were shops built on piling over the water but, to establish and facilitate business, some ten or twelve wharves were planned. Several of these extended thousands of feet into the bay.

The long-pending doubt about the admission of California to the Union was resolved on the eighteenth of October. On that day the steamer *Oregon* arrived, flag-draped and firing salvos as a sign that the long struggle was over. There had been much offense taken at the delay of Congress and not a few had spoken of an independent republic along the Pacific; but, at the sight of the *Oregon* and at the news it brought, every other thought died. The harmonious feeling of patriotism flared up, and hearts, hands and voices united in a jubilant welcome. For the rest of the day the colors of all nations were displayed, and there was rejoicing and song everywhere.

The thirtieth of the month was set as the day on which the people were to reveal themselves as a united and harmonious community, to rejoice at the successful issue of the struggle for statehood. It was to be a holiday and a day of celebration. For that occasion, a long parade through the streets was arranged; Judge Bennett made a brilliant speech; bonfires blazed and fireworks illuminated the night; and more than fifteen hundred persons took part in a ball at the California Exchange. But that day was also marked as a day of misfortune: the first steamboat-explosion in the history of California occurred. The boiler of the *Sagamore* exploded as it was about to leave the wharf, and about thirty people lost their lives. Scenes of life and death, of joy and sorrow, mingled.

The proposal of Captain Wilson to build a street with wooden pavement across the sand-hills to the mission, Dolores, was considered at the meeting of the city council on November eighteenth and an ordinance authorizing the street was passed. Work on it was begun and completed in five months. It was a striking contribution to the further development of the city and to more comfortable going about in it. It contributed greatly, likewise, to increasing the value of property. In general, the streets of the city were greatly improved. They were covered with planks and much better adapted for the rainy season than in the previous year.

During this year, more than 650 vessels arrived in the harbor, and the population greatly increased again. This influx of strangers and the great quantity of gold that poured into the city more than made up for the destruction by the great fire. Thus, the year 1850 drew to a close. There were backward steps, to be sure, but in spite of these the development of the city continued. The location had proved to be extraordinarily healthful; even cholera, except for a few eccentrics, ceased to terrify people. The retrogressions were visible only in political and financial matters; the city began to plunge deeply into debt and its credit sank. Respect for the courts ceased and they failed to make their authority felt, so that there were many violations of law and order.

Chapter XVII

THE YEAR 1851 AND ITS EVENTS: CONFLAGRATIONS

THE YEAR 1851 WAS USHERED IN, RIGHT OFF IN JANUARY, WITH THE excitement caused by the "gold bluff." The propeller *Chesapeake*, an "old sea-loafer," that had taken twelve or fourteen months to come from some place on the Atlantic coast to California — since it did not float on an even keel, came stern foremost, and was delayed otherwise as well — was not completely useless. It took along a company of "coast scouts" to a place in the neighborhood of some spot later known as "Red Bluffs," where magnifying eyes, not unassisted by imagination and by exaggerating tongues, saw an unheard-of and immeasurable wealth of gold dust lying stored in the sand-wastes of the seashore. This news threw the people into the wildest excitement.

Those who took part in the expedition and the discovery were assured that each would have at least fifteen million dollars as his share. The old specification "white sand and green sand" was changed to "black sand and gold sand." When one of these lucky gentlemen was told of this, in true American style he put his feet on the mantelpiece and called out: "Now I will buy Rhode Island for my summer-home and Cuba for my winter residence." Much as this sounds highly exaggerated, it was nevertheless accepted by many as simon-pure truth. They put everything they had into the expedition and set out to acquire immeasurable wealth. The whole story was a fraud; the tales were lies that depended only on a little gold dust that was washed down from the "bluffs," mixed with sand by the pounding waves, and gathering it amounted to very little daily compensation for risking one's life. This was the last glimmer and flicker of glory!

The condition of the city, with respect to law and order, rapidly grew worse. Robberies, assaults and murders became more and more the order of the day until, on February nineteenth, audacity and crime reached their peak in an attack, early in the afternoon, on Mr. Jansen in his own store on Montgomery Street, by two scoundrels. They knocked him down with a blow from an iron slingshot; took two thousand dollars from inside his desk and left him lying on the ground, seemingly dead. This ghastly crime created no end of excitement. Two individuals, Burdue and Windred, were immediately captured by the people and, without law or court, almost lynched. A mob, numbering thousands, gathered about the city hall and tried to get hold of these two in order to hang them without further ceremony. Nevertheless, a jury was enrolled from among the people; judge, prosecutor, sheriff and an attorney for the prisoners designated; and the prisoners were brought to trial on the twenty-fourth of February. Nine of the jurors thought them guilty; three not guilty.

Many of the people were dissatisfied with this and shouted for the execution of the prisoners, but cooler reflection gained the day and the people agreed to an adjournment of the proceedings. Later, it appeared that both the accused were, in fact, innocent of the assault upon Mr. Jansen and the robbery. However, in the trial that was set for them by the court, they were sentenced to fourteen years' imprisonment. Windred slipped out of jail and escaped to Australia. Burdue who, during all this excitement, was identified as someone named Stuart, the murderer of Sheriff Moore at Auburn, was later taken to Marysville in a judicial investigation of this crime and sentenced to be hanged. Before the sentence was executed, the real Stuart was captured, proceeded against by the "vigilance committee" that had established itself in San Francisco, and declared guilty. He confessed the murder of Moore as well as the assault upon Jansen and the robbery, and was at last hanged. As a result, Burdue was set free.

His resemblance to Stuart was remarkably deceptive; it extended even to the loss of part of a finger. The arrest of Stuart and his punishment seemed an act of Providence. He had set out for the city, visited the Mission, and, to attract no attention, entered the city by way of the sand-dunes. By doing so he fell into the hands of some members of the "vigilance committee" who were about to search in the neighboring bushes and was arrested by them as a robber. This led to his imprisonment, trial, sentence and execution for crimes that were no longer subject to investigation. The fact remains: "Sooner or later, truth will out."

William Walker (who was recently shot in Central America) was then one of the editors of the *San Francisco Herald* and had begun to describe the character of Judge Levi Parsons, of the District Court, in outspoken articles. This vexed the judge so that he had Mr. Walker brought before him, convicted him of contempt of court and imposed a fine of $500. He had him imprisoned until the fine should be paid. This aroused the people. They gathered at the plaza on March ninth and resolved that Mr. Walker had been right to act as he did and that the resignation of Judge Parsons should be demanded. Mr. Walker was later brought before the Superior Court by a writ of habeas corpus and set free. Judge Parsons was brought up on charges in the legislature but found not guilty by this body.

The first bill with respect to the water lots was passed on March twenty-sixth; it authorized the State to rent for ninety-nine years places that lay on the coast. The second water-lot bill followed this on May first; it surrendered the right of the State to these lots forever. Both acts aroused much discussion and led to many law-suits. An ordinance to incorporate these lots again within the city, which had enlarged its boundaries, was passed on April fifteenth.

In the elections of April twenty-eighth, the Whigs were victorious and elected Carl H. Brenham as mayor and took almost all the other candidates from their own party. Shortly before, the city had shown itself to be Democratic in its political sentiments. On May first, the legislature passed an act proposing to fund the city's debt. The disbursements for one and a half years had exceeded the sum of $100,000 monthly. Moreover, the value of paper money had fallen. It was clear to everybody that the city had been defrauded; its property had been sold; its revenues were squandered; its debts had increased at an alarming rate; its credit was almost completely undermined; and, before the city suspected it, it saw itself drawn into bankruptcy. It was burdened by more than half a million in debts and, except for taxes and licenses, had little that it could look to as of value. Moreover, the income from taxes and licenses was insufficient to cover the current expenses of the municipal government. To save its credit from complete ruin, the legislature permitted the city's debt to be funded.

The fifth great fire occurred on the third and fourth of May — the anniversary of the second fire. It began in a painter's workshop on the south side of the plaza between eleven and twelve o'clock. Within a few minutes the neighboring buildings were in flames. The fire spread rapidly in all directions. Nothing could stop it; it raged all night and, when the sun rose next day, two thousand buildings were in ashes. Not only wooden buildings were destroyed but the heat was so great, and the destruction spread so rapidly, that almost every brick house, of the sort that had previously been fire-proof, shared the same fate. Many estimated the damage caused by this frightful fire at more than ten million dollars. Sadder, however, than this enormous loss of property was the loss of human life; several were wholly consumed in the fire. In the raging of this vehement tornado of flame, wood changed in a flash into fire and glowing ashes; walls of brick became ovens; buildings of iron were rolled together like parchment and fell down in ruins. It was a night of horror followed by a morning of destruction.[*]

One of the worst privations from which the inhabitants suffered was the insufficient supply of good, fresh water. To remedy this, a plan was devised to bring water from a mountain lake. The lake lay in the hills between the Presidio and the Pacific, about four and a half miles from the plaza. A company was formed for that purpose and authorized by an ordinance of the city council, its rights being confirmed thereafter by the legislature. According to later ordinances, these rights were enlarged and the time for completing the project extended. Difficulties arose that made the execution of the project questionable but they were overcome and it is now fully completed. It has proved to be a great blessing for the city and at the same time brings in a rich return on the capital spent in carrying out the project. The great conflagrations that from time to time afflicted the city, as

---

[*] Such devastation can no longer occur so easily, in spite of the fact that fires break out daily, because the excellent and numerous fire-stations on hand, as well as companies of well-drilled and efficient men, prevent it. This will be shown later in the text.

well as the daily needs of individuals, taught the necessity of such an undertaking, which is for San Francisco what the Cochituate Works are for Boston, or the Croton water system for New York.

Chapter XVIII

Continuation: The Vigilance Committee

A NEW ORGANIZATION CAME INTO BEING THAT COULD ONLY — AND HAD to — arise here, and which received support from the most varied of sources. Inasmuch as disorders and excesses of all kinds occurred in growing number, a large part of the energetic citizens organized themselves, at the beginning of June, into a "vigilance committee." By the morning of the eleventh, it dispatched John Jenkins by hanging him from a cross-beam of the old adobe building that then stood on the northwest corner of the plaza. He was caught in the act of carrying off a small money-chest that he had brazenly stolen from a merchant's store. He was tried by the committee and punished between one and two o'clock in the morning. This act of spontaneous justice was a scene of festivity that no one who witnessed it will ever forget.

Only the absolute conviction that the courts of the city were wholly powerless to punish the lawbreakers and that terrifying examples of the administration of justice were necessary to check the lawlessness that was perpetrated on so large a scale and which was steadily growing worse, could have reconciled a law-loving people to such procedure. The majority approved of the committee's way of doing things and thought it right. Although the police and certain private individuals among the citizens were opposed to it and went to the trouble of hindering it, their number was not sufficient to free the accused. The thousands that milled about in excitement; the cold-blooded manner of the committee; the apathy and obstinacy of the prisoner; the terrible sight of a human being swinging from a beam — seen not too clearly against the dark horizon — all this contributed to a picture that made an indelible impression. Many hoped that these exemplary punishments of crime would bring to a stop the course of the desperados within the city and that the threats that were uttered to set it on fire again would not be carried out. But such hopes, it turned out, were not to be fulfilled completely.

On the morning of June twenty-second, just as the clocks showed that it was time for religious services — for the day was a Sunday — the fire alarm was sounded. The hour for the sixth great conflagration had arrived. It broke out near the corner of Pacific and Powell Streets — clearly the work of an incendiary — and in four hours left fourteen blocks in ashes. The destruction of property again amounted to three or four million dollars. During the preceding great fire, the office of every newspaper in the city, with the exception of *Alta California,* was wholly or partly destroyed; in this fire, the same misfortune overtook this profession again. Since this fire followed so soon after that in May, it caused great discouragement; but the active life and the energy of the people quickly revived again after this crushing blow. Several were financially ruined, but the hopes of others grew out of the heaps of ashes and they gathered their strength to begin all over again. It took longer now than at any time previously for new buildings to cover the marks of devastation that the flaming bride of the wind had left.. It was not the last conflagration; since then there have been countless others, but none is to be compared to the six mentioned. The best precautions against the danger of fire that have been devised anywhere saved the city later from similar catastrophes.

The Vigilance Committee punished John Jenkins, as has been mentioned above, with death on the eleventh of June; on the twenty-fourth of August, it re-imprisoned two men — Whittaker and McKenzie — who had been set free by the authorities and hanged them within twenty minutes after they had been taken from prison. About two months after this incident, the Committee discontinued its activity after it had executed four criminals and had frightened away from the city a fairly large number of abandoned characters. The Committee was a necessity. Only those who were residents of the city during the reign of terror, now over, are in a position to judge the activities of the Committee fairly; if the courts had been what they should have been, it would never have come into existence.*

Theatrical entertainment was put on a new footing by the opening of the Jenny Lind Theatre on October fourth. It is now the City Hall.

---

* For details consult the ANNALS OF SAN FRANCISCO, pp. 562-587. My comments depend only on oral reports.

It was the fourth or fifth theater to be built on the site; the others, one after another, had fallen prey to the flames. On the thirtieth of the same month the American Theater was opened — a splendid temple for the dramatic muse, splendid inside as well as outside. It was a large and comfortably-furnished building on Sansome Street, where only a year or two before the shore had been.

Immigration this year was markedly lower than the year before, and only amounted to 36,000. Many of the newcomers came from China; the most corrupt and beastly of all human creatures at that time living on the continent — the effeminate Chinese race — they seemed more numerous, although still represented by a small number. They were a detestable evil — the ruin of a future generation.

Nevertheless, the city increased in population and improvements continued constantly. Hills were moved into the harbor; houses that had been standing forty feet below the level of the sandy plain were raised; and shops were built where only a year before ships had been moving up and down. Comfort, yes, even luxury, took the place of the dangerous conditions and bad food of the year before; the markets were plentifully provided with the meat of animals raised for food and with game, with venison and all kinds of vegetables. The city was rapidly becoming an American city, but with characteristics that to a certain extent were like those of no other: for the numerous foreign population had implanted not a little of their own national characteristics upon the character of the city and its appearance. It had the Yankee's crafty look of business; the vivacity of the Frenchman; the German's readiness to work and his intelligent diligence; the dreamy and thoughtless indolence of the Mexican; and the strange, pigtailed, almond-eyed appearance of the Chinaman — a source of amazement to mankind that nature and custom should have combined to produce such a specimen of ugliness.

On the thirtieth of January 1852, the last great sales of the city's property took place, under the auspices of Peter Smith. During the preceding year, Dr. Smith had been authorized by several decisions of the city to dispose of almost all its possessions in wharves, water lots and lots on the solid ground, and did so that year and the present year. They were worth millions of dollars. He insisted that they were not to be disposed of for less than $65,000. In general, people did not believe that the sale would be valid and only few had the courage to make any offers. The property was certainly sacrificed. The highest court finally upheld the sales and the princely inheritance of the city was lost to it forever. This was either the result of a great conspiracy or of ignorance.

Although the property of the municipality was sacrificed in this way, this was no worse than the reckless spending and the resultant crippling taxation. During the fiscal year that ended on May 31, 1852, the city had paid more than $1,700,000 in taxes, including license-fees, taxes for municipal, national and state purposes, and custom duties; in addition, there was still about $300,000 to be collected. Among the city's debts was the sum of $200,000 for the purchase of the Jenny Lind Theater, on June fourth, which was to be turned into a city hall. A considerable amount was spent, in addition, on redecorating the building and to this very day there is a mortgage on the building lot of about $30,000.

The residents of San Francisco, although far from the East, were no less devoted to their country and, as a result, their admiration for the gifted politician, for his eloquence and shrewdness, was just as marked. This was clearly seen again on August tenth, in the exceedingly large procession and other signs of respect and sympathy that were solemnly paid to the memory of that great man, Henry Clay, soon after the news of his death reached the city. The city was wrapped in mourning. All parties, sects, classes and callings forgot for a while their discords and contentions and united in paying the last sad honors to one of the greatest and best of orators, citizens and statesmen. The diverse aims of the politicians united at the sepulchre in which lay greatness and merit; men knew no nationality at that hour when all heads were bowed.

The sad news of Clay's death and the solemnities that took place after it were followed, on November twenty-first, by the news of the death of another great man of the same political party — Daniel Webster. All possible honor was likewise paid to his memory. Daniel Webster possessed all the attributes of a great man, an important statesman and a remarkable orator, in greater measure than any other man whose spiritual greatness illuminated the continent. His name is encircled by immortal light.

These remarks about both statesmen have no direct connection with the course of the history of San Francisco. Nevertheless, the death of both men had a lasting influence upon the people and, besides, I think remarks about such men are seldom out of place. Whatever serves to throw more light upon the character of a civilized society may properly be regarded as an historical event.

The progress of the city became more evident, to some extent, by the appearance during December of a city directory, published by Mr. James A. Parker. It contained almost a hundred pages, octavo size, with a list of about 9,000 names. It was a reliable book and the third or the fourth to appear in the city.*

On the tenth of the month, the first legal execution within the city limits took place: José Forni was hanged on Russian Hill for the murder of José Rodriguez. To the very last he insisted that the death blow was in self-defense. Many thousands were witnesses of this event and here, as in all lands and societies and in all ages, it was seen that people, for the most part, are frankly curious and try to find pleasure even in death.

Almost 70,000 persons arrived during 1852 by sea, and only somewhat more than a third of that number returned by sea. This increased the population of the city greatly, even if the number of those who went on to the gold mines and other parts of the State is deducted. As always, there were among them representatives of almost all the nations on earth; an important section of that great number were from China — at least 20,000; and opinion is divided as to whether their immigration was a blessing or a curse. As the year drew to a close, the city was thriving and even if it was only a transit point for those hurrying to the gold mines, its own wealth soared, and it was easy to visualize the great future that lay before it.

The number of ships that arrived in the harbor that year amounted to 1147, with cargos of more than half a million, compared to 847 ships, with cargos of not more than half that amount which arrived during 1851. Customs-duties exceeded that of 1851, but not in tonnage. The output of the mines may be seen in the shipping of gold dust which amounted to the value of $46,500,000 during the year.

---

* For my notes I tried, as far as possible, to obtain city directories from their first appearance to the year 1862. I was unable, however, to find copies for the years 1854 and 1855.

Chapter XIX

ONE OF THE FIRST MEMORABLE EVENTS OF 1853 WAS THE ESTABLISH-
ment of the Mercantile Library Association: it showed the progress of
the city in intellectual matters. This institution has enjoyed the warm-
est support of the community and is flourishing at present. It has a
large and constantly growing library of worth-while books and the
beneficial influence that it exercises upon the spirit and manners of
the community can hardly be measured. Public libraries, like schools
and the established philanthropic societies, have not only an effect
upon the progress of knowledge, but also upon manners and the heart.
The essentially material nature may not be drawn to them, but for
spiritual natures capable of self-improvement these means of delight
and self-improvement have an irresistible attraction. They rate higher
than the distractions in which the ignoble nature takes refuge, even as
virtue is not only much mightier but far lovelier than vice. Considered
from this standpoint, the foundation of the Mercantile Library Association is a blessing which cannot be treasured sufficiently as an incen-
tive to virtue and as a remedy for depraved pleasures, quite apart from
its intellectual influence and the great convenience it offers everybody
as well as the scholar.

The obstacles to the progress of the city were many. These consisted
not so much in matters outside of the city, nor in the great fires, as in
the decisions regarding property rights. Under various titles, many
claimed the same ground; each buyer of property could be sure in
advance that, in spite of research and investigation prior to his purchase, he would have a bonus of one or more lawsuits. During February, the infamous claims of Limantour to a large tract of land along-
side the city were laid before the board of land commissioners and,
finally, held valid by this tribunal in spite of everything that was advanced against the claims as fraudulent. In support of these, Limantour asserted that he had a right to the land by virtue of a grant from
Governor Micheltorena in repayment of money that he had advanced
to the agents of the Mexican government. These claims were met with
contempt and ridicule, for they covered an enormous tract that in-

cluded not only four leagues of land within the city limits but numerous other places, islands in the bay and in the Pacific, and extended to other parts of the State. But since lawyers and courts had to decide this matter, everything had to be left to their opinions and views. When the hearing took place, he created further doubts as to his claims to title — doubts already as numerous as the sands of the ground itself — until, finally, the commission made its surprising decision.

An election of three delegates from each ward for a revision of the city's charter was held on the sixteenth of February and among the names of the delegates elected were those of Harry Meiggs, Edward McGowan and William Carr for the first ward. The first absconded of his own accord because of forgery; the second was glad to slip away to escape various charges, including an accusation of murder; and the third was set aside against his wishes by the Vigilance Committee of 1856 because of stuffing a ballot-box and other knavish tricks: these were the sort of men elected.

The proposal of Governor Bigler and those who supported him to extend the waterfront of the city met with decided opposition on the part of residents. The municipal government opposed the measure in April on various grounds, and a petition against it was presented to the legislature. The bill was passed, however, since two of the representatives from San Francisco were in favor of the measure. The five representatives who had voted against it resigned and returned to the city, but were elected again as a reward by an overwhelming majority. Those who opposed the measure contended that the limits of the city had been permanently established by a previous act of the legislature, that rights had accrued under it, and that to change these boundaries was an unjust violation of an implied agreement since great damage would result and that on the other hand, it would enrich only a few speculators who were instigators of the measure. On the twenty-sixth of April, the bill reached the senate for a vote: thirteen were for it and thirteen against. Lieutenant-governor Purdy, who was in the chair, voted against it and the evil results of the measure were avoided. Further attempts to pass the bill, or others like it, failed ignominiously, although Governor Bigler supported them with vigor.

On April seventh, the corner-stone of a marine hospital of the United States was laid at Rincon Point. The building is very beautiful. It is two hundred feet in length and one hundred feet broad and has accommodations for 500 to 800 patients. It cost almost a quarter of a million dollars. In this way, the first State building which the government of the United States erected within the city-limits is dedicated to charity and set apart specially for a class who make themselves very useful, even if they are frivolous — the sailors.

As mentioned before, many foreigners introduced their native customs into their new home. But no Europeans cling more steadfastly to the social pleasures of their youth than the Germans. Accordingly, on the first of May, the very large German singing and gymnastic society celebrated its founding in German fashion, by a parade, gymnastics, a concert and dance in Russ' Garden. The good fellowship and pleasures of youth that they had enjoyed on the Rhine, the Danube, the Oder and the Zuyder Sea were revived by the sport and entertainment of that day; and the great harmonies that had poured from the soul of a Handel, a Mozart, or a Beethoven and which were sung in the palaces and cities of Germany itself, found, even if they lacked the original tones and accent, an echo on the shore of the Pacific. To be sure, music is in itself a universal language that needs no explanation. All understand the nightingale if she soars up from a green English meadow or the bleak landscape of Sweden; and in the same way the harmonious tones that delighted a royal court in Berlin, or an imperial assembly in Italy, are understood and felt in the cities of Washington and Montezuma, and by the residents of Melbourne, or by those who live along the San Francisco bay.

On that day the Germans reminded themselves of their fatherland, listened to its great symphonies, and were happy: all revelled in the memory. On the following day, a Monday, the school-children celebrated May Day by a parade and various ceremonies, brought forward their Queen of the May, whom they crowned, and amused themselves freely. A thousand children, boys and girls, dressed for the holiday, took part in the parade, and such a gathering of fresh and healthy young faces had hardly ever been seen here before. No sight in the city gave those who wished it well more pleasure: this was the imprint of the future.

The electric telegraph sent its first current in this land between San Francisco and Point Lobos. On the twenty-second of September, progress took a step forward by means of the wires along the coast of the Pacific Ocean. Messrs. Streeny and Baugh, owners of the Merchants' Exchange, had it erected to facilitate their business. This was the first line in the net of telegraph wires which now enables the citizens of the principal and smaller cities of the State to communicate with each other as though they were sitting side by side.

In October, Judge Heydenfeldt of the Supreme Court handed down an opinion with respect to the rebate of land values proclaimed by the mayor. The other judges concurred. It was a decision of great importance. Although, as may be supposed, it opened the door to many fraudulent concessions, it succeeded in silencing many claims and some of the difficulties of settling the land were now brought to a happy end. This meant that progress was being made towards a more settled state of affairs.

On the twenty-fourth of October, the mountains spoke to the sea, as it were, by means of a lightning flash over the wires between Marysville and San Francisco, a distance, as the telegraph line ran, of more than two hundred miles. The price of the first ten words was two dollars and even at this high price it was considered a great convenience.

Filibustering, introduced by American adventurers a few years earlier along the Atlantic Ocean and around the Gulf of Mexico, appeared here during the year. It received its baptism on the thirteenth of December when the bark *Anita* sailed from San Francisco with 250 men to join a small band that had landed in Lower California under Col. William Walker. The first troop can only be regarded as the investiture of the child, for they dressed it in long clothes and brought it to the ocean. Although a new Republic of Sonora had been sketched on paper, it was only a pioneer movement. It led, however, to the successful conquest of Nicaragua by the father of this excursion. It may have the further result that all of Central America will be plunged into a full-scale revolution and that its old people and governments will be replaced by younger and more energetic ones. The fate of nations is like that of individuals: the weaker must give way before the stronger. The partition of Poland is not the only example of this; all southern Asia has had to experience a similar judgment at the hands of God. In the five states of Central America, similar causes may produce similar results.

The drama, for the production of which the Metropolitan Theater was erected, had homage paid to it by the opening of the building on December twenty-fourth. This, with respect to its interior, was one of the most beautiful and comfortable theaters on the continent. From the time of the opening it continued to enjoy a remarkable attendance, so that the sum it earned in a year and a half was enormous. And that was not surprising, for Kate Hayes, Mrs. Anna Bishop, James E. Murdock and other famous actors and actresses permitted themselves to be engaged just as soon as they could. Julia Dean Hayne enjoyed, during the present year, the greatest success that any actor or actress ever had: her run for four weeks was a continuous triumph. Nevertheless, the owners of this splendid theater lost all their capital for various reasons and the architect and the first shareholders were completely ruined when it was sold. Stars of the first magnitude had made fortunes of $20,000 to $30,000 during an engagement at the Metropolitan Theater, but the shareholders and builders who had added to the public resorts of the city so beautiful a place of entertainment and who had at heart the improvement of public taste in so amiable a fashion, saved nothing for themselves out of all the great revenues.

The incomes that were paid the city for the water-lots were sold on the twenty-sixth and twenty-seventh of December. Both sales brought a sum of more than a million and a half dollars. Several of these lots rented for $16,000. The gold dust shipped in the course of the year, according to the statement of the custom-house, amounted to almost fifty-five million dollars. An important share of the gold dust remained in private hands and for this reason could not be estimated accurately, but very likely exceeded the sum of five million. The output of the mines had, accordingly, not fallen off. Prosperity was also evident from the appearance of the houses; during that year it had greatly improved. Fire-proof brick as a rule predominated and the style of building was much better. The front was of granite and free-stone and regard was had for appearance as well as usefulness. The real estate within the city was valued at about thirty million dollars. At the end of the year the city was richer in many ways: eighteen churches, ten public schools, fourteen fire-houses, 160 hotels and public rooming-houses, fifteen flour-mills and saw-mills were erected; nineteen banking firms, six military companies, many literary, social, charitable, religious and professional societies had been founded; twelve daily and various weekly and monthly newspapers appeared; and six theaters, a music-hall, and a gymnasium were available for amusement. Imports during the year amounted to at least twelve million dollars; custom-duties received more than two and a half million; 1028 ships arrived and 1653 departed. By means of these incomplete figures, it is possible to obtain an approximate idea of the progress and commerce of the city.

One of the best signs was the constant arrival of women. Their influence cannot be overestimated. At this point, we are inclined to indulge in the greatest eulogies of women. Firstly, she creates the home, and without a home the majority have nothing that merits the name of happiness. When a toast was proposed to the wife of Daniel O'Connell in a public assembly, that great orator said, among other things, the following: "No man is capable of great undertakings until he has a warm nest at home." As soon as women came, homes were started, and, for the first time, man looked on California as permanent residence.

Chapter XX

THE BEGINNING OF THE YEAR 1854 FOUND SAN FRANCISCO IN MANY respects a great city. One improvement had followed hard on the heels of another, although the city had also been visited by misfortunes. Little by little, the printing of books and the steam-engine were introduced, and on February eleventh the city was illuminated by gas for the first time. The dirty streets of necessity gave way to pavement; the darkness of 1849 and the still greater darkness of oil-lamps which had a tendency to flicker down to a mere suspicion of a light, were gone forever. The illumination by gas, produced by the gas-company of San Francisco, with three hundred lamps, along a total distance of three miles, lit up and brightened the streets and also the hearts of the people. Like every occasion, this was also celebrated by a delightful reunion at the Oriental Hotel.

Great blessings are often mixed with pain and seldom, or rather almost never, is success in mercantile or other business achieved without sooner or later being darkened by shadows. In March of this year, the result of the heavy imports of the previous year was severely felt in that prices were forced down until goods threatened to become worthless and financial embarrassments grew constantly worse. Many had foreseen this approaching crisis in mercantile affairs some time before, and were greatly worried, but few had prepared themselves for it and the great majority kept their courage buoyed up by the hope which the previous year's business had instilled, and as a result of which not a few of the thoughtless ones were ruined. As the State began to grow its own food supplies and as the number of local manufacturers increased, much of the city's commerce disappeared. Good times began to slacken; the high rents and prices for real estate and goods fell, and considerable hardship followed.

The branch mint at San Francisco began to function on April third. The building of Curtis, Perry and Ward, the assayers for the mint of the United States, was rebuilt in part, bought by the government and provided with machinery; it became, although too small for the space that the work required, of inestimable value to the city and state. Congress should have appropriated at least a million dollars, instead of $300,000, for the building of a mint that would have been worthy of the city, the country and the mines whose treasures it had to change into cash. In this small building, at present furnished for the purpose, more coin was stamped and ingots cast than in all the other mints of the country, not excepting the principal mint at Philadelphia.

The trial of the Mexican consul, Don Louis del Valle, in the district court of the United States for a breach of the neutrality laws by conscripting or sending emigrants to Sonora, came to an end on April twenty-eighth with a verdict of "guilty." This trial, with its attendant circumstances, caused great excitement and much discussion. The injury that the consul had caused by sending to Sonora people who preferred this California could not have been great and could only be regarded as a breach of international etiquette. Monsieur Dillon, the French consul, was later accused of a similar offense. In this case, the jury could not agree, the district-attorney entered a *nolle prosequi* on the twenty-ninth of May, and the accused was acquitted. No further judicial proceedings were instituted against the Mexican consul. Mr. Dillon claimed to be free of any obligation to appear as witness before the court and invoked the treaty with respect to consuls between France and the United States. In this position he was energetically — and successfully — supported by his own government and the American government.

On the twenty-ninth of this month there appeared in San Francisco a Chinese journal with a title that meant, more or less, *Golden Hill* — the Chinese name for San Francisco. It was a monthly, printed in Chinese characters, and represented the fifth foreign language to be used for a periodical in the city.

Although the city had shown itself to be healthful, many, nevertheless, had to journey along the dark street from which no one returns. The old burial-grounds within the city-limits had to surrender their dead; the growth of the city had surrounded most of them with buildings, or cut streets through them. Only one cemetery was left within the city itself, Yerba Buena Cemetery, which by this time contained a large number of graves, and the relatives of the dead wished to be able to get quickly to the quiet resting-place where the dead were lying in eternal sleep. New and larger grounds that were more suitable for the cemetery of a great city were wanted. Two or three persons selected a place in the neighborhood of the Pacific, about three miles from the harbor, and bought it for this holy purpose. It is very uneven, consisting of hill and dale, almost completely covered with evergreen oaks or other trees and bushes, and offers, in many spots, a splendid view of the city and the ocean. This place, measuring 160 acres, was consecrated as a cemetery on the thirtieth of May, under the name "Mountain of Love," with appropriate ceremonies, addresses, delivery of an ode and other poems, a prayer service and the singing of hymns. A poem for this occasion, alluding to the chemical dissolution and transformation of animal bodies, by which the human organism becomes an ingredient of bush and tree under which it is buried, closed with the following verses:

> From every nation and from every zone
> Have virtue, innocence, and beauty here assembled
> To show themselves again in life renewed
> When warmth of spring returns and with it days of joy;
> In every rustle of a leaf their voices whisper,
> Their beauty makes its way through bud and blossom still,
> And though the life of these is fleeting like their own
> It strengthens our weak faith and makes it glow
> And lifts our hopes on wings unto the blessed shore
> Where Love, offspring of God, is never more extinguished.

From that time on, many a beloved form was carried to this last home, and many improvements that love and reverence suggested were made, so that beauty, holiness and love might emulate each other there. The course of time has covered it with an unfading green, and the wildly foaming waves of the ancient sea sing their eternal funereal song; solemn, beautiful and sublime, Nature furnishes the death-watch.

Chapter XXI

CONTINUATION

FOR A LONG TIME, THE DISORGANIZED CONDITION OF THE LAND TITLES, as has been often mentioned, caused much trouble. The pitch to which such an unsatisfactory state of affairs led reached such a height that during June a regular battle took place between individual settlers and another group who tried to drive them off some land that Captain Folsom claimed. A member of his party was killed. A few days later, a woman likewise lost her life in another part of the city on the occasion of a similar unfortunate riot. These incidents caused landowners to meet in order to organize a special body of police to protect their property; and about a thousand signed their names to the subscription list. It is to be expected, accordingly, that all such encounters will be avoided and will no more be repeated and that no similar provision, furthermore, will become necessary to avoid disagreements that arise out of the conflict of land titles and land claims.

Social conditions had improved in many important respects; in other respects, however, conditions had made little or no progress. The corrupting vice of gambling had greatly diminished, and other reprehensible habits had also abated. This was the result of developing social relations. There were more attractive dwellings now; people began to take a greater interest in their homes, whose inviting interiors provided increasing comfort and opportunity for social intercourse.

Outside, conditions had changed little. Little offenses and improper behavior were certainly almost always punished, but great offenses came within the rule that had applied in former years, that is, they remained unpunished, at least such as called for severe punishment according to the wording of the law. If it could be seen in advance that an offense would result in imprisonment in a state prison, the offender was brought up on charges; but the murderer, in almost every case, went scot-free. Technicalities, hair-splitting, sharp practices and the prejudices of the jury — not always composed of reliable people — combined with a feeling of sympathy for the still living criminal, forced into the background the implementation of justice on behalf of the murdered victim and injured society and served to protect the defendant, however definite the the implications of his guilt or revolting his crime. In addition, since the witnesses of bloody scenes generally belong to that class of residents who change their residence frequently, their testimony is hard to get and, as a result, it is difficult to convict an offender.

On the twenty-eighth of June, Wm. B. Sheppard was found guilty of killing Henry C. Day and on the twenty-eighth of July he was condemned to be hanged. The mandate of the law led to his execution, although Sheppard always insisted upon his innocence. On the scaffold, he acted the hero; but he had been justly condemned for a murder executed in cold-blood. The deed is established beyond doubt. There are still witnesses living near the city who were present at the trial, who with their own eyes had seen the crime committed. Sheppard left behind him an avowal of his innocence! Of what value are these declarations of innocence on the gallows? No more than death-bed conversions; both as a rule are no more than wasted breath.

The establishment of the newspaper, *Alta California*, built of fireproof brick, was bought for $50,000, in scrip, to be the hall of registry. This is one of the very few instances the city can show that for all its great expenditures it secured a building worth the cost.

At this time the great hostility to the immigration from China that many entertained was fed afresh by the dreadful condition of recent immigrants from that land. Shiploads of them — or, more correctly, as many as managed to reach the bay still alive — were landed on Goat Island. Here the mortality among them was very great. The sickness that killed so many of them was scurvy. The terrors of the African slave-trade seemed to be revived on board the few old vessels which had left China for California freighted with these pitiful creatures.

There were soon two synagogues among the great number of churches that had been built. The cornerstone of the first, known as Congregation Sherith Israel, was laid on July twenty-third. Details will be found later.

Since a "house of refuge" had become necessary, the supervisors set about to supply this need and bought, west of the Mission, some land at an enormous price. After this had happened and the money paid in cash or scrip and divided, the whole matter died down and was forgotten. The plaza was enclosed by an ornamental iron railing and the ground improved — made even and planted with trees and bushes. On the seventh of September there was an election. For this a very large gathering took place: there were 10,833 votes in the city alone. On October first, the steamer *Yankee Blade* was wrecked near Point Conception and many passengers were drowned. Shortly afterwards, the city was again thrown into a state of great excitement; it was discovered that Harry Meiggs, "Honest Harry," who had been a member of the city council for several years and enjoyed the reputation of being an honorable, enterprising, energetic and charitable man, had slipped away by boat with all his family and his brother who, shortly before, had been elected city comptroller. He left behind him $100,000 in fraudulent city securities on which he had borrowed as collateral and for which he had received considerable sums in cash. Harry headed for South America where he is at present.

Colonel Walker was at this time accused of having fitted out an armed expedition against Lower California. But he was acquitted on October nineteenth. That was the end of this filibustering tragedy. Property within the city, subject to taxation, was worth more than thirty-four million dollars at this time. The schools, too, were flourishing. According to the census, the number of children of school age amounted to 3780. An attempt was made to encourage immigration and a meeting held for this purpose. Nothing came of it, however, except resolutions.

The last important event of 1854 was the decision, by the Board of Land Commissioners of the United States, that San Francisco was a "pueblo" under Mexican rule and that as such it was included within the frontiers of that country. Many welcomed this decision and saw their salvation in it; others decried it as a trick, even though issued by the Commissioners. Since this is a matter about which the answers of those most learned in the law differ radically, one should excuse a layman from expressing his opinions. This Commission confirmed land claims and concerned itself with overlapping territory. The advocates of this law claimed that these rulings contain no contradiction as they only make decisions regarding the United States and the claimants, but not as to the value of the claims. In this way the United States is protected against any proceedings, and Limantour, Bolton, Barron and Company, and others have no recourse but to settle this point as well as they can.

So ended the year. It brought much to rejoice at and also much to regret. Wealth was lost and won. Gold, worth millions, reached the city and nevertheless many found themselves in want. Many who were well-off before are now badly off. Many are unhappy that the fine days, the prices and the business of years gone by for which they had hoped, did not return; it is hard completely to abandon a cherished idea and to see a cherished hope buried. So city and people go along the street of time, leave the well-trodden track of the old year and peer forward to the path that leads to the new, which imagination, hope and desire place among splendid landscapes, embellished, like a new Jerusalem, with gold, gold and more gold.

In January 1855, the new Merchants' Exchange, a very beautiful structure at the Battery, between Washington and Jackson Streets, was built and opened. Later, the circuit court of the United States and the district courts were removed to its main building where their sittings are now held. The city was greatly excited by the rumors of the discovery of gold along the Kern River in extraordinary quantities. The rumors reached their height in the course of the month. The news was like that of the "gold bluff" exaggerations and like those left many expectations unsatisfied. The gold-diggings proved to be very poor and because of hopes based on these false rumors hundreds lost their money and many even their lives.

On February seventeenth, the worst financial panic that had ever held the city in its power, broke out. On that day, a run began against Page, Bacon and Company as the result of news from the East. The firm suspended payment on the twenty-second. This firm was, and had been, the leading bank of the city for a number of years; the closing of its doors caused a panic. The bankruptcy of other banks followed — drawn into the whirlpool — and right afterwards, on the twenty-third, Adams and Company, Wells, Fargo and Company, Robinson and Company, and Wright and Company suspended payment. Riots, conferences and countless lawsuits were the result. Arrangements were made by which Page, Bacon and Company was able to resume business on the twenty-ninth of March; but this was only for a short time. After a few weeks, the firm had to close its doors again because of the attitude of Page and Bacon of St. Louis, Mo., with whom the San Francisco firm had business relations. Wells, Fargo and Company likewise began to do business again and continued to do so successfully from then on. Many who had faith in the other firms lost their entire deposits and not a few saw themselves robbed in this way of all they possessed. The uncertainty, injustice and partiality of the law with respect to bankruptcy and endorsement of negotiable exchange, not to mention the cunning of our lawyers, had the result of increasing the amounts spent in legal proceedings and, by such expenditure, of depriving the insolvent of whatever else they possessed, so that only a few could save themselves. Lawyers and others became rich, and the average honest man who had saved his money lost everything.

In April, several brokers and houses that imported their goods failed, one of the latter with liabilities of more than $200,000. Because of these events and other causes, business at this time came to a complete standstill and hard times lay like a blight over the city. The new charter for the city was approved by the legislature and there was hope that by this means the interests of the city would be more secure and the expenditures considerably reduced. This expectation was fulfilled.

At this time, the steamer *Charmer* left for New York with a cargo consisting, for the most part, of California products — wheat, oats and flour. The page had been turned, it seemed, and, instead of having grain shipped from the East, the State was in a position to supply other sections with its surplus. The branch mint coined in June money amounting to two and a half million dollars. Although so great a fortune existed in the city and there was so much money coined, businessmen left the city in droves. In the course of two and a half months, fifty-six insolvency petitions were filed, besides a frightening amount of liabilities of those still in bankruptcy, which was estimated by them at more than three million dollars. A dark picture was unfolded.

An Italian newspaper appeared in July or August and thus the speech of another nationality found expression. I. C. Woods, of Adams and Company, bankers, absconded secretly in August for South America. Many believed that he took along a large sum from the funds of Adams and Company which, it was known, they had lying in their vaults during the night before their suspension of business. An election was held on September fifteenth after the grant of the new charter: the number of votes in city and country amounted to 12,724; that of the city to about 11,700. The steamer *Uncle Sam* of the Nicaragua Line reached the city on the fourteenth of September with cholera on board. During the trip, 120 of the 550 passengers had died of it, and a great number died after landing. Luckily, the sickness did not spread in the city. The sale of the "city-slip property," held December 1853, that had brought in a million dollars, was declared invalid by Judge Norton and the city was obliged to refund what it had received. This gave its credit a powerful blow. Between October 1, 1849 and July 1, 1853, $4,324,650 had been spent of what it had in the treasury, and no one knew where the money had gone.

Under such circumstances, the national spirit awoke and the English, French and Sardinians of the city commemorated the twenty-sixth of November by a great festival in South Park, in celebration of the success of the Allies in the Crimea. A large tent was set up, decorated with flowers, evergreens, flags, inscriptions and views of Crimea, and all efforts were bent to making the festival impressive by music, speeches and so on. Warships anchored near the tent and fired their guns, and shots were also fired from a neighboring hill called "Malakoff." All went on in perfect harmony until a band of rowdies caused an uproar: they tore down the flags, interrupted the mid-day meal, smashed the tables and made the continuation of the festival quite impossible. There has never been a worse incident during a peaceful gathering; it was disgraceful that it should have occurred although only the lowest of the low were responsible for it.

The difficulty in which the consuls of Mexico and France found themselves because of the legal proceedings referred to above was obviated on November thirtieth by an agreement between the French and American governments. The American ship *Independence* saluted the French ship *Ambuscade* at the reinstatement of Mr. Dillon; the tricolor was again hoisted over the office of the French consulate and friendship was restored — never to be broken again, we hope.

It is possible to obtain an idea of the business depression during the last year — or the last two years — from the fact that in 1855 one hundred and ninety-seven petitions of insolvency were filed in court for relief from legal proceedings. Many of these failures amounted to large sums and, although much of the loss concerned persons who did not live in the State, the results were nevertheless very serious and crushing. Business was in a state of depression such as had never before been experienced; the city's head was bowed, and as a result of these vicissitudes the city's business became unsteady. Nevertheless, more than forty-five millions in gold were shipped away, without counting the sums taken out by private persons which, without doubt, amounted to millions and were not entered in the records of the custom-house. More than 31,000 persons arrived during the year. The number of ships that arrived from foreign harbors was 1163. Seventy-two million pounds of flour were exported from the State to other markets. Total exports were valued at more than four million dollars. The total of registered and licensed tonnage amounted to 79,319 at the end of the year. Within two years, thirty million dollars in coinage had been minted. Within three years, 117,292 persons had arrived, 76,407 had departed — leaving an increase in population of 40,885. Customs-duties on merchandise from foreign ports amounted to four million dollars. There were 267 marriages in the city during the year; out of all proportion to this number, seventy-two petitions for divorce were filed, and forty-one petitions for release from the silken bonds granted. All these suits were brought by the wives of these no-longer-harmonious marriages. Everyone can judge for himself from this what married life is like in California. Losses caused by fires during the year amounted to more than two million dollars.

A great sale of 309 lots of the real estate of the late Captain Folsom was held on January tenth and brought $607,695. Soon afterwards, the claims of Limantour were recognized by the Land Commission of the United States. About 20,000 persons live on this enormous tract of land which includes almost, or perhaps just, two-fifths of the city's surface. This decision, recognizing the claims as valid, resulted, as had all such previous decisions, in great excitement, for a number had bought their lots more than once because there were various claims on them.

Discord of quite another kind was occasioned by a sudden earthquake on the sixteenth. It caused no little fright. It was the severest that had ever been experienced and violent enough to send sustaining walls crashing and to cause other gaps. Luckily, the tremors lasted only seconds, and the work of destruction soon ceased. It began with a loud noise like the explosion of a boiler or a powder-magazine. Directly afterwards, one felt a roaring and trembling motion. This occurred towards the end of the night and startled those who were resting peacefully out of their morning slumbers. That part of the city that was built on the new land, where shortly before the water of the harbor had flowed, felt the shock more than the other parts. The shock, luckily, was greater than the damage.

A Mormon newspaper, under the name of *The Western Standard*, appeared on February twenty-third. At present, almost every party, sect or religious denomination has its representative among the editors of periodicals so that, for the immediate future at least, there does not seem to be any vacant place for a new periodical. What is required is an enterprising person, bent upon acquiring the fame of an editor, who is willing to set a stream of low prices flowing: here there would be a chance for a genius.

Chapter XXII

CONTINUATION: DISSOLUTION OF THE VIGILANCE COMMITTEE

THE SUIT BROUGHT BY HENRY M. NAGLEE, THE RECEIVER OF ADAMS AND Company, against Alfred A. Cohen, who had recently been appointed manager, was decided against the defendant on March eighth, and a judgment for $269,046 entered. This was followed by the arrest of Cohen. He was set free at the end of September by the Supreme Court.

Glancing at the figures with respect to the yearly mail between the State and the great foreign world, it may be worth while to note that during the first three months 257,175 letters were sent from the city to the eastern States and 216,175 received. During my stay in California, I learned that in one day, January 9, 1861, 9824 letters were sent by the overland post. The postage for each letter amounted during recent times to ten cents — an excessive amount, more than three times as much as the remaining thirty-three States had to pay for their correspondence with each other. However, California is accustomed to such exactions in the form of burdensome and unjust distinctions.

In April, the opportunity of traveling comfortably that had been offered the city and State was curtailed with the suspension of travel by steamer by way of Nicaragua. General Walker would not permit the steamers of the steamship company of Nicaragua to leave and had also attached other property of the same company. Service was accordingly interrupted and no ship could sail, except the *Sierra Nevada* which was under the control of, or owned by, Messrs. Garrison and Morgan and did not suspend its monthly trip.

The great "bulkhead project," to build a dam, was laid before the meeting of the city council that month and before the citizens, and it caused much discussion because it was severely criticized in the press and by the public generally. A company had made and supported the proposal most eagerly for the purpose of obtaining permission to build this wall along the water front of the city, but its efforts were in vain. The strong opposition to this project won, and forced its rejection.

All these matters, which had provided sufficient material for discussion, were overshadowed by one incident and its results. The foundation of an orderly society in the city as well as in the State was endangered, and the incident struck the peaceful people here and elsewhere like a thunderbolt. On the fourteenth of May, Mr. James King, of the firm of William King, publishers of the *Evening Bulletin*, was attacked on his way home along Montgomery Street by James P. Casey and badly wounded by a pistol shot in the left breast. Mr. King lingered, suffering indescribable pain, until the twentieth, when he died.

Casey had served a sentence in Sing-Sing (a prison on the Hudson in New York State). He sent a statement to the *Bulletin*, in which he explained his reasons for the murder of its editor, and the manner in which it had been carried out. This infamous deed caused great excitement in the city, as never before, in spite of many similar crimes. Instantly a desperate attempt was made by many to get hold of Casey, and on all sides rang the cry: "Hang the murderer! Hang him, hang him!" The police intervened and were fortunately able to prevent further acts of lawlessness and to bring Casey to jail. The city was still far from quiet and the mayor realized the necessity of calling out the military companies, who were thereupon quartered in the prison and its vicinity. The militia was called to arms and stationed before the building to keep an armed watch over it. Many of the enraged citizens were much inclined to attempt to storm the prison. However, cooler proposals gained the upper hand.

The nucleus of another vigilance committee that should have the final say in this case was organized that night. Its number increased rapidly. By Sunday, the nineteenth, the committee appeared in the streets in great strength, provided with weapons and divided into companies and battalions. They seized all the entrances to the prison and the places that commanded it, occupied the length of Broadway, planted a cannon directly opposite the entrance to the prison and demanded that the sheriff surrender Casey who was imprisoned inside. After some delay, the members of the committee were permitted to enter and take possession of him. He was led into the street to a hack, guarded carefully, and then brought to the headquarters of the vigilance committee on Sacramento Street. As a sequel, Charles Cora, accused of the murder of a Federal marshal, General Richardson, was also taken from prison and brought to the committee's building. It all took place very quietly and with resolution and presented a fear-inspiring sight — as was intended.

On the twenty-second Mr. King was buried. The people of the city dressed themselves in mourning as soon as they heard of his death and attended the burial in great numbers. While the funeral service was taking place in church, Casey and Cora, who had been prosecuted, some time before this, in a proceeding conducted by the vigilance committee and condemned to death, were hanged in front of the windows of the committee's building in the presence of a great crowd. An immense procession followed the remains of Mr. King to his resting-place in Love Mountain Cemetery.

Later the committee seized many other persons who were accused of crimes and evil conduct. Between thirty and forty were either banished from the city, or went away of their own accord at the suggestion of the committee. The charge against many was that they had stuffed ballot boxes or had become guilty of other election frauds. Almost nobody could have much sympathy for them.

The proceedings of the committee and its existence were, however, questioned by many because of its forceful action and they pronounced it might without any right, and its appearance dangerous because unconstitutional, and unlawful, and a threat to all the guarantees of a republican government. For this reason, those who were against the committee declared that the arrests, proceedings and punishments by hanging, that the committee had ordered with respect to those who were punishable to a greater or lesser degree, were unlawful, unjust and very dangerous; that, indeed, they were in themselves crimes against the commonweal and treason against the government of the state and nation. The committee and its adherents replied that it represented the people and the public; that the people have an inherited right to revolt in case the government fails to protect them, and that, furthermore, the committee was justified in improving an evil situation without the aid of the law if the law itself, by means of the courts, would not or could not furnish any redress! Moreover, they declared, the evil, which was spreading, could no longer be endured and there was no other way to stamp it out but that which they had undertaken.

In the meantime, the grand jury had discovered substantial evidence that Edward MacGowan and Peter Wightman were accomplices in the murder of James King. The police immediately with all zeal tried to hunt them down, while the police of the vigilance committee, likewise, made every effort to find them. In vain! To this day, there is no reliable information about their whereabouts; it was rumored that MacGowan was seen in Santa Barbara, but that has been doubted by many.

On the twenty-ninth of June, the third legal execution in the court of the prison took place: Nicholas Graham, who had been accused of murder some time before, was executed. He was still a young man and had killed a fellow-passenger on one of the steamships along a wharf of the city, after making sure that he was defenseless by getting him inebriated with brandy. A fear-inspiring result of intemperance! Another person arrested by the vigilance committee was the well-known prizefighter, Yankee Sullivan. His prizefights and defeats had made him known throughout the world. Although brave and fearless in a fight against another man, he did not have the moral courage to face the dangers which he imagined were awaiting him, during his imprisonment in the committee's building. He was convinced that he was to be exposed to the most frightful torture, hanged or sent to Australia, and therefore preferred to die a suicide rather than await the fate he saw befalling him. On the morning of May thirty-first, his jailers found him dead in his cell, bathed in blood, leaning against his bed, his left arm above the elbow gashed by a dreadful wound. He had committed this dreadful deed in his cell when he was unwatched, and so by his crime of suicide gave the finishing touch to actions at which mankind shuddered.

Exports in the month of May amounted to $4,575,408. Imports amounted to 38,789 tons. So the streams of wealth poured through the heart of the State, although the business of the city was almost at a complete standstill. Gold came and went; ships arrived, were unloaded, spread their white wings again, and sailed away; merchandise was put ashore, transported inland and distributed; some of the freight was paid for here, some of it there; and yet the rumor and talk still persisted that business was not active. Indeed, the existence of the vigilance committee was the only circumstance that kept minds busy; their connection with it was for many more important than any other occupation.

On the fourth of June, Governor Johnson's proclamation appeared in the newspapers together with the orders of General Sherman. By the former, the district of San Francisco was declared in a state of insurrection and the soldiers of the Third, Fourth and Fifth Divisions ordered to hold themselves ready to suppress it. General Sherman's orders announced a call for volunteers, and recruiting was commenced at various places in the city and elsewhere. Several companies were equipped for service to the State. These measures did not frighten the vigilance committee. It placed its headquarters in a state of defense; erected a breastwork with loop-holes in front of the building; piled sand behind the breastwork and planted cannon; turned the building itself into an arsenal and a fort; set sentinels day and night at the breastwork, the entrances to the building and on the roof; and took every measure against a surprise attack, so as to be able to resist a possible

170

assault. At the same time, the Law and Order Party enlisted recruits and concluded military exercises. It all had a warlike aspect.

In the midst of all this excitement, a new bulkhead project was brought before the city council and approved by the aldermen in spite of the decided condemnation of any such project by the public. However, the project was stopped in its course by the intervening decision of the board of assistant aldermen and so again defeated. Even if there had been no such decision, it is hardly likely that the project of the bulkhead corporation would have become law.

On the ninth of June, General Sherman resigned and Volney E. Howard became his successor. Persons who were not at all connected with the vigilance committee tried to effect an understanding between the governor and the committee, have the proclamation rescinded and obtain an adjustment of the dispute by the dissolution of the vigilance committee. The attempt failed. At the same time, an address of the committee to the people was made public.

On the tenth, eleventh and fourteenth, there were mass-meetings at public places where the people expressed their opinion about the questions of the day. A meeting was called for the fourteenth where the views of those were made public whom the conduct of the vigilance committee fully satisfied, although they were not members of it. It was a very large assembly. Prominent lawyers addressed it and praised the conduct and purpose of the committee, and the meeting expressed its agreement with these opinions in several resolutions. A short time before, a large meeting was held at the Plaza by the opponents of the committee to gauge the strength of those in favor of the constitution, the laws, the courts, trial by jury and the right to a writ of habeas corpus; and at this meeting the committee was bitterly accused. This organization announced on the twentieth of the month that it had six thousand members and four thousand muskets. This was certainly an exaggeration, although no one could have any doubt that it was strong both in men and in weapons. There was soon an opportunity to show its strength.

On the twenty-first of June, an attack was made against the Law and Order committee, by a contingent of the Vigilance group under the leadership of a certain Hopkins, in order to arrest J. R. Maloney. During this incident, Hopkins and Terry (a judge of the Supreme Court) encountered each other and in the fight that ensued Hopkins was stabbed in the throat by the judge. Maloney, Terry and the rest of the Law and Order party fled to the arsenal at the corner of Dupont and Jackson Streets, near which the fight had broken out. The arsenal was immediately surrounded by members of the committee. Presently troops, in companies and battalions, appeared under arms. Very soon, by means of infantry, cavalry and artillery, they were masters of all the arsenals of the Law and Order Party. The committee's troops demanded the surrender of Judge Terry and his companions and, after a short delay, these gave themselves up as prisoners, since they had no chance of successful resistance. At the same time, the troops of the committee secured all the weapons in the arsenals; all those found in the arsenals were made prisoners and, together with the weapons, were taken to the committee's building. After these events, all attempts to oppose the committee in the city seemed useless.

The arrest of Judge Terry, as well as the circumstances that brought it about and accompanied it, enraged both sides, in the full sense of the word. Some demanded the dissolution of the committee, others the freeing of Terry, and still others his execution. In the midst of all this excitement, the executive body of the committee instituted its proceeding against Judge Terry. This lasted a long time and disgusted both parties. For a long time Hopkins' recovery was in doubt and upon this depended, as was generally admitted, Terry's life. The public found itself in a very difficult situation that was only a little less distressing than that of the judge's friends. Hopkins eventually recovered and the proceeding against Terry could be terminated. He was found guilty of some of the charges; but, upon the condition that he resign his post as judge, set free by the committee on August seventh.

This proceeding was quickly followed by another. On the twenty-fourth of July, Dr. Andrew Randall was shot in the bar-room of the St. Nicholas Hotel by one Hetherington who had often threatened him previously. Dr. Randall died after lying unconscious a day or two. The killing was intentional and executed in cold blood. The committee seized Hetherington, instituted proceedings against him, found him guilty and condemned him to death. It was particularly ready to do so because a few years before he had killed Dr. Balduin under circumstances that showed great ferocity on his part. On the thirtieth of July, Hetherington and another murderer, by name of Brace, were taken by the committee out of their cells, led to a scaffold in Davis Street and hanged. Brace had taken part in the murder of Captain Best near the Mission two years before. He was also suspected of having killed his companion in another crime — a certain Marion — in Alameda County. Hetherington conducted himself quietly on the scaffold, showed self-control and even wanted to make a speech, but was interrupted by Brace whose expressions and behavior were revolting and aroused disgust. Compared with the moral conceptions that this man had and the character that he displayed on that dreadful platform, such depravity as often shows itself here appeared to be virtue. There had been so many examples of wickedness and depravity that anything worse seemed almost impossible, and yet something new always came along that exceeded anything that had gone before. How low can a man sink!

On August eighteenth, the vigilance committee appeared in all its strength at a great parade and muster: it was the last act before its dissolution. About three thousand armed men arrayed themselves in ranks, were inspected by their officers and the executives of the committee and paraded through the principal streets of the city. They appeared as organized might. Soon afterwards the organization was dissolved and their rooms opened to the public, which visited them in the thousands.

It was feared, later, that the committee would re-assemble to save two of their members from the severity of the law. Durkee and Rand were indicted by the Federal grand jury for piracy because, on the committee's orders, they had taken by force, weapons belonging to the State from a small vessel in the bay. They were proceeded against under the law but absolved, and so, for the time being, every fear of another conflict with the courts vanished.

Chapter XXIII

EVENTS OF THE YEARS 1856 AND 1857

WITH THE DISSOLUTION OF THE VIGILANCE COMMITTEE, PEACE AND quiet descended. Little occurred since that time that is worth particular mention. Whatever else might claim some discussion or comment was swallowed up in the political excitement of the times, and we limit ourselves, accordingly, to minor information.

On a Sunday morning, the fifth of October, the effigy of the Rev. Dr. Scott, pastor of Calvary Church, was found hanging in front of the building with a rope around its neck. A strange sight! People had discovered that Dr. Scott was quite able to express his opinion about events in the city in an effective fashion; but this was not liked and it is to be supposed that this was the reason for the mischievous insult which, it may be added, could only dishonor its perpetrators. To hang a man in effigy in broad daylight would be a pitifully weak and contemptible way of expressing hate. Such an act is certainly contemptible if, in addition, as was the case here, it is perpetrated in darkness like a theft, or the robbery of an individual. Those who do this kind of thing have lost all shame except the shame of having their names known. It is like anonymous letters of insult and the like. The result is that since then the church of that esteemed gentleman has been thronged as never before. Oppression and persecution do not belong to the disposition of a free people.

The number of arrivals during the first three-quarters of the year reached the total of 23,511; of departures, 15,905; the result was an increase in population amounting to 7606. This was not a striking increase compared to earlier ones. An overland route from the Eastern states by means of a railway had become necessary for many reasons. California and San Francisco could not expect a share of the emigrants from the Atlantic states equal to those of other states and cities in view of the routes then in use. The journey around Cape Horn, or over the plains, is not only too long but also too expensive; likewise, the journey by steamers over two oceans and across the territory of a foreign and only half-civilized nation, a territory subject at all seasons to dangerous epidemics and contagious diseases as well as the dangers of highway-robbery and rebellion, is risky and uncertain. Besides, it takes too much time and for the class of immigrant that the city and land especially need — for the hard-working, respectable man with a family, for whom a few hundred dollars is the fruit of many years of bitter labor — it is too expensive. The month spent in travel is an additional loss that is not easily borne. A railway, uniting the Pacific and the Atlantic Oceans, would prove, of necessity, the only effective way by which the population of San Francisco and its state could be multiplied; by means of a railway the broad and rich lands of the State would be settled and made productive, factories would be built, and all of the land, city and State set upon the road of enduring prosperity for which its splendid natural gifts and its abundant productivity seem to entitle it.

The activity of the mint during the last two years and the first three-quarters of the current year shows the following results in coin and ingots. In 1854, it amounted to more than nine million dollars, of which more than five and a half-million was in ingots. The mintage amounted to almost twenty-four million: of this more than three million was in ingots. The mintage of silver during the past and present years amounts on the average to $170,000 — only a small yearly increase. The total value of the mintage for three years exceeds the sum of fifty-five million dollars. At times the activity of the mint was interrupted by a lack of acid. This, as well as the inadequate size of the mint, must reduce the output. It is easy to see that the erection of a much larger and more suitable building would certainly prove advantageous.

On October first, 1856, the first paper-mill in California began to operate. It was situated near Tomales Bay, about ten miles above Bolivas, and was built by Messrs. V. B. Post and Samuel B. Taylor. This undertaking proved to be very profitable and the paper of this mill was used by the newspaper publishers of San Francisco and preferred to imported paper.

On the seventh of this month there was an outrageous attempt to sink the new steamer *Orizaba* as it lay at the wharf at the foot of Washington Street. A malicious person came on board and opened the valves in the engine-room. The water poured in rapidly and in the morning, when the mischief was discovered, there were several feet of water in the hold. It was immediately pumped out and the valves closed and so the danger of sinking was avoided but the damage was considerable.

On the fifth of November, James Kennovan, a native American, showed his strength by his accomplishment in walking upon a platform for 106 hours without stopping. This was regarded as the best entertainment that had ever been offered. He surpassed himself a few months later — also in this city — by increasing his record by a few hours. Kennovan is now forty-seven years of age and is at present in England, where he is challenging the world to a walking-contest.

December first was the important day of the presidential election. The following was the official vote of the State:

Buchanan	51,925
Fillmore	35,113
Fremont	20,339

Fremont is a resident of Maripon County.

On December fifth, Maguire's new opera-house, the building of which was commenced on October fifteenth, was finished. The first performance took place on the evening of December sixth. José Y. Limantour was arrested on December tenth as the result of a complaint against him: it was asserted, and this was later shown to be true, that he had offered a false claim to land before the land commission.

The claim extended to a large part of the city of San Francisco, the island of Alcatraz and other property. This arrest aroused much bitterness in many parts of the city. He furnished $30,000 bail for his appearance before the court. A social gathering to honor Monsieur P. Dillon, formerly the French consul at this port, was held at the International Hotel on the evening of December fifteenth. It was a farewell festivity, shortly before his departure from California, and was crowded.

The divorce calendar of the District Court in San Francisco shows that 110 suits for divorce were filed during 1856. Of these, thirty-nine were granted shortly before the end of the year. In 1855 there were seventy-two suits for divorce pending and all were granted.

During 1856, 146 petitions of insolvency were filed; forty-two of these in the Fourth District Court and 104 in the Twelfth. The amounts involved were the following:

liabilities	$3,401,042
assets (claimed)	637,908
amount of failures	2,763,134

In the year 1855, the number of these petitions was 197, and the bankruptcies were much more important:

liabilities	$8,377,827
assets on hand	1,519,175
amount of failures	6,858,652

The list of non-residents shows that in 1856 the number of arrivals and those leaving by sea was as follows:

total of arrivals	29,630
departures	22,747
surplus of arrivals	6,883

Accordingly, the population was increased by such arrivals by 6,883 — a very unfavorable showing. About 8,000 were added to the population by land and brought with them, it is estimated, 25,000 to 30,000 head of cattle.

The grave-diggers of the city reported the total number of deaths in the city and environs of San Francisco, during the year 1856, as 1346 — 54 more than in the previous year and 359 less than in 1854. Of the dead, 292 were men, 460 boys, 119 women, 262 girls, 133 stillborn; and twenty-three were colored. In the course of the year, fifteen persons were killed or murdered; four were hanged by the vigilance committee and one by the civil authorities; sixty-two were drowned and there were forty-nine suicides. Of the dead, 622 were born in the United States and 727 in other lands.

The new year began with a meeting of the legislature at Sacramento on January fifth. During the session, David C. Broderick was elected United States senator for the long term and William M. Gwin for the short term. The annual report for 1856 of the superintendent of public instruction was read aloud: he reported that at the end of the year there were 316 schools in thirty-four counties; thirty of these in the county of San Francisco. In all, there were 26,160 children attending school; of these, 4751 in the city.

On the ninth of January the city was subject to a severe earthquake, which seemed to affect the whole State. It was first noticed in San Francisco at a quarter past eight in the morning; in Sacramento it occurred half an hour earlier, and San Diego and places along the whole south coast were affected about eight-thirty. It has been described by the oldest inhabitants as the most severe earthquake they could recall. In some places clocks stood still; cans and goods fell off the shelves; a little wooden house which stood at the corner of California and Market Streets was hurled several feet away from its original site. This, too, is part of the dangers of the country. Within the last five years no less than six earthquakes occurred in this city and its environs.

On January twenty-eighth, José Y. Limantour was brought to trial in the circuit court of the United States and found not guilty on the charge of perjury for which he had been indicted by the grand jury.

The seventh anniversary of the San Francisco Bible Society was celebrated on February first. Its report stated that the number of copies of the Bible distributed during the previous year amounted to 4815; 325 were in foreign languages, the rest in English; 2386 were given away free, the rest sold. In the evening, a destructive fire broke out in Washington Street near Kearney in the building next to the chemical laboratory of Dr. Lanzweert, and several wooden buildings with their contents were destroyed before the fire could be brought under control. The damage was estimated at $50,000.

At a meeting of the board of supervisors on February second, they refused to pay the amount claimed by the San Francisco Gas Company for lighting the streets and the City Hall. The result was that the gas was cut off and hall and streets remained for the time being in darkness. At later meetings of the board, everyone had to bring his own light with him that business might not be transacted in darkness.

We continue our account of events in the form of a diary. If one or another of these may be of slight importance, it will nevertheless contribute to the completion of the entire picture and many a reader will be grateful for it.

February fifth. Sixty-five men embarked on board the steamer *Sea-Bird* to reinforce the troops of Gandara in the Mexican state of Sonora. The original number recruited in this State amounted to eighty-six, but twenty-one of these withdrew at the roll-call. They were well provided with weapons and ammunition from the United States. Two distinct earthquake shocks were once more felt towards seven o'clock in the evening, and new scenes of terror were feared. This time, however, there was no damage and the shocks caused only fear.

February sixth. The Chamber of Commerce of San Francisco named a committee to petition for postage of no more than one cent for letters within the State and the reduction of the rate for letters by messenger, for by this time the mail had greatly increased in volume and the high postage was causing a falling off in business.

On February tenth the Seaman's Home on Front Street, between Pacific Street and Broadway, was dedicated with suitable ceremonies. The institution was placed under the care and supervision of the ladies of the Sailor's Friend Society.

March third. A fleet of clipper-ships and other vessels entered the bay. Among them were the clippers *War-Hawk, Morning Light, Wind, Beaver,* and *Harvey Birke,* as well as the Danish clipper *Cimber.* The latter made the trip from Liverpool in 106 days, the quickest that has ever been made from that port. It was built at Darmstadt, Germany, and does its builder credit, for it is one of the finest examples of the ship-building craft afloat.

June twenty-second. The annual meeting of the Masonic grand lodge of California was held in Masonic Hall and the following officials were elected and installed: Louis L. Mortimer, M.W.G.M.; Charles W. Parker, D.G.M.; Wm. Isaacs, G.G.W.; Henry C. Cornist, Jr., G.W.; Anthony Osborne, G.T.; James G. Marshall, S.S.; R. W. Freeman, Cor. S.; John P. Scott; G. Tyler. The meeting lasted for three days.

The Fourth of July was celebrated by a small municipal parade in the city. This ever-memorable day in the history of America is one of great significance and of great importance. As the anniversary of the Declaration of Independence, it is usually the most important holiday of the American people and is celebrated by noisy, unrestrained jubilation. The celebration commenced at a quarter of five with a salvo by the Old California Guard under Captain Johns, and immediately the bells of the churches and the fire-houses loudly proclaimed the

178

return of the anniversary of American independence. Stores, banks, markets and all other places of business were closed and the city was completely taken up with the holiday and in celebrating it.

July ninth. There was a landslide of seven hundred tons of earth at the government's works at Alcatraz Island and two workmen, Daniel Pewter and Jacob Unger, were buried under it.

July twenty-sixth and twenty-seventh were days of song. The first annual jubilee of the United German Music Societies of the State was was celebrated by a great concert, a picnic and a ball. It was delightful from beginning to end. The tickets sold amounted to $3408.

August ninth was "the hot day." At 12 o'clock the thermometer in the city rose from 102 to 115 degrees in the shade. The sun was so strong that in many gardens the leaves were curled like hair.

August fifteenth. The public building known as the Metropolitan Theater, mentioned above, was destroyed by fire. It was discovered at 8 o'clock and burned until midnight; all the interior of the building was destroyed. The cisterns in the immediate neighborhood were quickly drained dry in the evening and all thought of saving the building was abandoned. This temple of the muses belonged to Messrs. H. Hentsch and L. E. Ritter. They suffered a loss of $80,000, for the building was not insured.

September fifth. The cornerstone of the new German hospital on Brannan Street was laid with suitable ceremonies; the Freemasons, Oddfellows and all other charitable institutions, as well as the German Fusiliers, took part. N. Green Curtis, M.W.G.M., of the Freemasons, with the assistance of the officials of the Grand Lodge, performed the dedication ceremony.

The most splendid spectacle that was ever seen on the Pacific coast was the celebration of the centennial of Lafayette's birthday on September seventh. Preparations for it had been made months before and committees named for every aspect of the celebration. A cannon was fired at daybreak and in no time flags were waving and fluttering in the streets; every flagpole and every vessel was decorated, several quite magnificently. The pavillion of the Mechanics' Institute was ornamented from every corner to the top of the cupola with hundreds of flags of all nations. The banks and stores were closed; work of every sort was put off; the streets were crowded; and every window and balcony of the main streets was occupied by women and children. It took several hours to arrange the procession and to furnish all that was necessary for it. In the meantime, various companies and societies marched through the streets with suitable flags and music. At ten o'clock the procession commenced. It was divided in six parts; each was under a marshal and his assistants; the procession as a whole was led by P. J. Haven as marshal-in-chief. Almost 3500 persons took part and almost the entire military force, the fire department, the Masonic and Oddfellow societies and other charitable organizations appeared in it, as well as officials of the United States, of the State and of the country, and the foreign consuls. After the procession had marched through the city for two hours, it halted in the square in front of the Oriental Hotel: this was the most suitable place in the city and large enough for so great a gathering. Upon the roomy platform erected here, the foreign consuls, the officials of the United States, and the representatives of the Press took their places; M. S. Satham, Esquire (the present United States senator), delivered a fiery, spirited address, and F. Soulé, Esquire, recited a poem suitable for the occasion. The ceremonies were over at five o'clock. Thereupon the various societies went to various places and broke up into small groups. Those days will be ever memorable in the annals of San Francisco.

For December thirty-first, we review again circumstances characteristic of the life and activities of the city and find that the number of those who declared their insolvency amounted to 130 during the course of the year: liabilities, $2,719,497; assets remaining, $271,507; deficit, $2,447,990. The number of petitions for divorce in the city during 1857: 106. Forty cases were decided in favor of the petitioners.

The total of land claims under Mexican grants in the Northern District of California amounted to 426; 211 of these were decided in favor of the claimant. These claims affected, all in all, more than 2,469,338 acres, each, on the average, somewhat more than 11,000 acres. Of the remaining claims, seventy-two were rejected or completely refused; seventy are as yet not decided, and the rest have been appealed to the highest court of the United States.

The fines imposed in the police-court during the last thirteen months amount to $34,686. Of this, $20,560 has been collected.

Chapter XXIV

THE YEAR 1858: TRADE AND INDUSTRY

THE YEAR 1858 BEGAN WITH THE OPENING OF A CHARITABLE INSTITU-
tion near the docks. On January second, the new German hospital
was dedicated and presented to the board of directors by the building
committee. It consists of a beautiful two-story brick building. The institution will act as a home for poor and helpless Germans who, sick
and infirm, will find here a ready reception. The cost of the lot and
the erection of the building itself amounted to $17,500 and was de-
frayed almost completely by the Germans of the city.

January tenth. The French ship *Asia* has left for a voyage to Hong-
Kong. It had the embalmed bodies of Chinese on board, prepared in a
peculiar fashion and shipped as freight, that they might rest in the soil
of their fatherland. All true Chinese regard the sending home of their
dead to their own Flowery Kingdom as a sacred duty. In the course of
three days, $900,000 was withdrawn from the banking-house of Tal-
lant and Hilde. This case alone shows how much unused capital there
is in San Francisco.

January twenty-seventh. There was a duel between Mr. A. H. Rapp,
an associate publisher of *Le Phare*, and Mr. Thiele, publisher of the
Spectator. They used short swords as weapons and Mr. Thiele received
a severe wound in his leg. Mr. Rapp was only slightly wounded. The
cause of the duel is not known in detail.

This year and the following passed without important events, and
I found little to notice, in spite of much trouble and research.

On January 29, 1859, the annual dinner in memory of the services —
theological as well as political — of Thomas Paine, was held at the
Hotel Richelieu.

On September ninth there was another earthquake. This did not
prevent Judge Terry from challenging Senator Broderick to a duel
because of insulting remarks made by Broderick about Terry in June
of the current year.

September thirteenth. Judge Terry and Broderick met again in a
deadly duel. It cost them both their lives. At the first exchange of

shots, the latter fell mortally wounded to the ground, struck in the right breast by the bullet of Terry's pistol. Mr. Broderick suffered for three days and then died, deeply mourned by all California.

October sixteenth. Winfield Scott, lieutenant-general of the United States Army, arrived on his way to the disputed island of San Juan and was received with great enthusiasm.

December thirtieth. The calendar of insolvents for the year 1859 was: petitioners, 56; liabilities, $827,641; assets, $96,831; petitions granted, 35.

Divorce calendar for the year 1859: petitioners, 69 (wives, 56; husbands, 13); petitions granted, 38.

Total number of insane in 1859: 90.*

January 30, 1860. A monster of a document, 247 feet in length and provided with 11,000 signatures, the beginning containing a protest against Chinese "coolieism" in the State, was sent on the twenty-fourth of March to the legislature in Sacramento. The clipper *Andrew Jackson* arrived after a trip of eighty-nine days, according to reports, in the best time yet from New York.

March twenty-ninth. The United States steamer *Sowhatan* brought the embassy from Japan, consisting of twenty delegates and twelve subalterns. For a while, they were the heroes of the day, but the inhabitants of San Francisco were soon tired of them, for they bore too many resemblances to the children of the Flowery Kingdom who are hated because of their dirty ways.

June twenty-fifth. The cornerstone of a new Masonic temple was laid by the Freemasons with ceremonies to celebrate the occasion. The lot and building will cost $162,000.

With this we end the list of events and turn to the consideration of trade and business, of the schools and of other institutions.

Trade and Business

Figures provide an insight into business, trade and commerce better than any words. Accordingly, we enumerate all the various kinds of occupations and the number of those in each:

bookkeepers	6	assayers	8
business advisers	4	astrologer	1
stores selling farm implements	14	lawyers	296
drug-stores	48	auctioneers	23
architects	17	bakers and bakeries	76
artesian-well diggers	1	banks	17

---

*   This probably means either the number of proceedings to have a person adjudged insane or such adjudications. *Tr.*

billiard parlors*	13	carvers of taps	2
boarding-houses**	161	butchers	89
workers in brass	5	preparer of caviar	1
bookbinders	8	chemical works	3
booksellers	30	chemists	11
shoes and boots (wholesale)	16	fortune-tellers	4
bathing-establishments	16	chronometer makers	4
beds and bedding sellers	7	cigar dealers and importers	26
bedstead manufacturers	2	cigarmakers	23
bell-founders	3	cigar retailers	91
billiard-ball manufacturers	3	clergymen	46
billiard-cue manufacturers	1	makers of clothing and mantillas	3
billiard-table manufacturers	11	importers of clocks and watches	3
tinsmith	54	clothing (wholesale)	33
pulley and pump manufacturers	3	clothing (retail)	116
wooden type manufacturers	1	oiled clothing	1
carpet manufacturers	11	importers of clothing	
carriage and wagon agencies	5	and woolens	4
carriage and wagon		kerosense, lamps, etc.	6
storage-places	5	coal-yards	19
carriage and wagon		coffee-roasters	5
manufacturers	23	coffin dealers	3
copperplate engravers and gliders	9	collectors	4
shoes and boots (retail)	73	butter importers	4
shoe-and-bootmakers and		cabinet-makers	22
repairers	128	camphor distillers	7
dealer in bottles	1	capmakers	6
cigarbox-makers	2	carpenters and builders	134
jewelry-box maker	1	coppersmiths	12
makers of salesmen's cases	3	rope maker	1
paper box makers	7	cork cutter	1
brass-founders (polishers)	6	corkscrew maker	1
beer brewers	26	corset makers	2
brick kilns	7	makers of costumes	2
brokers (generally)	53	dealers in earthenware	
brokers of houses	3	and glass	20
licensed business brokers	29	cutlers	13
freightage brokers	12	dealers in daguerreotype	
real-estate brokers	67	material	3
stock-and-money brokers*	18	daguerreotypists	16
broom-makers	4	dentists	37
brush manufacturer	1	molder of diamond letters	1

---

* Although every saloon — whose number is very great — has a billiard-table, under this heading of 13 are included places in which several billiard-tables are to be found.

** In addition to these regular boarding-houses, there are a large number of private boarding-places.

* Many of those designated here as brokers of this or that are engaged in some business or other and are brokers with their surplus funds.

distillers	3	interpreters	4
makers of doors, window-frames and window-blinds	8	iron railings, fences, etc.	2
		Japanese goods	1
makers of iron doors and shutters	5	jewelry (importers)	13
tailors	63	manufacturers of jewelry	17
fringe makers	2	jewelers	49
confectioneries	17	hairdressers	106
commission-agents	36	ironmongers	37
notaries	2	saddlery	26
coopers	26	hat and cap factories	6
flour dealers	28	importers of hats and caps	10
force-pump seller	1	hat makers	24
foundries	10	hay and grain	7
fruit stores	79	wool and skins	13
fur dealers	2	dealers in hops	1
dealers in furnaces and andirons	6	hotels	68
dealers in household utensils for men	21	rubber	2
		ink factories	2
dealers in household utensils for women	1	agencies for instruments	4
		insurance	11
furniture dealers	49	opticians	5
public gardeners	4	oyster-saloons	20
makers of gas-pipes	11	painters (house, sign and wagon)	65
gas-works	2	portrait painters	8
glass cutter	1	painters in oil and on glass	18
dealer in glassware	1	pawnshops	9
glue factory	1	doctors	173
maker of gold-leaf	1	printers (7 steam presses)	24
makers of gold pens	2	dealers in ink	6
granite yards	4	laundries	34
grocers (wholesale)	42	dealers in leather	6
grocers (retail)	348	lime and cement	4
armorers	12	liquor dealers (wholesale)	77
drugs (wholesale)	10	liquor dealers (retail)	388
dry goods (wholesale)	44	lithographers	5
dry goods (retail)	79	locksmiths	10
dyers	4	lodging-house keepers	40
dyes	1	agents for lotteries	2
electrotyper	1	timber	35
embroidery supplies	8	sewing-machines	11
machine makers	9	machinists	32
furnace cleaners	7	marbleyards	7
engravers	41	markets	66
expressmen	5	commercial agents	2
fashionable articles (wholesale)	26	merchants (commissionmen for products and glassware)	363
fashionable articles (retail)	28		
maker of taps for barrels	1	midwives	16
feed stores	27	milliners	39
fishing tackle manufacturer	1	flour mills	10
fishmongers	14	paper mill	1
information bureaus	9	rice mills	2

publishers	4	tanners	6
keepers of restaurants	101	teachers	61
riggers	6	tobacco dealers (wholesale)	13
roofers	10	upholsterers	29
rope-makers	12	veterinaries	6
makers of sewing-machines	6	watchmakers	44
shipwrights	19	watch-case makers	2
forwarding-agents and		dramatic artists	17
dealers in ships	41	makers of wicker-work	7
silverplaters	5	salt mills	3
livery-stables	48	newspapers and newspaper agents	12
dealers in stationery	23	dealers in wood and coal	71
warehouses	34	public notaries	20
stoves and tinware	58	nurseries for plants	6
tailors and dealers in			
woolen cloth	136		

Chapter XXV

Statistics about Business Enterprises and Improvements

We consider it the task of a faithful reporter to provide statistics of the enterprises of the State and its progress, based upon reliable sources. With this in mind we have paid attention to all institutions intended for the general good, to all enterprises, and to all branches of industry. From the compilation thus made, we present the following.

The endurance and energy displayed in the digging for gold are truly astonishing and deserve mention first of all. The gold diggers did not limit themselves to gold. We find, in addition to their herculean exertions in that respect, that they dug ditches and canals extending for 5632 miles to bring water from the streams to the dry ditches below. This work was carried out at an expenditure in money and labor amounting to $1,487,200 — at an average of $2,500 a mile. El Dorado County has the greatest mileage of ditches, and Tuolumne County the greatest expenditure.

Almost $800,000 has been invested in digging for quartz. The number of mills add up to 210: this does not include arastras. They cost $2,300,000, and the machinery for them $3,785,000.

There are 170 flour mills in the State; ninety-seven of these are driven by steam and seventy-three by water. They have 330 sets of mill-stones and can produce 300,000 barrels of flour annually. The total value of this industry is estimated at $1,800,000.

California possesses 405 sawmills; of these 186 are driven by steam and 218 by water. The building of these mills cost $2,810,000. Under favorable circumstances they can produce 550,000 feet of timber annually. This approximate calculation does not include cutting mills.

The State has thirty miles of railway, including Fremont's railway in Mariposa, costing $1,400,000. The capital spent on spanning rivers amounts to $263,000 and that for toll-bridges to $910,000.

The telegraph-line, now spanning the State, extends for 1097 miles, including the side lines. The amount of capital spent for this has not been made known.

As against this bright side, there is the fact — throwing its shadow on the soul of California — that there are already five distilleries in the State, in which $200,000 has been invested, and ninety-five breweries which have a working capital of $250,000.

With respect to factories, progress has also been made. There are three starch and three lime factories; three potteries which produce enough to supply the demand of the State; eight broom factories; three factories making articles of wicker-work; two match factories; two manufacturers of perfumery; twenty-six tanneries; several soap and candle factories; three factories making macaroni and noodles; a woolen mill that is able to produce forty pairs of blankets daily; a rope-work and a place where tow is made; twenty-four iron foundries; two paper-mills; a sugar refinery; a glass-works and a place for cutting glass; a factory for producing acids and others that need not be detailed.

The organization of fire-companies went on rapidly. The California Engine Company was organized on September 7, 1850, and George M. Garwood was elected foreman. On the tenth of that month, the Monumental Engine Company was organized with George H. Hossefrosz as foreman. It consisted, for the most part, of former members of the fire-department of Baltimore. The Knickerbocker Engine Company was organized on October seventeenth, James H. Biller, foreman. On February 22, 1852, the Vigilant Engine Company was organized with Martin B. Roberts as foreman. In the same year, on September fourteenth, the Pennsylvania Fire Company was organized. H. S. Brown was elected foreman. For the most part, it consisted of former members of the Philadelphia fire-department. The Columbia

Engine Company was organized on October twelfth of that year. John D. Rower became foreman. On October twenty-fifth, the Crescent Engine Company was organized and elected James Herbert as foreman.

On June 1, 1853, the Lafayette Hook-and-Ladder Company was organized, of which H. A. Cobb was elected foreman. It consisted, for the most part, of citizens of French descent. On October second of that year, the Pacific Engine Company was organized, Brierly Tackley foreman. The Manhattan Engine Company was organized on October 13, 1854, and David L. Beck became the foreman. On the seventh of February of the same year the Young America Fire Company was organized and elected James G. Dennison foreman. The Volunteer Fire Company was organized on the seventeenth of June of that year, Caleb Clapp foreman. On the twenty-second of February, 1855, the Tiger Engine Company was organized and elected Caleb Clapp as foreman.

Those mentioned are all the fire-brigades that at present belong to the fire-department. The Sansome Hook-and-Ladder Company was organized in 1852, but dissolved its organization in 1859. In 1859 the Independence Engine Company of St. Anna's Valley was organized, but did not join the department. An independent firemen's association was organized in 1858 with George H. Hossefrosz as president.

The first chief-engineer of the department was F. D. Kohler. He was followed by George H. Hossefrosz, Charles S. Duane, James E. Hultmann, F. E. R. Whitney and David Scannel in that post of honor.

Since the organization of the fire-department no member of it has ever failed to show the utmost activity and readiness in answering a call for help, and in countless cases they have heroically ventured into danger to save life or property. By day and by night, in sunshine or in storm, the firemen of San Francisco have dashed out to help their fellow citizens at the first signal of fire and in that task accomplished truly herculean deeds without compensation or any thought of gain — except that satisfaction which every man of noble feelings has when he knows that he has done his duty. The value of the property that the firemen of the population of San Francisco have saved during the last ten years has been estimated at one hundred million dollars. Several of them have paid with their lives in their praiseworthy efforts while doing their duty. How necessary such companies have been is shown by the fact that, as far as records indicate, since the organization of the Empire Engine Company in 1849 the firemen have offered their services at 3900 fires so that, on the average, there is a fire alarm every day.

The department has established a fund for the beneficent purpose of assisting members who have become sick and unable to serve, as well as a fund for decorating the graves of members and for lightening the burden of the funeral expenses of those who die in needy circumstances.

The fire-department of San Francisco consists of fourteen engine companies and three hook-and-ladder companies. It has 950 members. The length of its hose is 12,000 feet. The outlay of the department for repairs and so forth during 1859 and 1860 amounted to $35,000.

The region where gold has been found extends from the farthest point of the northern boundary of the State to Kern River in the south: it is about five hundred miles in length and from forty to one-hundred-and-fifty miles in width. It covers an expanse of about 14,000 square miles. According to the most exact calculation, the annual production of gold for the last ten years has amounted to sixty million dollars. However, it is certainly to be expected that in the next fifty years the annual production of gold will exceed that sum. Gold worth 660 millions of dollars has been taken from the soil of California since the first discovery of gold to the thirty-first of December, 1859. We may with all certainty count upon 550 millions of dollars worth of gold for every decade of the future.

Silver was discovered in several parts of the State. The silver mines in the counties of Mariposa and San Diego were productive. Silver ore is also to be found in no insignificant amounts in the counties of Santa Barbara, Santa Clara and El Dorado, and promises to become a profitable asset and a significant addition to the prosperity of the State. Lately, some extensive deposits of silver have been discovered at Washoe in the territory of Utah. Several millions have already been spent to take advantage of the ore and thousands have streamed to Washoe and Carson where the deposits of silver are said to extend for miles.

In 1859, eighty-three companies for mining gold and silver were incorporated in California.

Copper. Rich deposits of this metal have been found in the counties of El Dorado, Placer, Shasta, Calaveras and San Joaquin. Some have been worked with good results and others are now about to be exploited. Although the wealth that has been gained from the deposits of this metal has at yet amounted to little, nevertheless they certainly promise a significant addition to the prosperity of the land.

Iron is to be found in quantities, more or less, from one end of the coast-line to the other. The ore is rich enough in some places to cover the cost of exploiting it. Ore, 80 per cent of it pure iron, has been discovered in Placer County.

Copperas (ferrous). This was found by natives in the neighborhood of the city of Santa Cruz in great quantity. Dr. John B. Trask asserts that an area of several square miles is rich in this metal and that the day is not far off when Santa Cruz will be famous for its output of this metal as it is already for its vegetables.

Platinum, according to Dr. Trask, is to be found in as wide an area as gold, and he asserts that the value of the gold mines will be increased by at least 25 per cent by this metal. That it is to be found so widely in all of California, and in such quantity, may well support an expectation that in the future it will become an important source of wealth.

Chromium is to be found in great quantities in the northern mines. It is worth $80 a ton of unprocessed ore and, according to Dr. Trask, many tons of it may easily be obtained in the State. It is to be found in great quantity at Nelson Creek near its junction with Feather River, at the mountain ridge between the northern and middle forks of the American River; in the Coyote mines near Nevada; and at Hart River, two miles below Nevada. It is chiefly used for coloring porcelain. It is also much employed in dyes and rouge.

Nickel. This article, which is a by-product of the manufacture of hardware and household utensils from German silver, is to be found in important quantities in the counties of Contra Costa and Monterey. The scarcity of this metal, which has been often felt, makes the discovery of this ore in California important. From its wide distribution in these counties, it may be assumed that it exists in sufficient quantity to justify a business enterprise and there is not the slightest doubt that money so spent will in a short time yield a revenue.

Quicksilver. The quicksilver mines of California are unquestionably the richest and most productive in all the world. Without exaggeration, they alone can fully supply the demand. At present, the largest mine — which has also been completely explored — is that of New Almaden in Santa Clara County. When it is worked, it produces annually more than a million pounds of quicksilver — worth $400,000. The New Idria, Guadalupe, and Enriquita mines at present produce on the average two million pounds every year and, now that the openings of the mines have been enlarged so that the quicksilver has become easier to dig, they are in a position to yield still more. In addition, mines have been discovered in Napa County that are rich in quicksilver. The production of quicksilver of all the mines that at present are fully worked will amount to at least three million dollars annually, figuring 30 per cent to the pound.

Sulphur. Rich deposits of this mineral are to be found in the counties of San Luis Obispo, Santa Barbara and Los Angeles. Their yield is rich and plentiful.

Gypsum is to be found in abundant quantities in Santa Cruz and other districts of the State and will likewise yield a rich contribution to the productivity of the land.

Salt. This article, which plays so great a part in housekeeping, is obtainable in great quantity in this State. The Pacific salt-works in Los Angeles can produce each year more than 1500 tons, and the salt produced in the neighborhood of San Francisco Bay amounts to six hundred tons annually.

Saltpeter exists in great quantities in Santa Cruz County.

Borax. This article is derived from a great lake in Napa County. At present it produces more than two hundred pounds daily, but this can be increased by the use of suitable machinery. Many are absolutely convinced that this lake will produce enough borax to supply all of the United States. In that case, its value as an article for export would be immeasurably greater.

Coal. At present there has been little successful coal-mining in this State, although it is known that coal is to be found in many places. It is believed that in the northern counties, as well as in the neighborhood of the San Joaquin River, mining of coal would be very successful, but inasmuch as means of transportation is lacking these mines must remain as yet unused.

Marble. Great quantities of excellent marble are to be found in the counties of El Dorado, Calaveras, Tuolumne and Solano. The marble obtained from a vein in the last-named county is especially suitable for use in household furniture.

Alabaster is found in considerable quantity in Monterey County. Its quality is said to be excellent and to rival that of the finest Italian kind.

A kind of quartz, from which the excellent mill-stones known as "burr stones" are made, is to be found in quantity in a cliff near the Pit River in Klamath County. It promises to become an article of great value for California.

Limestone. There is no limit to the possibility of gain for the State as a result of its limestone, because in all parts of the State great quantities may be quarried.

Asbestos. This mineral is to be found in the counties of Contra Costa and Tuolumne and may also, it is possible, prove to be a source of profit.

Tin. In Nevada County, quartz has been found containing a metal that an assayer has declared to be tin.

Diamonds. Not long ago, a stone was found on a mining-claim in Butte County that a jeweler of Croville took to be a diamond. Two stones were found in another place and the owner sent them to New York for examination: these were likewise pronounced to be diamonds.

With respect to the mines in Washoe County, we offer the following report taken from a German newspaper in California: The *Territorial Enterprise* is exuberant with joy over the richness of the Washoe mines. If the report is not exaggerated, the treasure which the mountains along the Washoe valley hold must be immeasurable. The newspaper says in its description of Mt. Davidson that the Mt. Davidson Company has now advanced its tunnel four hundred feet and has already found in pieces of rock unmistakable evidence that it is near a rich vein of ore. Mt. Davidson lies 300 feet above Silver City and Gold Hill. It may be assumed, therefore, that water will be found on this mountain and in such quantity that the company will be able, not only to provide its own mining-works with it, but also the ore-mills in the places named. The tunnel of the company has already passed through several veins of rock containing good ore and the discovery of other ore, just as rich, is to be expected, for experience has long since shown that the Comstock vein is not at all the only one that the Washoe mines have to offer. It is even assumed that Mt. Davidson together with the surrounding mountains forms, as it were, a gigantic warehouse in which lie stored precious ores that now will gradually be extracted.

The tunnel of the Mt. Davidson Company is to extend for 2500 feet. It is six feet six inches in height and four feet six inches wide and, as stated above, has been advanced four hundred feet. The company plans another tunnel, three hundred feet below this one, to be three to six thousand feet in length, depending upon circumstances.

Thus we see how rich and full of hope the future of California is, even if one day no more gold should be found.

Chapter XXVI

PLACES OF ENTERTAINMENT

WHERE THERE IS LABOR THERE MUST BE RECREATION; AND MAN RE-quires after exertion and toil the pleasure of rest and the rest of pleasure. It is therefore natural that in a land of activity and unremitting work, places of amusement soon make their appearance. Strangely enough, the city of San Francisco would not have many of which it could be proud and which, indeed, it could not dispense with, were it not for the German element in its population. For the Germans brought over with them their love of pleasure and distraction which must be found socially: the love of music and of athletic exercise. It is to their tastes that the Americans have to be thankful for the pleasure-grounds of Russ' Garden, Pacific Garden, People's Garden and, in recent times, Hayes' Park.

The first mentioned began the series of amusement-places. It was opened by Christian Russ who arrived in California in 1846 with Stevenson's regiment. He gave up the profession of arms and established himself at the place that now bears his name; and he lived there until his death three years ago. In this garden the first German May festival was celebrated and it is still one of the leading places of amusement. In the manner of their arrangement most of these gardens are alike: they have swings, horizontal bars and other equipment for gymnastics; nor are roomy halls for dancing and rooms for refreshment lacking. On Sundays they are crowded and gay. Whoever has worked hard during the week takes his pleasure on that evening in music and dancing, with turns at athletic exercises and drinking lager beer. To the credit of the Germans who celebrate their May festival here and other festivities, it should be mentioned that at such occasions there is no violence or disorder. The spirit of gaiety and pleasure reigns supreme and they do not let glum sorrow in. The useful influence exercised by these places has shown itself in the spirit of contentment and happiness that animates those who frequent them and in the glow of good health that every feature expresses. The people of San Francisco would be the better for it if they had more such places of amusement, where everyone may go to refresh himself after a hard day's work and to indulge in exercises that are designed to preserve strength and vigor and to leave the spiritual faculties fresh and undamaged.

"The Willows" is a beautiful recreation center in the suburbs. It lacks a dancing-school and a gymnastic establishment. The absence of these, however, is fully compensated for by the shady walks that have been laid out to wind in and out of lovely groves of trees with thick foliage.

Since the opening of the Market Street railway, Hayes' Park with its peaceful spaces has attracted thousands. The proprietors have done what they could for the amusement of their guests: they have orchestral concerts, installations for playing ball and for bowling, shooting-galleries and other arrangements to make the visit enjoyable for the public. Plenty of tables and chairs have been placed in a beautiful little wood close by, and nothing is lacking for comfort.

In addition to the two places mentioned, there is the Ocean House which offers the pleasure of a drive along the shore. It is most enjoyable to watch the play of the waves and to listen to the eternal, continuous murmur, now soft, now loud! One is never weary of listening to that unceasing song, as indeed one is never weary of nature and of hearing the continuous lamentation and moaning for the loss of those who sleep their eternal sleep beneath the waves.

The Press

Having discussed places of amusement, let us take a look at the Press. These two have enough in common to justify consideration in this order.

Periodicals appear in California in great number. It is difficult to judge their merit, or lack of it, and the less said the better. Their owners are tireless in gathering the events of the day. No scrap of news, no matter how unimportant or worthless, is overlooked. From early morning until late at night the reporters are on the hunt for news: anything that sounds strange, that arouses astonishment or is sensational, is closest to their hearts; and it must be confessed that they heap up a monstrous amount. But it consists only of the day's gossip.

The number of periodicals appearing in the State amount to 118. Of these twenty-three are dailies. Four appear twice a week; five are monthlies; one is a quarterly; one appears every three weeks, and the rest are weeklies. Two dailies and two weeklies are in French; two dailies and one weekly are in German; another daily is in Spanish and a weekly in Italian. In addition, there is a Chinese newspaper that appears as often as news arrives from the Flowery Kingdom. Of the dailies, thirteen are published in San Francisco, four in Sacramento, three in Marysville, two in Stockton, and one in Nevada. The monthlies and the quarterly as well as two of the weeklies appear in San Francisco. Two of the weeklies are devoted to the law and two to Jewish learning. One of these, the *Weekly Gleaner*, has appeared for five years now; Dr. Julius Eckmann is the publisher. The other, *The Faithful Messenger of the Pacific*, only a recent addition, is edited by the Rev. H. M. Bien.

During the last five years, five publications of San Francisco have discontinued and thirteen new ones have appeared.

When one considers the haste with which people rush for newspapers, one is apt to think that this is a very profitable business. However, such is not the case. On the contrary, it is one of the least profitable businesses in the State. We doubt very much that more than a third of the newspapers appearing in English in the city of San Francisco cover their expenses. Another third just about make a modest profit, and that is due to an enviable circulation, which other papers do not enjoy.

It is impossible for the Press, under such circumstances, to assume the lofty, proud and independent attitude which is proper to it. Lacking in means and spiritual strength, the Press has become fawning and sycophantic; it seeks to gain profit from bowing and scraping, and on the whole the San Francisco Press has deteriorated into being nothing but a weak echo of the whims and fancies of anyone able to give it support — however little it may be. That newspaper which, under all circumstances, thinks for itself and acts accordingly; which presumes to express its own opinion without first troubling itself about that of its leading patrons, will soon feel the impropriety of such conduct. All newspapers appearing in California, with the exception of the monthly periodicals, carry the colors of a definite party and its leaders; they have no regard whatever for the state of mind of the public, do not try to guide it or direct it, and do not trouble themselves at all to reach a higher status than that of a trader in news. Many of the owners of newspapers involve themselves, in fact, in plans that would only be injurious to the public if ever carried out, and use their power to defend aims that are as disadvantageous as they are unjust. If an insignificant, unknown man, who is, however, rich, takes it into his head to become an outstanding personality and a candidate for an office — naturally the income from which averages several thousand dollars annually — he first bribes a publisher to laud his merits in ostentatious and charlatanlike notices, known as "puffs." If he wants to make certain of a following, he has a paper come out as an undertaking at his own expense and supports his own pretensions in the columns of his own paper. What has been said, in all truth, about the newspapers of

California and their conduct is true to a certain extent of every other section and state of the United States.

There are, of course, honorable exceptions, but unfortunately very few. No one turns to the Press if he wishes to read a powerful expression of a thought; no one expects the Press to be an agent in spreading noble ideas or to furnish an extensive review of questions of the day; it is known that all that the Press does is to fill its pages with cheap commonplaces and superficial paragraphs. If a question of the day arises, a writer must, of necessity, first study how much it can be made to contribute to his newspaper's "pocket"; and, since he has no further scope and dares not extend his usual sphere of activity beyond the prescribed narrow limits, the subject is treated superficially, as well as possible. Under such circumstances, the Press, naturally, cannot exert any moral influence. By way of an extraordinary exception, we must mention the *Evening Bulletin*. It has great influence and is free of all the base vulgarities that characterize many other newspapers.

From the not very cheering aspect of the Press we turn to the more encouraging appearance of the educational system. It gives me great pleasure to be able to congratulate the citizens of San Francisco upon the good state of their system of education. Their schools are making progress upon the wide and useful field that lies before them — progress that is not transitory but enduring and forever valuable. Unlike the public schools of many cities of the East or even of European lands (where only the poor are taught in public schools), the public schools of San Francisco are attended by children of all classes of society. The well-to-do and the influential as well as the poor are rivals of equal rank in acquiring a higher education and the upbringing that is here enjoyed; there is no separation between them.

The number of pupils in the public schools amounts to 6304; the disproportionate daily attendance figure is, on the average, 2830. The total number of boys and girls from four to eighteen years of age, according to the last census, is 7767; the total of boys and girls who have not yet reached the age of four, 6091. The total number of children of all ages is 13,858; the total number of girls between four and eighteen, 3882. There are 341 orphans in the city.

There are thirteen public schools in San Francisco, as well as a Chinese school and a school for Negroes.

It is quite impressive to find almost every nationality represented in these schools. There are pupils from scarcely known continents and every island of the Indies and the Pacific.

Industrial School. This school, or rather house of refuge for young law-breakers, was established by an act of the legislature in 1858.

It is supported by private donations in addition to the thousand dollars received every month from the city and State as a sustaining fund. The expenses of the school department are paid for out of the school fund of the city of San Francisco. The total number of children taken in up to March 1861, was 65. Of these, only one was committed by his own father; sixty-four were sent there by the police-judge. Three of them are Negroes, sixty-two white; five of them are girls and sixty boys. In age they are divided as follows (in so far as, in many cases, their age may be judged by appearance):

Age	No.	Age	No.
three years old,	1	thirteen years old,	11
five years old,	1	fourteen years old,	9
seven years old,	3	fifteen years old,	7
nine years old,	2	sixteen years old,	8
ten years old,	1	seventeen years old,	7
eleven years old,	6	eighteen years old,	4
twelve years old,	4		

The youth of San Francisco is very well represented and could furnish a much larger contingent, for there are plenty of rascals who would be much better off in the Industrial School. Parents (naturally, only those who are thoughtless and yet have the misfortune to have children) aim too little at the fulfilment of their obligation, and so it is nothing new if little boys are found guilty in the police-court of theft and other petty crimes.

Private Schools

San Francisco has, likewise, several excellent private schools.

Saint Ignatius College is a Catholic institution, founded in October 1855. It has about seventy students. The subjects taught consist of the ancient and modern languages and the higher classical studies. The number of professors at present is seven. It was the first college in San Francisco to be chartered.

The University of the Pacific is a medical institution with six professors. The lectures are conducted with the utmost order and regularity.

San Francisco College was founded in March 1854. It offers all that is necessary for an education to be found in a university and, besides, is free of all sectarian influence. It has a well selected library and complete equipment for all scientific experiments.

Ladies Institute of San Francisco. This institution has enjoyed, since the beginning of 1855, a blessed activity and is under the direction of Madam M. B. Swedenshierna.

With this we leave these new plants with best wishes for their continued thriving and blossoming.

It is a remarkable phenomenon, well worthy of attention, that California, in proportion to its population, has more cases of insanity than any other land. Hardly a day or two passes that one does not hear of one or two cases in some part of the State and that the unfortunate victim of this frightful affliction has been sent to the insane asylum in Stockton. The shining hopes, the dreams of gold and wealth, which enticed those who were far away to California, may have led more than one victim to insanity.

The average annual number of mentally sick sent to the above institution during the last three years was 210. Now, at an alarming rate, the number has risen about 20 per cent. Many cases have been cured at the institution in two to ten months, and the afflicted individuals released. The number of chronic cases probably does not exceed one hundred. At present there are seventy in the asylum who have been sheltered there for three years or more. The institution has, unfortunately, no less than ninety-five per cent of this territory's insane. In order to understand this number, we must not forget that the cause of all the many suicides that occur is a kind of madness. Furthermore, very many cases are of a mild and harmless character, so that they are not considered insane by the authorities and are not accepted by the asylum. Thus, it is possible to see daily on the streets of San Francisco a strong, robust man, dressed in a military uniform, who discusses the events of the day with all the gravity of a statesman. He was born on one of the islands of the Pacific and calls himself Norton I — Emperor of the United States. From time to time he writes proclamations for the Press in which he accuses the American people and summons his loyal subjects to arms for his defense. He does no one any harm and idle people amuse themselves with him. He is not the only one of these unfortunate dreamers.

During the last year there were thirty suicides in San Francisco — and, to the extent of reliable information available, almost as many in other parts of the State. It is astonishing! Sixty deaths a year by suicide, caused and brought about by madness, and this in a population that does not exceed 600,000!

It may well be asked, what is the reason that there is more insanity in California than anywhere else? There is more than one reason. We have already indicated the first above: a multitude came to this State with shining hopes and great expectations; they forsook their home, their friends and comforts in the almost certain hope that in a very short time they would here succeed in attaining an independent position in life. Only too often they find themselves dreadfully deceived in their expectations and their shining hopes lie shattered on the ground. Finally, their unsatisfied longings appear in the dark clouds of despair. This frightful disappointment and their privations result in the loss of their physical health and their spiritual strength; harsh trials and hardships throw reason from its throne and madness seizes command. A second cause is in the excessive use of stupifying beverages, which in this land are nothing better than foul-smelling poison. They heat the blood, shatter the nerves and disorder the brain. A third, although to be sure remote, cause, is to be found in the hurry and excitement that prevails throughout the entire State and which keeps the spirit at the highest tension. Joined with losses and damages suffered in business, all this has in many cases the direst results. Reason gives way under the constant strain; the ability to think breaks down at last; the voice of judgment is finally hushed. Insight is lost; all the spiritual powers, which make man superior to the mere animal, are gone with the wind and he, who only the day before was full of hope and expectation, is a shipwrecked man without any prospect of rescue, who wanders about on the stream of life without rudder and compass until death leads him to his rest.

On this darker side, California is also the land of contrasts. It has produced an abundance of wealth, but it has also been very productive of misery. Hundreds and thousands have sought its shore in the hunt for fortune, but have lost everything that makes life pleasant or, at least, endurable. But it must be confessed that it is comforting to see that the State does a great deal to alleviate as much as possible the misery of the unhappy poor. Its insane-asylum is an excellent institution, in which the utmost care is provided for the hopelessly undone and where many have had their health and their joy in life restored. It is a melancholy and mournful spectacle that the inside of a mad-house offers — to gaze with astonishment at the insane victims of dismal fortune. Here hearts are bleeding because of sorrows; there several patients are subject to a sort of good humor that by its expression eases their hearts; and elsewhere the visitor sees people acting in such fashion that involuntarily he asks himself: Are these really mad? On one side, there is raving, frenzy and cursing, indistinct, confused murmuring and the strange speech of the completely mad; on another side, the fantastic expressions of those who would have us believe that they possess the world as they brag about the millions in their treasury and their fleets at sea. Still others wander about the rooms of the asylum crushed by melancholy and despair. Thus their conduct in its various ways is often a true expression of the direct cause of their insanity.

Chapter XXVII

Jewish Affairs: Congregation Sherith Israel

WE TURN NOW ONCE MORE TO JEWISH AFFAIRS AND BEGIN OUR SURVEY with the description of Congregation Sherith Israel, mentioned above.

This congregation was organized in San Francisco in 1849. Having no permanent building of its own, it held its religious services in various places which, from time to time, were destroyed by fire. Finally the congregation became tired of shifting about and in 1852 bought a place on Stockton Street and asked for contributions to build a synagogue. They were successful in securing enough money: the cornerstone was laid by Dr. Julius Eckmann on August sixth, and the building itself consecrated on September eighth. Thus the building was completed in the incredibly brief period of a month, although, it is true, with only a brick front. It is very beautiful and roomy, too, since it is one hundred feet in extent.

The congregation has about 110 members. They all come from northern Europe or England.

The service follows the correct Polish *minhag* (rite) and is strictly Orthodox. From the very beginning the congregation was founded on these principles and they are embodied in its construction so that they remain in force to this day and, according to all appearances, it is very unlikely that innovations will be made since the Rev. Dr. H. A. Henry, who conducts the services, is an Orthodox teacher in Israel. We shall have the opportunity, later, to say something about this gentleman. Until the autumn of 1857, the congregation had no regular minister, and the *mohel* (performer of of the rite of circumcision) or the *shohet* (slaughterer of cattle or poultry according to Jewish laws) conducted religious services. In the autumn of 1857, the congregation elected the Rev. Dr. Henry of New York to preach and conduct the services. He has occupied that post to this day with the deepest respect and complete confidence of his congregation. He receives a salary of $1500 and the emoluments of his office. Mr. Israel Solomon, an Englishman, is the dearly beloved president of the congregation. He has been honored by this office for four successive years.

In 1849 the congregation bought a cemetery. For this purpose, subscriptions were solicited among the few Jews in San Francisco at that time, and the deed was made out in the name of three trustees for the benefit of all the Jews of San Francisco. When, in 1860, it was seen that this cemetery, small to begin with, was already filled, a suitable place for a cemetery was bought near the Dolores mission. It is surrounded by a brick wall and has a gate and a splendid building that serves as *metaher* house (mortuary, in which the dead are prepared for burial) and is provided with all modern improvements. The cemetery and house called for an expenditure of $16,000.

I was present at the elaborate ceremony of the consecration. The Jews of the city, generally, participated, as was evidenced by the presence of a large representation from the various congregations. This took place on May fifth. A platform was erected at the *metaher* house and very beautifully decorated. On the platform stood those who were conducting the ceremony, such as the preacher together with the officers and committee of the congregation, and guests. Dr. A. Kohen, the rabbi of Congregation Emanu-El, delivered the consecration-prayer in English, in a very elevating and touching manner, before those who were assembled; Dr. Julius Eckmann and others in turn chanted several psalms; the president of Congregation Sherith Israel then made a suitable address, at the conclusion of which he gave the president of the cemetery, M. Morris, the key to it, and the latter replied briefly. The ceremony concluded with a longer address of consecration by the Rev. Henry.

All hearts were deeply touched by the swift progress and rapid prosperity of the community. In a few years, plains and mountains had been converted into peaceful habitations; out of a Sahara of the desert they had come into a Canaan. That which in Europe had been barely possible in a long period of time was accomplished within eight years in America. The Jewish communities have fully organized themselves by the appointment of rabbis, the building of beautiful synagogues and erection of schools, and in this way they promise to become a blessing for the generations to come. The impression of this ceremony will remain ineffaceable for all who were present. The ful-

200

filment of the noble prophecies, if only in part and on a small scale, was here manifest. The worshippers of the Lord of Hosts have re-assembled after their dispersion among all peoples; they have come from the most distant parts of the world, separated from each other by high mountains and wide seas, faithful to the religion of their fathers based upon divine revelation; and with pride one could cite the verse of the wise king: Many waters cannot quench the love [of learning and for the word of God]; neither can floods drown it (*Song of Solomon* 8.7).

The cemetery is thickly planted with all sorts of bushes and trees by the members of Congregation Sherith Israel. (*Sherith* means in Hebrew "remnant" or "remainder".) The cemetery is called *Gibath Olam* or "Hill of Eternity."

We cannot refrain from mentioning the pleasure that a visit to the synagogue of Sherith Israel always affords us. The service is still conducted in the true Jewish manner, as our ancient ancestors used to conduct it. During my stay in San Francisco I had the pleasure of visiting Dr. Henry frequently. I was introduced to him by Dr. Raphall of New York, and I gladly take advantage of this opportunity to thank him for his ready furthering of my interests by deed and counsel. I took the trouble to become better acquainted with the Jewish ministers of California and other places and so learnt that Dr. Henry is a native of England and is a disciple of the late Rabbi Herschell. He was a junior teacher, when still quite young, in the Free School of London, which was organized according to the Lancaster System (followed by the British and Foreign School Society of London). At the age of twenty he was appointed an assistant teacher in that school, which is in Bell Lane, Spitalfields. Three years later, according to the information received, he became a senior teacher and inspector. In the year 1842, he received a call to the synagogue on St. Alban's Place in the West End of London, was ordained a rabbi by the late Rabbi Herschell, and remained at this post until 1849. While in London, he acted as tutor for several years in the famous Rothschild family by whom he was greatly valued and respected. Many young men, natives of London, who are now ministers in various parts of the world, owe him their first acquaintance with Hebrew and English learning. This reverend man is now in his fifty-second year.

Following a call to New York by Dr. Simeon Abrahams, he went to the United States in 1849. He had become a close friend of Dr. Abrahams during his travels in Europe and Asia in 1848. Dr. Henry has become known as a writer through the publication of several useful elementary books for Jewish children. He has also become well known among the Freemasons. He belongs to the Order and, when a resident of London, was greatly esteemed by his late Highness, the Duke of Sussex, Grand Master of the Masonic Lodges in England. In this field, Dr. Henry published a pamphlet in Cincinnati on the origin of Free-masonry. This was well received by his fellow Masons.

The titles of his books are: "Class Book for Jewish Youth"; "Prayers for Jewish Women after Child-Birth"; "A Series of Sermons on the Faith of the Jews"; "A synopsis of Jewish History"; "An Edition of a Jewish Prayer-Book, according to an Improved Method with a Guide in English."

Since my journey through the American states was a fairly search-ing one, I had extensive opportunities to examine the libraries of vari-ous American rabbis and ministers. I found none, however, that was the equal of Dr. Henry's. It is not only large and select, but includes the best authors and editions of all our Hebrew literature. I spent many hours there reading the splendid writings of our sages — writings that are the monuments of our holy religion. And along with the memory of that pleasure that brought my childhood and youth vividly before me — for they were devoted wholly to study — I shall some day, when again on foreign soil, recall the far-off coast of the Pacific Ocean where my brothers worship the God of their fathers in peace and quiet and count those hours as among the fairest of my life.

Presentation of a Torah by the Hebra Bikur Holim
(Society for Visiting the Sick)
to the Congregation on May 19, 1861

Upon invitation by the secretary, Mr. F. Phillips, I visited the syna-gogue on Stockton Street on May 19, 1861, andw as a spectator at a scene the like of which I had not seen for many years. The presen-tation of a Holy Scroll of the Torah for the use of the synagogue is always accompanied by a festive ceremony. There was one here, too. The Holy Scroll in its mantle of silk and velvet, encircled by dark-gold fringe, with a shield of solid silver, the splendid work of the famous craftsmen, Nahl and Brothers, was presented to the congregation of Sherith Israel as a gift by J. P. Davis, the president of the society. Mr. Davis, on this occasion, made some felicitous remarks about the origin and progress of his society and closed with the wish that the organi-zation, still small, might soon be able to number all those present among its members. Israel Solomon, Esq., president of the congregation, thanked the donors in a few, but effective words. Thereupon the Rev. Dr. Henry delivered an address that aroused general interest.

A beautiful detail of the ceremony and, in fact, the best and most useful that could be devised for such an occasion, was the sale of the privilege of filling in the last words of the Holy Scroll. A blank space had been left in the letters for this purpose. The first word that was sold was *uMosheh* ("and Moses"). It was sold to Moses Morris, Esq., for $50. The second word was bought by C. Meyer, Esq., for $22; the third by H. Meyer, Esq., for $20; the fifth, *shanah* ("year") by L. King, Esq., for $17.50. In this way every word was disposed of to a different person; the average price was $12; and the total obtained increased the funds of the congregation by $800. The Jews consider it quite an unusual favor to be able to fill in a complete word, or even a letter, of the Holy Scroll. Therefore, most of the spectators compete with each other for the privilege of leaving in the Holy Scroll some memento which, unlike themselves, only the inexorable hand of time can destroy.

I cannot fail to mention with thanks that the president of the congregation bought me a word for ten dollars.

A large number were present at the occasion and several were by no means disinclined to underwrite the needs of Sherith Israel: an event worthy of mention.

This congregation is very friendly and generous to strangers and travelers. In witness of this noble disposition on their part, here is a transcript of a document sent me: "Congregation Sherith Israel, San Francisco, October 7, 1860. At a general meeting, held on the seventh of the current month, it was agreed and decided that the sum of two hundred and fifty dollars ($250) should be presented to Mr. I. J. Benjamin (the Second), traveler, of the Jewish faith, to help him in his research. It was further decided that the congregation, in case further help should be necessary, will gladly and in like measure give the matter their further attention. A copy of the above resolution shall be transmitted to the above Mr. I. J. Benjamin.

L.S. Fr. Phillips, *Secretary*."

This aid was all the more welcome because my money just then was pretty much exhausted and by its prompt payment I was in a position to continue my research in California.

Chapter XXVIII

Congregation Emanu-El

THE SYNAGOGUE OF THIS CONGREGATION WAS DEDICATED ON SEPTEMBER 14, 1854, by the Rev. Dr. Julius Eckmann, their first rabbi. It is the largest and costliest synagogue in the city: it cost $35,000. Unlike Congregation Sherith Israel, this congregation has had many changes since its organization, particularly since Dr. Elkan Cohn,* the present preacher, became the head of it. Averse to all Orthodoxy, he has introduced "Reform" in its place. Dr. Cohn is a very eloquent preacher, a scholar and a gentleman, and much beloved by every Israelite of San Francisco. He receives an annual salary of $3,000, besides the emoluments of his office. Since he has been appointed for five years, it may be expected that in the immediate future there will be no more changes in the ritual and the congregation will continue along the path it has entered upon.

The congregation numbers 260 members, chiefly Germans and French. Heinrich Seligmann, Esq., president of the congregation, has been elected to that honor for the fifth time. Mr. M. Sachs is vice-president. He is the owner of an important business and an enthusiastic supporter of whatever is noble and beautiful; his poor and needy brothers have much to thank him for and they have always found him a charitable man.

Mr. Daniel Levy, the cantor, is highly respected by his co-religionists and merits their respect because of his noble character, united, as it is, with learning. (I made his acquaintance in Algiers where he translated my first book into French.) In addition to his post as *hazzan* (cantor), he is also employed as a teacher by the congregation and in Dr. Cohn's school.

The "Reform," mentioned above, was introduced on the first evening of the New Year before last. It consists of the following: contrary to the usage until now, men and women sit together; *piyyutim*

---

* Dr. Cohn is a native of Kosten in the duchy of Posen in the kingdom of Prussia and completed his studies in Berlin. His wife, Caroline, is a very lovely and learned lady.

(religious poems) are omitted from the service; and the Torah is read through in three years (instead of one). The last change, as well as shortening the service and other changes in it, has not yet been fully carried out. A choir and organ are used during the service. The congregation is now planning to build a new synagogue for $100,000 and to donate the old synagogue to the Eureka Society for turning into a hospital. A cemetery was bought last year and dedicated. It cost $16,000. This cemetery and that of Sherith Israel are near each other: the latter is larger and more showy.

To show the spirit that prevails in Congregation Emanu-El, I present the report of its president, mentioned above; it also offers a good deal of insight into American life.

San Francisco, October 7, 1860

To the Officers and Members of Congregation Emanu-El

In accordance with tradition and in harmony with the principles of our constitution, I beg leave to present herewith my annual report and at the same time offer a brief review of the condition of our organization. I shall try to bring before you a true and impartial description of all that has happened and been transacted since the last annual meeting.

First, and above all, it should be said that we have good cause to congratulate ourselves and to lift up our thanks to the Lord of all creation that He has preserved the lives of all our members during the past year, so that, with the exception of the death of the wife of one of our most respected members, we have, fortunately, no deceased to mention among us. May this continue to be the case and may we continue to be blessed with health and prosperity. However, kind Providence prepared a sad blow for us among the children of the members of our congregation, and many have to mourn the untimely loss of innocent beings who have been called to a better world. According to the report of the vice-president, eighteen children of the members of our congregation have been buried. As we extend our heartfelt sympathy to those parents whose children have been unexpectedly snatched away, we pray from the bottom of our hearts that Providence will spare us in the future from similar misfortune, so that our young ones will grow up to be the pride of parents and society.

It gives me great pleasure to be able to inform you of the rapid increase of our membership. According to the lists and records, fifty-three new members were admitted; of this number, only two withdrew. There were two resignations, and four names were stricken from the list of members. Thus we have gained forty-nine (*sic*) good members. Our membership is now 227 and, if our number continues to increase as it has in the last twelve months, Emanu-El will soon be the largest congregation in the United States.

I am also glad to be able to make a satisfactory report of our finances. At present our expenses are very great — ever since we had the good fortune to acquire our eloquent and learned preacher and leader. Disbursements for the choir have also increased as well as other expenses for the needs of so large a congregation. The board has tried to be as economical as possible but, nevertheless, the regular expenses come to $750 a month and will probably amount to $800 after the establishment of the new school. The sale of seats this year was very welcome in order to cover this great sum and, as you can see from the report of the Seat Committee, $5008 was collected and $60 is still outstanding. This is an increase of almost $2000 above last year. This is more than necessary to meet the additional regular expenses. Many of our members are in favor of dispensing with the *Gaben*,* but to bring this about another way must be found to enable us to cover our heavy disbursements. If we figure the monthly contributions of 110 members at $200 every month and consider that our interim loan-certificates are soon due, we cannot easily do without the $2500 or $3000 which the receipt of the *Gaben* amounts to on the average, without increasing the monthly dues; and I do not consider this advisable or just. We have many good and useful members who would regard such an increase as too heavy a tax and — if I may be permitted to express my own opinion — they would be quite right. Therefore, I consider it best to make no change in this respect and let things remain as they are.

Our loan-certificates have, fortunately, been reduced to $5919, including interest — a good sign of the liberality of our members, who have reduced a debt of $35,000 for our building, to so insignificant a sum. You will see, from the report of the financial secretary and treasurer, that there is a sum of $5737 in the treasury, plus the dues for the current month and the offerings during the holidays. And if you add the bills due us and, on the other hand, the bills that have as yet not been presented to the board for payment, the sums will balance exactly, and we remain free of debt. If in addition we consider that since our last annual meeting we have taken out of the congregation's funds approximately five thousand dollars for the cemetery, we may be proud of the satisfactory state of our finances and look forward to excellent prospects for the future.

Furthermore, we cannot overestimate our good fortune in having acquired as our preacher a noble, learned and eloquent man like the Rev. Dr. Elkan Cohn, who now lives among us and with us. I believe I express the conviction of almost all when I say we could have made no better or wiser choice. He is a faithful teacher who shows us and instructs us in the true faith that was given to our forefathers. It is therefore our duty to assist him in his difficult office and to offer our aid that we may encourage him in his sacred task, so that this new field — for which he left the place where he was settled, happy, be-

---

* Upon being called up to the reading of the Torah, offerings are made in many places. In many congregations these amount to a considerable sum.

loved and respected — may prove satisfactory to him, and prove blessed and instructive to us and our children.

The most important task that remains to claim our attention is that of the erection of a school for our children, and it is the wish of our preacher that quick measures may be taken to carry out this most essential objective. At the last quarterly meeting this matter was put before the board for a final decision, but since it was not in its power to appoint teachers and to expend money for salaries, it could not carry out the project. I trust that you will now take all the necessary steps to carry out this praiseworthy work, so that the children will soon derive benefit from the favorable opportunities that will then be offered, and will be able to receive all the instruction necessary to their becoming some day good and useful members of our congregation.

Furthermore, the great growth of our congregation points to the necessity of providing a house of worship adequate for all. It is clear that in a short time our synagogue will not be large enough for our needs, and I take the liberty of urging you to select soon a suitable plot of ground in the center of the city that a new house of worship, enough to meet our needs, may be erected. Then the attempt might be made, if possible, to employ our present house of worship for some other, though similar, purpose. I take the additional liberty of proposing that a fixed sum be set aside from the rental of seats in our present synagogue for the specific purpose of buying a plot so that later, and as soon as possible, the needs of the congregation may be satisfied.

At our last meeting an improvement of our organization was proposed, namely, that the office of the secretary in charge of the minutes and that of the secretary in charge of correspondence be consolidated and that a fixed salary be set aside for the post. The necessity of adopting this proposal has already been explained to you and, much as I am opposed to any increase in our expenses, nevertheless I consider this to be beneficial for the congregation. Although individual members are most willing to serve the congregation without payment, the demands of the office of secretary at present are too great for anyone to undertake without recompense and, should we grant this, we on the other hand would have the right to demand that those in office devote part of their time to our affairs.

I might further suggest that a certain amount be given the Jewish traveler, I. J. Benjamin. I believe that we would be performing a righteous act for our cause here and for the benefit of all the earth if we extend a helping hand to this estimable representative of our cause. San Francisco has rightly erected a glorious memorial for itself by the generous way in which it came to the help of its poor brothers in Morocco and will also, I hope, show its beneficence in this case and not hold back. I will bring this matter up again for your approval.*

---

*   With respect to this recommendation of the president, the following letter was later sent to me: "San Francisco, October 16, 1860. To I. J. Benjamin, Esq. Dear

I take the liberty of calling your attention to another fact. Before we were informed whether or not our highly esteemed preacher would accept the call to become our minister, I was, in the interval, instructed to write him and, accordingly, I informed him that, in case it seemed to him that an appointment for three years was too short a period and he would prefer to have it extended to five, the congregation would gladly enter into that stipulation. I consider it, therefore, only just for us to do as we promised and to extend the term of the appointment to five years. We may confirm the promised term unconcerned, for at last we have a man according to our wishes and needs; and in the choice of a conscientious and faithful teacher of our dear religion we could do no better.

With feelings of pride and of bliss, we saw at last the completion of our new cemetery, which we needed so badly, and in your name I express our thanks to those who furthered and hastened the completion of this excellent work. This was accomplished by the effective efforts of the board of road surveyors of both societies and by the

---

Sir: I have been instructed to inform you that at a meeting of Congregation Emanu-El, held on the fourteenth inst., it was decided to set aside the sum of $250 in order to assist you in your purpose to journey to the Orient. Respectfully yours, A. Eger, Secretary. (L.S.)" Since, at that time, my financial condition was very weak because of my rather lengthy stay in California, the high cost of living and particularly because I spared no sacrifice for my researches, I tried to collect the above sum quickly, but my efforts were unsuccessful. This was all the more disagreeable for me because withholding this payment was the base work of a man who in his petty egoism begrudged others everything and only worried about himself and thought no means too base to achieve his ends. In order to place this matter more fully before my readers, I see myself compelled to give the due measure of publicity and deserved contempt to the name of this man, and I beg the reader, if my words seem to betray too much irritation, to take into consideration how much I was embarrassed by him. In every congregation there are those who have crept into its midst and have enrolled themselves as members and who bring with them no additional life but rather death, and give no light but throw shadows. This was also the case in this distinguished congregation, most highly respected by the author. One of these "darkeners" was discovered by me in the person of Mr. Mayblum — unworthy of the name, for this "mayflower" does not blossom with a refreshing odor but spreads a stupefying smell. Mr. Mayblum has now been a member of the congregation for a year, does the least that he should do as a member or only what he must, namely, he pays his regular dues and has no higher interests. Therefore, when this model congregation is inclined to show its benevolence and spend more or less, he is quickly ready to hinder this at every opportunity and, by inducing others who think as he does to support him, tries to start a rebellion. As result, there were no less than five sessions held about me that decided now "aye," now "nay," until the nays won. I believe that it is to such a man that the Mishnah refers in the tractate *Aboth*: (*Lo yitten v'lo yittenu aherim, rasha'*) "He who will not give himself and is minded that others should not give — he is a wicked man" (5: 13). Because of my straightened circumstances at that time and my many sacrifices, a few who were well-intentioned towards me privately offered me a hundred dollars, but I refused this categorically because a traveler who finds himself embarrassed financially is not to be put in the same class as a beggar.

ample means provided them by the Emanuel and Eureka Societies, as well as by fellow members.

I take the liberty of further proposing that the post of delegate to the old board of supervisors of street-laying be abolished, with the remark that we are always ready and willing to pay our share of the expenses to keep the old cemetery in good order. By doing so, we only do our duty to our friends and relatives whose mortal remains are at rest there.

Now that I have presented all the points of our history for the past year worth mentioning and have recommended for your kind attention the proposals that I believe a successful guidance of the congregation requires, I cannot refrain, in conclusion, from expressing my gratitude to the board of officers for the effective and capable assistance that they gave me. They were punctual at their meetings and always ready to assist me in carrying out the duties of my office. By doing so, they contributed much to making my work easier.

I, likewise, take advantage of this opportunity to express my thanks to the members of the seating-committee. They performed their difficult task well during the holidays and we have to thank, in part, their effective and prudent management for the order and decorum that prevailed during services as well as their sound judgment that so great a sum was obtained for the seats.

My thanks also to the ladies who assisted so cheerfully and readily in the choir. I take the liberty of proposing that suitable presents be given them: they were always ready and zealous to assist us in glorifying our religious services and richly deserve our acknowledgment.

Finally, it gives me pleasure to be able to tell you that the harmony and concord that has so long prevailed among us was little disturbed. There was, it is true, a difference of opinion with respect to the laws and regulations as well as to the kind and manner of religious service as introduced among us a little while ago — a difference of opinion that has still not been resolved. But there is no doubt that we, although under obligation to respect the wishes of the minority, for that very reason conscientiously have in view — and this is just what all friends of progress and reform demand — an impartial critical examination of the new kind of religious service and worship and an acquaintance with the manner of it and its success. And I am now convinced that after this has been attained nothing can further disturb the harmonious feelings which fraternal members cherish for each other. That this will be fulfilled is my deepest wish and most ardent desire as well as that Emanu-El may take a worthy place among the foremost sister congregations of the United States. Very truly yours, Heinrich Seligmann, president.

This congregation is at present the largest and richest in California and may well be included among the great congregations of America.

The French members of the congregation are distinguished particularly by their wealth and charity. I mention some names that they may be remembered as worthy of honor, without any reflection upon those I do not mention: Lazard Frères; Leopold Cohen and family; Godchaux; Isaac Levy, the brother of my friend, Daniel, and his family; L. Tichner from Bavaria, an extremely charitable man, and his brother-in-law, Heller.

Shomrai Shaboth Congregation

This congregation consists of about thirty members, almost all Russians or Poles. They consider it an indispensable duty to keep the seventh day sacred and to worship their God in the good old way of their forefathers.

They have a spacious hall. Here services are held on Mondays, Thursdays and Saturdays, in addition to fast days and festivals.

Chapter XXIX

THE EUREKA BENOVOLENT ASSOCIATION

IT WAS ORGANIZED IN OCTOBER 1850, TO ASSIST POOR AND NEEDY JEWS, sick or in want. Its growth is truly astonishing, not only with respect to the number of members, which amounts to more than three hundred, but also with respect to its capital: it has at present $22,941.65 on deposit. It must be said in its praise that it has done much for needy fellow Jews: nursed the sick, assisted the widowed and buried the dead. The success of the society, as in the case of all others, must be ascribed principally to wise management by its directors, and the members are particularly indebted for the success of their society to Mr. August Helbing, its first president. At present, Mr. Helbing has been the president for seven years, and the manner in which he has conducted the office has gained the confidence and respect of all I know.

The society is devoted not merely to serious matters and the quiet joy of benevolence; joyful occasions are not excluded, and the annual balls of the society merit mention. In the case of these, too, benevolence is the object, and the sale of tickets for the last one held amounted to no less than $2504. I was invited to this celebration as a guest and I must admit that a more brotherly harmony and a better table are to be found nowhere else in the whole world. But this is of little importance and relegated to the background as compared to the fact that during the last year the sum of $5002.92 was spent in the relief of the poor. The amount brightly illuminates the benevolence of this society, one of the many benevolent societies of San Francisco, particularly if we consider that Jews are seldom the recipients of its charity.

As an addition to the general fund of the society, they established in 1858 a "Widows and Orphans Fund," for the assistance of the widows and orphans of former members. It already amounts to the respectable sum of $5402 and is constantly increasing because, as yet, there have been no claims upon it.

The monthly dues are $1.25.

However, the president of this society has apparently exposed himself to much attack and, although he is most highly regarded by his fellow members and richly merits this regard by the manner in which he has conducted his office, he has encountered bitter enmity; and I consider it my duty to furnish a true and impartial report of this situation. Since in San Francisco it is on the daily agenda that there should be a conflagration either by day or at night (a conflagration can be counted on at least once in twenty-four hours), it happened that a fairly large fire broke out on May twenty-seventh. This destroyed eight large warehouses in Commercial Street alone, for the fire spread to both sides of the street. In one of the houses destroyed there lived a very religious, generally respected Polish Jew, Moses Minz, who honorably supported himself and his large family — which included several children of the most tender age — by running a restaurant. The family escaped literally with only their lives, dressed in the lightest clothing. In this desperate plight, of which I was a witness since I lived in an adjoining house, the father of the family saw himself placed in the sad situation of having to apply for help to the president of a society consisting of Germans and Frenchmen and only a single Pole. But the unfortunate man was flatly rebuffed because, it is supposed, he was a Pole — so I have heard from many sources. Thus refused, he went to an American Christian and told him the whole story. The latter called upon the president of the society and as he could not honorably leave a fellow Jew helpless and suffering in the presence of a non-Jew, he gave the visitor $40 for the man.

Unfortunately, this is not the only instance of a hardness of heart that is with difficulty touched by misfortune. A member of the society, a very respectable man, told me that he had likewise applied to the president in behalf of a family in great distress, but without results. The refusal was accompanied with the explanation that the board knew best what it had to do.

This is still not all. The president has been blamed for even greater harshness in another matter. There was in San Francisco a certain Dr. Hermann Bien. Several years before he had been, for a short time, the preacher of Congregation Emanu-El. He published a newspaper, the *Pacific Messenger*. He had consented to becoming a member of the benevolent society, some years before, and he remained a member for several years and paid the usual dues regularly. But, as his financial circumstances became much worse, he was eight or ten months in arrears, hoping to pay his dues later under more favorable circumstances. However, in spite of his financial distress, he never asked any aid of the society. The president called a meeting of the trustees and had Dr. Bien suspended.

Dr. Bien protested this action. We take the following from his paper, *Pacific Messenger*, under date of June 7, 1861, at San Francisco:

A Personal Complaint

A True Picture of an Experience in California

The strongest heart, when the torments of care have pressed it to the ground, will struggle violently. Whether or not such a struggle is perceived by others, it at least affords some relief for the depressed. For this reason, I must lift my voice in most heartfelt complaint, compelled by the power of the grief under which I suffer. Pen and heart tremble as I write these lines, but there is no help for it: they must be written. For the first time in my life I write about myself. I do it with a heavy heart, slowly and hesitatingly. But there is a time for everything — for silence and for speech. I beg the reader to follow me willingly and patiently.

Five years have passed since I landed on these shores. I was then still a young, zealous man, ready and willing to work — to work so that I might make use of the strength and gifts which God had conferred upon me and which my education had provided. I was then called to the first post that the Jews of this State had to fill — that of preacher of Congregation Emanu-El of this city. In this post I enjoyed — I may say so — the respect and confidence of a good and intelligent congregation. However, there were soon fundamental differences of opinion in what was then a very young community inhabited by a mixture of persons from the most different countries and with even more diverse views. My heedlessness, in that I could not hide from the world that which does not please the multitude, namely, the truth, as well as my inexperience in hypocrisy, brought us into a difference of opinion with several influential members of this congregation. The latter quality I have to this day been unable to acquire and, alas, I believe that the Almighty has completely denied me the ability to learn it. Under those circumstances, I did not seek the renewal of my appointment after its term had expired.

Since then I have struggled to earn enough at least to keep body and soul together; there is no kind of work, no matter how difficult or humiliating, that I did not undertake. I had a good reputation as a teacher. But, though I had twelve hours a day in which to work, I could not earn enough for the barest necessities; I found much gold in my books, but nothing in my pocket. After a severe examination, the Board of Education of this city gave me a glowing testimonial — but no position. And so, under compulsion, I left the class-room.

I have likewise tried to become a business man. But one who understands no more than how to study books and guide a pen can at best be a very poor merchant and, since I was also honest, I lost what few dollars I had in order to repay — as much as I could — those who had trusted me. As a writer, I had a marked success in various kinds of writing, considering the little effort I put into it, and I harvested great praise. My *Sampson and Delilah* received from the entire California press the highest praise, of which I have a right to be proud (if an exception be made of the *Gleaner*, that had not the least mention of it, and two German papers that stooped to slander and personal insults). On the stage, too, the play was taken up by stars of the first magnitude and crowned with success. Although I had spent twelve years in writing it, the amount I received was not enough to pay for the paper used in printing it. I have on hand at present other writings, but I can begin to do nothing at all with them for lack of means.

I was the pioneer for Jewish periodicals in California and the first to publish the *Voice of Israel*. It now appears under the name of *The Faithful Messenger of the Pacific*. It has great prestige here and abroad; as is proved by the many articles quoted from it.

I not only had to struggle along in great need because many of my subscribers were in arrears with their payments, but I had to endure vexations of all sorts because of absolutely wicked notices and slanders. It almost seems as if, among the few who have any reason to cherish any feeling against me, there are several who cannot be absolved of a diabolical character. Some time ago, when in my great need and want I accepted a very humiliating position in Portland,

Oregon, I received a letter from here which placed before me a post after my own inclination and at the same time promised suitable compensation. It was from S. Harvis, of the firm of Harvis and Coleman, director of a newly established company, signed with his name and saying that, in case I was interested in taking the position, I was to return at once. I did so and discovered upon presenting the letter that it was one of the meanest forgeries that had ever been perpetrated. I could not trace the scoundrel who in so infamous a fashion had committed a crime that I would not be guilty of for the wealth of all California.

I was again penniless, without a steady position, and had to make my way in San Francisco as best I could. During the last three years, I heard no friendly word, saw no sympathetic glance. I do not know if I have any claim to either, but the heart is chilled to be so forsaken and forgotten and at that slandered, and to have to work day after day and week after week. The receipt of a letter from a Jewish benevolent society, where I had been a member for years and to which I paid my dues as long as I had a dollar to spare, set the crown upon the vexations that had already been heaped upon my sunken head. It read as follows:

"To H. M. Bien: We hereby inform you that you are expelled from membership in the society because you have not paid your regular dues for one year."

Some time before, I had given the financial secretary, in writing, adequate reasons as to why I did not pay these dues. Gentlemen, this was neither just nor fair on your part. Charity begins at home, and a man who hardly knows how he is to live from day to day should not be expected to contribute to the capital, already large, of a benevolent society. This letter, gentlemen, has caused me more grief than you are perhaps able to understand.

This is now my quite unenviable position in California, in a land that is so badly in need of men who understand somewhat more than buying and selling. The place where I live does not disgust me so much that I would move away and return, if I were so inclined, to the more suitable climate from which I came; besides, I have not sufficient means. But for the time being I have no such inclination because I know that the time must come and will come when my energetic and uninterrupted strivings will obtain recognition. However, since I must live among such harsh and painful circumstances, I make a modest request that I be treated with somewhat less spite and malice, that my enemies drag down my efforts and my person somewhat less into the common dust, and that my friends show somewhat more generosity and more activity in my behalf. I close with the hope that my remarks will not be misinterpreted and that this sincere wish of mine will find an echo here where one has the right to expect humanity and common-sense.

214

As a result of this protest which caused a great deal of excitement in the society, the president called a meeting at which the letter to Dr. Bien was recalled. Dr. Bien personally told me the story of his life and, later, I convinced myself sufficiently of the truth of it.* The president is also, in my opinion, very ungenerous to travelers in case these come unprovided with grandiose letters of introduction. Nevertheless, the society has the right to a testimonial for the great benevolence that animates it and deserves to rank with the foremost Jewish benevolent societies of America.

Before we close the long list of Jewish welfare organizations, which are strong evidence of the generosity of the Jews, and which show that even on the other side of the ocean one has not forgotten that benevolence is a hallmark of the descendants of Abraham, we want to acquaint our readers, as it were, with one of these societies and we therefore quote below the statutes of the most important—the "Eureka Society."

Constitution and By-Laws of the Eureka Benevolent Society of San Francisco, Cal.

Founded October, 1850

Foreword

The need of a benevolent society among the Israelites of this place induced a number of philanthropic-minded men of this faith to found one, and it was accordingly organized on the second of October, 1850.

The object of the society is: "Aid for the needy, care for the sick and burial for the dead."

To outline in detail how the object of the society, mentioned above, is to be carried out, a constitution and by-laws were framed and, after repeated revision, adopted as follows at a general meeting held on the fifteenth of December, 1860.

Although the activity of the society proved to be extensive and useful, the further need became apparent of providing means for offering help and aid in case of need to the families left behind by deceased members.

---

* Upon my return to Hanover, I learnt from a most respectable source that Mr. Bien had functioned as a teacher in several small congregations and had been compelled by circumstances to emigrate to America. There he conferred upon himself without any right the title of "doctor." As rabbi of Congregation Emanu-El, he wore the head-gear of the high-priest with an inscription in Hebrew meaning *Kodesh l'Adonai,* "Sacred to the Lord."

As a result, the "Eureka Widows and Orphans Fund" was created and for the administration of it provisional laws were framed and adopted at a general meeting held on the seventh of March, 1858.

Likewise, in the course of time, regard for the sacred duty that we owe the deceased was fully taken into account and sufficient means set aside to prepare a worthy resting-place for the remains of our dead fellow Israelites.

The society now has, in common with Congregation Emanu-El, a cemetery in accordance with the resolutions of the general meeting of November 12, 1859. The cemetery is under the supervision of a board of directors elected for that purpose.

Contents

Constitution. Article I: Name of the Society. Article II: Purpose. Article III: Officers. Article IV: Meetings. Article V: Dissolution. Article VI: Amendment.

By-Laws. Paragraphs 1-6: Duties and Rights of the Board. Paragraph 7: Duties of the Secretary. Paragraph 8: Duties of the Collectors. Paragraph 9: Members. Paragraph 10: Honorary members. Paragraph 11: Life Members. Paragraph 12: Dues. Paragraph 13: Basic Capital. Paragraph 14: Purpose. Paragraph 15: Fines. Paragraph 16: Resignation. Paragraph 17: Suspension. Paragraph 18: Loss of membership. Paragraph 19: Order of Business. Paragraph 20: Amendment of By-Laws. Act Authorizing the Eureka Widows and Orphans Fund. Act Authorizing the Cemetery.

Officers for 1861

August Helbing, President. Benjamin Schloss, Vice-President. L. B. Wertheimer, Treasurer. Julius Beer, Recording-Secretary. Trustees: M. Mayblum; Max Frankenthal; Leonard D. Heynemann; Moritz Meyer; Abraham Wolf. H. Greenbaum, Secretary. M. Steppacher, Collector.

Constitution

Article I

1. The Society shall be called
"Eureka Benevolent Society"
and this shall be its name forever.

Article II

1. The purpose of the Society shall be: *Aid for the needy; care for the sick; and burial for the dead.*

Article III

1. The administration of the Society shall be delegated to a board of nine members consisting of: a president, a vice-president, a recording-secretary, a treasurer and five trustees.

2. Election to the board shall be by ballot and requires a majority of the members present.

3. The board shall be elected for one year and the election shall take place in December.

Article IV

1. There shall be four general meetings annually; namely, on the first Sundays in March, June, September and December.

2. In urgent cases, the president has the right to call a special meeting.

3. The request of a member for a special general meeting must be supported by twenty members and must be accompanied by a written statement of the reasons for it addressed to the president. The president is then required to fix a date for such a meeting, which is to be held within ten days.

4. Special general meetings must be limited to the purpose for which they were called.

5. The society is authorized to frame by-laws; but in no case may these be contrary to the constitution.

Article V

1. The dissolution of the society may not be proposed as long as it has twenty members, and can only take place if three-fourths of the members vote in favor of dissolution.

2. In case of dissolution, the property on hand is to be applied to a charitable purpose in California. The majority is to designate the purpose.

Article VI

1. A proposal to change the constitution or amend it, presented in writing to the president, is only admissible at a regular general meeting. After it is read, it may not be discussed until the following regular general meeting. Its acceptance requires the consent of two-thirds of the members present.

By-Laws

Duties and Rights of the Board

1. The president presides at all meetings. He grants permission to speak and has the right to withdraw it. It is his duty to maintain the constitution and by-laws in all respects. At elections, he has the right to vote and is eligible for election. During debates, he may vote only if the members are equally divided. He signs all the minutes that have been accepted and particularly all documents authorized by the board or the society. He must resign his office in case he leaves the State for more than two months.

2. In the absence of the president, the vice-president has all his rights and duties. At the resignation or death of the president, the vice-president takes his place until the end of the term.

3. The recording-secretary is to take the minutes of the transactions of the society, as well as of the board, and after the minutes are accepted he shall certify that they are correct.

4. The treasurer is bound to furnish the board satisfactory security. He shall receive from the secretary, and give receipts for, the money of the society. He shall follow all instructions for the payment of money directed to him by the president in the name of the Society. He shall keep an accurate record of all income and expenditure, inform the board monthly of the financial condition of the Society, and likewise at the general meetings in June and December present an accurate report of income and expenditures with receipts for these. At these two general meetings, he shall have the cash-book in order for examination by a finance committee.

5. The trustees shall work for the good of the Society at the meetings of the board, together with the board-members named above.

In the absence of the president and the vice-president, the trustee who was next elected shall take their place.

6a. The board is obliged to have monthly meetings at which five shall be a quorum. The president shall appoint from the members of the board the following committees: (1) a financial committee; (2) a committee for assisting the needy; (3) a committee for the care of the sick; (4) a committee for burying the dead; as well as other committees for extraordinary matters.

6b. The board is authorized to hire a salaried secretary, physician, and collector, as well as to discharge them.

6c. The secretary and collector must be members of the Society.

6d. The secretary shall not receive more than $300 annually.

218

6e. If a member of the board leaves the city for more than fourteen days, he shall notify the president of this so that the latter may transfer the duties of the board-member to someone else for the duration of such absence. Upon the absence of a board-member for more than two months his office shall be considered vacant.

6f. Whenever the board shall lack a member, it shall make up the full number.

6g. After its term of office is over, the board shall transfer to the newly elected board the complete inventory of the Society as, for example, its property, books and utensils.

Duties of the Secretary

7a. The secretary is required to furnish security satisfactory to the board.

7b. He shall keep a correct record of his accounts in a book; receive all monies and turn these over weekly to the treasurer; take receipts and prepare all bills as well as notices of general meetings and board meetings to be held and give them to the collector at the proper time. Within eight days after a new member has been accepted, he shall inform him of the fact and send him a copy of the constitution and by-laws by means of the collector. He shall, above all, attend to whatever writing the society or board may ask him to do.

Duties of the Collector

8a. The collector is required to furnish security satisfactory to the board.

8b. He shall collect all the monies due the Society and receive whatever payment the board shall decide.

8c. He shall carry all oral and written messages that the Society or board may ask him to.

Members

9a. Whoever wishes to join the Society must be at least eighteen and may not be more than fifty years of age.

9b. In all cases, petitions to be admitted as a member of the Society must be presented to the president in writing, must be sponsored by three members and must be accompanied by the initiation fee.

9c. At a meeting of the board, the president shall appoint an investigation committee of three. The committee shall report its finding with respect to the character of the applicant by the word "favorable" or "unfavorable" at the next general-meeting.

9d. Admission to membership is by ballot and requires the approval of four-fifths of the members voting.

9e. Within three months after admission, every new member is obliged to sign the constitution.

9f. Every member must attend the general meetings and vote, if asked to do so, whenever a vote is taken or an election held. A member will be excused from voting only with the consent of the meeting.

9g. It is the duty of a member who learns of the sickness of any other member to report it at once to the president.

Honorary Members

10a. The board, as well as every member, has the right to propose honorary members. The acceptance of such proposal requires the consent of four-fifths of the members present. Honorary members enjoy all the rights of members except that of voting on motions or at elections; but they are excused from any duties.

Life Members

11a. Members may become life members upon payment of $125. Of this sum, one hundred dollars is to go to the general fund and twenty-five dollars to the Widows and Orphans Fund.

11b. Life members shall be excused from any further payment, but they remain subject to all other duties of a member.

11c. Acceptance as a life member requires a separate vote by ballot.

Dues

12. Every member must pay ten dollars initiation fee and monthly dues of $1.25. Voluntary offerings shall be accepted and recorded in the minutes.

Capital on Hand

13a. The Society has agreed upon the sum of ten thousand dollars as capital on hand. This is to be used only in extraordinary circumstances and for this use the consent of two-thirds of the members present at a general-meeting is required.

13b. The management of the capital of the Society is to be left to the board.

13c. The Society is authorized to buy real estate and to sell it.

13d. Decisions with respect to the purchase or sale of real estate shall be taken at a general-meeting especially called for this purpose, and such decision shall require the consent of three-fourths of the members present.

13e. In the invitations to the meeting, the members shall be intrusted with the particulars of the proposal.

Purpose: Aid

14a. The president has the right to give a member, by way of assistance, for the first time, a sum not exceeding $25. A sum not exceeding $100 may be granted with the consent of the committee for assisting the needy. Assistance, beyond this sum, requires the consent of the board.

14b. The president is authorized to give one who is not a member, by way of assistance, for the first time, a sum not exceeding $10. Assistance, beyond this sum, requires the recommendation of a member and may then be granted, with the consent of the respective committee, but not in excess of the sum of $50. All larger amounts are to be decided upon by the board.

Care of Sick Members

14c. When the president is informed of the sickness of a member, he shall instruct the committee for the care of the sick to visit the sick man without delay, discuss the matter with the physician and put all necessary provision for the care and comfort of the sick man within his reach. If visits are desirable, the president shall take the necessary steps to provide them.

Assistance of the Sick Who Are Not Members

14d. If the president is asked to help a sick man who is not a member, his condition shall be investigated by a committee. The president with the assistance of the committee shall decide upon the manner and amount of help.

Burial of the Dead

14e. At the death of a member, the board shall see to his burial and, if necessary, defray the expense of it, provided this does not exceed the sum of one hundred dollars.

The president shall appoint at least twenty members to accompany the body to the grave and shall ask all members present in the city to take part in the funeral. If the grave of a dead member has not been provided with a grave-stone after eighteen months, the Society is obliged to erect one, but may not spend more than forty dollars for this purpose.

In case of the death of members who leave no relatives in this country, it is the duty of the board to notify their families by letter or notice in the Press. At the death of a member, it is desirable that the board watch over the property he has left.

Fines

15a. A member of the board who is absent from a meeting incurs a fine of two dollars.

15b. Members who participate in calling a special general-meeting and do not attend it themselves are subject to a fine of five dollars.

15c. Any member who leaves a meeting without the permission of the president is to pay a fine of one dollar.

15d. A member who leaves a meeting and thereby deprives it of a quorum shall be fined five dollars without the right of appeal.

15e. If in a meeting a member is called to order twice by the president without complying, he shall have to pay a fine of at least a dollar and not more than five dollars.

15f. A member who does not comply with his duties, according to Paragraph 14, section e, forfeits a fine of ten dollars.

Upon a satisfactory excuse, the president may remit a fine.

All fines collected shall go to the Widows and Orphans Fund.

Resignation

16. A member who wishes to resign must present his resignation in writing to the board. It shall accept the resignation provided the member in question is not in arrears.

Suspension

17a. The board is authorized to deprive, for a fixed time, members who have not paid their dues six months in succession, as well as those who refuse to pay fines imposed upon them in spite of repeated demands, of all rights and benefits of the Society without relieving them from their duties.

17b. If a member of the board fails to attend three meetings of the board in succession without satisfactory excuse, the majority of the board may deprive him of his office.

Loss of Membership

18. Members who have not paid their monthly dues for twelve months in succession as well as fines imposed, after repeated demands for payment, may be stricken from the list of members by two-thirds

of the board, and the board is without authority to receive them as members again until their arrears have been paid to-date.

Members who have been convicted of a crime are considered expelled.

Order of Business

19a. Twenty members shall constitute a quorum. The president shall take the chair at the exact time set for the meeting and call the meeting to order. All business shall be conducted in German. However, upon request, the president shall permit discussion in English.

The following order of business shall be observed:

(1) Reading of the minutes of the previous meeting. (If accepted, they are to be signed by the chairman and the recording secretary.)
(2) Reading of the minutes of the board.
(3) Introduction of new members.
(4) Reports of committees.
(5) Agenda.
(6) Proposals.

19b. The president shall observe parliamentary rules and regulations during the meeting. He has the right to decide all points of order, subject to appeal.

19c. At the request of the president or a member, a proposal shall be committed to writing.

19d. Where the vote is in doubt, the president may order a division. It shall also be ordered at the demand of five members.

19e. Every speaker shall confine himself to the question under discussion. No member may speak more than twice about one and the same matter unless the meeting consents.

19f. Committees shall be named by the president. The first named is always the chairman of the committee unless the meeting provides otherwise.

19g. If a decision has been reached about a proposal, a member who voted with the majority may move that the same subject be thrown open again for debate and a vote. If this does not take place at the same meeting, such notice must be given at the next meeting.

Amendment of By-Laws

20. A proposal to change the by-laws or amend them shall, after it is read, be tabled until the next meeting for discussion and a vote.

Such change or amendment requires the consent of two-thirds of the members present.

Act Establishing Eureka's Widows and Orphans Fund

adopted at a regular general meeting held on the seventh of March, 1858, and amended September fifth, 1858, June fifth, 1859, and March fifth, 1860.

1. There shall be established a fund, completely separate from the capital on hand and other capital of the Society: its sole purpose shall be the assistance of widows and orphans of deceased members, and its name shall be

Eureka Widows and Orphans Fund

2. The Widows and Orphans Fund shall consist of: (a) half of the initiation fees; (b) a fifth of the monthly dues; (c) a fourth of all the extra income of the Society such as income from balls, concerts, theatrical benefits and the like; (d) and all fines collected.

3. The secretary shall keep a separate account for the said fund.

4. The fund is not to be drawn against until it has reached the sum of five thousand dollars. The board of the Society is to administer the fund.

5. Further particulars about the administration of the fund, after it has reached the sum designated in the foregoing section, is to be decided upon by the Society in the future.

6. The foregoing sections shall take effect April 1, 1858.

7. A proposal to change or amend these is subject to Paragraph 20 of the by-laws.

8. Special voluntary offerings for the Widows and Orphans Fund shall be accepted and recorded as such in the minutes.

Act for Establishing the Navo Shalom Cemetery

adopted at a special general meeting held on the twelfth of October, 1859. In view of the fact that the Eureka Benevolent Society, together with Congregation Emanu-El, is in possession of a cemetery and, upon further consideration, that the same is to be

> turned over to the exclusive control and direction of officers expressly elected for that purpose,

it is decided that:

(1) A board of directors shall be organized, consisting of nine members, to be elected as follows:

> (a) This Society shall elect by ballot at this meeting four directors who, together with five elected by Congregation Emanu-El, shall constitute the board of nine directors.

(b) In January of each year, such an election shall be held, and the directors elected shall enter upon their duties on the first Monday of February.

(c) At the election of directors to be held in January 1861, this Society shall elect five directors and the Congregation Emanu-El four, and this annual alternation of the number to be chosen shall be the rule for the future.

(d) In case of a vacancy the president shall name a substitute.

(e) The board of directors shall proceed to organize themselves without delay and from among themselves elect a president, vice-president, treasurer and secretary.

(2) The exclusive management of the cemetery shall be turned over to the board of directors under resolutions to be made public by the respective societies.

(3) The directors are hereby authorized and requested to solicit voluntary offerings from the members of both societies to be able to make at once the improvements required, and such contributions shall be credited to the respective contributors in the purchase of cemetery plots later.

(4) The directors are further authorized to sell parts of the cemetery to other societies and individuals of our faith for burial-grounds, upon the condition that such burial-grounds remain under the exclusive control of the board of directors.

Members

J. Ackermann
H. Ackermann
S. Altman
Henry Adler
M. Adler
Elvin Adler
Leon Ach
D. Abrams
Julius Adler
L. S. Ackerman
S. S. Arnheim
Jonas Adler
Joseph Aron
Julius Beer
J. A. Brunner
Leopold Blum
Wm. Brand
S. H. Böhm
Felix Bachman
L. Brown
Martin Blumenthal

Wm. Bloch
Isaac Bachman
Abraham Bloch
Max Brandenstein
Nathan Bachman
H. M. Bien
E. Bloomingdale
Isaac Bloch
Julius Blumenthal
Isaac Bernhart
Joseph Brandenstein
E. Blochman
S. Bauman
Siegmund Bettman
J. Baum
L. Bergstein
M. Bernheim
F. A. Benjamin
Leopold Boscowitz
B. L. Brandt
Aaron Cahn

David Cerf
Isaak Collin
Henry Cohn
Nathan Cohn
Louis Cohn
Julius Cerf
Elkan Cohn
Israel Cahn
Sylvain Cohn
L. Dinkelspiel
Chs. Dahlman
Julius Dettelbach
M. Dinkelspiel
L. P. Dormitzer
S. Elsasser
M. Engel
Moses Englander
Leopold Englander
A. Eger
Meyer Ehrlich
A. D. Ellis

M. Essberg
S. Fuhrman
Chs. Frank
Moses Frank
B. Frankenheimer
A. Frankenbach
Nathan Feldheim
H. Falkenstein
Israel Fleischman
Joseph Figel
Wm. Fischer
Henry Friedman
Max Frankenthal
Joseph Frankenheimer
J. Frank
L. P. Frank
A. Fleischacker
C. A. Fletcher
J. Greenebaum
L. Godchaux
Alexander Goldsmith
A. Godchaux
Amson Goldsmith
Bernhard Goldsmith
E. L. Goldstein
Solomon Goldsmith
Jacob Goodman
L. Greenberg
I. A. Goldman
Louis Goldsmith
A. Goldsmith
M. Goodman
H. Goldsmith
Henry Greenberg
Isaak Glazier
Isidor Gutte
G. S. Goodman
Herrman Greenbaum
Simon Gruenwald
Arnold Gerstle
Louis Goldstone
A. Goldsmith
A. Galland
Chs. Greenberg
Wm. Greenhood
August Helbing
Leonard D. Heynemann
Michael Hellman
Salomon Haas
Leopold Herzog

Levi Hess
Chs. Hess
B. Hagan
Max Hellman
B. Hamburger
A. Heineberg
S. Hahn
Moritz Heller
H. Herzog
B. Heineberg
G. Holz
I. A. Halphin
Isaak Hecht
Herrman Herz
E. Hochstadter
M. Heyman
Martin Heller
K. Heller
Samuel Haas
Albert Hiller
Adolphus Hollub
H. Hönigsberger
Isaak Herrman
Joseph Isaac
S. L. Jacobs
S. Jacobs
Louis Jacoby
Chs. Krauss
Ferdinand Königsberger
A. Kline
Simon Koschland
Marcus Kohn
Joseph Krauss
I. Lustig
Simon Lazard
Eli Lazard
Isaac Levy
John Levy
Henry Levy
Abraham Lindauer
J. L. Lang
H. Loupe
Chs. Levy
Daniel Levy
Georg Lehmann
Wm. Langermann
Hermann Levy
Isaac Levy
S. Lengfeld
Frank Livingston

Julius Levy
Max Levy
Michael Lewis
Seligman Langstadter
Julius May
M. Mayblum
Moritz Meyer
Wm. Meyer
M. Morgenthau
Joseph Messinger
Cauffman H. Meyer
M. Meyerfeld
Simon Messinger
Chs. Moore
Isaak Mannheim
J. J. May
Samuel Marx
Nathan Meyer
Leon Meyer
L. Newman
Louis Neustadter
H. Newman
H. Neustadter
Herrman Neubauer
Elias Newburger
Joseph Neubauer
Meyer Oppenheimer
H. Oppenheimer
A. Pinna
B. Price
M. Pincus
Elkan Pollack
Chs. Popper
Benj. Reinhart
S. Rosenthal
H. Regensburger
S. Regensburger
Nathan Rhine
I. Regensburger
F. M. Reinhart
F. Rosenbaum
Siegmund Rosenthal
Joseph Rosenbaum
Michael Reese
H. Robitscheck
D. Rosenberg
Julius Rosenfeld
S. W. Rosenstock
Julius Robinson
Sigmund Rosenfeld

226

J. Rothfeld
Levy Roesner
L. Rosenberg
Louis Rosenberg
Salomon Rosenberg
S. G. Rosenbaum
Meyer Rosenberg
S. Rosenstock
Julius Simonsfeld
Adolph Sutro
L. Schoenwasser
A. J. Saulman
Jacob Scholle
Benjamin Schloss
Wm. Scholle
L. Strauss
David Stern
S. L. Simon
H. W. Stein
U. Simon
A. Silberman
M. Siegel
K. Strauss
Siegmund Steinhardt
H. L. Simon
E. Schubart
Moses Selig
M. Sachs

Marx Strauss
David Stern
Phillipp Silbermann
Henry Seligmann
Levi Strauss
Isak Scholle
L. Seligman
L. Strauss
Maurice Strauss
Henry Schmitt
Isac E. Stoeckler
L. Sachs
M. Siegel
Bernhardt Strauss
S. Sweet
Wm. Steinhardt
Louis Strauss
Bernhardt Schweitzer
Gustav Sutro
Emil Sutro
M. Steppacher
L. Tichner
B. Triest
Wm. Thurnauer
A. Tandler
S. Uhlfelder
Adolph Unger
B. N. Vogelsdorf

B. Wolf
L. Werthheimer
L. Wachenheimer
A. Wassermann
H. Woodleaf
Henry Weill
E. Wertheimer
Samuel Wasserman
Louis Wormser
Simon Wormser
M. Wellhof
H. Wilstadter
David Walter
Edward Walter
Alexander Weil
Lewis Wormser
Heymann Wolf
Louis Wertheimer
A. L. Wangenheim
Emanuel Walter
S. Wangenheim
S. Wolf
Simon Wormser
Raphael Weill
L. B. Wertheimer
Abraham Wolf
Abraham Yehl
Philip Zadig

The First Jewish Benevolent Society

This Society was founded in 1849 and took as its task the aiding of poor and needy Hebrews. It has 225 members and spends about two thousand dollars annually for benevolent purposes. Mr. L. King was lately elected president and Mr. M. B. Ashim, the first president and founder of the Society, is now vice-president. The Society has about four thousand dollars in its treasury. Monthly dues are one dollar. This Society does not seem to be particularly liberal to strangers and travelers. It consists only of Polish and English Jews.

B'nai B'rith

The name B'nai B'rith means "Sons of the Covenant." It is a secret society, like the Freemasons, and consists only of Jews. There is no other society of Jews like the B'nai B'rith in America. It has a charter from the District Grand Lodge of New York. The purpose of the society is the mutual assistance of members and the spread of Judaism.

It has two lodges in the city: the Ophir Lodge with ninety members and the Modin Lodge with forty-five.

Hebrah Bikkur Holim Ukedusha
(Society for the Aid of the Sick)

The society was organized in February 1857, to provide needy and sick fellow members with medicine and care and all that they might need in the event of sickness. The society has about two hundred members and a capital of six thousand dollars. The president, Mr. J. P. Davis, was connected with other Jewish societies for a number of years and has done much for the growth of this society — as well as for replenishing its treasury which, at times, has been drained of funds — by attracting members from other circles where he was a distinguished member. Messrs. M. B. Ashim and L. King, whose praiseworthy efforts I shall have the opportunity of mentioning again elsewhere in this book, are among the few tireless founders of this laudable society.

Hebrah Berith Shalome
(Society of the Covenant of Peace)

This society received its charter in July 1860, and has for its purpose the mutual assistance of its members if in need. Among the rules of the organization are provisions for the care of sick members, the furnishing of medicine and the obligation to be of assistance under all circumstances. In case a member dies, the society is obliged to erect a gravestone that must not cost less than seventy-five dollars. They must also support the widow of a deceased member and extend their fatherly care to the orphans: in a word, to do all that a true Jew should for his fellow-man. Mr. I. N. Choynski is president of this *hebrah*. It has at present 105 members and, although founded only eight months ago, has a thousand dollars in its treasury.

Jewish Young Men's Literary Society

This society was founded as early as 1854, at a time when gold and gain was the watchword of every young man who set out to hurry through the newly-discovered places along the Pacific. The Jew, however, by founding this society publicly showed that materialism had never completely consumed him. Although, as I must regretfully say, this society has lately not made the progress it should have, still it has kept going in spite of all storms. It has lost many members through the departure of young men who left to find their fortune elsewhere, in places where better prospects appeared, or who, after gaining sufficient wealth, returned to their homes where a loving father or a tender mother waited for them. Still, enough members remain who have the interest to improve themselves intellectually and to exchange opinions about subjects of general concern.

The society has a valuable library consisting of Hebrew, English, French and German classics, in addition to numerous newspapers from all parts of the world. The membership consists of all possible nationalities and the halls are always full of listeners to their debates and learned exercises. It is to be regretted, however, that the intelligent Jewish residents of San Francisco do not show more interest in furthering the society's aims. This would be especially desirable because the present membership cannot meet the regular expenses of their club. Public applause and smiles of agreement certainly please the members but do not assist them or relieve them of their financial difficulties.

Union Debating Society

This club was founded by a number of young Jews in March of last year (1861). Their aim was to hold weekly debates upon some previously assigned subject at every meeting. The members are young men, mostly natives. For this reason, their speech lacks the sweet, soft, German accent that distinguishes the debates of the "Literary Society" — often to the great amusement of the listeners. Mr. Grünbaum was elected president and he seems fully capable of leading the society.

The Israelite Ladies Society

Its purpose is to assist Jewish women in all cases of necessity. It was founded August 12, 1858. The president is Mrs. C. Regensburger.

The United Benevolent Society of Jewish Women

This was founded in 1855 for the mutual assistance of Jewish women. The president is Mrs. S. F. Tandeller.

Both of these societies for women merit great praise. Fortunately, there are no claims upon them, for there are very few poor Jewish women in San Francisco.

Heftsi-Vah (My Delight is in Her)*

This Jewish school was founded in 1854 by Dr. Julius Eckmann. Although it often lacked the assistance due a thoroughly religious in-

---

*   B. translates this as "My Delight is in Him" but the reference is to Zion (Isaiah 62. 4). Tr.

stitution such as this, nevertheless it is firmly established at present through the enterprise and the perseverance of the pioneer rabbi on the Pacific Coast. Sixty children attend the school daily and are instructed in all branches usual at English and Jewish educational institution. On Saturdays and Sundays there are probably one to two hundred pupils in attendance, and they are instructed in the Bible and the main principles of Judaism.

The above-named founder of this institution, with whom the author had the honor of becoming acquainted personally, deserves to be known as a philanthropist who has to his credit many good deeds and great benefactions. He exerts himself to the utmost to make Judaism ever more firmly rooted, spends most of the day at the school, and allows all poor children to attend free of charge. Indeed, he assists these out of his own means with all that they need, such as books, clothing, food and the like. It is no wonder that he is generally regarded by them as a father, so that they even show him their affection on the street and hang on to his coat-tails on all sides — to help empty his full pockets.

Quite recently, he also opened a kindergarten. Many children of the tender age from three to five years are received in one of his houses. Here they are under the supervision of a lady and are prepared for attending school. In addition to these splendid qualities of heart and soul, Dr. Eckmann (who is a man of about fifty) has equally distinguished qualities of spirit and understanding. He is a learned man and has studied at German universities. Because of his great sacrifices, his income for his own purposes, that would otherwise be very good, has been much reduced and, as a result, as I know personally, he lives very poorly. I remember that once, to mention only a small matter, I found him sleeping in his newspaper-office on a very old couch, the springs of which were quite unreliable. What a difference between many European learned men and this American! One becomes rich writing books, the other remains poor and pale at it; one fills his head only with knowledge in order to shine as a star, the other is like the warming sun that with its light spreads life and flourishing growth at one and the same time; one strives after orders, titles, letters of homage and other distinctions, the other has hardly a coat to his back and considers it his greatest delight to sit among children on a low, dusty school-bench, unknown and unregarded by the rest of the world. Their innocent and grateful glances fill his soul with joy and rapture and awaken emotions and sensations in him that he would not exchange for millions nor all the wealth in the world.

I could cite many illustrations of his noble characteristics, but shall

230

tell only one. One afternoon, when it was almost two o'clock, I came upon him busy at a cupboard and saw that he was grinding coffee. I asked him why he was doing that. He took some bread and sugar and said: "This is my lunch. I must be sparing for the sake of my children and cannot permit myself anything better." It is not necessary to show more explicitly that such a man is always affectionate and helpful to the stranger and the traveler and exerts himself to the utmost to assist a necessary and meritorious undertaking. Unfortunately, I must add that this worthy man, even to this day, has found little recognition and assistance among the residents of the place — even among his fellow-Jews. Daily experience has shown a million times that a man will squander thousands in good living and for luxuries, but, often enough, will not have a penny to spare for art, science, charitable institutions and religious purposes. It is the same here; and this is why a man like Eckmann has so little assistance!

Academic Seminary

This school was opened only recently by the Rev. Dr. Elkan Cohn. It has four classes.

The seminary building is in a very healthful part of the city. Since the choice of teachers was a fortunate one, Dr. Cohn, in the course of time, may not only be useful to those who wish to provide their children with a thorough education, but may make his own future more secure, for the number of children in attendance is constantly increasing and promises to bring the enterprising rabbi great profit.

At present, the number of pupils is about ninety. Ten poor children have not only been accepted free of charge but have also been provided with books. Tuition fees are from four to eight dollars a month. Four languages are taught, Hebrew, English, German and French, in addition to other branches of learning of great benefit in the education of the young. Both boys and girls are admitted. Daniel Levy, the French teacher, formerly appointed by the French government to teach in a Jewish school in Algiers, is particularly excellent. The worthy Dr. Cohn himself conducts the classes in religion and Hebrew and very conscientiously supervises the school. I had the opportunity of visiting this institution often and was always delighted at the good spirit of the place: may it continue to thrive and flourish!

Chapter XXX

General Survey of the Israelites in California

Since san francisco is the chief center of the jews of california, we will at this point offer a general survey of the Jews in this State. Their number amounts to ten thousand. Of these half live in San Francisco. Almost all of them are doing well. The few who are rich maintain themselves and their families at least in an honorable fashion. It is only in San Francisco that a very small number of poor Jews is to be found, by way of exception, and it is rapidly diminishing. They are generously assisted by their fellow Jews. The great industry of the Jews of California, their temperance, their activity — all distinguish them favorably and here, too, they have a great influence in mercantile affairs: they have contributed not a little to the rapid rise of trade. This is generally acknowledged, and whoever will not admit it may know better from an occurrence of not so long ago.

It happened that two years ago the steamers for the East, chiefly to New York, were about to leave on the Jewish Day of Atonement. But since all the Jewish places of business were closed, the steamers had to postpone their departure for a day. So marked is the Jewish preponderance in trade! Their number and influence is also not without effect upon State affairs. The fifteen hundred votes that they have to offer in San Francisco on election days have some weight in the scales and they know how to rebuff and repay wrongs and infringements of their rights at that time. This may be shown by facts. For example, the principal of a public school rejected the services of an educated lady as a teacher simply and bluntly because she was a Jewess. In a land of religious liberty and tolerance, of equality of standing and of equal rights, this caused great and justified excitement, and it was decided at the first opportunity to requite such an act. When the time came for the election of school-principals, all the Jews voted against this intolerant man under whose guidance they did not believe their children to be safe. As a result he lost his post and was replaced by one more tolerant. The teacher thereupon received at once the work she had sought. The principal who was discharged betook himself, complaining bitterly, to Mr. Henry Seligmann, president of Congregation Emanu-El in San Francisco, and asked him, for he was an old and intimate friend, why he had acted as he did against him. He was told by way of answer that fellow believers took precedence over business friends and, moreover, that friendship could fasten no firm roots beside intolerance.

Their influence extends naturally to all other elections and Israelites not infrequently occupy important posts in the cities without thereby causing complaint or dissatisfaction. The majority are inclined to be Republicans in their politics, as was shown in San Francisco in the last presidential election.

The Jews are greatly respected by the non-Jews and it may well be said that nowhere else are they regarded with as much esteem by their non-Jewish brothers, and nowhere else are they so highly valued in social or political circles, as in the above-named city. Business, banking as well as trade, is to a great extent in their hands. The market depends upon them completely, because they import the most, and the most expensive, goods; and shipping and the forwarding business have them to thank for a great part of their flourishing condition.

In social circles, as at balls and other public gatherings, or in private groups devoted to the pleasure of conversation and social diversions, the Jews with their beautiful, always fashionably-dressed women play a fairly important part. They are the principal supporters of the opera-house, for some of them are very fond of music and know a good deal about it. Whenever an undertaking of public interest or benefit is to be carried out, the Jews are looked to first of all, because they are always ready to contribute, and such undertakings are generally successful because of their assistance. A large part of the wealth of California is in their hands: they have acquired it by thrift and sobriety, by steadfast industry and toil. It is particularly the Jews from southern parts of Europe, that is, those who come from Germany and France, who are engaged in very profitable business; to these may be added a few from Poland and England. They are represented in every branch of business; but in California, as elsewhere, they are chiefly in trade and most of them have a wholesale or retail store. Jewish lawyers and doctors merit special notice and praise for they are well regarded and beloved as the best and most devoted.

Charity, as has been often said, is one of the ancient virtues of the Jews and has been transmitted from generation to generation. Here also, thank God, it maintains its place. No one, no matter who he is, asks in vain for help and there is hardly any difference to be seen in the treatment of Jew and non-Jew. The many charitable institutions and the thousands of dollars spent every year in aid of the poor are sufficient evidence that the Jew has retained a sympathetic heart for the suffering of others. In urgent cases, not only the resources of the benevolent societies are resorted to, but the hand of every man is that of a ready giver. Their charity is not seldom put to the test, for often enough a helpless man who can no longer defy the storms of life, as one must in California, would like to hurry back home to his family; or someone who has come to grief without the least fault of his own must be helped to his feet; no one then withdraws his hand. Thousands of Jewish immigrants have received help and assistance from their fellows in faith so that it was possible for them to seek their fortune in the world; thousands owe their present respectable positions to the noble and generous hearts of fellow Jews who in the hour of trial stretched out a rescuing hand. Thousands who have left these shores to seek again the native land and the friends of their youth and to enjoy on the soil they had come from the wealth they gained here have every right to be proud of the fact that they contributed to the erection of institutions that will continue to exist because of their noble actions when they themselves become dust and ashes.

There is less call upon these institutions now that the condition of the working-class is far better than it had been. Social conditions are now more orderly and, due to the decline in number and extent of the disasters and misfortunes that were characteristic of the early history of California, the helplessness of those who have large families to support has vanished. Now that almost everywhere food and the cost of living has become cheaper, everyone can make a living in a respectable and honorable way. At the last Passover, for the first time, no Jew applied to a charitable society for *matzoth*. Since it is the custom everywhere among Jews to provide generously for the poor during these eight days, this would indicate that the financial condition of the Jewish residents is satisfactory.

At the time when the Mortara kidnapping created so much excitement throughout the world, the Israelites of California replied most readily to the requests of the unfortunate father who had been robbed of his child — and in what a noble fashion they replied! Almost eight thousand dollars was sent from the State of California alone and, if money had been able to obtain the desired result and could have succeeded in freeing the Mortara boy from the clutches of the Inquisition, I have not the least doubt that in a very short time a much larger sum would have been raised. In a similarly generous fashion, the Jews in California acted towards the poor, unhappy Jews of Morocco to whom they sent the considerable sum of ten thousand dollars.

I should also like to mention the great mass-meeting held in San Francisco to express the indignation and outrage aroused by the Pope's conduct in the Mortara case. One of the largest meetings ever seen in California was then held, consisting not only of Jews but of non-Jews, too, for everyone was invited to it. Clergymen of all sects, except Roman Catholics, were present and all expressed their abhorrence of the conduct of the Catholic Church in this matter and condemned it. Rabbis delivered excellent addresses, but even more than these it was the Christian ministers who by their speeches spurred men into action. Citizens who occupied the highest positions in the political and social world were present at this meeting and a great number of these publicly expressed their indignation at this despotic act so unsuited to our enlightened age! Circulars were soon printed and distributed containing the resolutions of the meeting and inviting the Jews to work together for the freeing of the poor boy. In a short time contributions were received from every mining-camp. Thus the Jew has never acted contrary to his nature in whatever clime, under whatever sky and in whatever circumstances he may chance to live, and never does he forget his duties to his fellow men.

Politically, the Jew has the same rights as the Christian. He may rise to every office and every dignity. Several Jews hold office in this city. These posts call for much trust in those who occupy them and they fully meet this requirement. Their service as public officials is highly valued and their advice is often sought. At the last presidential election, Mr. Henry Seligmann, an ardent Republican, was often asked for his advice and counsel with respect to the campaign. In politics, every difference between Jew and non-Jew is gone; he who is full of ideas and understands the thousand other things that a politician must be clever at, is and remains the most suitable man. He may then run for office with confidence, will be elected and, when he has once gained a foothold, it will be easy for him to make his way to a more distinguished office. At present there are several Jews among the city officials. —two of them being employed by the Government at Washington.

Of the religious condition of the Jews of this place, since it is the least cheering, I speak last: there is little to say about their performance of religious duties and observances: they have thrown everything overboard as burdensome ballast. Only New Year's Day and the Day of Atonement have still some meaning for them. In this respect, San Francisco provides the most encouraging aspect, and here, too, there are a great many who observe the dietary laws. But the related laws and precepts are more and more neglected; and so the *matzoth* for the Passover feast are baked of the flour usually offered for sale in the

235

market, no attention whatever being paid to the regulation for grinding the flour. When I was in San Francisco (1861), a wedding was celebrated during the "middle days," or half-holidays of Passover, without regard to the custom of not having such a celebration during those days. One of the rabbis who formerly functioned there performed the marriage ceremony. After this, the table was spread and *matzoth* placed on it — but they did not fail to provide also newly-baked bread over which the rabbi was also expected to say grace. Such a request angered the rabbi; but in response to his reproof and earnest effort to explain, as he subsequently reported to me, he had to listen to the insulting remark: "We live in the enlightened nineteenth century!"

So close to freedom is license. But this time will also pass for Israel; the threatening danger that frivolity conjures up for it will fortunately not last, and fairer days will dawn in which it will willingly and joyfully acknowledge its God and see Israel's loftiest goal in the keeping of His laws.

Chapter XXXI

About Churches and Various Other Institutions

There are thirty-eight churches in san francisco that are used for religious services. The cost of erecting them was $696,000. The Catholics have the most beautiful churches. In all, there are six of these: the cathedral of St. Mary (the name of the archbishop is Alemany), St. Patrick's, St. Ignatius' (under the ministry of three fathers of the Jesuit order), St. Francis', Notre Dame des Victoires (Our Lady of Victory) and the mission Dolores. The last is situated two miles from the city, at the site where the first church on the Pacific coast was built in 1776. The building is at present in a state of ruin and must sooner or later give place to a new one, particularly since the numerous statues, which are by no means of the usual size, can no longer be supported by rickety rafters.

The various branches of the Baptists have four churches. The Congregationalists have three. The English High Church, or Episcopalians, has four churches, namely, Grace Church, Trinity, St. John's, situated in the mission Dolores, and the Church of the Advent.

The German Lutherans have one church.

The Methodists (the Methodist Evangelical Church) have nine churches. Three of these are for Germans and two for Negroes.

The Presbyterians have six churches. Among these are one for Germans, one for Chinese and one for sailors.

The Swedenborgians have one church.

The Unitarians, likewise, have one.

Two new churches are almost finished and promise a marked increase in the value of the land in their neighborhood.

Thus Africans and Chinese, Germans and English, Swedenborgians and Spiritualists have their churches, halls and meeting-houses and their religious services. There is hardly a religious sect on the face of the earth that has no representation here on Sunday.

Religious Societies

Of religious societies, such as Bible, Tract, and Temperance societies, there are twelve in the city. Their purpose is the spread of Christianity and the absolute prohibition of intoxicating liquor.

There are twenty-eight charitable societies. In this number are included the charitable institutions of the various religious sects and nationalities.

The city has twenty protective associations, such as medical, commercial, real-estate owners' associations and the like. Their purpose is to protect the members against competition.

Literary and Historical Societies

Eleven literary societies, each of which has a good library and a considerable fund, speak very well for so young a city as San Francisco.

Societies for Social Entertainment

There are fifteen societies for the purpose of social entertainment and they have very many members. Several are for the purpose of arranging pleasure-parties and dances; others devote themselves to athletic exercises.

Freemasons

The city has twelve Masonic lodges besides three grand lodges, a council and two commanderies. At present they are jointly engaged in building a temple which will excel all others in America and the cost of which will amount to half a million dollars.

In addition, there are three lodges for Negroes which have received a charter from Great Britain.

I.O.O.F.

The Independent Order of Odd Fellows is greatly respected in the State of California, principally because the order is founded on purely humanitarian principles and its purpose is to make men sociable and spiritual. The Oddfellows have eleven lodges in the city and nine hundred members. They not only have a splendid hall in the center of the city but, in spite of the amount spent on building, have a substantial fund.

Independent Order of Knights

This charitable organization originated in California and was first organized in 1858. It has two lodges in the city and its membership is increasing rapidly.

Independent Order of the Sons of Malta

This organization was recently introduced from the East and I could learn little about it. It is making rapid progress by means of charitable gifts made in great secrecy.

Military Organizations

There are eleven companies of State Militia. They are thoroughly drilled and provided with good quarters. They must parade whenever a famous person arrives or on the anniversaries of great events. For such services the poor soldiers receive nothing extra — except that in bad weather (and this is no rare occurrence) they may expect to catch cold and get stiff necks.

Insurance Companies

No less than forty-eight insurance companies do business in San Francisco, and this with an unknown capital — in any event, it consists only of figures.

Hospitals

The city has nine hospitals, including the French, German, and Italian hospitals. The French have a splendid hospital. My friend, Daniel Levy, is the secretary, and S. Lazard treasurer. It has three thousand members who are very charitable towards their people.

Cemeteries

There are five cemeteries in San Franciso. Two belong to the Jewish community and, partly because of their situation, partly because of their better arrangement and more substantial inclosure, they are the best in the State. They were only acquired and arranged a short time ago and cost almost $40,000. A large sum for the last resting-place! But it must be confessed that competition has much worse results.

Expressage Conveniences

There are five express companies which forward money, baggage and letters to all parts of the civilized world. The prices that the express companies demand are very high in California: a simple letter to be delivered within the State costs ten cents. This is a very high price and brings in a great profit to the owners, since almost everybody sends his letters by express — not because it is any more certain, but simply because it is much more expensive than mailing them and everything that is expensive, in the opinion of Californians, must be good.

Mail-Coaches

Seven mail-coaches leave the city daily for all parts of the United States. By a recent act of Congress, California was granted a daily mail-service by land. This offers the traveler a convenient opportunity to leave any nice morning for St. Louis, New Orleans, or New York. The necessity of a daily mail-service by land was long felt and it is now one of the most reliable conveniences of the State. In addition to the mail-coach service between California and the Atlantic states, there is also a pony-express. This leaves San Francisco three times a week for St. Louis and arrives in eight days. It is expected, however, that even these rapid ways of transmitting news will be out of use as soon as the telegraph across the continent is fully ready. This should occur in the course of next year.

Sea-Going Steamers

Steamers that are seaworthy leave the bay, five times a month, for Panama and the [East] Coast.

239

Steamboats

Seven steamboats run daily between the city and various parts of the bay. Several go to Sacramento, Stockton, San Jose and Benicia; others to Petaluma, Napa and still smaller places on the other side of the bay to the cities of which a steamboat leaves every hour.

Railways

The railway within the city and county of San Francisco is only three miles long, but it is rumored that all the near-by cities will soon be connected with San Francisco by railway.

Omnibuses

Four omnibus lines cross the city. They do very good business because the inhabitants of California are too lazy to walk, be it sunshine or rain. This is particularly true of the women who take an omnibus simply for amusement and also to go just from one street to the next.

Chapter XXXII

THE GERMANS IN SAN FRANCISCO AND THEIR SOCIETIES

A German May Day

IT IS A HISTORICAL FACT THAT THE GERMANS HAVE CONTRIBUTED MOST to the settlement of a territory wherever a new tract is to be cultivated, ground that has never been ploughed has to be tilled and the establishment of a new home is at stake. We do not say this perforce out of any partiality, but as a simple statement of impartial and historical fact. The reasons for it are in the German spirit and only the greatest conceit and stupidest national pride of others, inferior to the Germans but who, nevertheless, think themselves far more illustrious peo-

240

ples, will deny it. California adds another proof of this to the many that history has to offer.

The number of German residents of the city of San Francisco is more than 20,000. They very soon united in societies for the more ready satisfaction of their bodily and spiritual needs. We shall now describe the more important of these societies.

The San Francisco Society

It was founded in 1852 to improve and protect the interests of the German residents of California. They discuss matters of importance to the Germans, but social entertainment is not excluded. The society has an important library of literary and scientific works in German, English, French and Spanish.* In addition, it has all the important European and American newspapers. The society also possesses two billiard tables. It has a large room for meetings and balls and another for reading, games, billiards and conversation. It has almost one hundred members, among them the most distinguished Germans of San Francisco. A board of directors, consisting of thirteen members, directs the affairs of the society. The present officers are: Dr. Regensburger, a Jew, president; Kruse, vice-president; Helmken, second vice-president; Grosskopf, recording secretary; Dörmitzer, financial secretary; Wapler, treasurer; Rühling, librarian.

Natural History Society

After an American society for this pupose had been in existence for some time, a German society was also organized in 1861. Its purpose is to investigate the rich sources of California in mineralogical, zoological and botanical specimens, and to plan a museum for this purpose. The society has already many and worthy members and a fine mineralogical and zoological collection. The director is Dr. J. N. Eichel. Dr. J. Regensburger is the first and Mr. Jordan the second vice-president. Mr. Tilman is the secretary and Mr. Michelson treasurer. The curators for zoology are Dr. Scharlach and Mr. Schmidt; for mineralogy Mr. Riehn; and for botany Messrs. Bauer and Bisor, pharmacists.

German General Aid Society

This society has been in existence since 1855 and was founded with the benevolent purpose of assisting Germans without means by giving

---

*   I received from this society a letter of thanks for presenting it with my book of travels in Asia and Africa. The letter is dated December 4, 1860.

them money or work, and of taking care of Germans who are sick. The society built its own brick hospital in 1857. It has all the conveniences of a modern hospital and is suitable for receiving sixty to seventy patients comfortably. The hospital is in every respect arranged in the most comfortable and most useful way, especially with respect to the arrangement and construction of the rooms, ventilation, water-supply and bathing installations which include warm sulphur and steam baths. A large, beautiful garden offers patients the opportunity of taking walks.

The number of members is at present about 1200. Most of them live in San Francisco and some inland. Each member must pay a dollar a month as dues; the initiation fee is two dollars. Every German, or one who speaks German, has the right to become a member provided he is well. In case of sickness, every member has a right to apply for admission to the hospital and, if he has been a member for two months, he must be admitted. Furthermore, every German who is poor and sick and has not been in California more than two months must be admitted. Whoever is not a member will be admitted upon payment of two to two-and-a-half dollars daily. Briefly, these are the excellent and noble rules of the society.

The society elects its board of directors annually. This consists of a president, a first and a second vice-president, a recording and a financial secretary, a treasurer and seven other members. The board of directors is divided into various committees of which the hospital committee is responsible for supervision of the hospital and the aid committee is responsible for aid outside of the hospital. The board elects the superintendent of the hospital, agents outside of the city and the hospital doctors. At present there are three doctors in charge of the patients. The president of the society is Mr. Moebius. The hospital doctors are: Dr. Fr. Loehr, Dr. F. Regensburger, and Dr. Scharlach.

The number of members is growing daily and the hospital is always full of sick so that it was necessary this summer to add two large wings to it. It is an ornament of San Francisco and a monument of honor to the Germans of California who were not engulfed in struggling and hunting for gain. Nowhere else in the United States has a society like this been able to reach the heights of this organization.

In addition to the societies mentioned there is also a large athletic club, two male choral societies, Harmonie and Eintracht, and a choral society of men and women called Cecilia Society. All the singing societies of the country held a great song-festival this year in San Francisco.

At this point I must not fail to mention with gratitude that I was received in the friendliest manner by all these various societies, to whom I was introduced by the letters of recommendation of the greatest German scholars: a kindness only he can fully appreciate who has himself eaten the bread of loneliness in a foreign land.

A German May festival on the soil of California must arouse the interest of the traveler, and the reader will be grateful to me if I present a detailed picture of such a day. The Germans' inextinguishable (though not always tested) loyalty to the customs and traditions of their dear old Fatherland, was displayed in excellent fashion at the celebration of the third May Festival of the German General Aid Society, held in San Francisco in 1861.

The May festival of the society, which had already erected such important monuments to German charity in the midst of San Francisco, contributed much to drawing together and fusing the various elements of the German population. The third May festival was not merely an annual festival of the society, but a general festival for all who were of German origin; in addition to the material result, which was certainly a highly profitable one, it was also a stimulus to closer unity and greater harmony among Germans — a unity not otherwise to be found everywhere. The dissonances that now and then in past years disturbed the unity of the German people in California will certainly be silenced for a long time under the influence of this festival and, it is to be hoped, never again find expression. It is already a good omen for the future that a festival at which so many thousands moved about in a limited space went off with the greatest cheerfulness and without the least disturbance.

The parade formed in Schüppert's Hall at the corner of Stockton and Pacific Streets. Preceded by a band, it set out at one o'clock in the afternoon. At the head rode Mr. G. A. Bauer, marshal of the festival, and his adjutants, H. H. Mairisch and Chas. Kohler. The California Fusiliers, under their captain, F. T. Tittel, opened the parade with the Stars and Stripes gleaming in their midst. Then came the Social Turnverein (athletic club) with its black, red and gold banner, and the members of the Aid Society, at the head of which were Mr. C. F. Moebius, its president, and Dr. Löhr, the speaker at the festival. The Harmonie, the Eintracht, the Teutonia Männerchor, and the Schützenverein (rifle club) with its beautiful American flag ended the line of parade. It went along Stockton Street, then Washington Street, then through Montgomery, Market, Third, Howard, Fourth, and Folsom Streets to Russ Garden. At half past two, Dr. Löhr delivered his address, in which he pointed out the beneficial influence of German

festivals upon the spirit of the people and particularly their tranquil-
lizing and strengthening effect amidst the unrest and confusion of the
present. The address was received with applause and I am especially
grateful to Dr. Löhr for letting me have his manuscript. Here is the
address at the festival in full:

My fellow citizens:

When weary of the bustling activity of the world, where else can
a man find rest if not in the circle of his own people? There the struggle and strife of the outside world does not penetrate; there the vexations that made the day weary for him, that wore away his strength
and filled his soul with grief, are silent.

And where shall we take refuge when the world about us is torn
by the savage struggle of political parties; when all the bonds that tied
society together threaten to part; when brother lifts his hand against
brother; when in the midst of the general babble of tongues the speech
with which, only shortly before, all came to an understanding with
one another, seems to have lost all meaning?

And yet we do indeed know a place amidst this wild struggle where
we can take refuge if we wish to enjoy an hour of peace. For we, too,
have a beloved circle that opens its arms to us, a circle in which wild
passions are silent and where we can find rest in a few hours of recreation and recoup our strength for new endeavors. The memories of
home awaken in us, and we seek peace in the circle of those who were
brought up with us at the same maternal breast of German life; we
enter the circle of our brothers who with us form a great family, and
in the midst of the struggle we have a beautiful festival of peace, a
May Day whose greenery refreshes us; we shake hands with everybody whatever our views, and we celebrate *a German festival of freedom in the circle of our German family*. If only for a short time, let
us throw off the cares of the world without, let us forget the savage
brawl, and let us rejoice in the joy that radiates before us.

I welcome you all, my fellow citizens, who have crowded together
here today to awaken the memories of our dear home, to forget the
long difficult years that lie between today and that fair time when we
also, to be sure, gathered on this day but when all our days were one
happy holiday; when as yet we had no reason to seek forgetfulness of
the troubles of life; when our dear home still embraced us all with its
loving arms, and joy and rejoicing filled our breast.

Wherever the German sets foot on the wide earth, he finds the same
spirit; everywhere he finds the same altars on which German life is
sacrificed; everywhere we bring with us our festivals and our songs;
everywhere we cherish the spirit that unites us with the distant home-
land.

Few indeed are the cities, that in this respect are to be compared

244

with San Francisco. Here German life blossoms and flourishes mightily; here in a few brief years a German life has developed among the people as nowhere else.

Everyone feels, in the midst of the alien hustling of savage business and political life, the longing for a quiet corner in which, if only for a few hours, he can place himself again in the happy times of the past and recuperate from the hardships of his difficult migration.

That is the meaning of our folk festivals. They are green oases along the weary, thorny road through the dry wastes of business life. Everyone hurries to it to share in the folk-life of the home-land, to convey to his children a memory of the far-off home, to be merry once more with wife and child as he once was merry in the distant fatherland.

Wherever German is spoken, there is our fatherland; and at the dear familiar sounds we are at home. We shake hands with everybody joyfully, high or low, poor or rich, who with us is a link in the great chain that spans the whole earth with German life, German customs, German honesty.

And as the life of our people is German — and remains so, wherever Germans may tarry — the ends that we pursue in this German life of ours are always German, that is, they are always devoted to what is good, either benevolence or the development of German cultural activity, as these exist in such strength and beauty everywhere in the life of our German societies.

Today, both German benevolence and German culture, have brought us together. With joyful pride I greet the assembled societies of this city, who, working together as brothers, have come together to help further the sacred, beautiful interests of humanity and of benevolence. Even though our societies in their purposes diverge in different directions, in one respect they are always together: wherever it is a matter of stretching forth a helping hand to a hapless brother and of erecting a memorial that we can leave to our children as a proud structure that German unity and German co-operation have established.

With pride I mention the structure, the completion of which we further today: a memorial of German unity and German public spirit. Yes, my fellow citizens, there is unity and public spirit among the Germans here, even if now and then the powerful exuberant life is clouded; even if now and then the various tendencies collide somewhat violently; even if now and then views are defended with rather excited liveliness. We Germans are a debating people. There must be debates. When debating, one sometimes does not weigh his words with care; but when it comes to action, when it is a question of furthering a good intention, we are all one. And if we previously debated in a somewhat lively fashion about the manner in which this intention should be accomplished, we are afterwards, for that very reason, all the more united.

I have often enough heard sharp condemnation by non-Germans of this national characteristic of Germans: they speak of strife and brawling. But actually no people shows more public spirit in carrying out good purposes than the Germans. We argue. We have, if I am not mistaken, also argued about the May festival and, indeed, in lively fashion. But today we are all here, everyone animated with the best of good-will, everyone willing to contribute his mite. No one thought of division and of separation from the good work. So shall it be and so remain; and without debate all interest in doing good would soon be extinguished!

For all that, today we are all here in our places, and I bid you all welcome most heartily. I am happy to be able to tell you only good news of the progress of the building to which you have all contributed a stone. Last year I explained that we wanted means for the shelter of fifty instead of twenty-five sick. The means were furnished! Today we need room for a hundred sick, and the means for this, too, will be furnished. What a glorious realization for our German residents of California to know that they have created a place of refuge that opens its doors to a hundred who suffer and are in pain, a place the like of which the Germans of no other city of the United States can point to on so large a scale.

With pride, therefore, I bid you welcome today in the name of the good cause we are all furthering. May many May Days to come, as today's, unite us in a like noble purpose; may the spirit of benevolence remain in all of you as zealous as today; may German public spirit and German benevolence continue to develop with equal strength so that they continue to stand here as a firm, healthy tree to continue to give our children shelter and shade. Thus, in fifty years from now, when Germans gather together for a like purpose on a like day, their fathers, who had begun so gloriously this noble work that will continue to bring blessings to our children and our children's children, will be remembered and praised.

My poor words are insufficient to praise enough what the Germans of California have been doing for years for the hospital of this place. Its history is a history of sacrifice which the community at large, as well as the board of directors representing the society, have displayed. How small the beginnings were! With what anxieties was the bold idea of building our own hospital accepted! At the beginning, there was doubt whether or not the means could be found to provide place enough for only twenty sick persons. Finally — how quickly the undertaking has grown from year to year! — before this year is over, we shall be able to say that the society is free of debt and has the room to receive a hundred sick persons. This German public spirit has been able to do; go and do likewise. This people have accomplished who, for the most part, had a few years before entered a strange land without means. These men have not only established a modest estate for themselves that provides them and their families with a livelihood, but they have not forgotten their suffering brother and have opened a place of refuge for him that the foremost city of Europe need not be ashamed of. This was done not only by the well-to-do; no, even the poor man contributed his mite by stinting himself of the necessities of daily life in order to place a contribution at the altar of humanity.

Above all, let us remember — among those who have furthered our great work greatly — our German women and girls. When did woman ever lack zeal if there was something good and noble to be furthered? And, truly, in no year were we so richly provided for, on their part, as this when the liberality of the women of this place has really overwhelmed our festival with gifts.

The work will soon be finished! The temple of honor to German public spirit will soon be completed. All of you, in assembling here, have helped build this splendid achievement; you may all with pride call it your work and it will testify to the spirit which animates the Germans of San Francisco today. I do not ask for a more beautiful monument and there is none more lasting, for it will still endure when we ourselves crumble into dust and ashes. And when the structure of stone and mortar is overthrown by time, this monument will endure in the memory of man as long as there is still a tongue to praise the acts of good Samaritans; as long as good deeds find recognition, it will endure for all times as a memorial of the noble spirit of the Germans of San Francisco.

So ended this inspired and, under the circumstances, inspiring address. When it was over, the Teutonia choral society sang the song "Sängergruss" (singer's greeting) in an admirably precise manner. The excellence of the execution was all the more commendable because the choral society, we have been informed, was first asked to sing after the festival parade had arrived at the grounds of the Garden and sang without any preparation whatever. A poem for the festival, written by Mr. Otto Körnich, was without doubt one of the best productions of German poetry ever created on the soil of California. We believed that this poem would be recited. Surely, we believed, there was someone to be found whose gift of elocution was equal to the merits of the poem. But that was not the case. (Unfortunately, we cannot furnish the poem here: it is no longer to be found among our papers.)

The song was followed by concert music, dancing, athletic exercises (the strength and dexterity which characterized several of these cannot easily be excelled), and amusements for the young by way of sack-races and pole-climbing, just as these are all part of the day's program in the German fatherland. The greatest attraction at the festival was the booths in which were the contributions for raffling.

For this the ladies had contributed some of the finest examples of needle-work. At these booths there was an endless crowding about of gentlemen who cheerfully sacrificed their dollars in the hope of winning a piece of work prepared by the fair hands of a lady. The dancing crowds surged about in the hall until late in the evening and only returned to the city by the light of the stars.

We consider this the proper place to make a few remarks in point. Much as the Germans distinguished themselves in almost every respect, and much as they also assist all good and useful undertakings by money or other help, I must remark for the sake of truth that in all California, strange to say, there is not a single German theater. What an astonishing inconvenience! Can there be a greater artistic pleasure than to spend the long winter evenings before well-cast plays? Can anything exercise a more beneficial influence upon the minds of young ladies and gentlemen than to see the masterpieces of our great poets presented by great performers? Formerly, there were theatrical performances at least once a week, on Sundays. But the fairly good performers failed to find sufficient support and this year had to abandon their performances again.

It is likewise a matter deserving censure that the German newspapers have so little support. There are only three German papers in all of California. All three are published in San Francisco; two are dailies and the third a weekly. In spite of the fact that the newspapers are so few, the editors, as they themselves have told me, have no little trouble to keep going. That the existence of the German Press finds little support in California is also the result of the fact that a number of Germans, as I myself saw, have English newspapers in their hands, although, to my own knowledge, they cannot speak English and much less read it. This is again that contemptible aping of the stranger, the rejection by one's self of one's own nationality, this fawning after American favor that will not, and cannot, be won — since their stupid national pride will not give up its "God damn Dutch!"

Such conduct is not only ridiculous and contemptible — as an example of the comical and farcical merely it might easily be tolerated — but it is harmful, yes, dangerous. The German nature is in danger of being lost after German nationality has been completely sacrificed for a long time by such doings. A German will never become an American, no more than an American a German, because the national differences are so great that, like many chemical substances, they may not be mixed. The Germans would have been able to save their own nationality in this land and to preserve it right well. But they have completely failed to understand the splendid mission that was to be-

248

come theirs and therefore trifled it away frivolously: it was to be a light and a lamp and a guide-post for the American people to all that is good and beautiful. They themselves have extinguished this light or, rather, did not light it at all and broke the sign-post, so that they are now German, now American; they no longer know the right road and grope about in darkness like a blind man in broad day.

No nation was more clearly summoned for this lofty task: the Germans have never gone to extremes; they have developed science and art itself to its most flourishing state and ever taken the greatest part in all that is great, beautiful, noble and sublime. Here in California they have not shown this to its full extent. Every reasonable man can understand that in saying what we have said of the Germans we offend no nation; that we gladly grant that every nation has its superiorities, its gifts and its own mission from its Creator; but we cannot help granting the Germans, in view of all that we have said, the place of honor. I became acquainted with many excellent Germans in America who complained to me of what has been said above. Surely it is high time that the Germans in this land wake from their slumbers and, like a mighty man in armor who knows no fear, set to work with vigor to make their nationality felt and respected and to bestow its blessings upon other nations. May this time come soon!

Chapter XXXIII

OUTSTANDING PERSONALITIES

ALTHOUGH THE PERSON IS ALWAYS SECONDARY TO THE EVENT, OR IS lost in it and vanishes with it, it is nevertheless always interesting to become more closely acquainted with outstanding personalities who guide and control the fate of the group.

Daniel C. Broderick*

We begin this gallery with the late Hon. Daniel C. Broderick. He was born in 1824 in Washington, the District of Columbia, of poor but respected parents. His father was of Irish birth and emigrated to America a few years before Daniel's birth. He was a stone-cutter by trade and Daniel, as soon as he was old enough, became an apprentice at the same trade under the instruction of his father. When a young man, Daniel went to New York City where he remained until the California "gold fever" broke out, infected him also and carried him along. He had little opportunity in his youth for acquiring a good education, but all who became acquainted with him, or in any way came into contact with him during his youth, could easily see that he had a strength of spirit and traits of character that would sooner or later distinguish him and bring him to a position of honor. An inflexible will, a steadfast honesty, an indomitable persistence — these characterized him; he was as hard upon his enemies as he was true to his friends, and honest with every man. These qualities were already conspicuous in his youth and as he grew older came to full flower: they were also those which lifted him from obscurity to the loftiest posts of honor with which the residents of his new home could invest him.

During his residence in New York he had lived mostly in the Ninth Ward. He always kept open house and was generally regarded as a man of strict integrity and manly principles in spite of the peculiar

---

* Benjamin refers to him as Daniel C. Broderick. Hubert Howe Bancroft, *History of California*, vol. VI (San Francisco, 1888), refers to him as David C. Broderick and offers a biography varying from that given here.

influences which his business interests had upon him. Quickly he became acquainted with the politics of his ward and city. He always belonged to the Democratic Party, defended it and acted according to its principles. Yes, he was so resolute and curt in his opposition to all that was not "democratic" that soon he was regarded almost everywhere as a local leader of his party and exercised an influence that was felt and envied everywhere. At that time he had the right of designating the nominee for the Assembly.

In California, Mr. Broderick's career was brief but brilliant: he came as a plain and simple citizen and died a respected and meritorious senator, mourned by all. Not long after his arrival in California, Mr. Broderick became connected with the smelting and assay business of F. D. Kohler, conducted under the name of Kohler and Company. In this business he laid the foundation of his fortune.

In 1850, there was a vacancy among the representatives from San Francisco in the State legislature upon the resignation of Nathaniel Bennet, Esq., and Mr. Broderick was elected as his successor on August eighth. He afterwards became lieutenant-governor of the State and as such president of the senate during the governorship of John McDougal. As senator, Mr. Broderick showed great ability and promised to go far. During his term of office the struggle began, known as the Broderick and Gwin embroglios, which disrupted the Democratic party. All Mr. Broderick's struggles and efforts were devoted to being elected to the United States senate, and for this purpose he exerted all his strength. Thanks to his zeal, he was elected by the legislature in 1857 to represent his State in that body. He served in the senate conscientiously for two years and was a faithful representative of those who elected him.

During the bitter and memorable political strife in California before the election of 1859, Mr. Broderick and D. W. Perley had a falling-out. This was caused by some remarks Mr. Broderick let slip in a conversation about Judge Terry of the Supreme Court. Mr. Perley, an ardent follower of Judge Terry, took offence at Broderick's remarks and demanded satisfaction on behalf of the judge. Mr. Broderick declared Mr. Perley unworthy of any answer or satisfaction, but said that, after the election, he would hold himself responsible for anything that he had said or done. Immediately after the election, Judge Terry resigned as a member of the Supreme Court and challenged Mr. Broderick to a duel. This was accepted for September thirteenth and both, after the necessary arrangements had been made, went with their seconds to the place agreed upon. Mr. Broderick's seconds were the Hon. J. C. McKibben and General D. D. Colton; Judge Terry's, Calhoun Benham, Esq., the present district-attorney, and Col. Thomas Hayes. Mr. Broderick fell at the first shot, struck in the breast. Severely wounded, he lingered until the sixteenth of the month when death at last freed him from his great suffering.

Mr. Broderick's death evoked general sorrow throughout the country. Sympathetic grief was seen on every face and the State mourned aloud for the loss of its faithful representative by the tolling of bells during his funeral. On the seventeenth, his remains lay in state and thousands upon thousands came to pay their respects. At the soft, hardly audible, approach of each one to the remains of the dead senator, silent tears, lips tightly pressed together, and the general demeanor, disclosed the attachment of the people. Col. E. D. Baker, at present United States senator from Oregon, delivered an apt eulogy at the plaza on the eighteenth and the remains were brought to their final resting place, within the confines of Love Mountain, accompanied by the longest, most solemn and most impressive procession ever seen in California.

The fairest duty of a people remains that of commemorating with due solemnity the memory of those who devoted life and work to the service of the commonweal; and in this respect no one can say that the inhabitants of California are ungrateful. A splendid monument will be erected in the immediate future to the stone-cutter's son.

John A. Sutter

A book about California that does not mention John A. Sutter would leave the reader unacquainted with one of the most distinguished and interesting of personalities. Although this old pioneer enjoys a reputation as wide-spread and as lasting as that of the State itself — to whose flourishing condition he contributed effectively — we would be committing an injury to the old veteran and to the reader of this book if we omitted an honorable notice of the man.

John A. Sutter is of Swiss origin, but he was born in the city of Baden in the grand-duchy of Baden, on the night of April 1, 1803. Accordingly, he is in his fifty-eighth year. Tired of life as a soldier, he took ship to New York in July, 1834, and settled in the state of Missouri. From there he went to Oregon and came at last, on the second of July, 1839, to Yerba Buena. He received permission to settle at Sacramento and picked out the place now called Sutter's Fort after him. He was an excellent settler and did much to bring the neighborhood under cultivation. It was during the building of a new mill which he had proposed that gold was first discovered and therefore he is to be thanked for finding the vein of gold that made California what it is.

When the Americans came to the State, General Sutter gave them all possible assistance. At one time he owned so much land that, if he had not given it up, it would have made him the richest man in the State. As things are at present, he owns only his stock-farm, on the Feather River, and lives there. His name must naturally be followed by the chapter telling the story of the first discovery of gold.

Chapter XXXIV

THE STORY OF THE FIRST DISCOVERY OF GOLD

IN THE WINTER OF 1847-48, CAPTAIN SUTTER BUILT A SAWMILL ON THE southern fork of the American River, a tributary of the Sacramento. Mr. James W. Marshall undertook the construction. In the course of it, he found it necessary to direct water into the mill-race so that the force of the current might make it wider and deeper. The current carried away a good deal of mud and sand as it entered the mill-race and this settled on the bottom. One day Marshall, inspecting the place, noticed a few shining objects in a corner of this mass of mud and sand. His curiosity was aroused and he gathered them up, not a little surprised at the nature and value of his discovery. He immediately went to Captain Sutter and these are the captain's own words about the discovery:

> "One afternoon, after taking my nap, I sat down to write a letter to one of my relatives in Lucerne. Suddenly I was interrupted by the arrival of Mr. Marshall who burst into my room. At his state of unusual excitement, I supposed that something very serious must have happened and looked at once for my gun, as in that part of the world we used to do instinctively, to see if it was in its usual place. The mere arrival of Mr. Marshall at the fort at this time would have been sufficient to surprise me, since he had only gone away two days

before to make some changes in a mill for sawing pine boards. When he had collected himself, he told me that, if I were surprised at his unexpected return, I would be much more so at the importance of his news. 'News,' he cried, 'which if we both take advantage of it, will mean millions and millions of dollars for us!' I must honestly confess that at his words it occurred to me that he might not be quite right in the head, until his throwing down a handful of small leaves of the purest, finest gold very quickly dispelled all mistrust. I was greatly surprised and begged him to explain the meaning of what I was seeing for the first time."

He then went on with the story of the discovery as we have already told it above and continued:

"Mr. Marshall at first thought the sparkling objects were opals, a bright translucent stone, found in great plenty at the places exposed by the sudden breaking off of masses of earth from the bank. At first, then, he paid no attention at all to the objects. But when, later, he was giving the workmen new directions and again saw several shining pieces, his curiosity was aroused. He bent down to pick some of them up. 'I assure you,' Mr. Marshall said to me, 'I changed my mind two or three times if I should go to the trouble of bending down to pick them up, and had come to the conclusion not to bother about it when I caught sight of another piece — the largest I had as yet seen. I picked it up and found to my great astonishment that it was a small lump of purest gold!' He then gathered twenty or thirty little pieces that upon closer inspection confirmed his opinion that what he had found was gold. At first it occurred to him that it had been lost or buried there, perhaps by one of the earliest Indian tribes or by some of those mysterious inhabitants of the West about whom we have no longer any information but who were already living on this continent for centuries and who built the cities and temples the ruins of which are now scattered throughout the deserts and wilderness. When, however, he began to examine the surrounding ground more closely, he found that it had, more or less, gold in it. This decided him. He mounted his horse and rode as quickly as he could to bring me the news.

"When Mr. Marshall had finished his story and, by closer examination of the pieces he had brought with him, I had convinced myself that in all this there was no exaggeration involved, I became as greatly excited as he was. I asked him hurriedly if he had also shown these pieces to the workers at the mill and was happy to hear that he had not said a word to anyone. We promised each other to tell no one about the incident and got ready to go to the mill next morning. On our arrival, shortly before sundown, we dug up the sand at various places and soon had gathered more than an ounce of gold mixed with much sand. I spent the night at Mr. Marshall's and we continued our search next day in the neighborhood of the southern fork of the stream.

254

To our joy we discovered that gold was to be found throughout the whole neighborhood, not only in the bed of the main stream where it had settled thickly but also along every little dried-up stream and in every canyon. I believe that in the latter places it was to be found even more plentifully. I myself dug up, with just a little knife, a piece of solid gold that weighed almost an ounce and a half, and this was in a canyon where the water had dried out — not far up the mountain.

"In spite of the precautions we took not to be discovered, we noticed upon our return, from the excitement of the workmen, that we had been secretly followed and, to add to our dejection, an Indian, who had worked in the gold-mines near La Paz, with some pieces of gold that he had picked up in his hand, cried out: 'Oro! Oro! Oro!' ('gold, gold, gold')." This is Sutter's story.

Chapter XXXV

OUTSTANDING PERSONALITIES IN AMERICA (continued)

John B. Weller

JOHN B. WELLER FIRST SAW THE LIGHT OF DAY IN HAMILTON COUNTY, Ohio, January 1813. He received his preliminary education at Miami University at Oxford, Butler County, in the same state. At the age of eighteen he began to study law, and to practice it when he was no more than twenty. Soon afterwards, when he was twenty-one, he was elected district-attorney of the county in which he lived and had the honor of seeing himself in a position above that of his former instructor in law. He conducted his office to the general satisfaction of the residents of the county. At the end of his first term he was re-elected. Three years later, he became the representative of his district in Congress and took his seat December 1839. He was re-elected twice and his career in the House of Representatives ended March 4, 1845.

At the outbreak of the Mexican War, he was made captain of the Butler Guards and later lieutenant-general of the first Ohio Regiment of Volunteers. He had no lack of important posts. We cite the following: on January 8, 1848, he was nominated by the Democrats to be governor of Ohio but failed to be elected by three hundred votes; in January 1849, he was appointed by President Polk to the commission to fix the boundary between Mexico and the United States; in January 1850, he came to California and, as early as 1852, was named to represent the state in the United States Senate. His term expired in March 1857, but in the autumn of that year he was elected governor of the State on the Democratic ticket. His term as governor ended January 5, 1860.

Mr. Weller is at present forty-eight years old and, not counting his military service, has been eighteen years in public office. From the beginning of his career he has belonged to the Democratic Party and he has tried to realize its aims in every office entrusted to him.

In 1857, Mr. Weller was a candidate for the United States Senate, but in the Democratic caucus was defeated by D. C. Broderick. He was again a candidate for the Senate in 1860, but was defeated at the election by Milton S. Latham, the present incumbent of this office.

In January of this year (1861), Mr. Weller was appointed consul to Mexico by President Buchanan — an office he still holds.

Peter Lassen

Is there anyone, who is at all acquainted with the history of California, who has not heard of Peter Lassen? His name is immortalized among our mountains by Lassen's Butte, among our valleys by Lassen's Great Meadow, and among our hills by Lassen's Pass. Peter Lassen, although a man without great learning or much education, has fastened his name to places where it will remain until the rocks and mountains fall and chaos takes over. He deserves these tokens of honor because of his activity in bringing this new territory under cultivation.

He was born in Copenhagen, Denmark, August 7, 1800, and was murdered by Indians August 1859, near Honey Lake Valley. By occupation he was a blacksmith, having learned the trade in his twenty-seventh year. In 1828, he emigrated to the United States and settled in Missouri. He was too restless to remain there long, and in 1839 climbed the Rocky Mountains on the way to Oregon and then went to California, where he settled. He acquired land at various places and, devoting himself completely to cultivating his property, he was richly rewarded. Mr. Lassen took part in the Mexican War on the side of the Americans and gave Colonel Fremont and other leading officers material help. After the Americans settled in California, the bold pioneer met with many financial difficulties, so that all his property fell into the hands of swindlers and lawyers. He was compelled at last to set out for the mountains again and fell at the hands of Indians as he tried to help a band of emigrants.

James King, Son of William King*

Among those who played a great role in the annals of San Francisco, James King stands in the front rank. He was one of the pioneers of California, arriving in 1849. He was born in 1822 in the District of Columbia. He was educated to be a merchant and, when he was still quite young, entered the employ of a bank in Washington. He remained at such employment until the beginning of 1849. He then migrated to California, well provided with credit and other assistance by his former employer, to found a bank for himself. Unlucky speculation in draining mines as well as the panic of 1854 were sufficient to cause him grave financial difficulties. He threw himself into another field of work. Although inexperienced and new at the publishing business, he nevertheless began to publish the *Evening Bulletin* in 1855. His courage and originality of style very soon aroused general attention and placed his journal among the leading newspapers.

During his editorship, he took occasion to express himself about several persons in no flattering manner and incurred, by his comments about J. P. Casey, the man's deadly hatred. On May fourteenth, Casey attacked him in the street and shot him in the breast. The wound resulted in his death on the thirtieth of the month. His death aroused unusual sympathy and a large procession followed his coffin to the grave. Many, yes, very many, mourned his death from the bottom of their hearts, for with him a fighter for right and truth had departed.

Colonel John C. Fremont

Colonel John C. Fremont is, as a rule, regarded as the conqueror of California and his achievements with so small a force and against a much superior number place him in an equal rank with the famous heroes of chivalry. However, the final subjection of the province might very well, in fact, be ascribed to the bold, determined and energetic means that Commodore Robert F. Stockton employed and carried out. In his position as an officer in the Topographical Bureau of Engineers, it was a major part of his duties to explore the districts and

---

*   He is generally referred to as James King of William. Cf. H. H. Bancroft, ibid., vol. VI, p. 746f.

regions about the Rocky Mountains and find out better ways of communication between Missouri and California and Oregon.

In 1845, Fremont was instructed by the War Department to discover a shorter, more southerly and easier route to the Columbia River. In carrying out this commission he reached, in January 1846, Monterey in California. There was at that time on the part of the Californians — or rather among the Mexican authorities — great hostility to American immigrants. The result was that at the appearance of Fremont's little force in the neighborhood of Monterey, General Jose Castro, at that time commandant of the city, became suspicious and took precautions to contest any farther advance. To allay his suspicions, Fremont left his detachment and hurried to Monterey. His explanations, made in person to Commandant Castro, fully satisfied the latter and he was no longer uneasy.

Upon Castro's admission that he was fully satisfied, that he had no cause for uneasiness, Fremont returned to his troops. But he soon received a warning from the American consul in Monterey that the Mexican commandant was secretly planning to attack him. Fremont immediately occupied a strong position in the neighborhood and planted the American flag upon it. Meanwhile, Castro changed his mind, particularly after he had seen for himself the strong position of the Americans, and decided to pacify this "foolish and stubborn people."

Fremont pushed ahead on the route he was taking to Oregon; but he had not gone far before he met with hostile Indians who delayed him. He suspected that they were goaded on by the Mexican authorities. He also learnt, in the meantime, that Castro intended to attack the American settlers. Upon more definite and detailed information of this, Fremont took the bold resolution of taking warlike steps against California.

His complete force amounted at that time — incredible as it sounds, it is true — to sixty-two men. On the fifteenth of June, others, acting under his instructions, attacked the garrison at Sonoma and captured it. By this move he seized nine cannon and two hundred and fifty guns. From that time until the present, Fremont has been more or less involved in the history of California. In 1856, he was nominated by the Republican Party for the presidency of the United States. Although he received a large popular vote, he was not elected. He is the representative of those young men in America who in their struggle for political distinction know neither moderation nor limits; who, although animated by the most ardent desires for the welfare of their country, have not attained their goal. He was the first to plant the American flag on a peak of the Rocky Mountains. When the contest for the presidency was over, he returned to California. At his return, a brilliant reception was prepared for him — a triumphant welcome such as only a victorious prince might have on coming home. He retired quietly and since then has been more or less busy digging for gold on his property at Mariposa.

But the United States could not leave a man like that in idleness long and he was soon roused from his quiet life. In October 1861, he was made a major-general by Congress and placed in command of the army of the West. He has his headquarters in St. Louis, Missouri. He has met with the complete confidence of the people; he was greeted with cheers as one of the new heroes of the day and, in view of the fearlessness he had displayed and the enterprise he had shown, the people have placed the greatest hopes in him. Since he is fairly distant from the American capital and St. Louis is one of the most critical points at present, the president now in office has given him, as a sign of the confidence placed in him, almost unlimited power. He soon saw himself called upon to make use of it, but, as could have been easily foreseen, by his measures he could not escape the abusive tongues of his opponents, namely, the Democratic Party.

Chief item in the unfriendly criticism of Fremont is that he named only foreigners for his principal officers (although, to be sure, very worthy officers from foreign countries). This particularly aroused the envy of Col. Frank P. Blair. The latter denounced Fremont on twelve grounds and tried to have him removed from office. The grounds of complaint involved mostly accusations of neglect of duty: he had been too dilatory in entering upon his office; he had refused to receive officers bringing important dispatches; he had several times failed to reinforce the troops at a time of danger; he had been grossly negligent in not preventing the recruiting of enemy troops in Missouri; he had not removed an unworthy officer and, in addition, had appointed two unworthy men as officers; as well as that he had not carried out several decisions taken in Washington. By these accusations Fremont was placed in so harsh a light that it was only too obvious that they were dictated by hate and that Blair must be his bitterest enemy: that it was a bold attempt to overthrow a hated opponent. If Fremont were the man Blair portrayed he would certainly not have been entrusted with the most important post in the West, for only well-known personalities would be selected for such a post. By his accusations, Blair merely placed himself in a bad light. He will not succeed in his purpose, and his charges are only the deep groans of an embittered heart that wishes to ease itself. Besides, as I heard from the lips of the most important politicians of all parties, the removal of Fremont would not only be inexpedient but very dangerous and have the most harmful results because of his great following.

Chapter XXXVI

The Libraries of San Francisco

San francisco has every reason to be proud of its libraries, and a reporter in describing the city must not, for many reasons, overlook this point. In foreign countries, the generally prevalent opinion, held by almost everybody, is that the residents of California take pleasure only in the rage for money and that all their activity, their thoughts and feelings are given over to acquiring material wealth; that the purpose of their existence is to have well-filled pockets and well-stored warehouses and to possess fine clothes and splendid carriages. But a closer consideration of the matter shows clearly that in the midst of the bustle and external progress of San Francisco, and in spite of the running about and racing after wealth that infects everybody and spreads like a pestilence, provision has been made for spiritual development and in this respect, too, treasures have been gathered and accumulated. The progress that this city has made with regard to its libraries and schools is really astonishing and in these respects it can challenge comparison with any city in the Union. Generations to come, who will inherit what has been gathered and accumulated, will praise the noble liberality and the public spirit of the merchants, craftsmen and professional men, now alive, whose nobility of spirit and whose prudence have established these libraries that already have become important.

The largest and choicest library is that of the Mercantile Library Association at the northeastern corner of Montgomery and Bush Streets. It had, during my stay in San Francisco, 12,800 volumes, among them the works of the best authors and books in all branches of knowledge. In conjunction with this library there is a worth-while collection of minerals and plants. For more convenient use by the public, almost three thousand books of the library have been arranged in the rooms of the Association so as to be always accessible to everybody. The physical aspects of the library leave nothing to be desired: the rooms are bright, airy, comfortable and spacious, and the service is careful and attentive. In addition to the books, there is always laid out in the rooms a well-selected collection of newspapers and recent pamphlets from all parts of the world, and the walls are decorated with a superior collection of paintings and copper-plate engravings.

It is easy to obtain an idea of the rapid progress of this library if one considers that the Mercantile Library Association was only organized on January 24, 1853, and in such an incredibly short time has achieved so much. At the beginning three hundred joined it as members and the enterprise was finally inaugurated with the election of the following officers: David Turner, president; Joshua P. Haven, vice-president; C. E. Bowers, treasurer; W. H. Stevens, recording secretary; and Dr. Henry Gibbons, corresponding secretary.

Almost 34,000 volumes are lent annually by the library to readers and every year the society spends from two thousand to three thousand dollars to add to its collection of books. An initiation fee of two dollars and monthly dues of one dollar carry with it the right to make use of the library.

Another library with which it may, to some extent, be compared is that of the Odd Fellows Library Association, located in Odd Fellows Hall, at the corner of Kearney and Bush Streets. This society was organized in 1855 and at present its library has already 800 volumes, among them very rare and valuable books. It possesses, among other old books, the first complete history of the Pacific coast that has as yet appeared. A very valuable museum of curiosities of natural history is attached to the library; a splendid aquarium has been added to the museum.

The Mechanical Institute contains a valuable library of mechanical and scientific books, as well as those of general interest. The library has almost 5,000 books. It has also a cabinet of mineral and geological specimens, as well as various scientific apparatus. The society was organized in 1855 and towards the end of the year the library began to be collected. Its rapid progress offers striking evidence of the generosity, energy and competence of the members of this useful association.

In 1850, the Society of the Pioneers of California was organized and since then has been assembling a library: it has about a hundred volumes. However, these are not very valuable, for the society has only one object in mind: they wish to have in their archives reports and information about the first settlers in the State and to gather the earliest histories of the land. The library also has a valuable collection of zoological, geological and mineralogical specimens.

The St. Mary's Library Association

Its rooms are at the Cathedral of St. Mary. The library has about 800 volumes, chiefly of a religious or historical nature. In addition, there is an extraordinary and very valuable collection of letters of the old Spanish missionaries who were stationed on the Coast. The dates of the letters commence in the middle of the eighteenth century and treat of the earliest history of the country.

The collections of books that we have mentioned contain, approximately, 28,000 volumes extending to all branches of knowledge. Their true value cannot be estimated accurately any more than their future influence upon the residents of San Francisco. We should like to add also that the public and Sunday schools, as well as several hotels, have libraries. Altogether these amount to about 20,000 volumes and are readily accessible to the public.

Chapter XXXVII

GEOGRAPHICAL SURVEY

The City and Environs of San Francisco

THE LIMITS OF THE PRESENT CITY AND COUNTY OF SAN FRANCISCO extend north and east to the bay and the lower watershed along the shores of Marin County, south to the county of San Mateo, and west to the ocean. The southern boundary, as the crow flies, is six and a half miles from the plaza — a few yards north of the abbey. The plaza is a park, surrounded by an iron fence, in the middle of the city and right in front of the city hall. The line dividing the townships is numbered "2" and "3" and runs from the bay to the ocean directly west. The city and county are almost a square, six and a half miles from north to south and almost as much from east to west. This area measures forty-two square miles or 27,000 acres: 10,000 acres are under cultivation; 8,000 acres consist of rock, shifting sand and water; 6,000 acres are set aside for pasture; 2,000 acres belong to the city; and about a thousand acres are used for truck-farms. A brief description of the site of the "Bay City," or "Chrysopolis of the West," will not be without interest to the reader.

San Francisco is located on a narrow isthmus between a bay and the ocean; it faces the bay and the east. Five miles away the great ocean comes rushing in. The bay extends southward for thirty-six miles, parallel to the sea and separated from it by a narrow strip of land, from five to twenty miles wide. The city rises at the outermost point. For this reason its situation is beautiful and stately; upon a steep level, that measures half a mile from the water's edge to the hills in the background, the houses rise row on row. Two promontories, Clark's Point to the north and Rincon Point to the south, a mile from each other, project into the bay, and between them form a half-moon along which is the city's water-front. The city has already occupied all of this space and for the most part it is built up. The two headlands and the rising hills, up which in a very short time the city will climb, provide a very picturesque sight.

It would be difficult to find anywhere else more charming and more varied views than may be enjoyed from these hills. From Telegraph Hill, north of the city, one sees to the east the wide bay — six miles wide and crowded with ships from all parts of the world, flag fluttering beside flag — and the many-colored activity rivals in liveliness only the rushing, stormy sea. On the other side of the bay are the fruitful shores of Alameda and Contra Costa and the city of Oakland: behind these, rise hill after hill, crowned with forests of red sandalwood. Above these projects the summit of Mt. Diablo — that deserves its name. To the north is the entrance to the harbor, quite close to our feet, it seems; and six miles distant Sanzalito, on the fortress of the opposite mountains. The bay extends northward until it is lost in the distance, studded with smoking steamers that travel to countless points along the Sacramento and San Joaquin rivers. If one turns to the south, there is the busy city, the din of which can be heard even here; on the other side, lies the mission Dolores in a narrow valley, set in a background of charming hills; and farther south the bay again, losing itself in the distance, and the distant, indistinctly seen, ridge of mountains along the coast, running parallel towards the east. To the west, one sees the narrow straights through which the endless sea surges up and down and into which the sea air flows daily with its cooling and cleansing fogs; in the distance is the Golden Gate and the fortress of the Presidio; and, to the other side, the great ocean. Everywhere, the eyes feast on the beauties of nature that, forever new, never lose their charm.

The islands — Yerba Buena, Alcatraz, Angel, and the Farralones — lie within the legal limits of the city and county and, accordingly, belong to the land.

The island of Yerba Buena lies in San Francisco Bay, northwest of the city: more exactly, about one and a half miles from Rincon Point and the Market Street wharf, and about three miles from Contra Costa. The outermost tip of the island is five and a half miles from the Golden Gate (Fort Point). The island measures about 198 acres, seventy-five of which consist of very good soil for truck-gardening; on fifteen acres, good timber grows thickly; twenty-three acres consist of thick bush and underwood, and seventy-five of hilly, rocky and sandy soil covered with a plant, a kind of mint, from which the island has its present name. Springs of excellent water are plentiful on the east and west side of the island, in the midst of a fertile valley.

The highest point of the island is 339 feet above the high-water mark. Originally, it was thickly covered with impenetrable woods and therefore known to the seamen of old and the whalers as Wood Island. However, a certain N. Spear placed a number of goats on it in 1839; they lived on the underbrush. For this reason, the island had — and still has — also the name of Goat Island among the people. On the eastern side there is a wide, shallow bay that at low tide is completely dry and this could be filled in with material to be found on the island itself so that it would be more than twice as large. The island itself consists of continuous layers of sandstone, some of which range from a thickness of a few inches to six or eight feet. Its composition is almost alike in all layers: the grains are close together, even, and generally very fine. The plant, mentioned above, grows among the underwood, looks like a vine, and reaches the height of several feet. The leaves are six inches apart. The plant has a very pleasant odor, healing qualities are ascribed to it and it is often used as a substitute for tea.

The location of these layers of sandstone is most suitable for quarrying and the stone can be loaded at the wharf with little trouble and delivered to the city by water. Several quarries have already been established on the island and it has been found to be an inexhaustible source for the preparation of building stone.

264

The government intended to plant a few batteries on the island and classified it as a third-class fortress. The right to the island was one of the points reserved in 1852 for future decision. The Mexican government claimed it and invoked a gift in writing dated November 8, 1838. The Mexicans held that it was the first island included in a decree by Governor Alvarado entitled, "Recognition of the Gift of Islands Made to Mexican Citizens." However, this claim was recently rejected by the District Court of the United States.

The second island, Alcatraz or Pelican Island, is likewise in the bay, west of Yerba Buena, from which it is about a mile and a half away. It is not quite four miles from the Golden Gate and lies between Yerba Buena and Angel Island. It has its name Pelican Island from the countless number of these water-fowl which for a long time have made their home on it. The highest point of this rocky island is 154 feet above sea-level and it measures thirty-five acres. Its maximum length is 1673 feet and at its widest it is 590 feet. Part of it is overgrown with a kind of oak which here grows very thickly.

This little island is tax-free because it is one of the fortresses of the State. Fifty great cannon have already been planted on it and the ground prepared for forty-one others. It is particularly suitable for a fortress: except for two spots, the shores are so steep that a landing can be made only with the greatest difficulty. Of the three chief batteries on the island, one faces the city and commands the bay in the neighborhood of the Presidio. This battery has thirty-five cannon; another faces the Golden Gate and has sixteen cannon; and the third, facing north towards Sanzalito and Angel Island, has forty cannon. The first fortification that one encounters after landing at the wharf is a bullet-proof guard-house, provided with a draw-bridge and a heavy door. On the highest point of the island is a barracks or citadel, massively built and so designed that every point can be mounted with the heaviest cannon. There are also three bomb-proof magazines, a very large furnace to heat musket-balls and cannon-balls, a weather-bell and a lighthouse. The last is provided with one of Freznel's lamps (third class): it is a splendid piece of machinery and can project a very bright light.

Angel Island is likewise in the bay, almost three miles northwest of Yerba Buena and about a mile from Marin County. It measures about 750 acres and its highest point is six hundred feet above sea-level. At the southeastern end of the island, they have begun to quarry stone for building: it consists of sandstone like that of Yerba Buena but softer and none of it is as dark. Several pieces upon closer examination show a good deal of calcium carbonate. The strata stretch towards the west.

The quarry was opened on a projecting ledge and not, as on Yerba Buena, at the end of the strata. Where the stone is exposed to the water, the surface has the usual rusty color.

This island was originally part of Marin County but later acts of the legislature attached it to San Francisco. The northern end of the island reaches the waters of Marin County, the boundary of which begins at the shore-line, opposite Fort Point, and follows a straight line to a point northwest of the Golden Gate (Statutes of California, 1857, p. 209). However, in a recent criminal case it was decided that this island is still within the boundaries of Marin County so that the only reason for mentioning it here is that it is taxed by both counties.

The Farralones Islands or Rocks

lie in the Pacific and consist of a northern group, a single middle island or rock, and a southern group; the last is almost seven miles from the northern group. This consists of seven rocks. The southern group is the larger and is two miles in circumference. Here is the light-house, the top of it 330 feet above sea-level. It is twenty-nine miles west of the Golden Gate.

It is hard to imagine a more desolate and barren place than these rocky islands. On the other hand, they may also be characterized as the largest poultry-yard in the world. The species of birds called by Buffon "Guillemot" ("Uva troile" by Linné) are to be found here in myriads. They lay their eggs on the bare rocks. Latham has applied the adjective "foolish" to these birds because they cannot be moved to flight easily and would rather, particularly when they are sitting on their eggs, allow themselves to be caught than fly away. An idea of their great number may be had when one considers that at their brooding-time a bird lays only one egg and that since 1851 more than four million eggs have been sold in the markets of San Francisco. The color of the eggs is pale green mixed with a dark red. They are used in restaurants for cakes, pancakes and the like, and a single place will use eight to nine hundred of them per day. The brooding-time lasts about six weeks — from the middle of May to the end of June. In 1858, thirty thousand dozen eggs were sold, on the average at about forty cents a dozen. In the year 1861 the price rose to a dollar and a half a dozen. The expenses of the company that supplies them consume 60 per cent of the gross revenue.

For many years Russian fishermen had a fairly important settlement on the larger of these islands.

Chapter XXXVIII

Observations on Natural History

THE MOST REMARKABLE MOUNTAIN FORMATIONS IN THE NEIGHBOR-
hood of San Francisco consist of a fine-grained firm sandstone mixed
with slate-clay; in addition, there are juttings of trap-rock and serpentine, all very likely of later formation. Under the ground on which
the city is built is sandstone; it extends along the coast and forms the
principal peaks and projecting points. Upon entering the bay from
the Pacific, the rocks at Point Lobos are first seen. The ceaseless activity
of the sea has changed the rocks into steep cliffs and hollowed out
arches and cavities. Great masses of rock have become detached from
these cliffs and lie scattered about in the breakers. These solitary rocks
along the islands are the haunts of the sea-birds and the great sea-lions.

However, this rock formation can best be seen from Pacific Street
where Telegraph Hill has been cut through. There the stratification
is clearly defined and the alternation of thick strata of clay and sandstone and of slate-clay and slate stands out. As yet no fossils at all have
been found in it. The top layer of ground has been formed by the
decomposition of the strata and is admirable material for the manufacture of brick. Much of it is so used. This shows that the rocks contain a large percentage of alum, as well as oxidized iron, as is shown
by the rusty color of the rocks where they have been exposed to the
weather and in the dark-red color of the bricks.

Another rock, next in importance to that of sandstone because of
its quantity as well as its formation, is that of serpentine. It forms a
high and projecting ridge of hills between bay and ocean; at the Golden
Gate it stands out prominently and forms Fort Point. The width of
this ridge is about a mile and a half; its extent south is not known
exactly. In this direction, the formation is less evident because of the
sand, but it forms a knoll at the orphan-asylum near the Mission. The
dark parti-colored appearance of this stone was turned to use in the
building of this splendid institution. Still, it has no other exceptional
qualities to recommend it as a stone to be used in building — especially
since it hardly offers much resistance to the weather — except that it
does not have to be brought from a distance.

Along the shore of the bay, near the Mission, there are wide stretches of swamp, formed by alluvia. It is covered by a very thick turf that, when cut out and dried in the sun, can be used as fuel. On the hills that surround the city there is a weak formation, formed by alluvia, that does not extend far and that fills up the lower places of the hollows that had been there. In an examination of the ground at the custom-house, made by drilling with an auger, layers of sand, clay and gravel were found in regularly repeated succession to a depth of sixty to eighty feet. This place is lower than the level of the streams, and between these alluvia and the rocks there are to be found surfaces or strata that have become filled with water and which have been reached, at various places in the city, by artesian wells.

There is perhaps no spot along the Pacific coast that offers a more favorable opportunity for the study of sand dunes than the peninsula of San Francisco. On the Pacific side there is a long extent of shore that stretches north and south for miles and for a fairly long stretch extends into the interior. In this way a large area, covered with loose, dry sea-sand, has the appearance and nature of a desert. This great stretch, aided by the sea-wind, without doubt formed the mass of sand, blown together, to be found in a great layer in such amounts in the city itself. Most of the hills in the city where this layer of sand rests are, or were, overgrown with a thick growth of brushwood (chamisae) that kept the wind from the ground and prevented the sand from being blown away.

We should also like to mention that here there has been much boring to find water for artesian wells. But it is not possible to state exactly the number of attempts, successful or otherwise, and the places where they were made. Water can be found in all parts of the city near the hills: as a rule, no deeper than 150 feet, although the depth varies according to the locality. In Lucky Valley the borings are successful at a depth of only seventy feet. North of California Street, it is necessary to go deeper, so that a well in Montgomery Block reaches a depth of 160 feet. The depth to which boring extends is greater from the foot of the hills towards the bay and many wells are sunk below the salt water.

Observations on the Animal Kingdom and the Kingdom of Plants

We begin our observations with the

Salmon fisheries. These are the principal fisheries along the coast of California. The spring run up the Columbia River begins in April and lasts into July: that is the best salmon of all. The autumn run up the river begins in August and ends in December: these salmon are not as good. The salmon in the tributaries of the Columbia belong to another species and are not suitable for salting. They are only used by the Indians for food during the winter.

The spring run of salmon up the Sacramento begins in February or March and the catch continues until August. The autumn run is at the same time as that of the Columbia. However, the salmon in the spring are smaller here and the autumn fish are better.

The salmon run in the Rogue River begins in August, in the Chetcoe and Smith Rivers in September, and in the Eel River in October. These salmon weigh from two to seventy pounds and are admirably suited for salting. Those caught in the river-water have a firmer flesh and are more suitable for transportation to tropical climates than any salmon caught off the coast. Great quantities have been shipped to New York, the Sandwich Islands, China and Australia, and always arrive in good condition.

The fish are to be found in incredibly large numbers and occasionally a thousand fish have been taken at one haul in a net of one hundred fathoms. Each of the rivers last named can ship one to three thousand barrels a month.

This year's catch may be noted in the following table:

Columbia River	1500 barrels
Sacramento River	2500 barrels
Rogue, Chetcoe, Smith and Eel Rivers	3600 barrels
Total	7600 barrels

The quantity that, in addition to the above, is consumed smoked or fresh can only be estimated with difficulty. However, it is certainly half of the above amount. From all this it follows that this industry is only at its beginning and is bound to increase greatly. It is a rich source for improving the general welfare and we do not doubt that in time it will be taken advantage of.

Sheep-herding in California is an old occupation. The old missions had great herds of sheep. After the secularization of church property, the herds were neglected and not many sheep were left. It is only five or six years since the raising of sheep has received greater attention in California. Colonel Hollister, who in 1853 had only nine hundred sheep, has by this time sold more than $100,000 worth of wool and sheep and has ten thousand sheep, besides, and sixteen thousand acres of land.

The following is a list of the great herds in Monterey, Santa Cruz and Santa Clara:

Joaquin Pereira	30,000	Isaac Branham	3,000
Flint, Bixby & Cole	16,000	Patrick Breen	3,000
Col. Hollister	10,000	John Fitzgerald	3,000
James Dunn	10,000	Charles De Ro	3,000
David and Dennis Mahony	7,000	Mauricio Gonzales	2,500
John Winn	6,000	J. B. Crockett	2,500
John Searle	6,000	Eugene Casserly	2,500
Mr. Vaca	6,000	Julius Kreyenhagen	2,000
Mr. Leigh	6,000	Mr. Burton	2,000
Montgomery and Bodley	6,000	Lynch and Röding	2,000
Threlkeld and Dore	5,000	Wm. Bennett	2,000
Mr. Sherwood	4,000	Capt. Neville	1,800
A. L. Peebels	4,000	M. D. Sweeny	1,500
Mr. Lunes	4,000	Mr. Sayers	1,500
Wm. F. White	4,000	Charles Hobler	1,500
F. P. Pacheco	3,500	Dr. Burbank	1,000

Several of these sheep-breeders are Jews. In general, the Jews here are glad to be farmers and devote themselves with zeal to agriculture and cattle raising.

Most of the flocks mentioned above are in Monterey County.

These sheep have already been improved to a great degree, principally by interbreeding with Southdowns and Australian merinos. A New Mexico sheep, on the average, produces two pounds of wool, worth from five to seven cents a pound; the American sheep, four pounds, worth fifteen to twenty cents a pound; the half-ermine, six pounds, worth eighteen to twenty-four cents a pound; the Southdown, five pounds, worth twenty to twenty-one cents a pound; and the Australian merino, seven pounds, worth twenty to twenty-one cents a pound. Washed and sorted, this wool naturally brings considerably higher prices, but the cheaper grades by such washing often lose thirty to forty per cent in dirt and fat. French and Spanish merinos are also much imported. The Spanish variety is the smaller of the two but, in spite of this, has more wool.

The production of wool in 1860 may be seen in the following figures. There was shipped in that year:

To New York	11,767	bales
" England	315	"
" Mexico	2	"
" other lands	2	"
Total	12,086	bales

All together they weighed 3,060,000 pounds.

To this must be added the 200,000 pounds that were used in manufacturing in San Francisco. Comparison with the output of wool in 1859 shows an increase of 37 per cent or of 881,750 pounds.

The production of wool in the last seven years amounted to:

Year	Pounds	Percentage of increase
1854	175,000	
1855	360,000	105
1856	600,000	66
1857	1,100,000	83
1858	1,428,351	30
1859	2,378,250	66
1860	3,260,000	38

The output of the last year, deducting the autumn shearing, is divided as follows:

wool for fine cloth (one-tenth the output)	251,000	pounds
medium grade (half the output)	1,255,000	"
ordinary coarse	1,004,000	"

The wool of 1860 is somewhat better than that of 1859. However, much remains to be done if those who send wool to the market wish to receive full price. Only a few of these have shipped goods without fault and have, accordingly, also obtained proportionate prices. A large amount of the goods comes to the market dirty, badly packed or not packed at all, often filthy with straw, grease and all kinds of dirt: all this lowers the price considerably.

Thoroughbred, or partly thoroughbred, rams have now been introduced almost everywhere and in a few years the coarse wool of the original Californian sheep will have disappeared. For ordinary breeding purposes, French or Spanish merino rams are mostly used and most of the wool on the market seems to have been improved by these. Southdown rams have also been introduced in great number — less so the Cotswold and Leicester rams. All these multiply very quickly, suffer little sickness, and pass through the winter easily. The splendid climate and magnificent grazing-grounds make sheep raising easier here than anywhere else and seem to be ideally suited for it.

Shearing twice a year has now been abandoned, except when the sheep are mangy. The heat in summer keeps the fleece quite dry and the autumn shearing makes it too short if the sheep have been shorn in spring. Spring wool brings from sixteen to twenty-three cents; autumn wool about twelve and a half cents.

The factory using wool in this city makes only blankets. Another factory to make coarse flannel and other cloth is planned but has not yet been established.

There are plenty of cattle in California that likewise yield a handsome profit. In southern California there are great herds of sheep, horses and oxen extending for forty or fifty miles (for example, from Los Angeles to San Bernardino, a distance of sixty miles, and from Los Angeles to San Diego). One man assured me that he has close to 1,200 horses in his herd; others — old Spaniards — have from fifty to a hundred thousand cattle at pasture. In the old days, when the Jesuits had their missions in the land, they had so much cattle that there was not enough land on which to pasture them and people had to be specially assigned to slaughter the old cattle so as to make room for the young ones. They always received the hide in payment. This is no longer so, naturally, for the Catholic priesthood has pretty much lost its authority.

Along the Stockton and St. Andrew's highway, James Cole in 1860, with the help of good hunting-dogs, caught and killed two hundred foxes, racoons and wildcats.

A mushroom was exhibited in a Montgomery Street restaurant, as a natural curiosity, that measured thirty-eight inches in circumference and was sixteen inches high.

The upward trend in California agricultural products is most clearly shown in the following figures. In the last three years, the following quantities of wheat were shipped here from the interior:

1858 (July 1st to November 6th)	280,401 sacks
1859 (July 1st to November 6th)	534,147 "
1860 (July 1st to November 6th)	1,191,783 "

Chapter XXXIX

THE MISSION DOLORES AND THE PRESIDIO:
RAPID GROWTH OF SAN FRANCISCO

THE YEAR THAT IS CELEBRATED AS THE ONE WHEN THE GREAT REPUBLIC of the West was born on the Atlantic coast of North America also saw the first permanent settlement on the coast of Upper California. In the year 1776 there landed on the shore of the Bay of San Francisco two missionaries of the Roman Catholic Church, belonging to the Order of St. Francis, and set about establishing a center for their activity, namely, to civilize the native tribes and convert them to Christianity. Francisco Palon and Benito Cambon, natives of Spain, came here from Mexico. Finding a fertile place in the neighborhood of the present city of San Francisco (almost two miles from it), that could be watered easily, they chose it for their new home and founded a mission which, in memory of the suffering of the Virgin, they called "Dolores."

The Fathers showed their good sense in the choice of the site that they selected for building the mission: it was a small, fertile plain, entirely surrounded by green hills. Little streams of sweet, crystal-clear water met at this place and formed a larger stream that ran into the bay. It is still known as Mission Creek. The missionaries began their labors at once and the first baptism took place on December 27, 1776. According to Humboldt, the mission in 1802 had eighteen chapels with 15,562 converted Indians. A detailed report of the mission, as well as of others at a greater distance from San Francisco, is to be found in the *Annals of San Francisco* by Frank Soulé, John H. Gihon, and James Nisbet (New York, 1855), pages 41-79.

The Presidio was established the same year (1776). Its purpose was to assist the missionaries with military aid in becoming masters of the Indians and in civilizing them. There are only four such "presidios" in the land. The one mentioned here lies in a splendid and charming locality and is at present occupied as a station for soldiers by a small detachment of the United States Army. A detailed description of the Presidio is likewise to be found in the book mentioned above, pages 71,

262 and the following pages, and I do not have to go into the subject in further detail.

Just as California is the land of wonders and tales because of the fabulous stories of the discovery of gold and its wealth still buried in deep shafts, so San Francisco is itself a city of wonders and the source of wonders. If one is surprised at its great wealth, that still exists in spite of the fact that its financial condition has become somewhat worse, this surprise must become astonishment if one considers that in 1835 the village of Yerba Buena did not exist in fact or name and that for a long time until then the Bay of San Francisco was known to travelers only as "the ornament of the West Coast." The first house was built in 1836 and the site of San Francisco might still well have been called a wilderness thirteen years ago. Herds of cattle pastured quite undisturbed where now are stores crowded with customers, and the raven croaked where peaceful dwellings have now been built. A year later (1837) the whole village consisted of 150 persons and twenty wooden huts. In 1847, on the thirtieth of January, the name of the place, (Bay of) Yerba Buena, was changed to San Francisco. Six months later, a census was taken and it was found that the population had increased to 459; in the current year this city — the metropolis of the Pacific — has a population of more than 85,000 souls and boasts of a tax-list of more than forty million dollars.

All of California, in addition to 60,000 Indians, has about half a million inhabitants; about one in every eight is Chinese — a bad eighth of the population! With respect to exports, San Francisco is the first port of the Union and, if we consider its imports and tonnage, it ranks among the first. Its lot was most unusual and there is nothing like it in the history of cities — nothing that may be compared to it. The discovery of gold in 1848 was the lever of the migration by means of which San Francisco, in so short a time, received the name of "city." Its growth was sudden, rapid; it had no period of early growth and was placed at once on the heights. A mere existence of twelve years assigned it to its place among the cities of the world and it is now on a sure road to wealth and greatness after it has overcome strokes of unkind fate, financial storms and misfortunes.

No land on earth has in fact the inducements that California has at present to captivate men. Apart from its mineral wealth, the State has agricultural riches and favorable opportunities for the establishment of factories that no other state in the Union can excel. It has a great variety of climate — from tropical heat to benumbing cold; it is so geographically located that in this respect it can certainly rival most privileged lands. For twelve years California has annually con-

274

tributed between fifty and sixty millions of dollars to the wealth of the world and the advancement of trade; and all this must go through the Golden Gate. The interior of the State is adorned with many beautiful cities, pretty, flourishing towns and villages, places with industrious men digging for gold, great and rich farms and ranches; and all this is dependent upon San Francisco, as its great and sole center, from which all mercantile business branches. Factories are planned on a grand scale; the merchant fleets of the civilized world trade with its inhabitants; and all is directed to the harbor of San Francisco. Steamship lines are organized and unite the city with the East, with Oregon, Washington Territory and British Columbia, and with South America and Australia: all sail from the harbor of San Francisco. The arrangements that the government has made with respect to travel connections by land has invested many interests in the State with new value, interests supplied and kept active by means of the port of San Francisco. The recent treaties concluded with China and Japan afford prospects of an increased trade with much profit soon between these countries and San Francisco.

There is no doubt whatever that a railway will be built sooner or later between the Atlantic and Pacific Oceans. A bill providing for the railway was introduced at the last session of Congress and requires only the approval of the Senate. As soon as the railway is completed the greater part of the trade with the Orient from Europe and the Eastern states will certainly go through the port of San Francisco.

A pony-express across the continent was established by an enterprising company and enjoys a success no one could foresee. Horse and rider leave San Francisco with a saddle-bag of letters and it is carried across the continent in the brief time of thirteen days. Telegraphic dispatches are received from New York in nine days, so that the merchants and politicians of San Francisco are already in active communication with the rest of the world and are part of the network that receives news of the fall and rise of financial matters in the fields of commerce and politics. The telegraph has outsped the slow steamers and as soon as the wires have been laid across the plains — which may take place within the year — San Francisco will be within hailing distance of New York.

Another, and not unimportant, step forward has been the construction of a railway from San Francisco to the Mission — a distance of three miles. This stretch of railway is much traveled and, as a result, the ground near it has increased in value considerably. The railway is soon to be extended to San José, a beautiful city. It lies in a valley almost fifty miles from San Francisco and boasts that it has the best climate in the State.

The following is a table surveying the city's growth with respect to the number of commercial houses, between 1852 and 1860. I have taken it alphabetically from the directories for the two years.

1852			1860	
A	69 firms	A	505 firms
B	82 "	B	1973 "
C	214 "	C	1550 "
D	137 "	D	1018 "
E	49 "	E	346 "
F	89 "	F	839 "
G	142 "	G	851 "
H	202 "	H	1640 "
I	8 "	I	74 "
J	61 "	J	327 "
K	70 "	K	748 "
L	128 "	L	920 "
M	246 "	M	2052 "
N	50 "	N	365 "
O	33 "	O	318 "
P	113 "	P	810 "
Q	7 "	Q	54 "
R	127 "	R	972 "
S	245 "	S	1786 "
T	108 "	T	600 "
U	7 "	U	35 "
V	32 "	V	227 "
W	171 "	W	1170 "
Y	5 "	Y	52 "
Z	5 "	Z	45 "

The number of banking-houses has fallen from twenty to sixteen. The number of churches has increased from twelve to thirty-eight. In addition, the number of public schools, hotels and the like, has increased considerably.

In the directory for 1852, under the heading "Consulates," there were only twenty-one consulates listed. In the directory for 1860 there were thirty-seven, namely:

Austria	Hawaii	San Salvador
Belgium	Honduras	Sardinia
Bremen	Lubeck	Saxony
Chili	Mecklenberg-Schwerin	Saxony-Anhalt
Costa Rica	Mexico	Spain
Denmark	Netherlands	Sweden and Norway
Ecuador	New Granada	Switzerland
France	Oldenburg	Two Sicilies
Frankfort	Parma	Tuscany
Guatemala	Portugal	Uruguay
Great Britain	Peru	Würtemberg
Hamburg	Prussia	
Hanover	Russia	

The consulates added to the previous ones are:

Costa Rica	Lubeck	Sardinia
Ecuador	New Granada	Saxony
Frankfort	Parma	Saxony-Anhalt
Guatemala	Würtemberg	Sweden and Norway
Uruguay	Russia	Tuscany
Honduras	San Salvador	Two Sicilies

A consulate for Nicaragua is to be found only in the directory for 1852.

Chapter XL

THE CHINESE

ALTHOUGH THE CHINESE HAVE BEEN SO OFTEN MENTIONED IN PASSING, I do not consider it superfluous to devote a special chapter to this part of the population.

In the month of April 1852, more than ten thousand Chinese arrived at San Francisco, and a multitude in excess of this number had already embarked at their native ports. The number of Chinese living at present in San Francisco is estimated at about eight thousand. They have their temple and an asylum: in the former sits their great idol, firm and motionless like a rock, in an artistically-fashioned room; in the latter, the needy poor of their countrymen are helped.

There is a great deal of freedom in America; the thieves, gamblers and vagabonds know it well, and the wicked among them know it very well, for they make it their boast at lying down and at rising up; they brag of it when they injure their fellow man, and they are proud of it when, in spite of all the circumstances and all effort, they are acquitted. Freedom flourishes for all except for the poor Chinaman, who is a stranger to the customs and speech of the inhabitants; for him no blossom of freedom springs up; for this hard-working people, who make the wilderness into a garden and smooth the rough paths for the white men there is no freedom. Their customs and ways create aversion among the Americans; the Chinaman with his strange speech, strange religion and odd character, that physically and spiritually is on a lower plane, is treated by some only somewhat better than the Negro, by others even worse.

Those who come in contact with the former residents of the "Celestial Empire" soon feel an irresistible disgust for them. John Chinaman's person has no particularly agreeable odor; the color of his face and its features are odd; his poverty is too great; his lies, knavish tricks and innate cowardice have become proverbial. He lives apart from the white inhabitants; his companions are only his fellow-countrymen; he can express his ideas only to these and show the better side of his nature only to them. Anything for which a native is readily forgiven is a crime if a Chinaman does it. It is true that they are a dirty, wily people, but they are not in the category of criminals! They have also their superiorities and admittedly good qualities: they are as a rule quiet and industrious members of human society, generous towards their fellow-countrymen, temperate men who do not indulge in drink and who are unacquainted with the vices that follow in its train. Generally they earn great praise for showing a tender attachment to their parents and for having great respect for all elderly persons: they believe that these are the source of wisdom.

A little, and the poorest of sustenance is sufficient to keep a Chinaman alive and for this they work long and hard under the greatest hardships.

In this country, they certainly deserve the deepest sympathy, for they are treated worse than dogs. If someone murders a Chinaman and robs him of his few bitterly earned dollars, the murderer knows in advance that he has no punishment to expect, since no attention is paid in a court of law to a wrong inflicted upon a Chinaman and, besides,

no white man is inclined to be a witness on behalf of the lost "Celestial."
In the mines, where thousands of Confucius' countrymen work, they
are without the privileges of the others. They are not permitted to
work claims that they have rented and, at the first such attempt, are
driven away by the ferocity of those who fly the flag of freedom from
their masthead and entice the stranger to their shores with the bait of
liberalism. The claims that the Chinese work almost exclusively are
those which white men have given up as not paying enough for their
"grub." And even at such work, the Chinese are heavily taxed by the
State and are often compelled by certain tax-collectors to pay three
times as much as they earn in the end, because these tax-collectors
believe, or wish to believe, that the Chinese have no souls and therefore do not know what to do with their money. The Chinese often
revolt against such a display of authority, but their rebellion is always
repressed by force of arms and they are not permitted to seek public
investigation of their grievances.

In 1856, the Chinese at the mines fought among themselves: it was
almost a battle and many were killed and wounded.*

About two years ago, the legislature of the State passed an act for-
bidding the immigration of Chinese. The more intelligent and liberal
Americans were greatly shocked at this and the Chinese themselves
held a meeting at which they read aloud a long protest against the act.
Their protest was composed in very temperate language and will
always remain a very memorable document. The result of repeated
friendly attempts on the part of the Federal government and the governor was that the published act was declared unconstitutional and
therefore invalid.

A few of the Chinese live in almost every part of the city and carry
on their business there, but the chief locality where they have settled
is the upper part of Sacramento Street, the length of Dupont Street
and the neighborhoods adjacent to these streets. Here almost all the
residents are Chinese and this quarter is not seldom called "Little
China."

A fair number of rich and respectable Chinese mercantile and business houses are to be found in the city. Their chief trade, as one can
easily guess, consists of the products of their native land. They either
speak a fairly fluent English or employ an interpreter. However, a
great number of their countrymen are engaged in much humbler work;
for very many of them, who "work" in the true sense of the word,

---

* In the second part of this book, soon to appear, in which I describe my second
  journey in the interior of California and my journey to the Mormons, I shall
  furnish more details of this.

279

make their living at washing and mending clothes; others are porters in warehouses and shops or perform other humble work that no one else wants to do.

Many Chinese also try their luck at gambling, and a part of upper Sacramento Street, as well as almost all the east side of Dupont Street, is lined with Chinese gambling-houses in which they satisfy their passion for gambling. (A detailed, rather comic, description of these places is to be found in *The Annals of San Francisco*, by Frank Soulé, Gihon, and Nisbet, New York, 1855, pages 382-3.)

While a large part of the Chinese population gives itself up to gambling, the women carry on the still worse trade of prostitution. They are the most shameless and the least respectable of all the residents. Several streets are crowded with such abandoned creatures. A large part of the Chinese population of San Francisco earns its living solely by these two vices.

For the study of Chinese customs we submit the following, taken from one of the newspapers in general circulation. A young Chinese woman is at present locked up in the police station-house. She says that she has just recently come from China and was sold for three hundred dollars by her masters, Messrs. Ah Hen, Ah Gan and Ah Yan, to the Chinese proprietress of a house of prostitution. The latter gave the sellers a note for this sum and pledged the slave herself as security for the payment. The buyer died and the slave was sold to another proprietress of a house of prostitution. The original sellers demanded payment of the three hundred dollars by the present owner of the slave and, when they could not get their money, tried to take their prostitute back. This led to blows; and the police, who arrived at the scene, arrested the slave-dealers on the ground of attempted abduction. An inquiry into the matter found the delinquents guilty only of assault and battery.

The upright Chinese are scattered throughout the whole city or its suburbs and are lost in the confusion and bustle of the people.

In 1852, a troupe of professional Chinese actors tried their luck in California and produced plays in their own language. These productions were very well received by their fellow countrymen and also by the white residents for whom the Chinese plays were a great curiosity. In the following year, another Chinese theater was opened. Their taste in these matters, developed by the many ceremonies of their festivities, seems peculiar to us and the same is also true of their music.

Suicide, when a man can no longer pay his debts, is regarded as honorable. Even Chinese women try to acquire this honor by poison. On the whole, they are a peaceful people who cause the authorities little trouble and, when they do, it is only out of ignorance of the law. In their private circles, to which no lower-class Chinese are admitted, they enjoy all the higher — or lower — luxurious pleasures of cultured nations. Most of them retain their Chinese dress and particularly their pigtail also; only a few use modern clothing. They are very fond of pageantry and for this reason their festivals generally have public parades connected with them. Many bring their dwellings or huts with them from China and at night hang upon them colored paper-lanterns after the Chinese custom. For the city — to mention another of their pleasures — the Chinese are a benefit inasmuch as they rid the city annually of thousands of rats, since the Chinese regard these as tid-bits.

We take the following description of a Chinese funeral from an English newspaper (the funeral took place during my stay). Yesterday, in addition to being the annual memorial day of the Chinese, in celebration of which they bring offerings and burn joss-paper to the spirits of their departed friends of beloved memory, was particularly distinguished by the funeral rites of a Chinese who had been a respected man of authority among the residents from the Celestial Kingdom. The dead man, Áh Ching, Number 2, was placed in a metal coffin and escorted, with all honor and no pomp spared to the vault for the dead on Love Mountain. The procession, which passed through Montgomery Street, was arranged in the following fashion. It was led by a Chinese band of music consisting of five players. The chief instrument was an ear-piercing clarinet that, as a sign of mourning for the departed, uttered wild, shrill and weird sounds, and so accompanied the mournful tom-tom and gong-gong. This was followed by the hearse, drawn by two white horses and decorated on top with white plumes — the color of mourning among the Chinese. From the box, a Chinese scattered joss-paper among the crowds. The hearse was followed by thirteen carriages. The first had its blinds drawn and carried, probably, members of the dead man's family. Four other carriages were occupied by female mourners; four by professional female mourners regularly hired for such occasions. They wore across their foreheads long white veils and the Chinese men, too, wore bands of white crepe. A carriage that carried the funeral banquet, consisting entirely of cold dishes, closed the procession.

The usual ceremonies of this peculiar people, who in all their usages mix civilization and barbarous customs, so that in some ways they are advanced and in others backward, were performed at the burial-place itself. This burial-place is only a temporary one in California, for the corpse is merely entombed for the time-being: the Chinese, according to the statutes of their religion, must be buried in China. For this purpose, a ship leaves for Hong-kong every month. If one dies before or after the departure of this ship, his body is entombed for the time-being. Accordingly, in September 1860, fifty bodies were sent off, and on April 12, 1861, the ship *Mary Whitridge* had two hundred Chinese corpses on board. Only those are buried in the soil of California whom the nation considers without honor — such as those whose pigtail has been cut off, or when, for example, they are caught stealing, or if they change their religion and accept another.

The features of their faces are very ugly; their skin is shiny because of the enormous amount of pork that they eat, and they are almost always of a medium height and thin. The clothing of men and women, except for what they wear on their feet and heads, is quite alike.

What has been said here about the Chinese is to be regarded only as a brief sketch and has no pretensions whatever to being a detailed account.

Chapter XLI

Luxury in San Francisco

Human nature is provided with much innate capacity for a satisfied and happy life and there is truly no need to chase after happiness by means of outward pomp and show. However, the passion for magnificence seems to be a tendency so deeply rooted in the human disposition that it appears wherever the most essential necessities of life have been satisfied. But there is no land in all the world where the passion to cause a sensation is so prevalent as in California. The hunt for gain can hardly be compared to the eagerness to outdo others in the building of splendid houses, driving swift horses, or in dressing in costly clothes. I saw plenty of luxury and splendor on my travels — glittering diamonds in France, Arabians ornamented with precious stones, Asiatic men of wealth and aristocrats whose passion for externals has become proverbial. In California, the emphasis on appearance is not to be compared with that anywhere else. For elsewhere wealth is generally inherited: handed down from father to son, from mother to daughter, as particular families won, as it were, the privilege of ornamenting themselves. But here in California a woman sweeps along, dressed in silk and showing her diamond-studded jewelry — what the Yankees in their colloquial speech call "cutting a dash"— while her sister rides proudly through the streets, and both forget that only a little while before they supported themselves by taking in washing or at some kind of trade. The parvenues are nowhere else as numerous and nowhere else as unendurable as in California; they ride a horse and do not know how to hold the reins; they pretend that they were born in wealth and splendor, and they drive — no uncommon occurence — their husbands mad.

The aristocracy of Europe is a natural one and inherited from august forefathers. But this hot-house aristocracy of California, this gingerbread nobility, that owes its origin simply to the turn of a lucky card or a fortune scoop of the shovel in a mine, is unendurable and dangerous. The servant-girl becomes a lady overnight if it suits the mood of one of the many adventurers. But the difference is hardly noticeable. For by the clothes of the servant-class and their appearance in the streets who would ever suspect that these costly clothes, elegant hats and expensive jewelry are worn by such as have to work, who must labor to earn their bread? They live like mistresses and ladies, and the words "domestic servant" apply to a few Irish girls who make thirty dollars every month and send their wages to their relatives at home in Ireland. This is not only true of the servant-class; it appears in other spheres also.

Note well, you ladies and gentlemen, who have never seen San Francisco and its residents in all their splendor: here comes a poor doctor, poor at least in understanding, but rich in goods and chattels. Glowing advertisements, repeated again and again, and nothing but brag and bombast, have elevated him, and through the sins of his fellow men he has stored up heaps of money. Eyeglasses with rims of gold, rings of gold and diamonds, a walking-stick with a great gold knob, a diamond stick-pin and diamond studs for his shirt, large waistcoat buttons and perhaps a golden snuff-box and tooth-pick — these are his necessary and inseparable concomitants. Everything must contribute to give him an engaging, appealing appearance to allure the public. The physicians in California occupy an exceptional position and a chapter about luxury may well include a few words about them: it is not as unsuitable as it seems. Many of them belong in a chapter about luxuries. Like the women who in 1849 were nothing more than laundresses or women selling cigars and who now play the part of the rich and stylish ladies, so many of these doctors now-a-days, these medical aristocrats, were nothing better than barbers or waiters in the places that they came from. Although the winds are strong during the summer afternoons and the winters damp and changeable, on the whole the climate is not unhealthful. Nowhere else did I see children who looked in better health — more robust and stronger — than in California; they are the pictures of good health; and yet San Francisco has more doctors, or rather more quacks who have labeled themselves "doctors," than any other city of so large a population — doctors of all kinds from all parts and sections of the world. The Yankee quack, who battens on the sufferings of dissolute men and sickly women, hangs out his sign next to that of the grave Chinese doctor, who in turn lives next to a doctor who has received a scientific education.

There is no doubt that there are doctors of excellent scientific education, men who know how to deal successfully with the most desperate cases, whose reputation in theoretical knowledge as well as in practice cannot be attacked in the least; but these are the very ones who find themselves in the worst and most pitiable condition. They cannot scrape together hundreds of dollars every month for pompous advertisements and, even if they could, they would never bring themselves to discredit their profession by column-length advertisements of recommendations and put themselves in the class of every clairvoyant or the women who tell fortunes by cards. Unfortunately, the doctors are in the same situation as the representatives of every other branch of knowledge: the truly learned and gifted are hardly noticed and even less often valued. They would like to follow their chosen path peacefully and quietly; but it never leads them to their goal. The fine man of the world, who rides in a carriage, dresses splendidly, visits the opera, patronizes the gambling-hells, and does everything that would make an upright man blush, can count with certainty upon the favor of the public consisting, as it does, mostly of the vulgar. A doctor in the United States must, therefore, be born the perfect doctor. There are exceptions, of course, but as a rule an American doctor reads a book about medicine, becomes acquainted with the names of the various sicknesses, and then briskly sets about doctoring in that, to the great satisfaction and delight of the undertaker, he casts his own hook for fish. A few Germans and a fair number from other countries, who are too lazy and lack the spirit to work, in order to avail themselves of another respectable way of making a living have aped the example of shameless Americans and put "M.D." after their names. Every case of sickness is treated as if it were the first of its kind and they care little about the fate and finish of the patient.

This audacity is catching and even women are bold enough to practice medicine. Why shouldn't they? Why shouldn't women have an equal right to deceive, particularly since they are so constantly the victims of the stronger sex? "Clairvoyant doctors" is the name by which these female deceivers are known and with which they derive a profit from an actual or pretended condition. Their method of healing is too interesting not to be described. The patient pays a fee of five dollars on entering; the female doctor promptly falls asleep in her chair and has visions — which they call a condition of trance — and falls to prophesying. In this way she supplies the sick man with instructions. Naturally, he must return often and pay five dollars each time to receive new prescriptions for his sickness from the land of dreams.

Medical studies have not gone much beyond the first stage. To be sure, there is a medical school here where young men study how to be doctors; they generally receive their diploma within three years — provided they have the money for it. I myself know a man who peddled during the day and at night attended lectures in medicine. He did this for nine months, was dubbed doctor, and even licenced by the government. In this way science, literature and art go begging through the streets, while impudence and ignorance batten and revel in luxury.

Under the title of luxuries we include the craft of fortune-telling that is here conducted as a profession. In a land where Franklin's cradle stood, in a republic that boasts of its great enlightenment, there are men and women who derive their subsistence and livelihood from the credulity of the people. Fortune-tellers do a wonderful business; men and women fill their coffers with money taken from their stupid victims, in return for which they reveal the past, present and future — from a dirty pack of cards.

How long before simplicity will prevail and only the ornaments of the spirit will be sought?

On the eleventh of May, 1861, the city of San Francisco celebrated the greatest national holiday ever observed on the Pacific coast. The streets began to be lively early in the morning and, the closer the time for the ceremonies approached, the greater were the crowds. They grew ever greater and, when the Union parade began, all was animation and gay activity and one could not get through any longer without pushing and pressure. The heavens were friendly; clear, bright weather tempted all into the open, and in the clear air we forgot our sweat and the oppressive heat. We suffered it gladly because we received compensation enough and saw many a spectacle to delight us. The city was like a forest of pennants and flags of the Union; the Stars and Stripes floated from almost every house; even from the third story of the dwellings of the poor to the very ground flags and bunting fluttered. In one place, the national colors of the Union, tastefully entwined, made a brave show, and wherever one gazed one saw a bright red, white and blue flag or pennant.

Wherever the Union colors could be placed, they were to be found: the horsemen decorated their horses with flags, children carried little flags in their hands — it was a remarkable expression of love of country that was shown here. If from some high ground one looked down a street and saw the countless symbols of the Union and the surging multitude of its loyal sons and daughters, it was a gay sight. These were no politicians of a particular party who filled the streets, but citizens of all parties with their families, from the youngest to the oldest, and no one was to grow tired of the length of the great parade and its lines of marchers; all followed it, urged on by love of country.

The individual companies and societies of the parade gathered about ten o'clock at the plaza and the march began promptly at half-past ten to the spot where the celebration was to take place, at the corner of Montgomery and Market Streets. This was the order of march:

Six policemen on horseback
Sappers of the California Fusiliers
An American brass band
First Regiment of militia under command of Col. Doane
General Cobb and staff
First California Guards
Black Hussars on foot
California Fusiliers
National Guard
City Guard
Fife-and-drum corps
Second Regiment of militia under Major West
McMahon Grenadiers
San Francisco Rifle Club
Washington Continentals
Montgomery Guards
United States officers in carriages
United States band
Arrangements committee
City officials and judges
California Pioneers

Chief engineer and assistants

Fire-engine Companies Numbers 5 and 6

Fife-and-drum Corps

Fire-engine Company Number 8 with a wagon on which its flag was carried

Fire-engine Companies Numbers 12 and 14

Children of the Episcopalian Mission Sunday School

Slavonic-Illyrian Benevolent Society with two flags

The National Music Band, hired by the workingmen of Miners Foundry

The workingmen of Miners Foundry

Fire-Engine Company Number 10

Several Union clubs

Riggers and stevedores

A carriage drawn by four horses, the horses hung with red banners with the words: "Sumter, the cradle of patriotism, shall be the tomb of treason"; "Treason is only for a day, but our country for all time."

A great number of carriages

A hay-wagon, drawn by six horses, on which were a great number of persons with the flag of the Union

A wagon of the Pacific Glue Factory with the sign, "We stick fast to the Union"

A wagon of the Golden Gate Tannery with the sign, "Give us the hides of traitors and we will tan them"

A great number of carriages at the end

When the parade reached the place where the ceremonies were to be held, the citizens gathered about the three platforms erected there and the militia marched into the adjoining streets. In a few minutes, the place and its immediate neighborhood were filled with people and all outlets were blocked. Women gazed from the windows of adjoining houses and a great number of men and boys found the crowd in the street too great and preferred to see the spectacle from the rooftops. The platforms were decorated with flags of the Union, slogans and emblems, and thirty-four boys with the shields of the thirty-four states stood about the central platform. It was in impressive sight — at which eyes and hearts rejoiced — to see the endless multitude and their jubilee and enthusiasm. Mr. Sam Brannan's call for order put an end to the bustle and noise; the meeting proceeded to the purpose of the gathering; and a board of officers was nominated and unanimously elected. The following officers were elected: president, Henry F.

Teschemacher; vice-presidents, D. J. Tallant, J. A. Coolidge, Jacob Denth, J. Whitney, Jr., James E. Nuttman, Albert Dibblee, R. Morton, John Sime, P. B. Cornwall, George W. Goren, Capt. Seidensticker, J. M. Strobridge, Gen. G. H. Ringgold, U.S.A., James Donohue, G. W. Ryckman, Gen. W. H. Halleck, W. Morris, C. M. Brosman, Jas. H. Cutter, W. C. Ralston, Thos. H. Selby, W. A. Woodward, Leonidas Haskell, Louis McLane, Asa T. Lawton, Mark Brumagim, Joel F. Lightner, Henry A. Seligman, Michael Skolly, G. S. Fisher, I. R. Seyder, John Bensley, Frank Soulé.

Secretaries, John Hancock, F. McCrellish, H. S. Daliba, Wm. Hüfner, J. Cremony, W. C. Parker, Cornelius Storm.

Speeches in the following order followed the election. The opening address was that of

Senator Latham

He began by referring to the pleasure that the meeting of the citizens of the city on February twenty-second had aroused in the East and to the like pleasure that would be caused by the news of this day's activity. We live in a free land, he continued, in a land beyond the reach of tyranny, where people have come together from all parts of the world but where, nevertheless, concord animates the entire population, concord prevails, and the wish to maintain the constitution of the land unites them all. The moment of decision is now approaching: we can be only against or for our country, and we are for it when we assist its authorities. The speaker then invited every one to express his opinion, openly, freely and frankly. For his part, he was for the people of California gathering about the true flag and not the Palmetto flag; the true flag was the flag to follow; it had gleamed in the van in a hundred battles, from Concord and Lexington to Yorktown, from Palo Alto to Buena Vista, from the castle of San Juan d'Ulloa to Mexico, and one should not desert it at any price.

He had always recommended concessions, always demanded guarantees for those who did not find their propery sufficiently secure in the Republic, but had just as publicly declared that the South had snatched at the first chance for the present war without the least excuse. The principle of secession is incompatible with any government, and any nation that subscribes to it must perish. As Jackson said, this principle of secession is no remedy, but rather the food of every evil; and wherever states had claimed this right the result was unprecedented outrage. All possibilities had been tried: the remedy of a convention of all the states that should examine and remove grievances was re-

288

jected; offers of compromise were made and were disregarded; not the least regard was had for the security, the wishes and interests of the sister states; even the pleas of those friends who did not wish the Union left in the lurch were made to deaf ears; the memory of those who had made our Union great was scoffed at, the hopes of millions who had sought the sanctuary of freedom in America were laughed at, the property and the forts of the United States were seized and its troops driven with abuse across the borders.

The list of offenses is not yet ended; men conspire in the cabinet of the president; and those who swore to maintain the Union, who daily draw their per diem to protect the nation, betray it and abandon it, preach high treason in the halls of Congress, scorn the warnings of a Washington, Jefferson, Madison and Jackson, and go so far as to threaten to bring fire and sword with armed bands into the capital of the land. Must not the heart of every patriot cry out with rage and pain at this? The government continues to be peaceful and this peacefulness is considered fear, just as the wish that those who have become wild with excitement might return to their senses is considered an admission of injustice. The civilized world that held our government to be the strongest on earth is astonished at seeing our land becoming a prey to anarchy. But it must not go that far. The time for patience is over and our government is awake. It plunges like an avalanche from an alpine height, like the mighty wave of the ocean, and strikes with the force of lightning to maintain its dignity and to annihilate rebellion.

We must choose between anarchy and civil war — both dreadful evils. But anarchy destroys everything and loosens every tie; civil war is only a transitory fire. Therefore, there is no choice: we must either perish as a nation, admit our wretched condition before all the world, insult our forefathers resting in their graves, or seize our weapons and fight for our rights. Our government has already endured what it would not have endured from all the rest of the world because it was indulgent to our brothers; but now we must advance in one mighty column to recapture the Union. California, take your stand for the Union and declare yourself ready to carry out every duty that will be required of you. Wherever the battle rages, there California will battle by the light of the Stars and Stripes; and where these shine we will be there to defend the flag.

The bands struck up the *Star Spangled Banner* in token of agreement, as the speaker withdrew to the thunder of sustained applause.

Next, Senator McDougall mounted the platform.

"We have not assembled [he began] to indulge in arguments, but to express our resolutions and our feelings in order to convince our friends on the other side of the mountains that we are for the Union. The traitors stand armed against our country and at that every good citizen must speak out and then bravely set to work. At such a time no subordinate interests can be tolerated; we must feel as our fathers felt when they took up arms for our country and united it under one flag and one constitution — the wisdom of which has made us one of the leading nations of the earth.

"That system of government which those great men founded has been unjustly called only an experiment and, with even greater injustice, high treason has characterized this experiment as a failure. Within four generations under this experiment we became a mighty people. Until a few months ago, the peaceful heavens smiled above our land; we stood upon the heights of prosperity; we saw the blessings of freedom and order, rights and property, protected. No government has met all demands upon it as has ours and, in spite of this, there are those who have the insolence to say that it has failed. No government can be perfect but ours reached its appointed goal and the wisdom of the founders of our republic stood the test of time. The defenders of high treason point out to us the lucky forward steps made by the South; but I say to them: those whom the Gods wish to destroy they first blind by luck. The success of their crazy economy was only an illusory one, and events will show that the traitors have judged falsely when they thought our system of government powerless. That was the work of our former president, Buchanan — may his name not be accursed forever! (Thunderous applause.)

"Our system of government was founded for the purpose of avoiding the very evils that appeared. A traitor cannot have another traitor as his successor; presidents who are traitors have no power after they have left office. Our present president is no traitor; he differs with many in his political views, but he is an upright man who loves his country and is firm enough not to be frightened from performing any duty imposed upon him by the Constitution. As yet he has not had time enough to prove whether or not the government is strong enough for this crisis; but what he has not been able to do the people have already done. Money in untold amounts and men without number are at his disposal and he has the power to trample treason under foot, yes, he has already trampled it under foot: he will do his duty in this hour of trial. In this matter, there can be no question of party. For my part, I will do everything to protect the government from treason and to keep our country safe. The benefits that our Constitution has conferred upon us imposes upon us the grave duty of protecting it and defending it. No one should be given an office, even if of least importance, who is not ready to stand by the Union or fall with it.

"Even here they speak of treason everywhere. Let us ban the word. Now there are no longer any questions of party; there is only one rivalry and that is — rivalry for the Union. Our slogan is: the Union and only the Union!˙ Millions are ready to defend it with their lives!" (Sustained applause.)

After the address of Senator McDougall, Chairman Teschemacher proposed the appointment of a committee to formulate resolutions. The proposal was accepted and a committee named.

The next speaker was General Shields who, in a few words, stirred his audience to the wildest enthusiasm and prophesied that in six months the American flag would wave from one end of the Union to the other over a resurrected republic.

After this address, the following resolutions of the above-mentioned committee were read aloud and adopted without dissent:

It is resolved, first, that the full and free development of American civilization and the extension of civil and religious freedom to all the world require the continued existence of the American government and demand its support against any and all attacks whether from enemies without or within.

It is resolved, second, that the duties of an American citizen to the Federal government are superior to all other duties and obligate him, by law and honor, to assist in suppressing rebellion and in executing the law.

It is resolved, third, that in the present crisis in which our country finds itself our hearts, our spirits, and our hands are united with the constitutional authorities and, ready for any sacrifice of life or property, we promise solemnly to take our stand now and forever, without reservation, restriction, or condition, for the union of these states and of this government in peace and in war.

General Sumner, commander of the Pacific division of the United States Army, was now called upon to speak by the meeting and his name was shouted in an outburst of excitement. The grey-bearded soldier mounted the platform with unhurried steps and by his calm looks and words it was clearly seen that he did not consider the enemies of the Union more than a mouthful or two — enough for a light breakfast. General Sumner pointed to the meeting, this powerful support of the government, and to the government's resources. He explained that the expenses of waging war were not lost, but that the money merely passed from hand to hand and, what was even better, it went from the rich to the poor. He characterized the secession movement by a powerful expression: "a miserable attempt to break down our government."

He was further of the opinion that there was some sense in speaking of a peaceful secession for the secessionists had nothing good to get out of war but, if they relied upon the good-nature of the people and the president, they may have made a great mistake, to judge by his own experiences, because they would find in every official a devilish Tartar. At this there was a roar of laughter and the applause of thousands followed the joking general as he left the platform. He seemed to be a calm, cool-headed, resolute officer.

The meeting now called for Governor Downey, but he could not be present because of official duties and a letter was read aloud, sent by him to the committee, in which he declared his firm loyalty to the Union and promised every constitutional aid in his power to maintain the Union. Messrs. Vorbee and Pixley spoke next and, afterwards, Uncle Abe's choir sang the song, *The Union Forever*. This made a deep impression upon the meeting. At the same time, a kite in the shape of a star with a flag of the United States for a tail rose from a house opposite and the wishes of the multitude went with it — that the flag of the United States might rise ever higher and higher.

The next speakers were Messrs. A. Campbell, Baby, Briggs from Amador, and Th. Fitch. With their ardent words and practical good sense they set the already enthusiastic hearts of the people afire as if by a lightning-flash. The names of the Union Committee were then read aloud — the meeting had previously proposed the appointment of such a committee — and its duties explained: the first was to form similar committees in the interior and to keep in constant touch with them. After the matter of this committee had been disposed of, more speakers took the platform: of these we mention the Rev. Meyers, Mr. Lippitt, General Cobb, Mr. Sam Brannan, and Mr. Haigston.

General Cobb assured the meeting, in the name of the militia, that they had their hearts in the right place and were always ready to sacrifice themselves for the Union. Mr. Wallace, from Sacramento, delivered a political poem which he had composed himself; it breathed the great enthusiasm of the poet for the Union and was received with enthusiasm by the people. Uncle Abe's choir, after the last speech, sang several other songs and, likewise, showed its patriotism.

The speakers, mentioned above, spoke from the middle platform but the people who were gathered about the other two platforms did not remain without speeches to listen to. Colonel Turner, from Nevada, had charge of the arrangements for these platforms, and Messrs. Thomas, Fitch, Manchester, Briggs, Sawyer, Brown, S. Platt and others gave the people an opportunity to elevate their minds by hearing solid, pithy speeches.

The meeting lasted until half-past three and during the entire time showed the greatest enthusiasm. The demonstration for the Union was wholly worthy of its noble purpose and will instill new courage to fight in the people of the East when they see how hearts beat in sympathy for them.

At seven o'clock in the evening, a great display of fireworks was set off at the meeting place by way of celebration and tar-barrels ignited. The crowd present finally organized a regular assembly. Mr. Sam Brannan was elected president; Messrs. Eugene Casserly, Hog, Taylor, Poulterer, Willey, Donahue and others vice-presidents; and Messrs. Gould and Haigston secretaries.

This enthusiasm should not be permitted to evaporate, but should be rekindled from time to time so that, when the hour for sacrifice arrives, the people may be ready.

Chapter XLII

Observations About the Climate: San Francisco Then and Now

From the month of May until August there is usually a thick fog over San Francisco until about ten o'clock in the morning. Then the sun dissipates the fog and the air becomes rather warm. But even at the height of summer it is not more than 90 degrees Fahrenheit. In the afternoon, towards two o'clock, the sea-winds generally begin to blow and at times it is so cool, even in the middle of summer, that it is necessary to wear an overcoat. These winds, in addition, are very fortunate for the city, for the air is often rather close. Besides, some of it is built on swampy places from which impure and unhealthy vapors rise that the wind blows away. The spring is early; it begins towards the end of March and continues in all splendor and beauty. In the summer — from June on — no rain falls at all, but all the more in winter, often for days at a stretch. After the rain has stopped falling, it will often turn warm and the thermometer rise to 50 degrees. Autumn lasts until January. Accordingly, where weather conditions are such, there is not much to be said about winter. Here are some weather reports during the spring of 1861:

April 1, 8 A.M., 54 Degrees; noon, 50 degrees; 6 P.M., 57 degrees
”   2,   ”   57   ”   ”   59   ”   ”   55   ”
”   3,   ”   51   ”   ”   59   ”   ”   55   ”
”   4,   ”   54   ”   ”   59   ”   ”   55   ”
”   5,   ”   58   ”   ”   62   ”   ”   59   ”

In all my travels, I have found nowhere a more agreeable climate than that of San Francisco and of all California in the spring and autumn. In the interior, the summer is naturally much warmer, so that the thermometer will rise in the valleys to 115 and 120 degrees. However, the heat is never oppressive and troublesome as in other hot regions. There is no snow to be found in winter except in the mountains. Here, at times, the snow-storms isolate them. Here, also, there is much rain in the spring and it may last several days and interrupt the mails. As for the fertility of the soil, the following incident will be evidence of it: in the month of March 1860, some vines were planted that by October were bearing bunches of excellent ripe grapes. The soil and climate of California can best be compared to that of upper Persia. In one respect, the State differs very much to its advantage from the other American states, particularly those of the United States: the nights are rather cool from the spring till the middle of August so that a woolen blanket may well be needed. Towards the end of August – until the beginning of November – the nights become warmer.

(An extract from a daily morning newspaper.) The duties of a writer for a daily morning newspaper oblige him, compel him, for his own convenience, to get up and go to bed at unusual hours. Since, as a rule, his work ends in the "wee, sma" hours of the early morning, he usually makes up for his loss of sleep by sleeping a few hours longer in the daytime than the rest of mankind. We except, of course, printers and all others who must work at night. Accordingly, if there is no urgent reason for getting up early, that is, in other words, if his household is that of a bachelor's and he has no wife to arouse him from his sweet slumber, he may rest undisturbed until noon. We know several who seldom, almost never, leave their bedroom any earlier, and this does not cause them any inconvenience. The daily work of an editor

294

may be completed no matter how late he gets up; he will have time enough, for his day lasts long into the night.

The residents of San Francisco are not, as a rule, early risers, particularly when compared in this respect to the residents of other great commercial centers. We could not discover the real reason for this, for there are two reasons — but they contradict each other and both, it seems, are of equal importance. Business here is in a state of constant bustle which requires unusual activity of mind, in fact, almost uninterrupted attention and, therefore, it is quite natural that one should look for refreshment in sleep and prolong the enjoyment of it. The even temperature which is seldom disturbed and rarely interrupted by storm or other sudden changes is also conducive to sleep, and this has just the same effect as the climate in tropical countries. Both of these conditions, since both are present in San Francisco, certainly bear between them the blame for the fact that the residents sleep late, and we leave it to the reader to solve the riddle which is the real cause and to take into consideration the idiosyncracy of each individual.

We had no intention, however, to enter into a physiological or philosophical investigation of sleep, but wish to devote our space for a comparison between the city as it was at night, six or seven years ago, and as it is now. We return to our theme.

Seven years ago, we had the same chair in the office of our newspaper that we have now. It is the only memento of that time; much else is in a corner somewhere, unused and useless. We used to find a big lantern necessary at night to make our way safely through the streets: we can dispense with it now as easily as in those days we found it difficult to do without it — and never did. We would never finish our labors before four or five in the morning and, exhausted by our work, often enough climbed the hill to our house just as the rising sun was gilding the eastern hills. San Francisco was awake and about and just as noisy as it is now in broad day. Whole rows of houses were alight and distinguished the streets along which were the gambling-houses and saloons — with doors that were never closed. Drunkards and revelers wandered up and down and about the city and troubled the night with their loud cries; in between these would be heard, from time to time, the *dulce note* ("agreeable sound") of pistols firing their lead bullets rapidly.

The anxious newspaper-editor, compelled to keep his eye open for news, always preferred to walk in the middle of the street and avoid the unreliable sidewalk: this was too uneven for a safe step at night. The saloons and liquor shops were rich sources of news for the reporter because everybody met there — the citizen, the merchant, the soldier and the stranger who had just arrived. Hardly was dinner over before everybody betook himself to these places: they were the "exchanges" of those days.

One had to avoid, whenever possible, a crowd standing at a corner, for in those days men reached at once for their weapons and very often persons were shot at for walking in that direction, quite innocently and often unaware of a syllable of the controversy. When bloodshed took place, it was always easy to learn the particulars without having to be mixed up in the occurrence oneself. In those days, the whole city seemed to be completely unconcerned about sleeping; and Montgomery Street, at two or three o'clock in the morning, was then as lively as it is now at the same hours in the afternoon. The habits that people had accustomed themselves to in 1850 were too firmly fixed to be easily gotten rid of. At four or five o'clock in the morning it was the habit of the "bloods" in those days to harness up, if they had their own carriage, or, if not, to hire a "shay" or "buggy," and go out for a drive along the sea and then have breakfast in one of the houses at the shore. The average price for the hire of a carriage was from sixteen to twenty dollars and most of the breakfasts at those places near the sea cost just as much. Today one makes use of the steam-engine, rides out to the Mission or Hayes' Park, and can have a much better time for two dollars.

Gradually things have assumed a settled order and the old "Frisco" has changed into the civilized and order-loving city of the present. If one goes home at twelve or one o'clock at night now, one meets only two or three passersby who have been delayed. Towards midnight the city is muffled in a deep silence and whoever is seen walking around at three or four in the morning, if not a policeman — they are rarely to be found at that time, anyway — should be looked at with suspicion. At four o'clock, a number of people are to be seen in the streets: those who deliver newspapers or sell milk, those who sell vegetables in the markets, and the butchers. At six o'clock, there are the first signs of life in the restaurants and hotels. At seven, porters begin to work in the stores, and the people who sweep out offices, open the shops, and perform similar work, are to be seen. At eight o'clock the whole city is awake and resumes its daily life, and the various places of business are more and more in full swing until towards ten o'clock just about everything is rushing along and steaming ahead until towards four in the afternoon; wholesale business than slackens off and retail business becomes slower and sleepier until, towards eight o'clock, everything is usually stock still.

Between five and seven in the afternoon the inhabitants are at dinner and, by way of praise, it must be said that at about ten, half of them are already buried in healthful slumber. A few hours later the city is as quiet as a cemetery and everything is fast asleep. Eighty-five thousand voices are hushed, eighty-five thousand souls lie under the spell of sleep, eight-five thousand bodies are motionless in houses of brick or houses of wood or iron; on beautifully ornamented rosewood or rough pinewood, on luxurious springs and horsehair-mattress or on wooden shavings and straw; wrapped in linen, cotton, or wool; in rooms fit for a palace or in disgusting filth; some in cellars, others in the storeys of buildings that soar upward to the sky; some in valleys and others on the hills, on water or over swamps; all in deep sleep, all happy until the morning, which brings again the toil and trouble of life and when sorrow is again awake. Such is the course of life and so a month is gone, a year, and one generation follows another.

Let everyone do his work, work at his calling with all his might and leave whatever he has succeeded in achieving to the weal and profit of those who follow him: the one the treasures that he has heaped up, another the experiences that he has gathered, here and there, near and far, with great trouble and often at the risk of his life.

Chapter XLIII

CONCLUSION

EVERYTHING RUSHES ALONG IN FEVERISH HASTE, WITHOUT PEACE, without rest anywhere. Pictures fly past us as at a magic-lantern show: one is hardly gone and there — another! Every day brings something new, something unknown, which is attractive for a moment until something else makes us forget it.

The events of a year in California would fill a decade in the old country, in the Fatherland where everything still goes ahead at an easy, regular pace, where it takes longer to build a house than a city here. Everything here is commotion without stop or stay; even the houses will not stand still, but play a part in the mad whirl: here today, they are off tomorrow to another street, and the day after they have found, perhaps, a new location. But how much is lost that is beautiful! Where is the joy with which a young man, after years of absence, returns to the home of his childhood — where the well-known rooms, familiar linden-tree, the garden bench, that silent witness of secret happiness, and the graves of those dearly beloved, all keep talking of the past. The graveyards themselves in California, the most fixed of places on this earth, go upon journeys; as, for example, one can see in the case of the Jewish cemeteries, the location of which has been changed; to say nothing of the Chinese who, hardly at rest in the quiet earth, must be on their way to China or Japan.

The city is built upon quicksand; the wind blows it about from day to day, Limantour today, Bolton and Barron tomorrow, Sherrebach the day after tomorrow. No one knows how it will end. Onward! Onward! That is the cry heard everywhere; one pushes his neighbor aside; no one bothers about his brother; all human feelings would often seem extinguished if we did not know that, in spite of everything, they do exist. On, on! That is the cry of every man as soon as he sets foot on this land. "Onward!" cried the miner as he left the richest of claims in a wild frenzy to follow a shadow somewhere else. "Onward!" has now been the slogan for ten years. No one is satisfied with the present; all are consumed by a restless drive; and here, where the table is spread for everyone more lavishly than anywhere else in the whole world, every one is dissatisfied and considers himself still unfortunate when he reaches his goal — which otherwise he would have valued as the greatest of good fortunes. He continues to hurry after shadows that beckon to him in a golden glitter from the misty distance.

In this mad drive people lose all moderation in their desires. Those whom fate provided for most lavishly were most dissatisfied and the result has been that it is just the oldest residents, for whom destiny spread the contents of its richest cornucopia, who are now often the poorest.

What drives, and drove, people to California? A vague idea of all sorts of untasted fortune hovers before those who tread this ground. No one has hurried to California to look for a decent income, nor has anyone come to find wealth as the late reward of persistent diligence: these were obtainable elsewhere. No, every man wants to become rich quickly, or else he accuses fate of having cheated him. The soil, fruitful as nowhere else, shall not reward his patient tilling; no, in one year it should pay for his farm twice over. Here one does not plough and sow as elsewhere; one does not give his property the care that in other lands the most careless husbandman does. One does not come to California for that. Two or three harvests must make the owner rich. In the meantime, he will ride around in a "buggy" and live like a lord; then go on, and leave behind him untilled the exhausted land.

The miner is driven from place to place just as restlessly, and the same precipitate speed has seized all classes of society. "Onward!" is the slogan: not through steady industry, but by the mad gamble of a risky undertaking. Onward into the midst of wealth! Onward until — the wealth has melted away.

Unhappy California, with all the splendor which a prodigal nature has poured upon you, with the untold wealth that lies hidden in your lap! Time and again your gold has been only the gold of dreams: it has vanished and gone like smoke. Those whom you have blessed have scattered your blessing like mad spendthrifts and the farmer in Wisconsin who ten years ago, in the primitive wilderness, took up his homestead on 160 acres of public land, who these ten years has worked industriously with wife and child, is today a richer man than many of those to whom the soil, almost without any effort, gave rich crops that brought them countless thousands. In Wisconsin, in fact, fruit so plentiful that it breaks the branches of the trees will be left to rot, if it cannot be sold at California prices without trouble.

Thou shalt earn thy bread in the sweat of thy brow: this is God's cry to every man. You shall work and sweat, for there is blessing in it. Gain without effort has never yet brought lasting good; the energy grows slack and many, who have spent years in luxury and at ease, in the end hunger and starve. "Onward!" has, it is true, been the mad cry for ten years, but this slogan has never yet brought anybody onward. In a wild chase they have been turning in a circle and have come at last to the spot from which they started.

Only moderation, only steady industry, only persisting in one direction, only perseverance, even with a small beginning, has brought anyone in California onward and forward. But these qualities will help one get ahead everywhere on earth.

Let us, therefore, stop just once; let us look backwards once; and let us settle accounts with the past.

The hearts that ten years ago were still beating proudly and joyfully are, in many cases, broken; discontent gnaws at them; and the feeling that their life has been a failure has stolen upon many. Many a man who believed that he had long forgotten an earlier contented existence today looks back with longing to that time, to the peace that an active life of toil offered. Well for him who can still say that he has kept that spirit! It is the only security for a contented life and whoever is animated by it surely enjoys today the fruits of industry in his new fatherland — fruits that are still denied his wild neighbor who has rushed onward.

The first decade, the wild year of California, has rushed by, and, praise God, we see signs of improvement everywhere. Men no longer build on the quicksands of blind luck, but on the solid foundations on which alone a sound life can be erected. Everywhere a new race of men is stirring, entirely different from those who first settled in this land, and at the same time one also sees the fruit of this change. Where formerly the miner traveled from place to place like a nomad, human industry has now created powerful structures to wrest the gold from the soil; the careless working of a farm that wastes this too-fruitful land will soon give way to orderly husbandry; the vine and the fruit-tree on the hills and in the valleys offer a rich return to the industrious hand; prosperity everywhere, everywhere wealth, but no one will become rich quickly and everyone must work.

Today, at the end of the first decade, let us stop, accordingly, for a moment, and let us look backwards over the road that has been traveled. Let us learn wisdom for the future from the illusions of the past and the mistakes that have been committed; let us learn to live according to the rules that nature has prescribed for us; let us learn to value greatly the little modest happiness that may be ours; let us learn to prefer industry, persistence, and contentment to the dreams of a wandering, always discontented nomad with his fantasies. Nowhere else, as in this land, are there so many sources of prosperity offered us. But this prosperity, if it is to be an abiding one, does not have its source in the gold-mines of the mountains but in our own earnest effort.

Whoever wishes to write the secret history of California during the last ten years, of this land of promise, will have to write a history of painful disillusionment. He will have to tell why so many thousands wander about, broken in body and spirit, and why they have lost all energy for further striving. He will have to describe, not the splendid castles-in-the-air, but the ashes left over after the fires that have wasted them are out. The long row of graves on Love Mountain Cemetery is a continued story of human happiness thrown away; the madhouses have many a sad story to tell of mistakes; the jails have their frightful reports of what unbridled passion leads to.

But in spite of all this, in spite of an entire class of people who went down in the wild throes of the first struggle, the development of the land goes forward; a new spirit is awake and grows stronger year by year — the spirit that alone can build a strong society — the spirit of industry and of temperance. Thus, on every hand, we are surrounded by a new life; the city, in which we tarry, is beginning to flourish exceedingly. No longer is the land the property of a great landowner, but the hard-working farmer possesses it. Every man has his small share; almost every one has his little farm where, surrounded by blooming children, confident and content with little, he faces the future. Everyone may find here the land of promise if he is temperate in his desires, and only those who are not easily content will not find it: like the children of Israel in the wilderness, they will never see the Promised Land.

Let it storm elsewhere: here, beside the Pacific, all is quiet. Here every man rejoices in the blessings of peace: even now, when the great battle of freedom against oppression is being waged without. The struggle for freedom against slavery had to be begun, sooner or later, so that the time might come in which the words of the prophet shall be fulfilled: "And it shall come to pass afterward that I will pour out My spirit upon all flesh" (Joel: 3, 1);* "the earth shall be full of the knowledge of the Lord as the waters fill the sea" (Isaiah: 11, 9). At that time there will also be fulfilled what Isaiah prophesied: "and they shall beat their swords into ploughshares and their spears into pruning-hooks; nation shall not lift up sword against nation and they shall not learn war any more" (2, 4). And Micah repeats this and adds: "they shall sit every man under his vine and under his fig-tree, and none shall make them afraid: for the mouth of the Lord of Hosts has spoken" (4. 3, 4). And there will be peace upon the whole earth and more attention paid to religion; as Zechariah says: "Thus says the Lord of Hosts: It shall yet come to pass that there shall come peoples, and the inhabitants of many cities; and the inhabitants of one city shall go to another saying: Let us go speedily to entreat the favor of the Lord and to seek the Lord of Hosts. [And they shall answer them:] I will go also" (8. 20, 21).

God grant that these prophecies may be fulfilled in our time and that we may see those fair days dawn.**

---

* Benjamin also has the original Hebrew of these quotations in German letters and with several typographical errors. Tr.

** The description of my journey in the interior of California and to the southern and northwest coasts of the Pacific as well as of my visit to Indian tribes is contained in the second part.

I have said elsewhere in the present work* that I would make a report at the proper time about each Jewish community. But, since no man knows the future and, therefore, must employ the present to the best advantage, I have undertaken to set down here some comments about each Jewish community of America that I visited. These comments may not be exhaustive, but they will be at least informative.

Philadelphia

On October 3, 1859, at eleven o'clock in the morning, I left New York and reached Philadelphia by railway, at half past three in the afternoon. The cities are about a hundred miles apart and the fare was $3. In Philadelphia, I stopped at the excellent hotel of Mr. David Höxter. It is conducted strictly according to Jewish ritual. This great and splendid city with its population of half a million has been described very often. I may, therefore, restrict myself all the more, to the principal purpose of this appendix, which no other description has paid attention to.

There are seven Jewish congregations in Philadelphia: Mikveh Israel (Portuguese ritual) was founded in 1782 (5542 after the creation of the world). It has an old synagogue and is fairly well provided for financially. However, the cost of its splendid new synagogue on North Seventh Street, built about two years ago at a cost of more than $100,-000, has caused it to fall into debt. The president of the congregation is Abraham Hart. The cantor and preacher is Sabato Morais, a native of Livorno, who studied under Abraham Baruch Piperno, chief rabbi of Livorno. Until six years ago, Isaac Leeser, editor of *The Occident*, was the minister. At that time there was a good deal of dissension in the congregation and it divided into two congregations. The seceding group formed a new congregation in 1856 — Beth-El Emeth. It bought a church to use as a synagogue and this was dedicated in the Hebrew month of Nissan, 1857. The congregation has not many members, it is true, but these are all very well-off. Neuhaus is the president. The vice-president is David Scholes. The third member of the board of officers is Alfred Jonas. Isaac Leeser, mentioned above, is the cantor and preacher. It is said that in Philadelphia there are about twelve Jewish families who no longer circumcise their children. For the most part these families, so it is said, belong to the Portuguese.

The third congregation, Rodeph Shalom, has a German ritual. It

---

*   In the text Benjamin refers to Volume I, p. 58 of the German edition; see this volume, p. 84.

was founded in 1802 (5562 after the creation of the world). In 1847, it built a synagogue and a Jewish elementary school. The *mikvah* (ritual bath for women) is in the southwestern part of the synagogue. Samuel Adler is the president of this congregation; the vice-president, Solomon Teller; the cantor, Isidor Frankel. During my first stay in Philadelphia Henry Vidaver was the preacher. Later, he left the post. I will go into the reason for this elsewhere when I discuss the rabbis of America separately.

The fourth congregation, Beth Israel, was founded in 1849 (5609 after the creation of the world). At the head of it are Benjamin Abeles and S. Ezekiel; the cantor and preacher is Gabriel Pape. The ritual is Polish.

The fifth congregation, Bene Israel, was founded in 1847 (5607 after the creation of the world). Its president is Hirschnow Henri; the cantor and preacher, Noot. The members are Netherlanders.

The sixth congregation, Adath Israel, was just recently organized. At the head of it is M. Blumenthal. The cantor is Samuel Breitenbach. The ritual is German.

The seventh congregation, Keneseth Israel, is Reform, It was founded in 1847 (5607 after the creation of the world). Abraham Klapper is the head of it. Dr. Deutsch was the preacher in 1859 but at present he lives in Syracuse as a layman. The *hazzan* or cantor was Mr. Naumburg. At present Dr. David Einhorn, editor of *Sinai*, occupies the post of preacher.

There are twenty-three Jewish charitable societies in Philadelphia:

(1) Hebrah Gemilut Hesed, founded in 1822 (5582). The annual membership dues are $4.

(2) Another society with the same name and dues, founded in 1842 (5602).

(3) Hebrath Nashim (Hebrew Benevolent Society), founded in 1819 (5579).

(4) Hebrath Mishan Almanot Veyetomim (Society for the Assistance of Widows and Orphans), founded 1844 (5604).

(5) Hebrew Hased Vaamet (to assist and care for the sick and bury the dead), founded in 1844 (5604).

(6) Hebrath Neshe Israel, a society of Portuguese women, founded in 1833 (5593).

(7) Hebrath Gomel Hesed Neshe Israel, the society of German women, founded 1845 (5605).

(8) Hebrath Yehude America, a society of American Jews, founded in 1846 (5606).

(9) Hebrew Sunday School Society, for the purpose of Hebrew instruction, founded by Rebecca Gratz in 1838 (5598).

(10) Hebrath Bikur Cholim Ugemilut Hasadim, a society to assist the sick and perform acts of charity, founded in 1814 (5574).

(11) Hebrath Education (Malbish Arumim), a society to clothe the poor. The men furnish the material and the women work it up and divide it among the needy. It was founded in 1848 (5608).

(12) Hebrath Bachurim, a society of young men to assist the poor and sick, founded 1841 (5601).

(13) Jewish Literary Society, founded 1850 (5610).

(14) Hebrew School of Congregation Rodeph Shalom, with classes held twice a week.

(15) Hebrew school of Congregation Keneseth Israel, with classes three times a week.

(16) Hebrath Etz u-Pehamim LaAnyim, a society to supply the poor with fuel.

(17) Hebrah Hinukh Nearim, a society to provide young children, irrespective of denomination, with religious instruction.

(18) Hebrah Harmonia.

(19) Hebrah Concordia.

(20) Hebrah Olympia. These three are social societies with charitable purposes.

(21) Hebrah B'nai B'rith, founded in 1850. This is divided into five lodges: Har Sinai, Har Nebo, Hamoriah, Elim, and Joshua.

(22) Hebrah Har Sinai Cemetery, founded 1853 (5613), has bought a burial-ground. One can buy the right to a grave for $10 and to a family-plot for $25.

(23) Hebrah Foster Home, founded by women, for the education of poor children. Twenty children are in the institution.

There are about five to seven thousand Jews in Philadelphia.

The following may not be without interest. During my stay in America a former empress died, the widow of the former emperor of Mexico, Yturbida. This lady had been living on Broad Street since 1825, the year in which her husband was shot in Mexico. Several of her sons lived in Mexico; one son and two daughters with her. Only a few friends were present at her burial. Philadelphia did not seem to know what a noteworthy person it had sheltered for so long.

Her husband, the brave Yturbida, freed Mexico from Spain and on the eighteenth of May, 1822, was chosen emperor of Mexico as Augustine the First. He accepted the crown only after considerable hesitation, and the year after his coronation it was made hereditary. However, a revolution broke out soon thereafter, a republic was proclaimed and, on the twentieth of March, 1823, Yturbida abdicated. He left the country but returned in 1824 and was shot at Padilla on July 19, 1824. He died like a hero. During his absence he had been declared a traitor, but Santa Anna later had his memory honored and his family received, as the gift of the nation, lands and an annual allowance which has been paid regularly to within recent times, even during the disorders.

Madam Yturbida was a very fine, well-educated woman of honorable character.

Baltimore

On December 8, 1859, at 8 o'clock in the morning, I left Philadelphia and reached Baltimore by means of the railway at one in the afternoon. The two cities are as far apart as New York and Philadelphia — about a hundred miles. The fare was $3. Baltimore has about 180,000 inhabitants, and the number of Jews are just as many as in Philadelphia. The city is very lively and has broad, beautiful streets. This was the first city I visited in America that had slaves. There are six Jewish congregations.

(1) Nidhe Israel, founded in 1823 or, according to the Hebrew chronology, 5583. The president is B. Himmelreich and the preacher Dr. H. Hochheimer, a native of Ichenhausen, Bavaria.

(2) Aden Street congregation, founded in 1845 or 5605. The president is M. Wiesenfeld. The *hazzan* (cantor) is the son of the deceased *hazzan* of Darmstadt and a grandson of the well-known Mendel Rosenbaum of Zell, near Würzburg. He has been educated as a musician and has introduced choral singing. The rabbi is Dr. Issachar Bär Illowy, at present in New Orleans.

(3) Howard Street congregation, founded in 1845 or 5605.

(4) Har Sinai is a Reform congregation. When I was in Baltimore, Dr. David Einhorn, at present in Philadelphia, was the preacher. His efforts were successful in inducing the members of his congregation to keep their places of business closed on the Sabbath.

(5) Key Street congregation, founded in 1852 or 5612. Its ritual is Polish.

(6) Oheb Shalom, recently founded, sent to Hungary for its preacher — Dr. Szold.

In addition, there is a small congregation whose rabbi is Abraham Reiss, a very pious man with a wealth of talmudic learning.

With respect to charitable societies, they are not as numerous as in Philadelphia. Still, the poor are assisted generously. During my stay, there was a banquet arranged to assist the poor and about three thousand dollars was subscribed in half an hour by the 230 persons present. To this sum the members of Congregation Oheb Shalom added about five hundred dollars. The instruction of children in Hebrew is taken care of in Baltimore just as well as in Philadelphia. There are also six lodges of the B'nai B'rith. They are called: Jedidiah; Sholom; Hermon; Judah or Jehuda; Heres. The name of the sixth lodge is unknown to me.

On December 22, 1859, I returned to New York. I stopped for a few days in Philadelphia and reached New York December twenty-seventh.

Washington

On March 1, 1860, I arrived in Baltimore, remained there until the fifth, and then went to Washington. Washington has only one Jewish congregation – the "Hebrew Congregation," founded in 1851. In 1858 the congregation divided into two and a new congregation with the name, Oheb Shalom, was formed; but in 1860 both congregations were re-united. They have a teacher for instruction in English and German. A Hebrah Bikur Holim has been founded by young people. There are somewhat more than a hundred Jews in the city.

Richmond, Virginia

At six in the morning on the sixth of March, I left Washington and embarked on the steamer *Baltimore* for Richmond. Two-thirds of the way I sailed along the Potomac and went the rest of the way by rail; at three in the afternoon I arrived at Richmond. The trip cost $5.50. Since this city has been playing an important part in the American war over slavery recently, I will try to give, in a brief and hasty sketch, the essentials about the origin and history of the place.

Richmond, the capital of Virginia and the present seat of Jefferson Davis and his assistants, is located on the north side of the James River in one of the most beautiful and romantic parts of Virginia, 122 miles from where the river flows into Chesapeake Bay. The city is built on hills and every part of it affords a splendid view of the river winding to the south and of the beautiful expanse of well-cultivated plantations in the neighborhood. Favorably situated and protected on all sides by fortifications and heavy batteries, there will be bloody battles there, sooner or later, before the Federal government will succeed in making good its just claims to supreme authority over all parts of the country. With Richmond taken, the entire state of Virginia will be won and the rebellion forced out of one of its strongest points.

Richmond was laid out in 1733 on the estate of Colonel Byrd and so named by him because location and scenery resembled that of Richmond in England. In 1742, Richmond received from the assembly of Virginia the rights and privileges of a city, and soon afterwards a fair number of newcomers settled in the new municipality. The seat of government of the state was removed in 1777, for greater security, from Williamsburg to Richmond. At that time, the city had at most 140 or 150 houses with six hundred or, perhaps, as many as seven hundred inhabitants and it was difficult to find quarters for the officials and employees of the government. In 1780, the public places and buildings were laid out and building begun. Benedict Arnold, the traitor, at the head of a thousand English, burnt down a large part of Richmond in 1781, including public and private buildings, and withdrew after twenty-four hours. Since then, the city has constantly grown in population and prosperity and today the number of residents is estimated at more than 60,000. Of these perhaps a tenth are German.

Richmond has more than fifty tobacco-factories, a number of iron-foundries, an arms factory and the state arsenal. A few years ago, a splendid monument was erected in the immediate vicinity of the capitol: it is ornamented with the statues of all Virginia's heroes and statesmen.

There are three Jewish congregations in the city. They are all well-off.

(1) Beth Shalom, founded in 1791 or 5551. The ritual is Portuguese.

(2) Beth Ahaba, a German congregation, founded in 1841 or 5501. The ritual is German. S. Strauss is the president. The *hazzan*, teacher, and ritual slaughterer is Mordecai Michelbacher. This congregation, as well as Beth Shalom, has its own synagogue.

(3) Keneseth Israel, a congregation recently organized with a Polish ritual. The president is Henri; the *hazzan*, Rosenberg. This congregation has no synagogue and has rented a house for its religious services.

Charitable organizations are:

(1) Hebrah Gemilut Hesed, founded by the Portuguese in 1852 or 5612;

(2) Hebrah Shebeth Achim, founded in 1848 or 5608 by the English and Portuguese;

(3) Hebrah Ahabath Israel, founded somewhat later than the preceding societies by Germans;

(4) Hebrah Achioth, founded by women to establish and take care of a *mikvah* (ritual bath).

As I was told by Jews of the city, there is not a Jew there in need of any charitable assistance and most of the Jews are well-to-do.

In the evening of March eighth I left Richmond and the following morning was again in Washington. I stayed there a few days to await the arrival of Col. Mendes Cohen and I. I. Blumenberg. On the thirteenth of March, those gentlemen introduced me to Gen. Lewis Cass, a member of the cabinet, who received me in a very friendly manner and requested me to come again the following day. At this second and final visit, he handed me a letter of introduction to Secretary Cobb, and he in turn gave me a letter addressed to his friend, the American ambassador to China. That day I also went to see several senators, among whom J. P. Benjamin, a fellow Jew from Louisiana, is particularly worth mentioning. On the fifteenth, Secretary Lewis Cass paid me a return visit but, to my regret, did not find me at home and left me his card.

Cincinnati

In the morning of March sixteenth, I left Washington again and went to Cincinnati. However, I spent the seventeeth as a day of rest, for the Sabbath had commenced. I reached Cincinnati at last on the eighteenth. The distance is about 500 miles. It is not in my power to describe this great city with its population of 180,000, its extensive trade by railway and by boat along the Ohio; nor the romantic beauty of the surrounding countryside, which is in a state of intensive cultivation and has especially many vineyards; nor the mountain called "Forest Hill" on the bank of the Ohio, across the river, near the border of Kentucky, of which Alexander von Humboldt said that from it one had the finest view in all North America (from the top one can look down upon the whole Ohio valley); to describe all this requires an Alexander von Humboldt. However, I will add just a word about the city and its environs. Cincinnati has been called "The Queen of the West." That expresses it all.

There are about five to seven thousand Jews in Cincinnati.—about as many as in Philadelphia. Most of them are well-off and there are even a few millionaires among them. The first Jewish immigrants, who settled here in 1816, were the following. Joseph Jonas, from England, whose acquaintance I was still able to make, is a watchmaker. I will tell a little story about him here. One day, a farmer brought him a watch and left it to be repaired. In a few days the farmer was again in town and wished to get his watch but, to his surprise and fright, found the shop of Mr. Jonas closed. He thought the man had gone bankrupt, or had run away with his watch. However, before hurrying to court, he went into a neighbor's house and asked why the store of the watchmaker was closed. Upon the reassuring answer that the man was a Jew and therefore kept his place of business closed that day for it was a Saturday, the farmer went home with his mind at ease. At home, he told his mother, an old American woman, why he had not brought his watch back. She was greatly surprised to learn that there were still Jews in the world, about whom she had read so much in the Bible, and urged her son to take her along with him to the city just once that she might see a Jew. Soon afterwards, the son went to the city again and took his mother with him. They went to the watchmaker together. After the farmer had his watch back, the old woman asked the watchmaker: "Are you really and truly a Jew — a descendant of Abraham?" When the watchmaker had answered that he was, she folded her hands and lifting her eyes to Heaven said: "How can I thank Thee, O Lord, that I have lived to see one of the descendants of Abraham before my death!"

The second Jew in Cincinnati was Moritz Moses, likewise an Englishman, in whose house the first *minyan* was held later. At this, he himself recited the prayers. This man, respected and honored by all, died during my stay in Cincinnati. Many acquaintances and friends were in the funeral procession. Soon after the arrival of Moritz Moses in Cincinnati, his brother, Solomon Moses, followed him and a certain David ben Ascher, as well as Mose ben Joshua and Joseph Nathan. At this time the city had about eight thousand inhabitants. But, because of its favorable location, in hardly half a century it became as important as it is today.

There are six Jewish congregations in Cincinnati.

(1) Bene Israel, founded in 1819 or 5519. In 1830, or 5590, the congregation built a synagogue, called the Broadway Synagogue, after the street on which it is. It follows a Polish ritual. The membership is partly English and German, partly French, and there are a few Poles: in all about 200. The congregation, to be sure, is Orthodox; but it has introduced a choir of men and women. Education is taken care of by a fairly good elementary school. The rabbi is D. M. Lilienthal. A delightful community festival was recently introduced by this congregation: this was held during the half-holidays (*hol hamoed*) of Sukkoth when I was in Cincinnati. All members, irrespective of position or means, send all sorts of food and fruit to the school-house. Then they assemble for a community meal that is animated by general conversation and at which all is cheerfulness and gaiety. It seems to be a revival of the *Simhath Beth ha-Sho'ebah* in the Holy Temple. It was introduced by the above-mentioned rabbi of the congregation — Dr. M. Lilienthal.

(2) Bene Yeshurun, founded in 5600 or 1840. Its synagogue, the Lot Street Synagogue, likewise called after the street where it is, was built by the congregation in 5605 or 1845. The congregation is well-off and consists of 220 German members. A few years ago they introduced some innovations and since then have been called a Reform congregation. They have an organ and a choir at their services, but men and women are separated and do not sit together as in other Reform congregations. In 5617 the rabbi of the congregation, Dr. I. M. Wise, arranged a new Hebrew prayer-book with the title, *Minhag America*. It is a shorter version of the old prayer-book and those parts, particularly, are left out that deal with sacrifices and the Messiah, which, however, constitute the principal parts of Judaism. Only the first section of the prayer-book has appeared; the second section, that was to deal with the services for the New Year and the Day of Atonement, did not appear and on those days the old ritual is followed. Perhaps they were afraid that God was awake on those days and they might be the worse for it in God's judgment.

Their president is Abraham Aub. They have the best Jewish elementary school in all America. This school, with good teachers and monitors, is under the direction of Dr. Wise. It has two hundred pupils, girls as well as boys. One of the best of the teachers is L. Buttenwieser, a distinguished Talmudist. The school is generally known as "Talmud Yelodim" and was founded in 1849 or 5509. Judah Touro bequeathed it three thousand dollars; a certain Simon Syman donated a thousand dollars; and with these sums it was possible to erect a large four-storey building. Every member of the congregation pays two dollars annually for the children of the poor who are pupils of this institution. The president is Henry Mack.

The above two congregations have a cemetery in common. It is four miles from the city and for the most part divided into family-plots.

(3) Shearith Israel. The members of this congregation formerly belonged to Bene Israel but withdrew and organized a separate congregation. For several years the congregation rented a house for its services, but in 1860 built a beautiful synagogue on Lot Street and next to it a *mikvah* (ritual bath) for women. It has about seventy members and follows a strictly orthodox German ritual. Its president is Nathan Maltser. He is very well-to-do, strictly observant and fairly well acquainted with the Talmud. He is also a *mohel* (one who performs the rite of circumcision) and makes it his business to provide and gather money for the poverty-stricken Jews of Palestine. Another member of this congregation is Moses Heinemann. He is an old man, truly charitable and strictly religious, who retired from business and

occupies himself only with visiting the sick and in caring for them and in aiding the poor.

(4) Adath Israel, founded in 1850 or 5610, has thirty-five members and follows a Polish ritual. It has no synagogue of its own and therefore rents a house for religious services.

(5) Beth Hamedrash has fifteen members, some German and some Polish. The ritual is German.

(6) Ahabath Achim (German ritual), founded in 5608 or 1848, has its services on the other side of the canal that flows through the city. About 120 members belong to it. The congregation has its own cemetery.

There are eighteen charitable organizations in Cincinnati.

(1) Hebrath Bikur Holim. A society to assist the sick, travelers as well as residents. It has about two hundred members and was founded in 1828 or 5588.

(2) Hebrah Beth Holim Hospital, founded in 1850 or 5610. Judah Touro, mentioned above, left this society five thousand dollars. Abraham Mack gave it five hundred dollars on the occasion of the death of both his sons in a railway accident, and Moses Rindskopf gave the society five hundred dollars upon the death of his wife. With these sums a hospital was built.

(3) Hebrath Almanoth vi-Yethomim, an asylum for widows until they remarry and for orphans until they are released from school. Four hundred members belong to it and each contributes four dollars annually.

(4) Hebrath Gemiluth Hassadim, founded by Dr. M. Lilienthal, the rabbi, in 1856 or 5616. It has a hundred and fifty contributing members. In addition, collections are made among the members that bring in about five thousand dollars. Half of it goes to the poor of the city and the rest to poor strangers on their way elsewhere.

(5) Hebrath Meshiboth Nefesh, a society of about a hundred members, founded in 1842 (5602).

(6) Hebrath Tifereth Israel, founded in 1848 or 5608. In addition to pious works, its purpose is to establish and care for a *mikvah* (ritual bath for women).

(7) Hebrah Lehahsik Aniye Eretz Israel, a society to aid the poor of Palestine, founded in 1853 (5613).

(8) Hebra Kadisha, consisting of about eighty members, for the purpose of aiding the sick and burying the dead.

(9) Hebrath Judah Touro, founded in 1856 (5616), by those who belonged to no particular congregation. The society has about one hundred members and each contributes six dollars annually. They have

bought a cemetery where strangers, who belong to no congregation, may also be buried.

(10) Hebrath Oneg veSimhah. This society likewise uses its income for charitable purposes.

(11) Hebrath Nashim Gomloth Hesed, founded by English women in 1838 or 5598. The purpose of the society is to aid the poor and orphans.

(12) Hebrath Nashim Zekenoth Ashkenaz, founded by German women in 1841, or 5601. This society has the same purpose as the preceding one.

(13) Hebrath Nashim Gomloth Hesed, a charitable society of women from various countries.

(14) Hebrath Neshe Gomle Hesed, a society with similar purposes as the preceding society and with a similar name.

(15) Hebrath Nashim Malbish Arumim was founded in 1858 (5618) for the purpose of distributing clothes among the poor.

(16) Two small societies of men, both with the name Hebrath Gomle Hasodim, likewise devoted to charitable purposes.

(17) Various social societies, namely:
    a. Allemania (200 members)
    b. Harmonia (100 members)
    c. Phoenix (120 members).

In addition to the meetings, once a week, for men, theatrical performances and balls are held every two or three weeks in winter. Balls are held particularly at *Simhat Torah, Hanukkah* and *Purim*, here as in all America. But in no American city are the Jews more sociable and more disposed to enjoy themselves than in Cincinnati.

(18) Independent Order Bnai Brith. This society has three lodges in Cincinnati:
    a. Beth El
    b. Jerusalem
    c. Moriah.

The Jewish population of this city is engaged chiefly in manufacturing and in dealing in groceries and produce. Joseph Braunschweig from Switzerland has an important factory making equipment for billiards. The beautiful opera house that Samuel Peik built for about $300,000 should be mentioned. In addition, he has an important liquor business.

I consider myself duty-bound to mention here also Mr. A. Adae, consul for the kingdoms of Prussia, Würtemberg, Bavaria, Hanover, Saxony and so forth, who was of great service to me. He is a man of scientific education who, irrespective of religion, does all he can to further the interests of science. In addition, he is very charitable to all and is always one of the first to contribute when it is a question of charity. Mr. Adae is a native of Germany. Mr. Henry Mack is very friendly with him and together they did much to assist me in my undertaking. I am also much indebted to Messrs. Joseph Trounstine and L. Rosenstiel. The latter was born in Königsberg in 1815 and was educated in Gross Glogau. After he completed his studies, he entered the employment of Stettiner Brothers in Königsberg. In 1840 he went to America and now, blessed with wealth, surrounded by a charming family, he is the enthusiastic patron of all that is noble and beautiful. Many a beautiful, elevating poem in English has been pubblished about him in the American press.

With respect to the steps initiated in Cincinnati to further my undertaking, I add the following report taken from the issue of March 30, 1860, of *Deborah* — a newspaper published there.

"On the twenty-fifth of this month, a meeting was held in the hall of the Allemania Society, as the result of the summons of several influential men, to welcome the famous Jewish traveler, Mr. I. J. Benjamin II, and to hear what he wishes the Israelites of Cincinnati to do.

"Mr. Joseph Trounstine was elected chairman of the meeting and Mr. Benjamin was introduced by Mr. Louis Seasongood, president of Allemania. The Rev. Dr. Lilienthal was then called upon to explain the purposes of Mr. Benjamin's travels and to suggest the means by which these may be furthered by his fellow Jews of America.

"After Dr. Lilienthal explained the purpose of the journey with respect to its relation to scientific knowledge generally and its significance for Jewish history and Jewish political rights, he recommended as the most effective way of assisting Mr. Benjamin in his travels the plan suggested by Mr. Michelbacher, president of the Temple in New York. However, in that too busy metropolis nothing had been accomplished. The plan was, namely, to organize a society for three years, the subscriptions of whose members, at least $5 a year, were to provide Mr. Benjamin with the means for his journey.

"Mr. Benjamin then delivered a discourse in Hebrew before the meeting, which the Rev. Dr. Wise translated and explained in detail. He compared Benjamin I and the present bearer of the name; called attention to the advantages that a Jewish traveler in the Orient has over a Christian, inasmuch as the Jews who were dispersed throughout the Orient were always ready to help a fellow Jew; pictured the sufferings that Mr. Benjamin had already endured and the dangers he had exposed himself to; praised the courage and perseverance of Mr. Benjamin in being willing to set out upon a second such journey in spite of its hardships; described the scientific results achieved by the first journey and the more important results to be hoped for from a second journey; and, in conclusion, recommended that the meeting adopt the plan proposed.

"The Rev. Dr. Lillienthal then moved that a standing committee be named, fully authorized to organize the society in Cincinnati and to establish branches throughout the country and to provide for the continuation of Mr. Benjamin's journey of three years.

"The motion was carried by acclamation and the chairman named as members of the proposed committee the Rev. Drs. Lilienthal and Wise, and Messrs. Ph. Heidelbach, S. Friedmann, and L. Rosenstiel. Mr. J. Trounstine also had to become a member of the committee according to the unanimous desire of those present.

"Upon the motion of Mr. L. Rosenstiel, the subscription list of dues for three years, payable annually in May, was begun at once, and in a few minutes annual dues amounting to almost three hundred dollars were subscribed by the participants in the meeting.

"There is no doubt that the annual dues will amount to almost a thousand dollars. The Israelites of Cincinnati should be honored, honored again and again and again, because they are always ready to help every good cause with heart and hand.

"The committee hopes that the Israelites of the West will participate in this undertaking in great numbers and in this way show that their hearts respond warmly to every Jewish interest."

In expressing my thanks again, at this time, to the noble-minded Jewish community of Cincinnati, I hope that I shall very soon be in a position to begin my journey to Asia and I will then request that the resolution of the meeting just mentioned be carried out.

It is worth noting that Cincinnati is the first place in North America where the cultivation of vineyards was carried on as a business. Nicholas Longworth, in particular, has made a good deal of profit out of this. He bought several thousand acres of land from the government, cultivated it and planted vineyards. The wine turned out to be extremely good and had so great a sale Longworth was unable to take care of all the business himself and had to lease part of his lands to young settlers. Recently he established a winery for making champagne. Although he is now worth about fifteen million dollars, he still lives modestly and very simply. His children, however, who were born to wealth, live in a grand style and reside in beautiful palaces. On April thirtieth I went to see him in the company of Dr. Lilienthal to make his acquaintance. I found him in his garden, dressed simply and doing the work of a gardener. After I was introduced to him, he invited me into his house and then brought me into his wine-cellar. This excelled anything of the sort I had ever seen. There we tried some of his best wines. As I went away with Dr. Lilienthal, he asked me what I really thought of the man. I did not know how to characterize him any better than as follows: the man is a North American Noah.

Another important business in the products of the land — although not engaged in by Jews — is the trade in salted pork.

As still another example of my previous statement that science in America has, so to say, to go begging, I cite the case of Professor Mitchell who, a few years ago, built an observatory here that cost $40,000. But since he could find no students who wished to be active in it, he was compelled to give up the post. He then drew up, as an engineer, the plan for an Ohio-Mississippi railway. Now that this work is finished, he is compelled to go from city to city and lecture, for he has no other way of making a living.

Gambling is in full swing in Cincinnati, although there are laws against it. Recently a gambling-hell was discovered in Baker Street, an alley distinguished for its dirt and heaps of rubbish. We borrow the following description from the *Volksfreund*, published in Cincinnati.

"In the midst of the desert of Baker Street, there rises a palace, four storeys high, in Gothic style, ornamented with architectural embellishments scarcely to be found upon the most modern buildings on Fourth and Seventh Streets. However, only a very hasty glance will deceive an observer as to the true character of the goings-on in the building. All those embellishments are covered with dust. The windows are dirty. The shutters are half-opened and swing moaning and groaning on their hinges in the wind. The entrance to the house is level with the street and the dirt of the street reaches into the vestibule. A golden figure, 4, is on the fan-light above the Gothic door; lit up by the gas-light behind it, it is clearly visible at night. Inside the door, one is led into a parlor by servants who are neatly dressed, but whose manner has a kind of insolence; the parlor is furnished with splendid chandeliers and has a dark Brussels carpet. Red gauze about the gas-light softens it to a twilight. The splendor of this room is to be seen in all the other rooms of the house; but dusty walls, spotted carpets, and quarreling servants draw attention to an irregular, tedious existence.

"On the second floor one sees that everything possible has been used to charm the senses. Richly decorated oil-cloth gives off a glaring reflection under the brilliant gas-lit lamps. At the slightest touch a door opens and a richly spread table, always set, catches the eye: here the finest liqueurs and the most expensive wines and cigars are waiting for those who visit the house. Players hurry to the table to calm themselves, after their losses in the enjoyment of fiery drinks, or to get the courage to try their luck again. In the adjoining room is the bank where the chips for playing are sold for cash and also cashed. Next to this room are several small rooms for private parties. On the third floor is the principal gambling-place. Here are the faro tables, the billiard tables (where a bet is laid on every stroke), "three-card monte" baize, in short everything that was ever discovered to swindle people out of money by gambling. The servants of the house live on the fourth floor.

The gambling-house, here described, was recently raided by the police. This was no easy task. Plain-clothes men were smuggled into the house to inform the police-chief waiting outside about the lay-out of the place. One of these found the exit, but not the other. He was recognized and the players and those who ran the house redoubled their watchfulness. A strong police-squad of twenty men waited a long time in vain. Finally, the door was opened for a gambler and that moment the entire squad of police entered the house. As quick as lightning the alarm-bell in the house was sounded by the guards, but not quickly enough to keep the police from their quarry. The consternation of the gamblers was such that many did not know where they were running to and so fell into the hands of the police. However, a few were fortunate enough to escape by the rear door. Eight men, including the owners of the house, were arrested and brought to the station-house on Ninth Street.

The gambling equipment was afterwards taken from the house by the police and brought to the office of the chief of police: this equipment alone was worth five thousand dollars.

The unhappiness brought upon many respectable families by these gambling-houses is dreadful. A few weeks ago, a young merchant from New York lost six hundred dollars gambling. In despair at his loss he was driven to trying to commit suicide. A Cincinnati merchant, a partner in one of the largest firms of the city, fell into the hands of the demon of gambling, and lost in this bank all he had in the world as well as his wife's jewels. Finally, he contracted debts that involved the property of his partners. Because of this, he was forced out of business and is now, morally and physically, a ruined man and with his family abandoned to the bitterest poverty. We could give hundreds of other examples of the frightful results of the goings-on in this house.

New Orleans

On April second, at eight o'clock in the evening, I left Cincinnati and on the fifth of the same month reached New Orleans. The distance of these cities from each other is about 800 miles. As soon as one crosses the Mississippi, one is, so to say, in another world. Until then one saw well-cultivated stretches of land, but now primitive woods and swamp alternate. The nearer one approaches New Orleans the more numerous the swamps seem to be and the greater in extent until finally one sees only swamp. A traveler, with whom I rode across this part of the country, told me that at one time he would often see snakes and crocodiles along this stretch of railway. On a branch road that likewise leads to New Orleans, these reptiles are still to be found. However, I saw none of these dangerous creatures in that section of the country.

It is not within the scope of these notes to write of this great and beautiful city and its extensive commerce. I restrict myself to a report about the community of my fellow Jews.

There are four Jewish congregations in New Orleans.

(1) Shaare Chesed, with two hundred members, follows a German ritual. It was founded in 1828 or 5588. In 1850 it built a synagogue. Until then the congregation used to rent a house for religious services. During my stay in New Orleans, L. Klappmann was the president of the congregation and M. Stiefel vice-president. The latter is a strictly religious man who keeps his place of business closed on Saturday and the holidays. I had the friendliest of receptions in his house and had many an opportunity to become acquainted with his noble spirit and his never-failing benevolence. His house is always open to every stranger, every visitor to New Orleans. S. Friedländer, a very rich, noble-spirited man, was later elected president. Solomon Jacob from London was the rabbi and *hazzan* (cantor). He established a newspaper, *Cornerstone*. He died towards the end of 1860 and at his death this periodical, a weekly, ceased to be published. His successor as rabbi is Issachar Bär Illowy, a very good Talmudist and able writer on Jewish themes. This congregation is the most charitable in all New Orleans.

(2) Nefutzoth Yehudah, a Portuguese congregation. It has about forty members and was founded in 1846, or 5606. The president is Mr. Jonas. The *hazzan* and preacher is J. K. Gutheim, a native of a place near Münster in Westphalia. He devoted himself to Jewish studies rather late in life. This congregation has a beautiful synagogue, built by money bequeathed to it by Judah Touro.

(3) Ahabath Achim, established in 1850, or 5610, in the suburban city of Lafayette. It has about eighty members and follows a German ritual.

(4) Temime Derech, founded in 1858 (5618), has seventy-five members and follows a Polish ritual. The members formerly belonged

to Shaare Chesed but withdrew because the Germans and Poles did not get along together.

Charitable Societies

There are eight of these in New Orleans, namely:
(1) Hebrath Gemiloth Hesed, founded in 1847 or 5607;
(2) Hebrath Nashim (a society of women), founded the same year;
(3) Hebrath Bikur Holim, founded in 1849 or 5609;
(4) Hebrath Mashmie Yeshuah, or Hebrew Foreign Mission, founded in 1853, or 5613.

This society has a capital of about ten thousand dollars, most of it from Judah Touro, who bequeathed it six thousand dollars. He left this money chiefly for the purpose of assisting Jewish travelers and to induce Chinese Jews to send their children to the society to be brought up. After his death several members united under the above name and adopted new rules and by-laws. Every member pays annual dues of $5. The society has seventeen members now. At the meeting of its board of directors on April 10, 1860, it was decided to assist me in my journey to Asia — God grant now that it will be soon! — with an annual contribution of three hundred dollars for three years. The board informed me of its resolution in the following letter (translated from the original):

To Israel Joseph Benjamin from Falticeni (Moldavia)

New Orleans, April 19, 1860.

Dear Sir:

I have the pleasure to inform you herewith of the following resolution, unanimously adopted by the Board of Directors of the Hebrew Foreign Mission, at their meeting on the tenth inst. It was decided that the sum of three hundred dollars be paid annually to Mr. Israel Joseph Benjamin from Falticeni in Moldavia from the treasury of this society, for three successive years, to defray the expenses of this seasoned traveler in his contemplated voyage to Arabia, Malabar and China for the purpose of discovering the condition of our fellow Jews in those lands and to report upon it; and the above sum, so granted, will be forwarded to the above-named Mr. Benjamin together with similar grants made by other corporations of this country, or through a consul in Europe.

318

Hoping that you will soon secure the necessary means and wishing you the utmost success in your contemplayed voyage, I have the honor to remain

Very respectfully,

L.S.

Your devoted servant,
James K. Gutheim,
Secretary of the H. F. M.

After a few weeks, however, this resolution was revoked for reasons to be discussed fully below.

(5) Orphan Asylum, an institution for widows and orphans, in which there are sixty-five widows and orphans.

(6) Hospital. Judah Touro left a building, worth about $30,000, and bequeathed it to this society.

(7) Hebrew Benevolent Society, a society to assist the poor, the sick, strangers in distress, and so forth.

(8) Independent Order of Bnai Brith, mentioned with respect to other cities. The society in New Orleans is no different.

The number of Jews in New Orleans is about two thousand. Most of them are well-to-do.

As a contribution to Americana the following story may be in place. In a small place, a few miles from New Orleans, there lived two Jews. The sister of one was the wife of the other. She died and before her death expressed the wish that she might be buried in the Jewish cemetery of New Orleans, for there was no such cemetery where she lived. However, at that time the level of the water had fallen so low it was difficult to transport the corpse to New Orleans. Accordingly, the brother of the deceased woman placed her body in alcohol in order to carry it to its last resting-place at an opportune time. So several weeks passed and the mourning husband could not show his deceased wife the final honors. No doubt for distraction, he went by land to New Orleans and — married again. Soon afterwards, it was possible to go by water to New Orleans and the brother brought the corpse of his sister to the city. The former husband, in a black suit of mourning, followed the bier beside his new bride.

On April twenty-seventh, several members of Congregation Shaare Chesed, including the president, published in different newspapers a call for a meeting in behalf of my projected trip to the Orient. As a result, a considerable number of the Jewish residents of New Orleans appeared at a meeting held on April twenty-ninth. Mr. Haver was elected president, Mr. Isaac Hart vice-president, and Messrs. M. Stiefel,

Louis Stern, and Schwarz assistants. Rabbi Solomon Jacob opened the meeting with an eloquent address that was very well received by all present. He pointed out that since Benjamin of Tudela, that is, for almost seven hundred years, there had been no Jew who ventured his life upon a long journey for the sake of increasing our knowledge of Jewish conditions in remote parts of the world. He emphasized, further, how necessary it was just then, when the condition of the Jews in Europe and America, had taken so fortunate a turn politically, to send a traveler particularly to China, Arabia and other lands of the Orient in order to have exact information of the condition of our fellow Jews in those lands. Since I, because of my previous long journeys on four continents, had attained insight into conditions in foreign lands, I was now the best suited because of my experience to undertake such a mission. I had such a journey in mind and to direct it in that direction, he recommended that I should be assisted with money in such a manner as to be able to continue my travels.

Mr. M. Stiefel then made a motion to organize a society for this purpose, to be known as the Benjamin Society; this was to continue in existence for three years and every member was to pay annual dues of five dollars at the beginning of each year for the three years. This motion was carried unanimously and the maker of it designated to set a subscription-list in circulation the next day. Thirty-five members were accepted immediately and paid their dues at once. The money was handed over to a member of the executive board and, for all I know, he may still have it. Not only was the money not received by me, but I have the loss of about eighteen dollars to complain of in this affair. I was billed for the announcements and for the hall in which the meeting was held. I paid these bills believing that I would surely be reimbursed out of the money that had been collected; but, when I asked the member of the board for what I had spent, he refused to pay me. I believe I know the probable reason: it lies in what took place later and I will describe this in the following section.

The Judah Touro Monument

After the discussion of my affairs at the above-mentioned meeting had been concluded, the president of Congregation Shaare Chesed, Mr. S. Friedländer, requested the meeting to remain a little longer because he had something else to say. He informed the meeting that the Portuguese congregation had disclosed to him that they wished to set up a statue of Judah Touro to the lasting memory of the man who had been a benefactor of so many congregations, and that they sought the assistance of the other congregations of New Orleans in the project in the hope that other congregations in America would also join in it. I was astonished at the proposal and asked my neighbors for more details about this proposed memorial: what it would be like, where it would be set up, and so on. I was told that the statue of the dead man would be cast in bronze and was to be set up in the outer court of the Portuguese synagogue. Hearing this, I was more astonished than ever and asked permission to speak.

"Gentlemen," I said, "although I am only passing through the city and, therefore, have no right to take the floor in the discussion of community affairs, I see myself forced to express my views in this matter because this concerns our religion, and in such a case every Israelite has the right to speak. When I was young I spent much time in Jewish studies and have recently seen four continents and have learnt something at first hand about millions of my fellow Jews. Nowhere did I see or find the statue of a Jew: because this is clearly against the principles of our holy religion."

My words caused great excitement among the religious Jews at the meeting and it was, accordingly, terminated.

In fact, to prevent the statue from being set up, I went next day to the *hazzan* and preacher of the Portuguese synagogue, Mr. J. K. Gutheim. I asked him if setting up the statue had been earnestly considered. When he said it had, I asked him further what he, as a rabbi, had to say about it. He answered that he was wholly for it. At my remonstrance that it was against our religion, he replied drily: "I don't see that at all." When I then said that it was clear from our books of religious law that setting up a statue was strictly forbidden and cited the legal statements with respect to it, he answered: "That was in ancient times. Now, however, we live in the nineteenth century." Thereupon I said: "If the world were twice as old as it is, our Torah would still be the same!" "Ah," he said, "all that doesn't bother me at all."

When I realized that he would not give up his project, I announced that I was compelled to protest publicly against setting up the statue. He ended our conversation with these words: "You may do what you like and the congregations may contribute or not. I will wager everything that this statue will be set up."

On May 19, 1860, I handed in my protest: it was printed in the *Cornerstone*, No. 12, and the editor of this periodical, who was also the rabbi of the German congregation, publicly agreed with me. The protest was as follows:

"I take the liberty of calling the attention of the Jewish community of New Orleans to a matter that has been rumored for some time but which I could not believe. When I first heard of this startling rumor, my hair stood on end. How is it possible that Jews can entertain the wish to carry out an act which is a clear violation of the Ten Commandments? These declare: 'Thou shalt not make for thyself a graven image'! No, I said, this can only be the idle invention of a man who has given the matter no thought. However, when I was present at a meeting of Congregation Shaare Chesed yesterday, I heard the proposal of the Sephardic congregation introduced, namely, in behalf of 'erecting a statue to honor Judah Touro.'

"Where is a precedent for this? Where can anything like it be found? Good and pious Jews have lived at all times and in all climes, but did any of our ancestors ever receive such a mark of respect? Were our prophets, kings, or the bards of Israel ever honored by such a token as this that men wish to set up to the memory of Judah Touro? One cannot say: the times have changed. One cannot reply: the men who lived in the days of Moses, Joshua, David, Solomon, Isaiah and the Maccabaeans were less patriotic, less grateful, than we! No, no, their patriotism was the true and grateful love of their fatherland. They shed their blood to defend their nationality and would never have permitted a monument bearing the likeness of a man — the image of God! — to be erected. Have we forgotten the fate of our brothers when 'the statute of Micah' was set up, or when Manasseh's picture was brought into the Temple?

"It is stated expressly in *Yoreh Deah* (141, 4) that we may not make the portrait of a man in relief. We also find in *Sifte Kohen* that it is prohibited to make a complete likeness and that, it is explained, is the form of a man with both eyes, nose and so forth.*

"Therefore, let us not carry out a project so decidedly in conflict with our holy religion and which, for this very reason, cannot truly honor the memory of a good Jew.

"Among Israelites, there is only one recognized way by which honor may be shown to a noble and great man and his name perpetuated, and that is to erect a hospital or an orphan-asylum or some other benevolent institution.

"May 7, 5620

Benjamin II."**

This protest caused a great sensation among the Jews of New Orleans. On May thirteenth, there appeared an article attacking me in No. 95 of *The Daily Picayune*. It was written by Benjamin da Silva, the *shammash* (beadle and sexton of a synagogue) of the Portuguese

---

*   Since I had no other digests of the Law at hand, I had to limit myself to these two citations.

** The "protest" as printed in *The Cornerstone* was in English. According to a statement in the text of the book, the German version is a translation. Tr.

congregation. I replied in No. 13 of the *Cornerstone*. This second article created even much greater excitement among the Jews of the city than the first. On the evening of the seventeenth of that month, the rabbi of the German congregation informed me that the son of the above Da Silva had expressed his intention of murdering me wherever he might meet me in the evening. The rabbi wanted to call on the authorities to protect me against this man, for when a threat like that is made in America there is little doubt that an attempt will be made to carry it out. But I prevented the rabbi from taking any such step, lest the authorities have the opinion that Jews, too, can hate each other so much because of a difference in religious views that they reach for a revolver or knife. At least, the worthy rabbi begged, I was to stay in his house that night and not expose myself to danger in the streets. But I, to show him that a traveler must know no fear, took my stick and wandered about several streets of the city until after midnight. Luckily for both of us, we did not meet. Indeed, I was not afraid of being overpowered by him, for I had been lucky enough to ward off many an attack; however, I had never yet had to fight against a fellow Jew.

The Hebrew Foreign Mission, mentioned above, that had assured me of three hundred dollars annually for three years, as I have also mentioned, consists for the most part of Portuguese Jews. It was their congregation that had first suggested setting up the statue of Judah Touro. I now received from a member of the society a demand to withdraw my protest, and this was backed up by the threat that otherwise the grant of nine hundred dollars would be terminated. I replied that I did not permit myself to be moved by any such consideration into changing a step dictated by my conscience. Thereupon a meeting took place at which eight members were present to decide whether or not to withdraw the grant. Three Germans were for me. The other five, however, including the president, Joseph Simon, although he was also a German, were for withdrawing it. The next day I received a letter in which I was informed that the grant of nine hundred dollars was withdrawn.

To avoid the danger mentioned above, I hastened my departure and left New Orleans on the twentieth of that month to return to Cincinnati. I reached this city the evening of the twenty-second.

What had happened in New Orleans also made a great stir in Cincinnati. The press took it up and discussed it more and more. *The Israelite*, edited by Dr. Isaac Wise, the preacher of the Cincinnati Reform congregation, justified my position and, placing itself resolutely on the ground of Jewish law, spoke out against setting up the proposed statue. But it is worth noting that, except for Mr. Jacob mentioned above, not a single Orthodox rabbi in America took my side, which was also theirs. Mr. Gutheim hounded me in the *Occident* to the utmost. He even went so far as to assert that I was not really the traveler, Benjamin, but his son. Mr. Isaac Leeser, the editor of this sheet, pretends to stand at the head of the Orthodox Jews of America. Does he think that he is justifying these pretensions not only by accepting an article such as that of Mr. Gutheim but also, as may be inferred from his remarks about it, by not taking exception to such a monument? Another truly religious man, *Hazzan* Isaacs of New York, publisher of the *Jewish Messenger*, would not for any amount print such an article in his paper. That article attacking me, caused a great stir when published in Cincinnati — among the Reform Jews as well as among the Orthodox. A meeting was called for June twenty-fourth, to be held in the Lot Street Synagogue. At the meeting, Mr. Gutheim's behavior towards me was disapproved of and Dr. M. Lilienthal commissioned to reply in the *Israelite* to Mr. Gutheim's personal attack upon me.

As further evidence that even the most zealous advocate of Reform Judaism did not sanction this project, so decidedly against the spirit of Judaism, I mention the fact that Dr. David Einhorn, who is certainly a radical Reformer, told me that he, too, was once asked if a statue might be set up to the memory of a deceased Jew. He answered that setting up a statue as a memorial to a dead person was not in accordance with Jewish views and, therefore, should not be done.

The committee that had been appointed in New Orleans to set up the Touro statue could not continue with its plans in view of the excitement that this matter stirred up everywhere. It saw itself compelled to obtain the opinion of important European authorities as to whether the project was permissible according to Jewish religious law and usage. Accordingly, Rabbi Adler of London, Rabbi Hirsch of Frankfort-on-the-Main, Rabbi Rapoport of Prague, and Dr. Frankel of Breslau were asked to express their opinion on this matter. All without exception were against setting up the statue of Touro. These opinions, together with the committee's questions, were published in the *Occident*, Nos. 2 and 6 for the year 1861, as follows.*

New Orleans, June, 1860.

At a meeting of Israelites of this city, it was resolved to erect a monument on some open public place, in honor of the late Judah Touro. The memory of the deceased is held in the deepest respect

---

* The English version of the letter by Gutheim, below, is drawn from *The Occident*, XIX, pp. 49-50.

for the benevolence and charity which characterized his life. His name, especially since the publication of his will and testament, has become known throughout the civilized world. — But it is in this city in particular, where the late philanthropist resided for the last fifty-one years of his life, that the virtues which adorned his heart and shed a bright lustre on the Jewish name, are best appreciated.

The deceased died in this city in the beginning of 1854, and his remains were transferred to his family tomb in Newport, Rhode Island, where a suitable monument is placed over his grave.

Now, it is the desire of the Israelites of this city — a desire which is shared by and is certain of the active co-operation of our non-Jewish fellow-citizens — to perpetuate the memory of the late honored philanthropist, by erecting a statue (of bronze or marble) or some other monument (a shaft, pillar or column) in honor of the deceased, *provided such action be not in conflict with the laws and usages of Israel.*

In order, therefore, to settle the doubts of the Jewish community on this point, it was resolved at the first meeting of the executive committee of the Touro Monument Association that, before taking any farther steps, the opinions touching the legality of the enterprise in a religious point of view of some of the most eminent Rabbinical authorities of Europe should be obtained, and that the matter, in all its bearings, be referred to the decisions of Chief Rabbi Dr. N. M. Adler of London, Rabbi S. Raphael Hirsch of Frankfort-on-the-Main, Chief Rabbi Dr. Z. Frankel, Director of the Theological Seminary at Breslau, and Chief Rabbi S. L. Rapoport of Prague.

As the representative of the Association, I therefore take liberty, reverend sir, to solicit your opinion on this matter, and your answer to the following questions:

I. *Primary questions.* —
1. Is it lawful for Israelites to erect a statue (cast in bronze or chiselled of marble) in some open public place of a city, in honor of a deceased fellow-Israelite?
2. Is it lawful for Israelites to erect a monument, say, a shaft, column, or pillar, in the same manner and for the same purpose?

II *Collateral questions.* —
1. Is it lawful for Israelites to subscribe or take any active part towards the erection of a statue or monument to an eminent non-Israelite, living or dead?
2. Is it lawful for an Israelite to devote himself to the art of sculpture or to any mechanical trade in which the manufacture of images, cast, moulded, or graven, not made for purposes of idolatry, form the principal occupation?

325

3. Is it lawful for Israelites to keep within their houses, for the sake of ornament, specimens of art, such as statues or statuettes of human beings, or of dragons and other animals?

III *Principal question.* —

Is it lawful for the Israelites of New Orleans, in conjunction with their non-Jewish fellow-citizens, or by themselves, to erect a statue or monument in honor of their late co-religionist, Judah Touro?

Your answers to these questions will tend to settle every doubt; and, as the subject is one of deep importance to our community, I trust that you will devote your attention to it, and send me a reply in either the Hebrew, German, or English language, at your earliest convenience.

I have the honor to be, with sentiments of profound regard,
Your humble servant,
JAMES K. GUTHEIM
Acting President of the Touro Monument Association.

Attest, JOSEPH MAGNER, Secretary.

Rabbi S. L. Rapoport's Opinion
Extract from a letter to Mr. Gottlieb Wehli of New York

ועוד דבר לי אליכם חכמים יקרים אחרי כי טוב לבבכם הסב לי הכבוד לבא
במרוצת חליפות מכתבים עמכם הנה יש לפני ענין גדול אשר לו נשאלתי מרבנים
חכמים שמה ואם זכרוני לא מכזבני היה גם הרב מהורר בער אילילאווי בתוכם
אשר מגמתם היתה למנוע את העושים במלאכה לעשות או לבנות את הנאסר לפי
דעתם והיא הישרה:

ועוד נדרשתי גם מעבר השני של רבנים אשר מגמתם היתה להשיב רשיון והסכמה
על מעשה או בנין כזה. ונושא השאלה הוא זה. איש אחד עשיר מאהב"י חלף הלך
לו שם מעולם החדש לנו אנשי איברופה אל עולם שכלו טוב לכלנו ועזב רכוש רב
אחריו צדקה לעניים ולא לבד לבני ארצו אך גם לבני ארצות אחרות וביותר סך
גדול לעניי א"י מאהב"י: ועתה הנה מיודעיו ואנשי משפחתו רוצים לעשות לו שם
זכרון נצח בתבל ארצה בעבור פתו נתן לאביונים צדקתו עומדת לעד. ויהי
הנקל לפניהם לבקש הרבנים והמורים רשיון מטעם התורה והדת לעשות פסל תמונתו
מאבן שיש ולהקימו על קברו. ובשגם לא נעשה עוד בישראל כזאת מלפנים חושבים
קצת בדמיונם כי כן בזמנינו באיזה מקומות כמה מנהגים חדשים מקרוב באו ולא
שערום אבותינו כמו המזמורים בביהכ"נ במקהלות נערים ונערות בנינוני אהבה העזה
כמות או לעזוב ביהכ"נ ביוהכ"פ אחרי תפלת שחרית על איזו שעות איש לדרכו
מקצתו והרומים לזה. ולא ידעו ולא יבינו ההבדל הרב אשר בין אלה הדברים
אשר אמנם זרים ומוזרים. ובכל זה נחשבים לקטני הערך נגד הדבר החדש הזה
אשר כל עובר עליו מדור אחרון ישום וישרוק אומר לא נראתה כזאת למיום התגברו
החשמונאים גם על רשעי עמינו המתהללים באלילי היונים ובכיבוד פסיליהם.
ויצה"ר כזה נחשב כמו נעקר ונתבטל אצל עם ישראל. ועתה הנהו מנסה עוד הפעם
לקום ממחילת עפר ולהגלות בדמות מוקיר ומכבד את איש חסד. וזאת תשובתי
לשואלים מן הראשונים והנזכרים:

326

א' כן אמנם אוהבי ישראל ואוהבנו תצדקו בדבריכם תזכו בשפטיכם כי מצד
הדת המסורה אשר כמונו תאמינו בכל חקותיה ומשפטיה לית דין צריך בשש. כי
עשית או הקמת תמונת אדם בולטת אסורה מה"ת וזה בברייתא ארוכה כל הפרצופין
מותרין חוץ מפרצוף אדם ומפרש שם בבולט (ר"ה כ"ד ב' ע"ז מ"ג ב') ורש"י אפילו
שלא לעבודי וכן בס' היד לרמב"ם (הל' ע"ז פ"ג ה') וכתב שם שלוקין מי שעובר
על זה (ש"ע יו"ד סי' קמ"א סעיף ד'):. . . . .

שלמה יהודה ליב ראפאפארט
רב ואב"ד בק"ק הנ"ל

החותם פה ק"ק פראג יום ג' י' תמוז תרכ"א.

Rabbi S. R. Hirsch's Opinion*
To the Touro Monument Association, New Orleans.

Much Respected Sirs:

You will kindly excuse the delay of my answer to your esteemed
communication of the 6th of June, being prevented by a press of
official business, to attend to the same ere this; and even to-day I am
obliged, in order not to defer my reply still farther, to limit my
answers to the essential interrogatories propounded by you.

You purpose to honor the memory of a deceased philanthropist
by the erection of a statue or of some other monument, provided
that such action does not conflict with the religious laws and usages
of the Jews, and you honor me with the request to express my
opinion.

Whether it be permitted, in accordance with the Jewish law, to
erect a statue of bronze or marble in some public place of a city, in
honor of a deceased co-religionist?

Whether it be permitted, in accordance with the Jewish law, to
erect a monument (pillar, &c.,) in the same manner and for the same
object?

To this I have the honor to reply:

The erection of a statue, *i. e.*, of a human figure, of bronze, stone,
or other material, is, according to Jewish law, prohibited in any
place and for any object.

In like manner does the Jewish law distinctly prohibit the erection
of a monument, utterly devoid of any image, of a pillar, a stone, &c.,
for purposes of divine worship, and be it even to gather around it for
the worship of the Holy One. (See Maim. Accum vi.6.)

Not quite as explicit is the decision concerning the erection of
such a monument, not for purposes of divine worship. According to
רש"ל on ש"ת מ"ב סמ"ג it almost appears that the erection of a pillar,
&c., not for purposes of worship even, was unlawful, and that, consequently, the passage of Maim. cited above had to be construed, that
the erection of a *Mazebah* in general, and be it even for the worship
of the Holy One, was not permitted. But the facts recorded in Joshua

---

* The English version is drawn from *The Occident*, XIX, pp. 55–58.

iv.24, 26, 27, 1 Samuel vii.12, testify that even *after* the promulgation of the Mosaic law, the erection of stones as monuments for profane purposes was not prohibited by the law.

But you have yourselves indicated in your esteemed communication, that you desire to observe in this question not only the express dicta of the law, but also the received usage in Israel, and that the project was only then intended to be executed, if it was not in conflict with the "laws and usages of Israel."

Looking upon this question in this light, it would indeed appear that the historical usage in Israel, prevailing throughout the whole Jewish past, would declare itself against the erection of a monument in honor of a man. As far as our knowledge reaches in ante-Mosaic or post-Mosaic times, monuments in commemoration of events or in relation to memorable localities are to be found; monuments as honorary mementoes of men are not to be found. Only one example is met with, that a monument was erected in commemoration of a man, and this — a vain man — Absalom, had erected to himself during his lifetime. However large the number of the great men of our nation (and there is assuredly no other nation which more gratefully cherishes the memory of its heroes in intellect and virtue), it has honored their memories by everything else except by monuments of metal or stone. And although no evidence can be deduced from the non-perception of a certain fact — לא ראינו אינה ראיה — yet (as shown at length by ש"ך, *Yoreh Deah*, חושן משפט 37) with regard to a custom, and more especially such a one that runs through a period of several thousand years with thousandfold opportunities, the non-occurrence may certainly serve as a proof that usage did not regard it admissible.

Let it not be objected, that the period of exile under oppression and persecution was not favorable to the erection of such monuments. The Spanish epoch afforded full liberty; and although it could boast of not a few great men who, during their lifetime, had been honored as benefactors of their nation, some even in a princely manner, yet nobody even thought of honoring their memory by a monument. Nay, still more. Even in the time of the second temple, when, especially under the kings of the Asmonean and Herodean houses, personal attributes were made improperly conspicuous, and love of pomp and the aping of Grecian and Roman customs particularly invited to the erection of such monuments, we find that towers, castles, towns, &c., were built in commemoration of men, but to erect columns and similar monuments — as far as memory serves* — was not ventured. Taking all this into consideration the assumption will appear well founded that Jewish custom is

---

*   Note by the Translator. — Statues of the daughters of King Agrippa I were extant. Vide Jos. *Ant.* xix.9.1.

decidedly opposed to the erection of columns and similar monuments to the memory of men.

Now you have intimated in your esteemed communication that in the settlement of this question not only the *laws* but also the usages of Israel should be taken into account. It is, moreover, a religious *law* of Israel to conscientiously observe the usages of Israel; hence the violation of a Jewish custom of this kind would be a direct infringement of the Jewish religious law.

It is true, honored sirs, that, according to this view of the case, you are prevented from executing your design, quite laudable in itself, to honor the memory of a philanthropist in this manner; yet, in the abstract, let us rejoice that Jewish custom denies to itself the erection of pillars &c. as honorary personal memorials, equally with those pillars &c. prohibited by the law.

Let us preserve this Jewish custom which, considering the un-titled name of the greatest distinction — גדול מרבן שמו — means also to honor most the memory of the distinguished dead by the very refusal of the commonest tomb אין עושין נפשות לצדיקים, because, as the motive expresses, דבריהם זכרונם, they have erected for themselves, by their words and deeds, the most indestructible monument.

Let us in particular, preserve the Jewish custom which, until now, has honored the memory of deceased distinguished men only by good, useful, and salutary works, and has thus in truth — זכר צדיק לברכה — caused the memory of the righteous after their death to redound to the blessing of the living.

Let us not forget that the Jewish mind does not recognize any thing praiseworthy in the erection of not useful and salutary, although magnificent structures. (End. v. ירושלמי שקלים.) A Rabbi who, on passing a magnificent Synagogue, boasted כמה ממון שקעו אבותי כאן, "How much money have my fathers sunk here?" received as reply, כמה נפשות שקעו אבותיך כאן, "How many souls have they sunk here!" לא הוי בנים דילעין באוריתא. Were there no people in need of assistance to enable them to study the law? — And thus I believe, honored sirs, will you perhaps share my conviction, that were you to devote, in honor of the name of the deceased, the interest of the amount which the erection of a monument would cost towards the annual bestowal of a physical, intellectual, or moral benefit upon a single human soul, you would honor his memory, the more he was actually deserving such honor, in a more Jewish, *i. e.* truer and worthier manner, than by the most magnificent monument which you may execute in bronze or marble.

Please accept the assurance of my most distinguished consideration with which I have the honor to be, honored sirs,

Yours, truly,

Hirsch.

329

Dr. N. M. Adler's Opinion*

Office of the Chief Rabbi,
London, August 1st, 5620

Reverend and Dear Sir:

I have the honor to acknowledge the receipt of your letter dated the 6th of June, concerning the erection of a monument in honor of the late Judah Touro, and beg to apologise for having, in consequence of my absence from town, postponed my answer.

I have given the subject of your communication the earnest consideration which it requires, embracing as it does questions of great theological and historical interest. I have, however, avoided writing you a diffused and learned disquisition, and proceed to give you briefly the result of my investigations in straightforward answers to your several queries.

I *Primary Questions.* —

1. It is *not* lawful for Israelites to erect a statue, cast in bronze or chiselled of marble, and to place it anywhere in honor of a deceased fellow-Israelite. Surely the prohibition does not apply with such rigor to a bust as it does to a statue; still, even to erect the former would not be Jewish.
2. It is, however, lawful for Israelities to erect a shaft, a column, a pillar, or a pyramid, with an inscription containing the virtues and acts of the deceased, and to place it in some open public place of a city. The words in the Holy Scriptures (Deut. xvi.22) refer only to pillars erected for the worship of God or for purposes of idolatry.

II *Collateral questions.* —

It is not unlawful for Israelites to subscribe or even to take any active part towards the erection of a statue in honor of a distinguished non-Israelite, living or dead; provided it is cast or chiselled by a non-Israelite, and it is known that the person thus honored is not to be considered a saint or to be worshipped.

2. It is not lawful for an Israelite to devote himself to the art of sculpture or to a mechanical trade, in which the manufacture of images of cast, moulded, or graven images, forms the principal occupation, in so far as it relates to *human* images, the sun and moon.
3. It is not lawful for Israelites to keep in their houses statues of human beings, images of the sun and moon, or of dragons. — Images of other animals, however, except of the חיות הקדש, are allowed.

---

* English version taken from *The Occident*, XIX, pp. 53–54.

III *Principal question.* —

It follows from the above, that it is not lawful for the Israelites of New Orleans to erect a statue, but it is allowed to erect a shaft, a column, a pillar, or a pyramid in honor of the late Judah Touro.— I should, however, advise, that the same be not erected in front or behind the Synagogue.
I have the honor to remain, reverend and dear sir,

Yours, very faithfully,
Dr. N. M. Adler

Rev. James K. Gutheim,
President of the Touro Monument Association.

Dr. Z. Frankel's Opinion.*

Rev. James K. Gutheim,
Acting President of the Touro Monument Association,
New Orleans, La.

Dear Sir:

Prevented by indisposition from immediately replying to your honored communication of the 6th of June, I perform this task to-day. You propound to me, in the name of the Touro Monument Association, several interrogatories, which, together with their answers, are subjoined in the English language; the argument, however, upon which these answers are based I have premised in the German language, which is more familiar to me, in order to avoid all ambiguity.

Above all, I beg to remark, that the erection of a monument, such as is proposed by your Association, is unknown to ancient Jewish custom and usage. The deceased benefactors of their brethren were honored by having their memory cherished long and vividly, or by the erection of charitable institutions in their honor and after their name. Even tomb-stones were seldom erected in olden times; the sentence אין עושין נפשות לצדיקים דבריהם הם זכרונם is known.

Historically it is established, that statues, even as marks of honor— hence not merely for purposes of idolatry — were considered extremely objectionable, and were not tolerated to perpetuate even the most important events. Thus, when Alexander the Great had entered Jerusalem and treated the city and inhabitants with the greatest kindness, no statue was erected to honor him, but the Jews resolved, as is related, to name, as an expression of their gratitude, every male child born in that year after the victor's name, Alexander! I will but incidentally mention the refusal to receive the statue of Caligula in Jerusalem and Alexandria, which, according to Philo (*Contra Gaium*) and Josephus (*Antiq.* 18), would have caused the extermination of the Jewish inhabitants of those

---

* The English version is drawn from *The Occident*, XIX, pp. 51–53.

cities, had not the death of the tyrant prevented the execution of his design. And yet this statue was a mark of respect. But that the Jews generally, from the oldest period, adhered in this point with the utmost rigor to the religious ordinances may be demonstrated from the fact, that those living in Alexandria under the Ptolemean kings regarded even painting as being prohibited. In Palestine they did not go so far, and permitted the art of painting; but it can certainly be perceived that the prohibition to erect statues has a very ancient historical basis.

After this brief historical sketch I pass to the religious sources in which this prohibition is discussed at length. These are Talmud Rosh-hashanah 24, Aboda Zarah 43, Tasafot in locis and Yoma 54, Rambam Accum 3, #10, 11, *Yoreh Deah* 141, ##34, et seq.

And now the answers to the interrogatories of your communication *seriatim*.

I *Primary questions.* —

1. Is it lawful for Israelites to erect a statue (cast in bronze or chiselled of marble) in some open public place of a city, in honor of a deceased fellow-Israelite?

Answer

The erection of a statue in honor of an Israelite as well as of any other man is prohibited by the Jewish religious law. (See *Yoreh Deah*, 141,4.)

2. It is lawful for Israelites to erect a monument, say a shaft, a column, or a pillar, in the same manner and for the same purpose?

Answer.

The erection of a monument in the foregoing described manner is lawful without hesitation.

II *Collateral questions.* —

1. Is it lawful for Israelites to subscribe or take any active part towards the erection of a statue or monument in honor of a distinguished non-Israelite, living or dead?

Answer.

To subscribe is not prohibited (see Tos. Rosh. Hash. 24, beginning שאני and ש״כ *Yoreh Deah*, l. c., litt. 17), nor to take active part, except the erection, viz: the sculpture.

2. Is it lawful for an Israelite to devote himself to the art of sculpture, or to any mechanical trade, in which the manufacture of images, cast, moulded, or graven, not made for purposes of idolatry, forms the principal occupation?

Answer.

The practice of the art of sculpture, comprising that of human beings, is prohibited, of other beings is not prohibited. (See *Yoreh Deah* ##4, 6.) The art of engraving is lawful.

3. Is it lawful for Israelites to keep within their houses for the sake of ornaments specimens of art, such as statues, or statuettes of human beings, or of dragons and other animals?

Answer.

Israelites shall never keep statues or statuettes of human beings in their houses. (See *Yoreh Deah*, l. c. #4.) But if mutilated on nose or eye, such a statue or statuette can be allowed a place in an Israelite's house. And such is also the practice. (See Tal. Rosh. Hash. l. c., סמי עיניו דרין.)

Statues of animals may be kept in the houses of Israelites (*Yoreh Deah*, l. c. #7), and in some instances those of dragons. (See *Yoreh Deah* #3.)

III *Principal question.*

Is it lawful for the Israelites of New Orleans to erect a statue or monument, in conjunction with their non-Jewish fellow-citizens, or by themselves, in honor of their late co-religionist, Judah Touro?

Answer.

The conclusion of all that has been stated above is: That the Israelites of New Orleans can, conformably to the religious laws, by no means erect a statue to the late Judah Touro, either by themselves or in conjunction with non-Israelites. The erection of a monument, however, such as a shaft, column, or pillar, in honor of Judah Touro, is lawful, and can be executed without scruple or hesitation.

I have the honor to sign myself,

Respectfully and truly,

Dr. Z. Frankel

Breslau, July 19th, 1860.

At this time, the Civil War in America broke out and "the Lord annulled their decision and made their purposes in vain." Although, because of this affair, I suffered much and had great losses, nevertheless I had the satisfaction of having acted according to my convictions and of having opposed, not without success, a memorial so public, so enduring and — so unJewish.

Louisville, Kentucky

I left Cincinnati on June first at noon. The steamer *S. Melinde* carried us along the Ohio past a well-cultivated countryside where the sight of fields, meadows and woods alternated with that of villages and small towns to please and charm us. We reached Louisville at eleven o'clock at night. There I stopped at the boarding-house of a widow, Mrs. F. Lango, who conducts it strictly according to Jewish ritual. There are two Jewish congregations in the city. They are: (1) Adath Israel and (2) Beth Israel.

Adath Israel, consisting of Germans, was founded in 1836 (5596). It built a synagogue on Fourth Street in 1849. The president is Moses Libermann; the *hazzan*, teacher and *shohet*, B. H. Gotthelf. The latter has made some changes in the traditional liturgy.

Beth Israel, with services according to a Polish ritual, was founded in 5611, or 1851, by Isaac Goldstein and his brother-in-law, Mordecai Goldberg. At that time it consisted only of about twenty members. In 1857 it had thirty-six. A tale that is chiefly told in Poland might be applied to this congregation. It is said that the prophet, Elijah, was once traveling about in the world and came to a town where he met with the friendliest of receptions and was entertained by everybody. As he was leaving he was asked for his blessing. He said: "May there always be only one of you who wants to be head of the community so that your peace will never be disturbed." In another town he had an unfriendly reception. When he was asked for his blessing here, too, he said: "I wish that each of you should strive for the honor of being head of the community, and let that be the payment for your inhospitality!" In this little congregation, likewise, every member wants to be the head of it and because of this there are perpetual disputes.

On June sixth, the German congregation met in the basement of their synagogue to welcome me at a celebration in my honor. I was escorted into the assembly-room by a committee especially chosen for this purpose, consisting of the teacher and several esteemed members. At this meeting, the president informed his fellow members that a Christian and his wife wished to become converted to Judaism and that the man had asked to be received as a member of Adath Israel. This request was no sooner placed before the meeting for discussion than a member rose to speak about it. He had the following reasons for not granting it: "When a man wants to become converted to our religion," he said, "he must first become thoroughly acquainted with its laws. Now we have been commanded, above all, to keep the Sabbath holy and, likewise, the holidays. With respect to women, we have

334

been commanded particularly to have a ritual bath — and there are other matters. But how can we, who do not obey these commandments ourselves and do not even have a ritual bath for women, impose such commandments upon others? We would only make public our shame to have strayed so far from the divine commandments." Embarrassed by this speech, they came to no conclusion and the matter was put off.

Charitable Societies

There are four of these in Louisville.

(1) Hebrah Meshibath Nefesh, founded in 1850, to aid widows and orphans. The president is Mr. Samuelson. It has eighty members with a fund of about a thousand dollars.

(2) Hebrah Nehamah's purpose is to care for the sick and bury the dead. It has fifty members.

(3) Hebrah Nashim Gomle Chesed, founded in 1854. The president is Karl Lichton (*sic*).

(4) Hebrah Nashim Gomle Chesed, No. 2. The president is Mr. Samuelson (*sic*).

There are about two thousand Jews in Louisville. Most of them are well off. It is said that they are charitable. I had, to be sure, no opportunity of finding this out for myself.

On June ninth I went back to Cincinnati. On the twenty-second I went on to New York. I reached it on the twenty-fourth. On August first, as I mentioned in the beginning of the book, I began my trip to California.